Contents

"Living with the Certainty of a Shaky Future," by John Burks 28

Maps

Foreword

While every care has been taken to assure the accuracy of the information in this guide, the passage of time will always bring change and, consequently, the publisher cannot accept responsibility for errors that may occur.

All prices and opening times quoted here are based on information supplied to us at press time. Hours and admission fees may change, however, and the prudent traveler will avoid inconvenience by calling ahead.

Fodor's wants to hear about your travel experiences, both pleasant and unpleasant. When a hotel or restaurant fails to live up to its billing, let us know and we will investigate the complaint and revise our entries where the facts warrant it.

Send your letters to the editors of Fodor's Travel Publications, 201 E. 50th Street, New York, NY 10022.

Highlights '95 and Fodor's Choice

Highlights '95

For residents and visitors alike, the major civic event of the year should be the January 1995 opening of the new, $60 million **San Francisco Museum of Modern Art** across from the Center for the Arts at **Yerba Buena Gardens** on Third Street. For decades, the museum has been housed in rented space on the top floors of the War Memorial Building. The new building, designed by internationally celebrated architect Mario Botta, is as distinctive looking, if not so controversial, as the glittering Marriott Hotel nearby: at its center is a 125-foot-high cylindrical atrium topped by a slanting skylight that's been compared to a gigantic donut. The 225,000-square-foot building will more than double the Museum's exhibition space, and also add to the appeal of the Yerba Buena Gardens development project. The museum bookstore and café will open first, in the fall of 1994.

Also in the news will be the **California Palace of the Legion of Honor** art museum in Lincoln Park, overlooking the Golden Gate Bridge. It has been closed for remodeling for two years and is scheduled to reopen in the fall of 1995. New features include an expanded restaurant, a bookshop, and six galleries built around a courtyard on the level beneath the museum's entrance colonnade. The collection of European paintings, sculpture, and other artwork that has been scattered elsewhere will be reinstalled. The museum will also have seismic bracing to protect the entire building from the kind of damage that some San Francisco Bay Area structures suffered in the 1989 earthquake.

On the city's eastern waterfront, the primary magnet for visitors, the new attraction will be **Underwater World at Pier 39**. Unlike traditional aquariums, this will take visitors through transparent tunnels on moving walkways, surrounded by marine life, all of which will be indigenous to San Francisco Bay—including the sharks. It is scheduled to open in the fall of 1995.

In the early 1980s, San Francisco's transit authority replaced streetcars on Market Street, the city's major thoroughfare, with an underground light-rail system. It was overcrowded almost immediately, so back came the streetcar tracks in a project that has taken years and caused endless traffic congestion. The result, expected to be completed by mid-1995, will offer more than additional transit capacity. The line will carry **historic San Francisco streetcars**—refurbished, shiplike cars from the 1940s and 1950s—between Transbay Terminal downtown and Castro Street to the west. On special occasions, a collection of older restored streetcars from cities around the world will be temporarily added to the line. The Castro section of Market Street has also been lined with 37 20-foot-tall Canary Island palm trees.

The city's traditional retail center around **Union Square** changes slowly, but it should be revitalized at several locations this year.

In 1994, a posh new branch of **The Gap** brightened the sometimes sleazy cable-car turnaround at Powell and Market streets. By early 1995, a **Disney Store** offering clothing, toys, and video entertainment will be open, across from Union Square and the Westin St. Francis Hotel, at Powell and Post streets. At Stockton and Market streets, another franchise of **Planet Hollywood**, the chain of movie-memorabilia restaurants, is due to open early in 1995.

Note that in early 1995 San Francisco's **Civic Center** will close for three years of seismic upgrading.

Fodor's Choice

No two people will agree on what makes a perfect vacation, but it's fun and helpful to know what others think. We hope you'll have a chance to experience some of Fodor's Choices yourself while visiting San Francisco. For more information about each entry, refer to the appropriate chapters within this guidebook.

Special Moments

Enjoying the sunset view and a drink at the Carnelian Room, Bank of America Building

Picnicking on sourdough bread and California wine on the shores of the lagoon at the Palace of Fine Arts

Attending a classic double feature at the last of San Francisco's great movie palaces, the Castro Theater, when the organist closes the intermission with a chorus of "San Francisco"

Browsing in the City Lights bookstore in North Beach, a cultural landmark from San Francisco's beatnik era

Walking across the Golden Gate Bridge

Watching the Giants beat the Dodgers at Candlestick Park

Memorable Sights

The view of the city and her bridges from one of the ferries in the bay

Flower stands at Union Square

Fog rolling into the city over Twin Peaks

The fresh food displays in the Chinatown markets

The sea lions howling in the surf at Cliff House and at Pier 39

Restaurants

Fleur de Lys (*$$$$*)

Masa's (*$$$$*)

Postrio (*$$$$*)

Stars (*$$$*)

Greens at Fort Mason (*$$*)

Lulu (*$$*)

Square One (*$$*)

Tra Vigne, Napa Valley (*$$*)

Khan Toke Thai House (*$–$$*)

Capp's Corner (*$*)

Top Seasonal Events

The Chinese New Year parade in February

Golden Gate park when the rhododendron dell blooms in April

The Bay to Breakers race in May

The Gay Freedom Parade in June

Opera in the Park in September

Halloween in the Castro

Hotels

Campton Place Kempinski (*$$$$*)

Four Seasons Clift (*$$$$*)

Ritz-Carlton (*$$$$*)

The Sherman House (*$$$$*)

Petite Auberge (*$$$*)

The Cartwright (*$$*)

Galleria Park (*$$*)

San Remo Hotel (*$*)

Night Spots

Club Fugazi

Club 36

Great American Music Hall

Harry Denton's

Kimball's East

Slim's

The Stud

Tosca Café

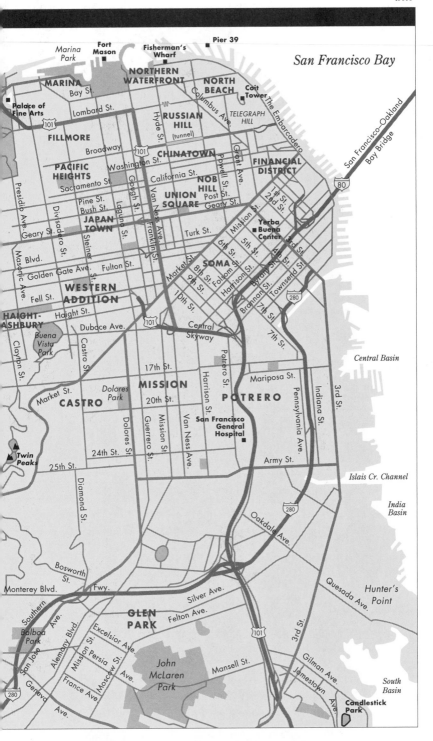

San Francisco Bay

Marina Park
Fort Mason
Fisherman's Wharf
Pier 39
MARINA
Bay St.
NORTHERN WATERFRONT
NORTH BEACH
Coit Tower
Palace of Fine Arts
Lombard St.
101
RUSSIAN HILL
(tunnel)
Columbus Ave.
TELEGRAPH HILL
The Embarcadero
San Francisco-Oakland Bay Bridge
FILLMORE
Broadway
101
Hyde St.
CHINATOWN
FINANCIAL DISTRICT
80
PACIFIC HEIGHTS
Washington St.
California St.
NOB HILL
Grant Ave.
Powell St.
1st St.
2nd St.
Presidio Ave.
Sacramento St.
Pine St.
Bush St.
Post St.
Geary St.
UNION SQUARE
Mission St.
5th St.
6th St.
3rd St.
4th St.
JAPAN TOWN
Divisadero St.
Gough St.
Van Ness Ave.
Laguna St.
Steiner St.
Franklin St.
Turk St.
Yerba Buena Center
Geary St.
Masonic Ave.
Blvd.
Golden Gate Ave.
Fulton St.
Market St.
SOMA
8th St.
9th St.
Folsom St.
Harrison St.
Bryant St.
Brannan St.
7th St.
Townsend St.
WESTERN ADDITION
Fell St.
10th St.
HAIGHT-ASHBURY
Haight St.
101
Dubose Ave.
Central Skyway
Clayton St.
Buena Vista Park
Castro St.
Central Basin
Market St.
17th St.
MISSION
Potrero St.
Harrison St.
Mariposa St.
POTRERO
Pennsylvania Ave.
Indiana St.
3rd St.
CASTRO
Dolores Park
20th St.
Dolores St.
Guerrero St.
Mission St.
Van Ness Ave.
San Francisco General Hospital
280
Twin Peaks
24th St.
25th St.
Diamond St.
Army St.
Islais Cr. Channel
India Basin
280
Oakdale Ave.
Bosworth St.
Fwy.
Monterey Blvd.
Silver Ave.
Quesada Ave.
Hunter's Point
Southern
Balboa Park
Alemany Blvd.
San Jose Ave.
Excelsior Ave.
GLEN PARK
Felton Ave.
101
3rd St.
Gilman Ave.
Geneva Ave.
280
Mission St.
Persia Ave.
Moscow St.
France Ave.
John McLaren Park
Mansell St.
Jamestown Ave.
South Basin
Candlestick Park

Northern California

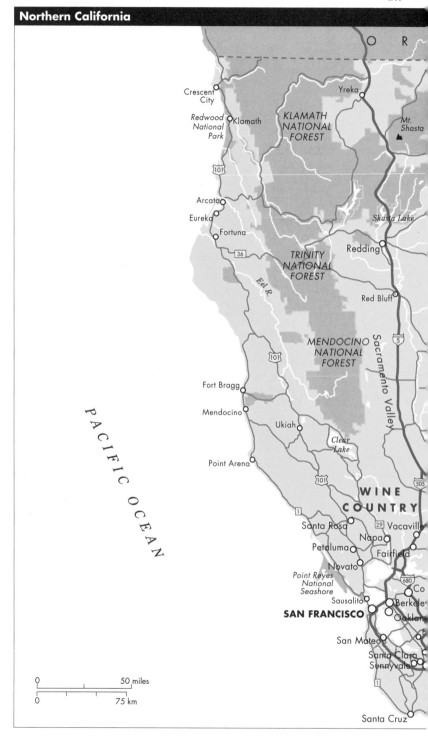

Crescent City

Redwood National Park

Klamath

101

Arcata

Eureka

Fortuna

36

Eel R.

KLAMATH NATIONAL FOREST

Yreka

Mt. Shasta

TRINITY NATIONAL FOREST

Shasta Lake

Redding

Red Bluff

I-5

MENDOCINO NATIONAL FOREST

101

Fort Bragg

Mendocino

Ukiah

Clear Lake

Point Arena

101

PACIFIC OCEAN

1

Santa Rosa

Petaluma

Point Reyes National Seashore

Novato

Sausalito

SAN FRANCISCO

San Mateo

Santa Clara

Sunnyvale

1

Santa Cruz

WINE COUNTRY

29 Vacaville

Napa

Fairfield

680

Co

Berkele

Oaklan

Sacramento Valley

505

0   50 miles
0   75 km

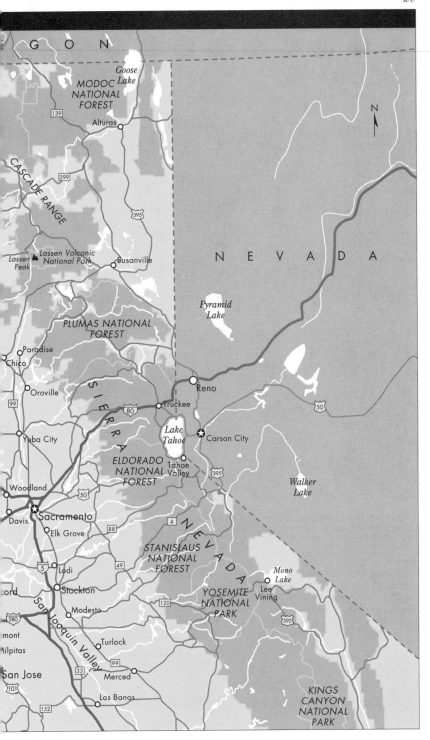

World Time Zones

International Date Line

MONDAY
SUNDAY

| +11 | +12 - | -11 | -10 | -9 | -8 | -7 | -6 | -5 | -4 | -3 | -2 |

Numbers below vertical bands relate each zone to Greenwich Mean Time (0 hrs.).
Local times frequently differ from these general indications,
as indicated by light-face numbers on map.

Algiers, **29**
Anchorage, **3**
Athens, **41**
Auckland, **1**
Baghdad, **46**
Bangkok, **50**
Beijing, **54**

Berlin, **34**
Bogotá, **19**
Budapest, **37**
Buenos Aires, **24**
Caracas, **22**
Chicago, **9**
Copenhagen, **33**
Dallas, **10**

Delhi, **48**
Denver, **8**
Djakarta, **53**
Dublin, **26**
Edmonton, **7**
Hong Kong, **56**
Honolulu, **2**

Istanbul, **40**
Jerusalem, **42**
Johannesburg, **44**
Lima, **20**
Lisbon, **28**
London (Greenwich), **27**
Los Angeles, **6**
Madrid, **38**
Manila, **57**

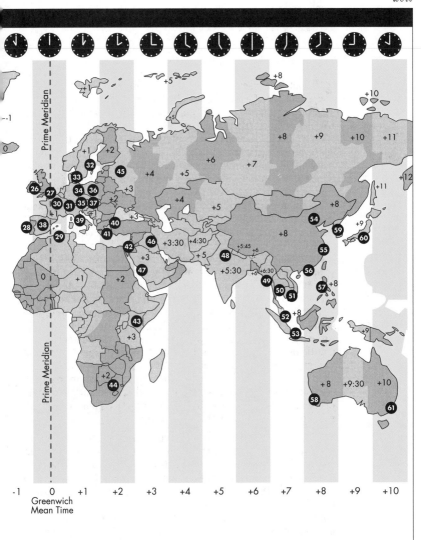

-1   0   +1   +2   +3   +4   +5   +6   +7   +8   +9   +10
      Greenwich
      Mean Time

Mecca, **47**   Ottawa, **14**   San Francisco, **5**   Toronto, **13**
Mexico City, **12**   Paris, **30**   Santiago, **21**   Vancouver, **4**
Miami, **18**   Perth, **58**   Seoul, **59**   Vienna, **35**
Montréal, **15**   Reykjavík, **25**   Shanghai, **55**   Warsaw, **36**
Moscow, **45**   Rio de Janeiro, **23** Singapore, **52**   Washington, D.C., **17**
Nairobi, **43**   Rome, **39**   Stockholm, **32**   Yangon, **49**
New Orleans, **11**   Saigon (Ho Chi Minh   Sydney, **61**   Zürich, **31**
New York City, **16** City), **51**   Tokyo, **60**

Introduction

San Franciscans tend to regard the envy of visitors as a matter of course and to look on whatever brought them to settle here (there's probably never been a time when the majority of the population was native born) as a brilliant stroke of luck. Certain local problems can be traced to this warm contentment with the city and to the attendant fear that somebody might do something to *change* it. The skyline, for example, which in recent decades has become clotted with high rises, has turned into a source of controversy. The city's Financial District is dominated by the dark, looming Bank of America—the sculpted lump of black granite out front has been nicknamed "The Banker's Heart"—and by the Transamerica Building, the glass-and-concrete pyramid that has made the city's skyline instantly recognizable. (Nearly two decades after its construction, San Franciscans still argue vehemently about its merits, or its utter lack of them. But nobody claims it isn't distinctive.) Admirers of the skyline defend the skyscrapers as evidence of prosperity and of San Francisco's world-class stature; detractors grumble about the "Manhattanization" that's ruining a unique place. Historically, San Francisco is a boomtown, and various periods of frantic building have lined the pockets of developers for whom the city's beauty was no consideration at all. Nevertheless, in 1986 the voters set limits on downtown construction; now the controversy has moved out to the neighborhoods, where entrepreneurs want to knock down single-family houses to make room for profitable apartment buildings.

The boom began in 1848. At the beginning of that year, San Francisco wasn't much more than a pleasant little settlement that had been founded by the Spaniards back in the auspicious year of 1776. The natural harbor of the bay (so commodious that "all the navies of the world might fit" inside it, as one visitor wrote) made it a village with a future. The future came abruptly when gold was discovered at John Sutter's sawmill in the Sierra foothills, some 115 miles to the northeast. By 1850, San Francisco's population had zoomed from 500 to 30,000, and a "western Wall Street" sprang up as millions upon millions of dollars' worth of gold was panned and blasted out of the hills. The gold mines began to dry up in a few years; but in 1859 prospectors turned up a fabulously rich vein of silver in the Virginia Range, in what is now Nevada; and San Francisco—the nearest financial center—prospered again. The boom made labor a precious commodity, especially since most of the able-bodied men were rushing off to the mountains to make their fortunes. San Francisco has remained a strong labor town, though not always happily so: During rough times, the unions found a scapegoat in the immigrant Chinese workers.

But contentiousness is part of the price San Francisco pays for variety. Consider, as an indicator, the makeup of the city's chief administrative body, the 11-member Board of Supervisors: Past boards have included a healthy mix of Chinese, Hispanics, gays, blacks, and women. The city is a bastion of what it likes to refer to as "progressive" politics. Leftish *Mother Jones* magazine publishes from an office on Mission Street; the Sierra Club, founded here by its first president, John Muir, in 1892, has its national headquarters on Polk Street. The two daily newspapers, on the other hand, lean heavily right, at least on their editorial pages. (William Randolph Hearst, whose father gave him the *Examiner* in 1887, turned the paper into a laboratory of yellow journalism; today the name at the top of the masthead is William R. Hearst III.) Political bitterness has sometimes led to violence, most spectacularly with the "Bloody Thursday" face-off between striking longshoremen and scab labor in 1934, and in the 1978 assassinations of the city's liberal mayor, George Moscone, and its first gay supervisor, Harvey Milk, by a vindictive right-wing ex-supervisor. (On a more eccentric note, San Francisco is also the city where, in 1974, the Symbionese Liberation Army and its most famous victim/inductee, Patty Hearst, held up the Sunset District branch of the Hibernia Bank.) But, despite a boomtown tendency toward raucousness, and a sad history of anti-Asian discrimination, the city today prides itself on its tolerance. The mix, everybody knows, is what makes San Francisco. On any given night at the Opera House—a major civic crossroads—you can see costumes ranging from torn denim and full leather to business suits, dinner jackets, and sequined, feathered gowns—expensive originals gracing society dowagers and the occasional goodwill-store find on a well-dressed drag queen.

Geographically, San Francisco is the thumbnail on a 40-mile thumb of land, the San Francisco Peninsula, which stretches northward between the Pacific Ocean and San Francisco Bay. Hemmed in on three sides by water, the land area (less than 50 square miles) is relatively small; the population, at about three-quarters of a million, is small, too. Technically speaking, it's only California's third-largest city, behind Los Angeles and San Diego and no longer very much ahead of nearby San Jose. But that statistic is misleading: The Bay Area, which stretches from the bedroom communities north of Oakland and Berkeley south through Silicon Valley (the cluster of Peninsula cities that have become the center of America's computer industry) and San Jose, is really one continuous megacity, with San Francisco as its heart—its hub.

Not so many centuries ago the area that was to become San Francisco was a windswept, virtually treeless, and, above all, sandy wasteland. Sand even covered the hills. The sand is still there, but—except along the ocean—it's well hidden. City Hall is built on 80 feet of it. The westerly section of the city—the Sunset and Richmond districts and Golden Gate Park—seems flat only because sand has filled in the contours of the hills.

But the hills that remain are spectacular. They provide vistas all over the city—nothing is more common than to find yourself staring out toward Angel Island or Alcatraz, or across the bay at Berkeley and Oakland. The hills are also exceptionally good at winding pedestrians. (The cable cars didn't become instantly popular because they were picturesque.) The city's two bridges, which are almost as majestic as their surroundings, had their 50th birthdays in 1986 and 1987. The Golden Gate Bridge, which crosses to Marin County, got a bigger party, but the San Francisco–Oakland Bay Bridge got a better present: a necklace of lights along its spans. They were supposed to be temporary, but the locals were so taken with the glimmer that bridge boosters started a drive to make them permanent; radio DJs and newspaper columnists put out daily appeals, drivers gave extra quarters to the toll takers, various corporations put up shares, and—close to a million dollars later—the lights on the Bay Bridge now shine nightly.

First-time visitors to San Francisco sometimes arrive with ideas about its weather gleaned from movie images of sunny California or from a misinformed 1967 song that celebrated the "warm San Franciscan nights." Sunny, perhaps; warm—not likely. That's *southern* California. (A perennially popular T-shirt quotes Mark Twain's apocryphal remark: "The coldest winter I ever spent was a summer in San Francisco.") Still, it almost never freezes here, and heat waves are equally rare. Most San Franciscans come to love the climate, which is genuinely temperate—sufficiently welcoming for the imposing row of palms down the median of Dolores Street but seldom warm enough for just a T-shirt at night. The coastal stretch of ocean may look inviting, but the surfers you sometimes see along Ocean Beach are wearing wet suits. (The beach, though, can be fine for sunning.) And, of course, there's the famous fog—something that tourists tend to find more delightful than do the residents. It's largely a summer phenomenon; San Francisco's real summer begins in September, when the fog lifts and the air warms up for a while. November brings on the rains.

The city has three trademarks: the fog, the cable cars, and the Victorians. Bay-windowed, ornately decorated Victorian houses—the multicolor, ahistorical paint jobs that have become popular make them seem even more ornate—are the city's most distinguishing architectural feature. They date mainly from the latter part of Queen Victoria's reign, 1870 to the turn of the century. In those three decades, San Francisco more than doubled in population (from 150,000 to 342,000); the transcontinental railway, linking the once-isolated western capital to the east, had been completed in 1869. That may explain the exuberant confidence of the architecture.

Over the years, plenty of the Victorians have gone under the wrecker's ball to make way for such commercial projects as shopping complexes, or for the low-income housing projects that went under the rubric of "urban renewal" but quickly degenerated into slums. The decrepit old houses were out of favor for a while, but once the era of gentrification arrived, those that were left standing were snatched up, fixed up, and sold at exorbitant prices. Parts of the city that not so long ago were considered ghettos are becoming expensive places to live.

By far the biggest annihilator of San Francisco's older buildings, of course, was the April 18, 1906 earthquake—or, more precisely, the fire that followed it. San Francisco doesn't lie precisely on the San Andreas Fault, and the violent shaking of the earth accounted for only about 20% of the total damage. The Victorians, in fact—most of them redwood, an ideally tractable medium for all the gingerbread—swayed and bent and withstood the quake admirably. But they were natural fodder for the blaze. Some 28,000 buildings—80% of the city's property—went up, and well over half the city's population was left homeless. But San Francisco bounded back quickly. The *Chronicle* observed that the people who had been burned out of their homes were "taking things as happily and philosophically as if they were out on a summer's camping trip." Entrepreneurs began rebuilding so rapidly that the city missed a golden opportunity to right some of its long-standing design blunders. (The streets have never followed the contours of the hills; they were laid out on a grid pattern that had—and still has—nothing to do with the natural features of the landscape. Hence their sometimes unbelievable steepness.) The catastrophe left its deepest mark on the city's imagination. San Franciscans are sensitive to the sudden rattle of dishes on the shelves, and no one who has lived here for any length of time hasn't heard it. The 1989 Loma Prieta earthquake, centered far south of the city near Santa Cruz, was not "the big one" that scientists had long predicted, although it resulted in widespread damage. Destruction within the city was limited—10 homes in the Marina district near the northern waterfront were eventually demolished, and about two dozen downtown buildings were judged unsafe. Since the earthquake, unstable elevated freeways along the Embarcadero, facing San Francisco Bay, and west of City Hall were torn down, opening vistas that had been blocked since the 1950s.

In terms of both geography and culture, San Francisco is about as close as you can get to Asia in the continental United States. (The city prides itself on its role as a Pacific Rim capital, and overseas investment has become a vital part of its financial life.) The first great wave of Chinese immigrants came during the gold rush in 1852. Chinese workers quickly became the target of race hatred and discriminatory laws; Chinatown—which began when the Chinese moved into old buildings that white businesses seeking more fashionable locations had abandoned—developed, as much as anything else, as a refuge. Chinatown is still a fascinating place to wander, and it's a good bet for late-night food, but it's not the whole story by any means. The Asian community, which now accounts for a fifth of San Francisco's population, reaches into every San Francisco neighborhood, and particularly into the Sunset and Richmond districts, out toward the ocean. Clement Street, which runs through the center of Richmond, has become the main thoroughfare of a second Chinatown. Southeast Asian immigrants, many of them ethnic Chinese, are transforming the seedy Tenderloin into a thriving Little Indochina. There was heavy Japanese immigration earlier in this century, but most of it went to southern California, where organized labor had less of a foothold and where there were greater opportunities for Asian workers. Still, San Francisco has its Japantown, with its massive Japan Center complex and scads of shops and restaurants clustered in and around it. In the past, Asians have tended toward a backseat—or at least an offstage—role in the city's politics; but like so much else on the city's cultural/political landscape, that, too, seems to be changing.

San Francisco has always been a loose, tolerant—some would say licentious—city. As early as the 1860s, the "Barbary Coast"—a collection of taverns, whorehouses, and gambling joints along Pacific Avenue close to the waterfront—was famous, or infamous. Bohemian communities seem to thrive here. In the 1950s, North Beach, the city's Little Italy, became the home of the Beat Movement. (Herb Caen, the city's best-known columnist, coined the term "beatnik.") Lawrence Ferlinghetti's City Lights, a bookstore and publishing house that brought out, among other titles, Allen Ginsberg's *Howl* and *Kaddish*, still stands on Columbus Avenue as a monument to the era. (Across Broadway, a plaque identifies the Condor as the site of the nation's first topless and bottomless performances, a monument to a slightly later era.) The Bay Area was the epicenter of '60s ferment, too. The Free Speech Movement began at the University of California in Berkeley (where, in October 1965, Allen Ginsberg introduced the term "flower power"), and Stanford's David Harris, who went to prison for defying the draft, numbered among the nation's most famous student leaders. In San Francisco, the Haight-Ashbury district was synonymous with hippiedom and gave rise to such legendary bands as the Jefferson Airplane, Big Brother and the Holding Company (fronted by Janis Joplin), and the Grateful Dead. Twenty years later, the Haight has become a peculiar mix. Haight Street itself is a shopping strip, replete with boutiques and nail-care salons and noted especially for its vintage-clothing stores. The once-funky Victorians that housed the communes have been restored and purchased by wealthy yuppies. The neighborhood's history and its name, however, still draw neo-hippies, as well as New Wavers with black lips and blue hair, and some rather menacing skinheads. The transients who sleep in nearby Golden Gate Park make panhandling one of the street's major business activities. It's not a completely happy mix; still, most of the residents remain committed to keeping the Haight the Haight. There's especially bitter resentment against the chain businesses (McDonald's, The Gap) that have moved in. In 1988 a chain drugstore's attempt to open a huge outlet sparked furious protest and, eventually, arson. The question of who set the fire, which gutted not only the unfinished store but several nearby apartments and businesses as well, has never been answered, but the fire accomplished its purpose: The chain pulled out.

Southwest of the Haight is the onetime Irish neighborhood known as the Castro, which during the 1970s became identified with lesbian and gay liberation. Castro Street is dominated by the elaborate Castro Theater, a 1923 vision in Spanish Baroque, which presents one of the best repertory movie schedules in the city. (The grand old pipe organ still plays during intermissions, breaking into "San Francisco" just before the feature begins.) There's been much talk, most of it exaggerated, about how AIDS has chastened and "matured" the Castro; it's still an effervescent neighborhood, and—as housing everywhere has become more and more of a prize—an increasingly mixed one. At the same time, gays, like Asians, are moving out of the ghetto and into neighborhoods all around the city.

The Lesbian and Gay Freedom Day Parade, each June, vies with the Chinese New Year Parade, in February, as the city's most elaborate. They both get competition from Japantown's Cherry Blossom Festival, in April; the Columbus Day and St. Patrick's Day parades; the June Carnival in the Hispanic Mission District; and the May Day march, a labor celebration in a labor town. The mix of ethnic, economic, social, and sexual groups can be bewildering, but the city's residents—whatever their origin—face it with aplomb and even gratitude. Everybody in San Francisco has an opinion about where to get the best burrito or the hottest Szechuan eggplant or the strongest cappuccino. The most staid citizens have learned how to appreciate good camp. Nearly everyone smiles on the fortunate day they arrived on, or were born on, this windy, foggy patch of peninsula.

1 Essential Information

Before You Go

Tourist Information

Contact the **San Francisco Convention and Visitors Bureau** (201 3rd St., Suite 900, 94103, tel. 415/974–6900). The attractive 80-page *San Francisco Book* ($2; from the SFCVB at Box 6977, 94101) includes up-to-date information on theater offerings, art exhibits, sporting events, and other special happenings.

The **Redwood Empire Association Visitor Information Center** (785 Market St., 15th Floor, 94103, 415/543–8334) covers San Francisco and surrounding areas, including the Wine Country, the redwood groves, and northwestern California. For $3 they will send *The Redwood Empire Visitor's Guide*; it's free when picked up at their office. For the Silicon Valley area, contact the visitor information center in **Santa Clara** (1515 El Camino Real, Box 387, Santa Clara, 95050, tel. 408/283–8833).

In addition, there are chambers of commerce in dozens of San Francisco Bay Area towns, including **Berkeley** (1834 University Ave., Box 210, Berkeley, 94703, tel. 510/549–7003), and convention and visitors bureaus in **Oakland** (1000 Broadway, Suite 200, Oakland 94607, tel. 510/839–9000 or 800/262–5526), **San Jose** (333 W. San Carlos St., Suite 1000, San Jose 95110, tel. 408/295–9600 or 800/726–5673), and **Santa Clara** (2200 Laurelwood Rd., Santa Clara, 95054, tel. 408/970–9825).

The **California Office of Tourism** (801 K St., Suite 1600, Sacramento 95814, tel. 916/322–1397) can answer many questions about travel in the state. You can also order a detailed 208-page book, *Discover the Californias*, which includes an informative section on the Bay Area (free; tel. 800/862–2543).

Tours and Packages

Should you buy your travel arrangements to the San Francisco area packaged or do it yourself? There are advantages either way. Buying packaged arrangements saves you money, particularly if you can find a program that includes exactly the features you want. You also get a pretty good idea of what your trip will cost from the outset.

You have two options: fully escorted tours and independent packages. Escorted tours mean having limited free time and traveling with strangers. Escorted tours are most often via motorcoach, with a tour director in charge. Your baggage is handled, your time rigorously scheduled, and most meals planned. Escorted tours are therefore the most hassle-free way to see a destination, as well as generally the least expensive. Independent packages allow plenty of flexibility. They generally include airline travel and hotels, with certain options available, such as sightseeing, car rental, and excursions. Independent packages are usually more expensive than escorted tours, but your time is your own.

While you can book directly through tour operators, you will pay no more to go through a travel agent, who will be able to tell you about tours and packages from a number of operators. Whatever program you ultimately choose, be sure to find out exactly what is included: taxes, tips, transfers, meals, baggage handling, ground transportation, entertainment, excursions, sports or recreation (and rental equipment if necessary). Ask about the level of hotel used, its location, the size of its rooms, the kind of beds, and its facilities and amenities, such as a pool, room service, or programs for children, if they're important to you. Find out the operator's cancellation penalties. Nearly everyone charges them, and the only way to avoid them is to buy trip-cancellation insurance. Also ask about the single supplement, a surcharge assessed to solo travelers. Some operators do not make you pay it if you agree to be matched up with a roommate of the same sex, even if one is not found by departure time. Remember that a program that has features you won't use, whether for rental sporting equipment or discounted museum admissions, may not be the most cost-wise choice for you.

Fully Escorted Tours Many tour operators make San Francisco a one-day stop on a multiday itinerary. Tours are usually sold in three categories: deluxe, first-class, and tourist or budget class. The most important differences are the price and the level of accommodations. Some operators specialize in one category, while others offer a range. Look into **Maupintour** (Box 807, Lawrence, KS 66044, tel. 913/843–1211 or 800/255–4266) and **Tauck Tours** (11 Wilton Rd., Westport, CT 06881, tel. 203/226–6911 or 800/468–2825) in the deluxe category; **Caravan** (401 N. Michigan Ave., Chicago, IL 60611, tel. 800/227–2862), **Domenico Tours** (751 Broadway, Bayonne, NJ 07002, tel. 201/823–8687 or 800/554–8687), **Gadabout Tours** (700 E. Tahquitz Way, Palm Springs, CA 92262, tel. 619/325–5556 or 800/952–5068), **Globus** (5301 S. Federal Circle, Littleton, CO 80123, tel. 303/797–2800 or 800/221–0090), **Talmage Tours** (1223 Walnut St., Philadelphia, PA 19107, tel. 215/923–7100 or 800/825–6243) and **Trieloff Tours** (24301 El Toro Rd., Suite 140, Laguna Hills, CA 92653, tel. 800/248–6877 or 800/432–7125 in CA), in the first-class category; and **Cosmos Tourama,** a sister company of Globus (*see above*), in budget programs.

Most itineraries are jam-packed with sightseeing, so you see a lot in a short amount of time (usually one place per day). To judge just how fast-paced the tour is, review the itinerary carefully. If you are in a different hotel each night, you will be getting up early each day to head out, travel to your next destination, do some sightseeing, have dinner, and go to bed, then you'll start all over again. If you want some free time, make sure it's mentioned in the tour brochure; if you want to be escorted to every meal, confirm that any tour you consider does that. Also, when comparing programs, be sure to find out if the motorcoach is air-conditioned and has a rest room on board. Make your selection based on price and stops on the itinerary.

Independent Packages
Independent packages are offered by tour operators who may also do escorted programs and any number of other companies from large, established firms to small, new entrepreneurs. Most of the airlines that offer packages to San Francisco also offer packages, among them **American Airlines Fly AAway Vacations** (tel. 800/321–2121), **Continental Airlines' Grand Destinations** (tel. 800/634–5555), **Delta Dream Vacations** (tel. 800/872–7786), **TWA Getaway Vacations** (tel. 800/438–2929), **United Airlines' Vacation Planning Center** (tel. 800/328–6877), and **USAir Vacations** (tel. 800/428–4322). **SuperCities** (139 Main St., Cambridge, MA 02142, tel. 617/621–9988 or 800/333–1234) has many programs. **Amtrak** (tel. 800/872–7245) tours include major California attractions.

These programs come in a wide range of prices based on levels of luxury and options—in addition to hotel and transportation, sightseeing, car rental, transfers, admission to local attractions, and other extras. Note that when pricing different packages, it sometimes pays to purchase the same arrangements separately, as when a rock-bottom promotional airfare is being offered, for example. Again, base your choice on what's available at your budget for the destinations you want to visit.

Special-Interest Travel
Special-interest programs may be fully escorted or independent. Some require a certain amount of expertise, but most are for the average traveler with an interest and are usually hosted by experts in the subject matter. When the program is escorted, it enjoys the advantages and disadvantages of all escorted programs; because your fellow travelers are apt to be passionate or knowledgeable about the subject, they can prove as enjoyable a part of your travel experience as the destination itself. The price range is wide, but the cost is usually higher—sometimes a lot higher—than for ordinary escorted tours and packages, because of the expert guiding and special activities.

Adventure/Hiking
Trek America (Box 470, Blairstown, NJ 07825, tel. 908/362–9198 or 800/221–0596) offers hiking, camping, and hotels on several tours inland and along the Pacific Coast that include San Francisco.

Ballooning
Napa Valley Balloons (Box 2860, Yountville, CA 94599, tel. 707/253–2224 or 800/253–2224) and **Sonoma Thunder Wine Country Balloon Safaris** (6984 McKinley St., Sebastopol, CA 95472, tel. 707/538–7359 or 800/759–5638) float over wine country valleys toward a champagne brunch.

Biking
Backroads (1516 5th St., Suite Q333, Berkeley, CA 94710-1740, tel. 510/527–1555 or 800/245–3874) has several trips that include San Francisco; you don't have to be an expert pedaler, and lodgings are often in country inns. **Mountain Travel-Sobek** (6420 Fairmount Ave., El Cerito, CA 94530, tel. 800/227–2384) offers a variety of free-wheeling tours in the Bay Area. **Napa Valley Bike Tours** (4080 Byway E, Napa Valley, CA 94558, tel. 707/255–3377) has day tours of the valley, with stops at three wineries and a catered lunch.

Food and Wine The **Robert Mondavi Winery** (Box 106, Oakville, CA 94562, tel. 707/944–2866) has two- and three-day weekend cooking demonstrations by celebrated chefs.

Horseback Riding **FITS Equestrian** (685 Lateen Rd., Solvang, CA 93463, tel. 805/688–9494 or 800/666–3487) leaves from nearby Oakland on a week-long "Ride of the Mustangs" around the many nature parks in the bay area.

Nature and Ecology **Earthwatch** (680 Mount Auburn St., Watertown, MA 02272, tel. 617/926–8000) recruits volunteers to serve in its EarthCorps as short-term assistants to scientists on research expeditions at Golden Gate National Recreation Area near San Francisco. **Lindblad's Special Expeditions** (720 Fifth Ave., New York, NY 10019, tel. 212/765–7740 or 800/762–0003) sail the historic waterways of the San Francisco Bay. **Oceanic Society Expeditions** (Fort Mason Center, Bldg. E, San Francisco, CA 94123, tel. 415/441–1106 or 800/326–7491) conducts whale-watching trips out of San Francisco December–April. The **Sierra Club** (730 Polk St., San Francisco, CA 94109, tel. 415/776–2211) offers guided tours to the regions surrounding San Francisco.

Tips for British Travelers

Contact the **United States Travel and Tourism Administration** (Box 1EN, tel. 0171/495–4466).

Passports and Visas British citizens need a valid 10-year passport. A visa is not necessary unless (1) you are planning to stay more than 90 days; (2) your trip is for purposes other than vacation; (3) you have at some time been refused a visa, or refused admission, to the United States, or have been required to leave by the U.S. Immigration and Naturalization Service; or (4) you do not have a return or onward ticket. You will need to fill out the Visa Waiver Form, I-94W, supplied by the airline.

To apply for a visa or for more information, call the U.S. Embassy's Visa Information Line (tel. 01891/200–290; calls cost 48p per minute or 36p per minute cheap rate). If you qualify for the visa-free travel but want a visa anyway, you must apply in writing, enclosing a self- addressed envelope, to the U.S. Embassy's Visa Branch (5 Upper Grosvenor St., London W1A 2JB), or, for residents of Northern Ireland, to the U.S. Consulate General (Queen's House, Queen St., Belfast BT1 6EO). Submit a completed Nonimmigrant Visa Application (Form 156), a valid passport, a photograph, and evidence of your intended departure from the United States after a temporary visit. If you require a visa, call 01891/234–224 to schedule an interview.

Customs British visitors aged 21 or over may import the following into the United States: 200 cigarettes or 50 cigars or 2 kilograms of tobacco; 1 U.S. liter of alcohol; gifts to the value of $100. Restricted items include meat products, seeds, plants, and fruits. Never carry illegal drugs.

Returning to the United Kingdom you may import duty-free 200 cigarettes, 100 cigarillos, 50 cigars or 250 grams of tobacco; 1

liter of spirits or 2 liters of fortified or sparkling wine; 2 liters of still table wine; 60 milliliters of perfume; 250 milliliters of toilet water; plus £36 worth of other goods, including gifts and souvenirs.

For further information or a copy of "A Guide for Travellers," which details standard customs procedures as well as what you may bring into the United Kingdom from abroad, contact HM Customs and Excise (New King's Beam House, 22 Upper Ground, London SE1).

Insurance Most tour operators, travel agents, and insurance agents sell specialized policies covering accident, medical expenses, personal liability, trip cancellation, and loss or theft of personal property. Some policies include coverage for delayed departure and legal expenses, winter sports, accidents, or motoring abroad. You can also purchase an annual travel-insurance policy valid for every trip you make during the year in which it's purchased (usually only trips of less than 90 days). Before you leave, make sure you will be covered if you have a preexisting medical condition or are pregnant; your insurers may not pay for routine or continuing treatment, or may require a note from your doctor certifying your fitness to travel.

The **Association of British Insurers,** a trade association representing 450 insurance companies, advises extra medical coverage for visitors to the United States.

For advice by phone or a free booklet, "Holiday Insurance," that sets out what to expect from a holiday-insurance policy and gives price guidelines, contact the Association of British Insurers (51 Gresham St., London EC2V 7HQ, tel. 0171/600–3333; 30 Gordon St., Glasgow G1 3PU, tel. 0141/226–3905; Scottish Provincial Bldg., Donegall Sq. W, Belfast BT1 6JE, tel. 01232/249176; call for other locations).

Tour Operators Tour operators offering packages to San Francisco include **British Airways Holidays** (Atlantic House, Hazelwick Ave., Three Bridges, Crawley, West Sussex RH10 1NP, tel. 01293/611611), **Jetsave** (Sussex House, London Rd., East Grinstead, West Sussex RH19 1LD, tel. 01342/312033), **Key to America** (15 Feltham Rd., Ashford, Middlesex TW15 1DQ, tel. 01784/248777), **Kuoni Travel Ltd.** (Kuoni House, Dorking, Surrey RH5 4AZ, tel. 01306/76711), **Premier Holidays** (Premier Travel Center, Westbrook, Milton Rd., Cambridge CB4 1YQ, tel. 01223/355977), and **Trailfinders** (194 Kensington High St., London W8 7RG, tel. 0171/937–5400; 58 Deansgate, Manchester, M3 2FF, tel. 0161/839–6969).

Airfares Fares vary enormously. Fares from consolidators are usually the cheapest, followed by promotional fares such as APEX. A few phone calls should reveal the current picture. When comparing fares, don't forget to figure airport taxes and weekend supplements. Once you know which airline is going your way at the right time for the least money, book immediately, since seats at the lowest prices often sell out quickly. Travel agents will generally hold a reservation for up to five days, especially if you give a credit card number.

Some travel agencies that offer cheap fares to San Francisco include **Trailfinders** (42–50 Earl's Court Rd., London W8 6EJ, tel. 0171/937–5400), specialists in round-the-world fares and independent travel; **Travel Cuts** (295a Regent St., London W1R 7YA, tel. 0171/637–3161), the Canadian Students' travel service; and **Flightfile** (49 Tottenham Court Rd., London W1P 9RE, tel. 0171/700–2722), a flight-only agency.

Car Rental Make the arrangements from home to avoid inconvenience, save money, and guarantee yourself a vehicle. Major firms include **Alamo** (tel. 0800/272–200), **Budget** (tel. 0800/181–181), **EuroDollar** (tel. 01895/233–300), **Europcar** (tel. 0181/950–5050), and **Hertz** (tel. 0181/679–1799).

In the United States you must be 21 to rent a car; rates may be higher for those under 25. Extra costs cover child seats, compulsory for children under 5 (about $3 per day); additional drivers (around $1.50 per day); and the all-but-compulsory Collision Damage Waiver (*see* Car Rentals, *below*). To pick up your reserved car, you will need the reservation voucher, a passport, a U.K. driver's license, and a travel insurance policy covering each driver.

When to Go

Any time of the year is the right time to go to San Francisco, which is acknowledged to be one of the most beautiful cities in the world. The fog rolls in during the summer, but it seems less an inconvenience than part of the atmosphere of this never-mundane place. As long as you remember to bring along sweaters and jackets, even in August, you can't miss.

San Francisco is on the tip of a peninsula, surrounded on three sides by the Pacific Ocean and San Francisco Bay. Its climate is quintessentially marine and moderate: It never gets very hot—anything above 80° is reported as a shocking heat wave—or very cold (as far as the thermometer is concerned, anyway).

For all its moderation, however, San Francisco can be tricky. In the summertime, fog often rolls in from the ocean, blocking the sun and filling the air with dampness. At times like this you'll want a coat, jacket, or warm sweater instead of the shorts or lightweight summer clothes that seem so comfortable in most North American cities during July and August. Mark Twain is credited with observing that the coldest winter he ever spent was one summer in San Francisco. He may have been exaggerating, but it's best not to expect a hot summer in this city.

If you travel to the north, east, or south of the city, you will find warmer summer temperatures. Shirtsleeves and thin cottons are usually just fine for the Wine Country.

Be prepared for rain in winter, especially December and January. Winds off the ocean can add to the chill factor, so pack some warm clothing to be on the safe side.

Climate The following are average daily maximum and minimum temperatures for San Francisco.

Jan.	55F	13C	May	66F	19C	Sept.	73F	23C
	41	–5		48	–9		51	11
Feb.	59F	15C	June	69F	21C	Oct.	69F	21C
	42	–6		51	11		50	10
Mar.	60F	16C	July	69F	21C	Nov.	64F	18C
	44	–7		51	11		44	–7
Apr.	62F	17C	Aug.	69F	21C	Dec.	57F	14C
	46	–8		53	12		42	–6

Information For current weather conditions and forecasts for cities in the
Sources United States and abroad, plus the local time and helpful travel tips, call the **Weather Channel Connection** (tel. 900/932–8437; 95¢ per minute) from a touch-tone phone.

Festivals and Seasonal Events

January The **Shrine East-West All-Star Football Classic** (1651 19th Ave., 94122, tel. 415/661–0291), America's oldest all-star sports event, is played every year in the Stanford University Stadium in Palo Alto, some 25 miles south of San Francisco.

January– April Whale-watching can be enjoyed throughout the winter, when hundreds of gray whales migrate along the Pacific coast. For information about viewing sites and special excursions, contact the California Office of Tourism (801 K St., Suite 1600, Sacramento 95814, tel. 916/322–1397).

February The **Chinese New Year** celebration in San Francisco's Chinese community, North America's largest, lasts for two weeks. It culminates with the justly famous Golden Dragon Parade. For a complete schedule of events, send a stamped, self-addressed envelope to the Chinese Chamber of Commerce (730 Sacramento St., 94108, tel. 415/982–3000).

March On the Sunday closest to March 17, San Francisco's **St. Patrick's Day** celebration is marked by a long parade through the downtown area and by snake races.

April The **Cherry Blossom Festival,** an elaborate presentation of Japanese culture and customs, winds up with a colorful parade through San Francisco's Japantown. A detailed schedule is available after mid-March; send a stamped, self-addressed envelope to Japan Center (1520 Webster St., 94115, tel. 415/922–6776).

May–June May's *San Francisco Examiner* **Bay to Breakers Race** (Examiner Bay to Breakers, Box 7260, 94120, tel. 415/777–7770) is crowded and jovial and takes runners across the city on a 7½-mile route from bayside to oceanside. There are abundant festivities before and after the race; it's a huge San Francisco event that can be enjoyed by participants and spectators. **Carnival,** held in the city's Mission District in May or June, is a Mardi Gras–like revel that includes a parade, a street festival, and a costume contest in which participants indulge their fantasies through masquerade, music, and dance.

July The city's **Fourth of July** celebration is held at Crissy Field in the Presidio and features family festivities beginning in mid-afternoon and a fireworks display at 9 PM.

September–
October
The **San Francisco Blues Festival** (tel. 415/826–6837) is held on the Great Meadow at Fort Mason every year in September. On weekends then or in October, the **Renaissance Pleasure Faire** (Living History Centre, Box B, Novato 94948, tel. 415/892–0937) is held in Novato, 20 miles north of San Francisco. Three thousand costumed participants stage an authentic Elizabethan harvest festival. The **Columbus Day** celebration (678 Green St., 94133, tel. 415/434–1492) begins with a weekend festival of Italian food and music, a blessing of the fleet at Fisherman's Wharf, and a parade through North Beach on the Sunday closest to the holiday. Also in October is the **Grand National Livestock Exposition, Rodeo, and Horse Show,** held at an immense San Francisco facility appropriately named the Cow Palace (Box 34206, 94134, tel. 415/469–6065); it's a world-class annual competition, with thousands of top livestock and horses.

December The **New Pickle Circus** (tel. 415/826–0747), a particularly joyous group that started out as a band of street performers during the early 1970s, performs annually during the holiday season at the Palace of Fine Arts Theater in the Marina District or at nearby Fort Mason.

What to Pack

Clothing The most important single rule to bear in mind when packing for a vacation in the San Francisco Bay Area is to prepare for changes in temperature. An hour's drive can take you up or down many degrees, and the variation from daytime to nighttime in a single location is often marked. Take along sweaters, jackets, and clothes for layering as your best insurance for coping with variations in temperature. Include shorts or cool cottons for summer. Always tuck in a bathing suit, because most lodgings include a pool.

Although casual dressing is a hallmark of the California lifestyle, men will need a jacket and tie for many good restaurants in the evening, and women will be more comfortable in something dressier than regulation sightseeing garb.

Considerations of formality aside, bear in mind that San Francisco can be chilly at any time of the year, especially in summer, when the fog is apt to descend and stay. Nothing is more pitiful than the sight of uninformed tourists in shorts, their legs blue with cold. Take along clothes that will keep you warm, even if the season doesn't seem to warrant it.

Miscella-
neous
Although you can buy supplies of film, sunscreen lotion, aspirin, and most other necessities in California, it's a good idea to take along a reasonable supply of the things you know you will need, to spare yourself the bother of stocking up. Also, pack a list of

the offices that supply refunds for lost or stolen traveler's checks.

Bring an extra pair of eyeglasses or contact lenses in your carry-on luggage. If you have a health problem that requires a prescription drug, pack enough to last the duration of the trip. Don't pack them in luggage that you plan to check, in case your bags go astray.

Luggage
Regulations
Free airline baggage allowances depend on the airline, the route, and the class of your ticket; ask in advance. In general, on domestic flights you are entitled to check two bags—neither exceeding 62 inches, or 158 centimeters (length + width + height), or weighing more than 70 pounds (32 kilograms). A third piece may be brought aboard; its total dimensions are generally limited to less than 45 inches (114 centimeters), so it will fit easily under the seat in front of you or in the overhead compartment. In the United States the Federal Aviation Administration gives airlines broad latitude to limit carry-on allowances and tailor them to different aircraft and operational conditions. Charges for excess, oversize, or overweight pieces vary.

Safeguarding
Your Luggage
Before leaving home, itemize your bags' contents and their worth in case they go astray. To minimize that risk, tag them inside and out with your name, address, and phone number. (If you use your home address, cover it so potential thieves can't see it.) Put a copy of your itinerary inside each bag, so that you can easily be tracked. At check-in, make sure that the tag attached by baggage handlers bears the correct three-letter code for your destination. If your bags do not arrive with you, or if you detect damage, file a written report with the airline before you leave the airport.

Insurance
In the event of loss, damage, or theft on domestic flights, airlines' liability is $1,250 per passenger, excluding the valuable items such as jewelry or cameras that are listed in the fine print on your ticket. Excess-valuation insurance can be bought directly from the airline at check-in. Your homeowner's policy may fill the gap; or firms such as **The Travelers Companies** (1 Tower Sq., Hartford, CT 06183, tel. 203/277–0111 or 800/243–3174) and **Wallach and Company** (107 W. Federal St., Box 480, Middleburg, VA 22117, tel. 703/687–3166 or 800/237–6615) sell baggage insurance.

Getting Money from Home

Many automated-teller machines (ATMs) are tied to international networks such as **Cirrus** and **Plus.** You can use your bank card at ATMs to withdraw money from an account and get cash advances on a credit-card account if your card has been programmed with a personal identification number, or PIN. Check in advance on limits on withdrawals and cash advances within specified periods. On cash advances you are charged interest from the day you receive the money from ATMs or tellers. Transaction fees for ATM withdrawals outside your home turf may be higher than for withdrawals at home.

For specific Cirrus locations in the United States and Canada, call 800/424–7787. For U.S. Plus locations, call 800/843–7587 and press the area code and first three digits of the number you're calling from (or of the calling area where you want an ATM).

Wiring
Money

You don't have to be a cardholder to send or receive a **Money-Gram from American Express** for up to $10,000. Go to a Money-Gram agent in retail and convenience stores and American Express travel offices, pay up to $1,000 with a credit card and anything over that in cash. You are allowed a free long-distance call to give the transaction code to your intended recipient, who needs only to present identification and the reference number to the nearest MoneyGram agent to pick up the cash. Money-Gram agents are in more than 70 countries (call 800/926–9400 for locations). Fees range from 3% to 10%, depending on the amount and how you pay.

You can also use **Western Union.** To wire money, take either cash or a cashier's check to the nearest office or call and use Master-Card or Visa. Money sent from the United States or Canada will be available for pickup at agent locations in 78 countries within minutes. Once the money is in the system it can be picked up at *any* one of 22,000 locations (call 800/325–6000 for the one nearest you).

Traveling with Cameras, Camcorders, and Laptops

Film and
Cameras

If your camera is new or if you haven't used it for a while, shoot and develop a few test rolls of film before you leave home. Store film in a cool, dry place—never in the car's glove compartment or on the shelf under the rear window.

Airport security X-rays generally aren't harmful to film with ISO below 400. To protect your film, carry it with you in a clear plastic bag and ask for a hand inspection. Such requests are honored at U.S. airports. Don't depend on a lead-lined bag to protect film in checked luggage—the airline may increase the radiation to see what's inside.

Camcorders

Before your trip, put camcorders through their paces, invest in a skylight filter to protect the lens, and check all the batteries. Airport security personnel may ask you to turn on the camcorder to prove that it's what it appears to be, so make sure the battery is charged.

Videotape

Videotape is not damaged by X-rays, but it may be harmed by the magnetic field of a walk-through metal detector, so ask for a hand-check.

Laptops

Security X-rays do not harm hard-disk or floppy-disk storage, but you may request a hand-check, at which point you may be asked to turn on the computer to prove that it is what it appears to be. (Check your battery before departure.) Most airlines allow you to use your laptop aloft except during takeoff and landing (so as not to interfere with navigation equipment).

Traveling with Children

Publications *Family Travel Times,* published 10 times a year by **Travel With**
Newsletter **Your Children** (TWYCH, 45 W. 18th St., 7th Floor Tower, New
York, NY 10011, tel. 212/206–0688; annual subscription $55), cov-
ers destinations, types of vacations, and modes of travel.
TWYCH also publishes *Cruising with Children* and *Skiing with
Children.*

Books Two books that can give you suggestions for traveling with kids
in the San Francisco area are *Places to Go with Children in Northern California,* by Elizabeth Pomada ($9.95; Chronicle Books,
275 Fifth St., San Francisco, CA 94103, tel. 800/777–7240) and
San Francisco Family Fun, by Carole Terwilliger Meyers
($12.95 plus $3 for shipping; Carousel Press, Box 6061, Albany,
CA 94706, tel. 510/527–5849). **"Kidding Around in San Francisco"**
is a feature in the SFCVB's *San Francisco Book* (*see* Tourist
Information, *above*).

Great Vacations with Your Kids, by Dorothy Jordan and Mar-
jorie Cohen ($13; Penguin USA, 120 Woodbine St., Bergenfield,
NJ 07621, tel. 800/253–6476), and *Traveling with Children—And
Enjoying It,* by Arlene K. Butler ($11.95 plus $3 shipping per
book; Globe Pequot Press, Box 833, 6 Business Park Rd., Old
Saybrook, CT 06475, tel. 800/243–0495 or 800/962–0973 in CT),
help you plan your trip with children, from toddlers to teens.
From the same publisher are *Recommended Family Resorts in
the United States, Canada, and the Caribbean,* by Jane Wilford
with Janet Tice ($12.95), and *Recommended Family Inns of
America* ($12.95).

Tour **Grandtravel** (6900 Wisconsin Ave., Suite 706, Chevy Chase, MD
Operators 20815, tel. 301/986–0790 or 800/247–7651) offers tours for people
traveling with their grandchildren. The catalogue, as charm-
ingly written and illustrated as a children's book, positively in-
vites armchair traveling with lap-sitters aboard. **Rascals in
Paradise** (650 5th St., Suite 505, San Francisco, CA 94107, tel.
415/978–9800 or 800/872–7225) specializes in adventurous, exotic, and fun-filled vacations for families to carefully screened
resorts and hotels around the world.

Getting On domestic flights, children under 2 not occupying a seat travel
There free, and older children currently travel on the "lowest applica-
Airfares ble" adult fare.

Baggage The adult baggage allowance applies for children paying half or
more of the adult fare.

Safety Seats The FAA recommends the use of safety seats aloft and details
approved models in the free leaflet **"Child/Infant Safety Seats
Recommended for Use in Aircraft"** (available from the Federal
Aviation Administration, APA-200, 800 Independence Ave. SW,
Washington, DC 20591, tel. 202/267–3479; Information Hotline,
tel. 800/322–7873). Airline policy varies: U.S. carriers allow
FAA-approved models bearing a sticker declaring their FAA ap-
proval. Because these seats are strapped into regular passenger

seats, airlines may require that a ticket be bought for an infant who would otherwise ride free.

Facilities Aloft Some airlines provide other services for children, such as children's meals and freestanding bassinets (only to those with seats at the bulkhead, where there's enough legroom). Make your request when reserving. The annual February/March issue of *Family Travel Times* details children's services on dozens of airlines ($10; *see above*). "Kids and Teens in Flight" (free from the U.S. Department of Transportation's Office of Consumer Affairs (R-25, Washington, DC 20590, tel. 202/366–2220) offers tips for children flying alone.

Hints for Travelers with Disabilities

California is a national leader in making attractions and facilities accessible to travelers with disabilities. Since 1982, the state building code has required that all construction for public use include access for the disabled. State laws more than a decade old provide special privileges, such as license plates allowing special parking spaces, unlimited parking in time-limited spaces, and free parking in metered spaces. Identification from states other than California is honored.

The **San Francisco Mayor's Disabilities Coordinator** (10 U.N. Plaza, Suite 600, San Francisco, CA 94102, tel. 415/554–8925) provides information on accommodations and attractions for visitors with specific disabilities.

The **National Park Service** provides a Golden Access Passport free of charge to those who are medically blind or have a permanent disability; the passport covers the entry fee for the holder and anyone accompanying the holder in the same private vehicle as well as a 50% discount on camping and various other user fees. Apply for the passport in person at a national recreation facility that charges an entrance fee; proof of disability is required. For additional information, write to the National Park Service (Box 37127, Washington, DC 20013-7127).

All stations in Bay Area Rapid Transit (BART) are equipped with elevators. Call the station agent on the white courtesy telephone. Stations also have wheelchair-accessible rest rooms, phones, and drinking fountains. For information on a Bay Region Transit Discount Card, call BART (tel. 415/788–2278).

Organizations Several organizations provide travel information for people with disabilities, usually for a membership fee, and some publish newsletters and bulletins. Among them are the **Information Center for Individuals with Disabilities** (Fort Point Pl., 27–43 Wormwood St., Boston, MA 02210, tel. 617/727–5540 or 800/462–5015 in MA between 11 and 4, or leave message, TTY 617/345–9743); **Mobility International USA** (Box 10767, Eugene, OR 97440, tel. and TTY 503/343–1284, fax 503/343–6812), the U.S. branch of an international organization based in Britain (*see below*) that has affiliates in 30 countries; **Moss Rehab Hospital Travel Information Service** (tel. 215/456–9603, TTY 215/456–9602); the **Travel Industry and Disabled Exchange** (TIDE, 5435

Donna Ave., Tarzana, CA 91356, tel. 818/344–3640, fax 818/344–0078); and **Travelin' Talk** (Box 3534, Clarksville, TN 37043, tel. 615/552–6670, fax 615/552–1182).

In the United Kingdom   Important information sources include the **Royal Association for Disability and Rehabilitation** (RADAR, 25 Mortimer St., London W1N 8AB, tel. 0171/637–5400), which publishes travel information for people with disabilities in Britain, and **Mobility International** (228 Borough High St., London SE1 1JX, tel. 0171/403–5688), an international clearinghouse of travel information for people with disabilities.

Travel Agencies and Tour Operators   **Flying Wheels Travel** (143 W. Bridge St., Box 382, Owatonna, MN 55060, tel. 507/451–5005 or 800/535–6790) is a travel agency specializing in domestic and worldwide cruises, tours, and independent travel itineraries for people with mobility problems. Adventurers should contact **Wilderness Inquiry** (1313 Fifth St. SE, Minneapolis, MN 55414, tel. and TTY 612/379–3838), which orchestrates action-packed trips like white-water rafting, sea kayaking, and dog sledding for people with disabilities. Tours are designed to bring together people who have disabilities with those who don't.

Publications   Two free publications are available from the U.S. Consumer Information Center (Pueblo, CO 81009): **"New Horizons for the Air Traveler with a Disability"** (include Dept. 608Y in the address), a U.S. Department of Transportation booklet describing changes resulting from the 1986 Air Carrier Access Act and from the 1990 Americans with Disabilities Act, and the Airport Operators Council's *Access Travel: Airports* (Dept. 5804), which describes facilities and services for people with disabilities at more than 500 airports worldwide.

Fodor's publishes *Great American Vacations for Travelers with Disabilities* (available in bookstores, or call 800/533–6478) detailing services and accessible attractions, restaurants, and hotels in San Francisco and other U.S. destinations. The 500-page *Travelin' Talk Directory* (*see* Organizations, *above*; $35 check or money order with a money-back guarantee) lists names and addresses of people and organizations who offer help for travelers with disabilities. Twin Peaks Press (Box 129, Vancouver, WA 98666, tel. 206/694–2462 or 800/637–2256) publishes the *Directory of Travel Agencies for the Disabled* ($19.95, plus $2 for shipping), listing more than 370 agencies worldwide. The Sierra Club publishes *Easy Access to National Parks* ($16 plus $3 shipping; 730 Polk St., San Francisco, CA 94109, tel. 415/776–2211).

Hints for Older Travelers

Organizations   The **American Association of Retired Persons** (AARP, 601 E St. NW, Washington, DC 20049, tel. 202/434–2277) provides independent travelers who are members of the AARP (open to those age 50 or older; $8 per person or couple annually) with the Purchase Privilege Program, which offers discounts on lodging, car rentals, and sightseeing, and the AARP Motoring Plan, which furnishes domestic trip-routing information and emergency road-service aid for an annual fee of $39.95 per person or couple ($59.95 for a premium version). AARP also arranges group tours, cruises, and apartment living through AARP Travel Experience from American Express (400 Pinnacle Way, Suite 450, Norcross, GA 30071, tel. 800/927–0111or 800/745–4567).

Two other organizations offer discounts on lodgings, car rentals, and other travel products, along with such nontravel perks as magazines and newsletters: the **National Council of Senior Citizens** (1331 F St. NW, Washington, DC 20004, tel. 202/347–8800; membership $12 annually) and **Mature Outlook** (6001 N. Clark St., Chicago, IL 60660, tel. 800/336–6330; $9.95 annually).

Note: Mention your senior-citizen identification card when booking hotel reservations for reduced rates, not when checking out. At restaurants, show your card before you're seated; discounts may be limited to certain menus, days, or hours. If you are renting a car, ask about promotional rates that might improve on your senior-citizen discount.

Educational Travel The nonprofit **Elderhostel** (75 Federal St., 3rd Floor, Boston, MA 02110, tel. 617/426–7788) has offered inexpensive study programs for people 60 and older since 1975. Held at more than 1,800 educational institutions, courses cover everything from marine science to Greek myths and cowboy poetry. Participants usually attend lectures in the morning and spend the afternoon sightseeing or on field trips; they live in dorms on the host campuses. Fees for programs in the United States and Canada, which usually last one week, run about $300, not including transportation.

Tour Operators The following tour operators specialize in older travelers: If you want to take your grandchildren, look into **Grandtravel** (*see* Traveling with Children, *above*). **Saga International Holidays** (222 Berkeley St., Boston, MA 02116, tel. 800/343–0273) caters to those over age 60 who like to travel in groups. **SeniorTours** (508 Irvington Rd., Drexel Hill, PA 19026, tel. 215/626–1977 or 800/227–1100) arranges motorcoach tours throughout the United States and Nova Scotia, as well as Caribbean cruises.

Publications *The 50+ Traveler's Guidebook: Where to Go, Where to Stay, What to Do* by Anita Williams and Merrimac Dillon ($12.95; St. Martin's Press, 175 Fifth Ave., New York, NY 10010) is available in bookstores and offers many useful tips. "The Mature Traveler" (Box 50820, Reno, NV 89513, tel. 702/786–7419; $29.95), a monthly newsletter, contains many travel deals.

Hints for Gay and Lesbian Travelers

Organizations The **International Gay Travel Association** (Box 4974, Key West, FL 33041, tel. 305/292–0217, 800/999–7925 or 800/448–8550), which has 700 members, will provide you with names of travel agents and tour operators who specialize in gay travel. The **Gay & Lesbian Visitors Center of New York Inc.** (135 W. 20th St., 3rd Floor, New York, NY 10011, tel. 212/463–9030 or 800/395–2315; $100 annually) mails a monthly newletter, valuable coupons, and more to its members.

Tour Operators and Travel Agencies The dominant travel agency in the market is **Above and Beyond** (3568 Sacramento St., San Francisco, CA 94118, tel. 415/922–2683 or 800/397–2681). Tour operator **Olympus Vacations** (8424 Santa Monica Blvd. #721, West Hollywood, CA 90069; tel. 310/657–2220 or 800/965–9678) offers all-gay and lesbian resort holidays. **Skylink Women's Travel** (746 Ashland Ave., Santa Monica, CA 90405, tel. 310/452–0506 or 800/225-5759) handles individual travel for lesbians all over the world and conducts two international and five domestic group trips annually.

Publications The premiere international travel magazine for gays and lesbians is *Our World* (1104 N. Nova Rd., Suite 251, Daytona Beach, FL 32117, tel. 904/441–5367; $35 for 10 issues). **"Out & About"** (tel. 203/789–8518 or 800/929–2268; $49 for 10 issues, full refund if you aren't satisfied) is a 16-page monthly newletter with extensive information on resorts, hotels, and airlines that are gay-friendly.

Smoking

Limitations on smoking are becoming increasingly common; if you smoke, be sensitive to restrictions. If you do not smoke, ask for and expect accommodations for nonsmokers on airplanes, in hotels, in restaurants, and in many other public places.

Most hotels and motels have no-smoking rooms; in larger establishments entire floors are reserved for nonsmokers. Most bed-and-breakfast inns do not allow smoking on the premises.

Most eating places of any size have no-smoking sections. Many cities and towns in California have ordinances requiring areas for nonsmokers in restaurants and many other public places.

The trend in California, a health-conscious state, is toward more NO SMOKING signs. Expect to see them in many places.

Further Reading

While there are many novels with a San Francisco setting, they don't come any better than *The Maltese Falcon* by Dashiell Hammett, the founder of the hard-boiled school of detective fiction. First published in 1930, Hammett's books continue to be readily available in new editions, and the details about the fog, the hills, and seedy offices south of Market continue to be accurate.

Other novels are John Gregory Dunne's recent *The Red White and Blue*, Stephen Longstreet's *All or Nothing* and *Our Father's House*, and Alice Adams's *Rich Rewards*. Many of the short stories in Adams's collection, *To See You Again*, have Bay Area settings.

Two books that are filled with interesting background information on the city are Richard H. Dillon's *San Francisco: Adventurers and Visionaries* and *San Francisco: As It Is, As It Was*, by Paul C. Johnson and Richard Reinhardt.

Armistead Maupin's soap-opera–style *Tales of the City* stories are set in San Francisco; they were recently made into a PBS series, much to the delight of Maupin's devoted fans.

For anecdotes, gossip, and the kind of detail that will make you feel almost like a native San Franciscan, get hold of any of the books by the longtime San Francisco *Chronicle* columnist Herb Caen: *Baghdad-by-the- Bay, Only in San Francisco, One Man's San Francisco,* and *San Francisco: City on Golden Hills.*

Arriving and Departing

From North America by Plane

Flights are either nonstop, direct, or connecting. A **nonstop** flight requires no change of plane and makes no stops. A **direct** flight stops at least once and can involve a change of plane, although the flight number remains the same; if the first leg is late, the second waits. This is not the case with a **connecting** flight, which involves a different plane and a different flight number.

Airports and Airlines   San Francisco International Airport (tel. 415/761–0800) is just south of the city, off U.S. 101. American carriers serving San Francisco are **Alaska Air** (tel. 800/426–0333), **American** (tel. 800/433–7300), **Continental** (tel. 800/525–0280), **Delta** (tel. 800/221–1212), **Southwest** (tel. 800/531–5601), **TWA** (tel. 800/221–2000), **United** (tel. 800/241–6522), and **USAir** (tel. 800/438–4322). International carriers include **Air New Zealand** (tel. 800/261–1234), **British Airways** (tel. 800/247–9297), **Canadian Airlines** (tel. 800/426–7000), **China Airlines** (tel. 800/227–5118), **Japan Air Lines** (tel. 800/525–3663), **Lufthansa** (tel. 800/645–3880), **Mexicana** (tel. 800/531–7921), and **Qantas** (tel. 800/227–4500). Several domestic airlines serve the Oakland Airport (tel. 415/577–4000), which is across the bay but not much farther away from downtown San Francisco (via I–880 and I–80), although traffic on the Bay Bridge may at times make travel time longer.

Cutting Costs   The Sunday travel section of most newspapers is a good source of deals. When booking, particularly through an unfamiliar company, call the Better Business Bureau and your local or state Consumer Protection Bureau to find out whether any complaints have been registered against the company, pay with a credit card if you can, and consider trip-cancellation and default insurance.

Promotional Airfares   Less expensive fares, called promotional or discount fares, are round-trip and involve restrictions, which vary according to the route and season. You must usually buy the ticket—commonly called an APEX (advance purchase excursion) when it's for international travel—in advance (seven, 14, or 21 days are standard), although some of the major airlines have added no-frills, cheap flights to compete with new bargain airlines on certain routes. These new low-cost carriers include **Private Jet** (tel. 800/949–9400), based in Atlanta and serving Miami, Dallas, St.

Thomas, St. Croix, Las Vegas, New York's Kennedy, Los Angeles, Chicago, and San Francisco. With the major airlines the cheaper fares generally require minimum and maximum stays (for instance, over a Saturday night or at least seven and no more than 30 days). Airlines generally allow some return date changes for a $25 to $50 fee, but most low-fare tickets are nonrefundable. Only a death in the family would prompt the airline to return any of your money if you cancel a nonrefundable ticket. However, you can apply an unused nonrefundable ticket toward a new ticket, again with a small fee. The lowest fare is subject to availability, and only a small percentage of the plane's total seats will be sold at that price. Contact the U.S. Department of Transportation's Office of Consumer Affairs (I–25, Washington, DC 20590, tel. 202/366–2220) for a copy of "Fly-Rights: A Guide to Air Travel in the U.S." *The Official Frequent Flyer Guidebook* by Randy Petersen (4715-C Town Center Dr., Colorado Springs, CO 80916, tel. 719/597–8899, 800/487-8893, or 800/485–8893; $14.99, plus $3 shipping and handling) yields valuable hints on getting the most for your air travel dollars.

Consolidators   Consolidators or bulk-fare operators—"bucket shops"—buy blocks of seats on scheduled flights that airlines anticipate they won't be able to sell. They pay wholesale prices, add a markup, and resell the seats to travel agents or directly to the public at prices that still undercut the airline's promotional or discount fares (higher than a charter ticket but lower than an APEX ticket, and usually without the advance-purchase restriction). Moreover, some consolidators sometimes give you your money back. Carefully read the fine print detailing penalties for changes and cancellations. If you doubt the reliability of a company, call the airline once you've made your booking and confirm that you do, indeed, have a reservation on the flight.

Discount   Travel clubs offer members unsold space on airplanes, cruise
Travel Clubs   ships, and package tours at as much as 50% below regular prices. Membership may include a regular bulletin or access to a toll-free hot line giving details of available trips departing from three or four days to several months in the future. Most also offer 50% discounts off hotel rack rates, but double check with the hotel to make sure it isn't offering a better promotional rate independent of the club. Clubs include **Discount Travel International** (114 Forrest Ave., Suite 203, Narberth, PA 19072, tel. 215/668–7184; $45 annually, single or family), **Entertainment Travel Editions** (Box 1014 Trumbull, CT 06611, tel. 800/445–4137; price ranges $28–$48), **Great American Traveler** (Box 27965, Salt Lake City, UT 84127, tel. 800/548–2812; $29.95 annually), **Moment's Notice Discount Travel Club** (425 Madison Ave., New York, NY 10017, tel. 212/486–0503; $45 annually, single or family), **Privilege Card** (3391 Peachtree Rd. NE, Suite 110, Atlanta, GA 30326, tel. 404/262–0222 or 800/236–9732; domestic annual membership $49.95, international, $74.95), **Travelers Advantage** (CUC Travel Service, 49 Music Sq. W, Nashville, TN 37203, tel. 800/548–1116; $49 annually, single or family), and **Worldwide Discount Travel Club** (1674 Meridian Ave., Miami Beach, FL 33139, tel. 305/534–2082; $50 annually for family, $40 single).

Publications The newsletter "Travel Smart" (40 Beechdale Rd., Dobbs Ferry, NY 10522, tel. 800/327–3633; $44 a year) has a wealth of travel deals in each monthly issue.

Smoking Since February 1990, smoking has been banned on all domestic flights of less than six hours' duration; the ban also applies to domestic segments of international flights aboard U.S. and foreign carriers.

Between the Airport and Downtown **SFO Airporter** (tel. 415/495–8404) provides bus service between downtown and the airport, making the round of downtown hotels. Buses run every 20 minutes from 5 AM to 11 PM, from the lower level outside the baggage claim area. The fare is $8 one-way, $14 round-trip.

For $11, **Supershuttle** will take you from the airport to anywhere within the city limits of San Francisco. At the airport, after picking up your luggage, call 415/871–7800 and a van will pick you up within five minutes. To go to the airport, make reservations (tel. 415/558–8500) 24 hours in advance. The Supershuttle stops at the upper level of the terminal, along with several other bus and van transport services.

Taxis to or from downtown take 20–30 minutes and average $30.

By Train

Amtrak (tel. 800/872–7245) trains (the *Zephyr,* from Chicago via Denver, and the *Coast Starlight,* traveling between Los Angeles and Seattle) stop in Oakland; from there buses will take you across the Bay Bridge to the Ferry Building on the Embarcadero at the foot of Market street in San Francisco.

By Bus

Greyhound serves San Francisco from the Transbay Terminal at 1st and Mission streets (tel. 415/558–6789 or 800/231–2222).

By Car

Route I–80 finishes its westward journey from New York's George Washington Bridge at the Bay Bridge, which links Oakland and San Francisco. U.S. 101, running north–south through the entire state, enters the city across the Golden Gate Bridge and continues south down the peninsula, along the west side of the bay.

Car Rentals

The best approach to renting a car in San Francisco is not to, at least for a day or two. First see how well suited the cable cars are to this city of hills, how well the Muni buses and streetcars get you around every neighborhood, how efficiently BART delivers you practically anywhere on the bay. Chances are that you won't want a car, unless you're preparing to take excursions into Marin County, the Wine Country, or Silicon Valley.

Most major car-rental companies are represented in San Francisco, including **Alamo** (tel. 800/327–9633); **Avis** (tel. 800/331–1212, 800/879–2847 in Canada); **Budget** (tel. 800/527–0700); **Dollar** (tel. 800/800–4000); **Hertz** (tel. 800/654–3131, 800/263–0600 in Canada); and **National** (tel. 800/227–7368). Unlimited-mileage rates range from $32 per day for an economy car to $47 for a large car; weekly unlimited-mileage rates range from $143 to $180. This does not include tax, which in San Francisco is up to 8% on car rentals.

San Francisco has many good budget rental-car companies: **American International** (tel. 415/692–4100), **Enterprise** (tel. 800/325–8007), and **Reliable** (tel. 415/928–4414) are a few. At the other end of the price spectrum, **Sunbelt** (tel 415/771–9191) specializes in BMWs, and Corvette and Miata convertibles.

Extra Charges Picking up the car in one city and leaving it in another may entail substantial drop-off charges or one-way service fees. The cost of a collision or loss-damage waiver (*see below*) can be high, also. Some rental agencies will charge you extra if you return the car *before* the time specified on your contract. Ask before making unscheduled drop-offs. Fill the tank when you turn in the vehicle to avoid being charged for refueling at what you'll swear is the most expensive pump in town.

Cutting Costs Major international companies have programs that discount their standard rates by 15%–30% if you make the reservation before departure (anywhere from 24 hours to 14 days), rent for a minimum number of days (typically three or four), and prepay the rental. More economical rentals may come as part of fly/drive or other packages, or even bare-bones deals that only combine the rental and an airline ticket (*see* Tours and Packages, *above*).

Insurance and Collision Damage Waiver Before you rent a car, find out exactly what coverage, if any, is provided by your personal auto insurer and by the rental company. Don't assume that you are covered. If you do want insurance from the rental company, secondary coverage may be the only type offered. You may already have secondary coverage if you charge the rental to a credit card. Only Diners Club (tel. 800/234–6377) provides primary coverage in the United States and worldwide.

In general if you have an accident, you are responsible for the automobile. Car-rental companies may offer a collision damage waiver (CDW), which ranges in cost from $4 to $14 a day. You should decline the CDW only if you are certain you are covered through your personal insurer or credit-card company. California, New York, and Illinois have outlawed the sale of CDW altogether.

Staying in San Francisco

Important Addresses and Numbers

Tourist
Information
The **San Francisco Convention and Visitors Bureau** (tel. 415/974–6900 or 415/391–2001 for a summary of daily events) maintains a visitor information center on the lower level at Hallidie Plaza (Powell and Market Sts.), just three blocks from Union Square, near the cable-car turnaround and the Powell Street entrance to BART. It's open weekdays 9–5:30, Saturdays 9–3, and Sundays 10–2.

The **Redwood Empire Association Visitor Information Center** on the 15th floor at 785 Market Street (tel. 415/543–8334) is open weekdays 9 AM–5 PM.

Emergencies For **police** or **ambulance,** telephone 911.

Doctors Two hospitals with 24-hour emergency rooms are **San Francisco General Hospital** (1001 Potrero Ave., tel. 415/206–8000) and the **Medical Center at the University of California, San Francisco** (500 Parnassus Ave. at 3rd Ave., near Golden Gate Park, tel. 415/476–1000).

Access Health Care provides drop-in medical care at two San Francisco locations, daily 8–8. No membership is necessary. *Davies Medical Center, Castro St. at Duboce Ave., tel. 415/565–6600; 26 California St. at Drumm St., tel. 415/397–2881.*

Pharmacies Several **Walgreen Drug Stores** have 24-hour pharmacies, including stores at 500 Geary Street near Union Square (tel. 415/673–8413) and 3201 Divisadero Street at Lombard Street (tel. 415/931–6417). Also try the Walgreen pharmacy at 135 Powell Street near Market Street (tel. 415/391–7222), which is open Monday–Saturday 8 AM–midnight, Sunday 9 AM–9 PM.

Getting Around San Francisco

Because San Francisco is relatively compact and because it's so difficult to find parking, we recommend that you do your exploring on foot or by bus as much as possible. You may not need a car at all, except perhaps for exploring the Presidio, Golden Gate Park, Lincoln Park, the Western Shoreline, and for making excursions out of town.

How to Get There from Union Square will tell you how to reach approximately 50 points of interest in the city by public transportation. It's free from the Redwood Empire Association Visitor Information Center (*see* Tourist Information in Important Addresses and Numbers, *above*).

By BART **Bay Area Rapid Transit** (tel. 415/922–2278) sends air-conditioned aluminum trains at speeds of up to 80 miles an hour across the bay to Oakland, Berkeley, Concord, Richmond, and Fremont. Trains also travel south from San Francisco as far as Daly City. Wall maps in the stations list destinations and fares (85¢–$3).

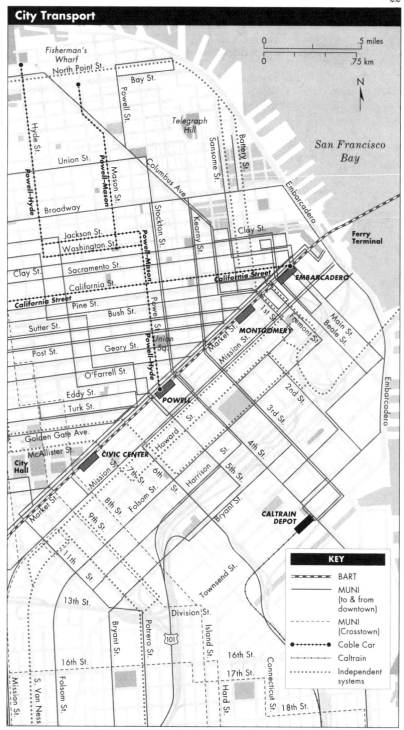

City Transport

Trains run Monday–Saturday 6 AM–midnight, Sunday 9 AM–midnight.

A $2.60 excursion ticket buys a three-county tour. You can visit any of the 34 stations for up to four hours as long as you exit and enter at the same station.

By Bus The **San Francisco Municipal Railway System,** or **Muni** (tel. 415/673–6864), includes buses and trolleys, surface streetcars, and the new below-surface streetcars, as well as cable cars. There is 24-hour service, and the fare is $1 for adults, 35¢ for senior citizens and children 5–17. The exact fare is always required; dollar bills or change are accepted. Muni no longer offers free transfers. Eighty-cent tokens can be purchased (in rolls of 10, 20, or 40) to reduce the cost of transferring; otherwise you must pay $1 each time you board a bus or light-rail vehicle.

A $6 pass good for unlimited travel all day on all routes can be purchased from ticket machines at cable-car terminals and at the Visitor Information Center in Hallidie Plaza (Powell and Market Sts.).

By Cable Car In June 1984, the cable-car system first introduced in 1873 returned to service after a $58.2-million overhaul. Because the cable cars had been declared a National Historic Landmark in 1964, renovation methods and materials had to preserve the historical and traditional qualities of the system. The rehabilitated moving landmark has been designed to withstand another century of use.

The Powell-Mason line (No. 59) and the Powell-Hyde line (No. 60) begin at Powell and Market streets near Union Square and terminate at Fisherman's Wharf. The California Street line (No. 61) runs east and west from Market Street near the Embarcadero to Van Ness Avenue.

Cable cars are popular, crowded, and an experience to ride: Move toward one quickly as it pauses, wedge yourself into any available space, and hold on! The sensation of moving up and down some of San Francisco's steepest hills in a small, open-air, clanging conveyance is not to be missed.

The fare (for one direction) is $2 for adults and children. Exact change is preferred, but operators will make change. There are self-service ticket machines (which do make change) at some terminals, kiosks at others; be wary of street people attempting to "help" you buy a ticket.

By Taxi Rates are high in the city, although most rides are relatively short. It is almost impossible to hail a passing cab, especially on weekends. Either phone or use the nearest hotel taxi stand to grab a cab.

By Car Driving in San Francisco can be a challenge because of the hills, the one-way streets, and the traffic. Take it easy, remember to curb your wheels when parking on hills, and use public transportation whenever possible. This is a great city for walking and a terrible city for parking. On certain streets, parking is forbidden during rush hours. Look for the warning signs; illegally parked cars are towed. Downtown parking lots are often full and always expensive. Finding a spot in North Beach at night, for instance, may be impossible.

Guided Tours

Orientation Tours

Golden City Tours offers 14-passenger vans and small buses for their 6½-hour city tours, which include such landmarks as Twin Peaks, the Cliff House, and Chinatown as well as a drive across the Golden Gate Bridge. Customers are picked up at all major airport hotels. A shorter afternoon tour omits Sausalito. *Tel. 415/692–3044. Cost: $39.50; afternoon tour $29.50.Tours daily. Make reservations the day before.*

Golden Gate Tours uses both vans and buses for its 3½-hour city tour, offered mornings and afternoons. You can combine the tour with a bay cruise. Customers are picked up at hotels and motels. Senior citizen and group rates are available. *Tel. 415/788–5775. Cost: $22.50 adults, $11 children under 12, $20.50 senior citizens. Tours daily. Make reservations the day before. Cruise combo: $30 adults, $15 children under 12, $28 senior citizens.*

Gray Line offers a variety of tours of the city, the Bay Area, and northern California. The city tour, on buses or double-decker buses, lasts 3½ hours and departs from the Transbay Terminal at 1st and Mission streets five to six times daily. Gray Line also picks up at centrally located hotels. **Gray Line-Cable Car Tours** sends motorized cable cars on a one-hour loop from Union Square to Fisherman's Wharf and two-hour tours including the Presidio, Japantown, and the Golden Gate Bridge. *Tel. 415/558–9400. Cost: $25 adults, $12.50 children. Tours daily. Make reservations the day before. Cable car tours, $12 and $18 adults, $6 and $9 children. No reservations necessary.*

The Great Pacific Tour uses 13-passenger vans for its daily 3½-hour city tour. Bilingual guides may be requested. They pick up at major San Francisco hotels. Tours are available to Monterey, the Wine Country, and Muir Woods. *Tel. 415/626–4499. Cost: $27 adults, $25 senior citizens, $20 children 5–11. Tours daily. Make reservations the day before, or, possibly, the same day.*

Superior Sightseeing Company operates 20-passenger vans and picks up visitors at hotels for 3½-hour tours of the city, ending at Fisherman's Wharf. There is also a full-day excursion to the Wine Country. *Tel. 415/550–1352. Cost: $24–$40 adults, $22–$38 senior citizens, $14–$20 children.*

Self-Guided Tours

San Francisco Scenic Route from **Near Escapes** (Box 193005-K, San Francisco 94119, tel. 415/386–8687) is an audiocassette with music and sound effects that will take you in your own car "where the tour buses can't go." It will guide you past Fisherman's Wharf, Chinatown, Golden Gate Park, Twin Peaks, Ghirardelli Square, Mission Dolores, the Civic Center, and other tourist attractions. A route map is included. The tape is available in a few local outlets, or you can get them mail-order for $12.

Special-Interest Tours **Near Escapes** (*see above*) plans unusual activities in the city and around the Bay Area. Recent tours and activities included tours of a Hindu temple in the East Bay, the Lawrence Berkeley Laboratory, the aircraft maintenance facility at the San Francisco Airport, and the quicksilver mines south of San Jose. Send $1 and a self-addressed, stamped envelope for a schedule for the month you plan to visit San Francisco.

Walking Tours **Castro District.** Trevor Hailey leads a 3½-hour tour focusing on the history and development of the city's gay and lesbian community, including restored Victorian homes, shops and cafés, and the NAMES Project, home of the AIDS memorial quilt. Tours depart at 10 AM Tuesday–Saturday from Castro and Market streets. *Tel. 415/550–8110. Cost: $30, including brunch.*

Chinatown with the "Wok Wiz." Cookbook author Shirley Fong-Torres leads a 3½-hour tour of Chinese markets, other businesses, and a fortune cookie factory. *Tel. 415/355–9657. Cost: $35, including lunch; $25 without lunch. Shorter tours, $15–$22.*

Chinese Cultural Heritage Foundation (tel. 415/986–1822) offers two walking tours of Chinatown. The Heritage Walk leaves Saturday at 2 PM and lasts about two hours. The Culinary Walk, a three-hour stroll through the markets and food shops, plus a dim sum lunch, is held every Wednesday at 10:30 AM. *Heritage Walk: $12 adults, $2 children under 12. Culinary Walk: $25 adults, $10 children under 12.*

Lodging

Home Exchange You can find a house, apartment, or other vacation property to exchange for your own by becoming a member of a home-exchange organization, which then sends you its annual directories listing available exchanges and includes your own listing in at least one of them. Arrangements for the actual exchange are made by the two parties to it, not by the organization. For more information contact the **International Home Exchange Association** (IHEA, 41 Sutter St., Suite 1090, San Francisco, CA 94104, tel. 415/673–0347 or 800/788–2489). These are some of the principal clearinghouses: **Homelink International** (Box 650, Key West, FL 33041, tel. 800/638–3841), publishes four annual directories (plus updates), with thousands of foreign and domestic listings; the $50 membership includes your listing in one book. At **Intervac International** (Box 590504, San Francisco, CA 94159, tel. 415/435–3497), with three annual directories, the membership is $62, or $72 if you want to receive the directories but remain unlisted. **Loan-a-Home** (2 Park La., Apt. 6E, Mount Vernon, NY 10552, tel. 914/664–7640) specializes in long-term exchanges; there is no charge to list your home, but the directories cost $35 or $45, depending on the number you receive.

Apartment and Villa Rentals If you want a home base that's roomy enough for a family and comes with cooking facilities, a furnished rental may be the solution. It's generally cost-wise, too, although not always—some rentals are luxury properties (economical only when your party is large). Home-exchange directories do list rentals—often second homes owned by prospective house swappers—and some services search for a house or apartment for you (even a castle if that's your fancy) and handle the paperwork. Some send an illustrated catalogue and others send photographs of specific properties, sometimes at a charge; up-front registration fees may apply. Among the companies are **Rent-a-Home International** (7200 34th Ave. NW, Seattle, WA 98117, tel. 206/789–9377 or 800/488–7368) and **Vacation Home Rentals Worldwide** (235 Kensington Ave., Norwood, NJ 07648, tel. 201/767–9393 or 800/633–3284). **Hideaways International** (767 Islington St., Box 4433, Portsmouth, NH 03802, tel. 603/430–4433 or 800/843–4433) functions as a travel club. Membership ($99 yearly per person or family at the same address) includes two annual guides plus quarterly newsletters; rentals are arranged directly between members, not by the club staff.

2 Portrait of San Francisco

Living with the Certainty of a Shaky Future

By John
Burks

*John Burks is
a professor of
journalism
and
humanities at
San Francisco
State
University. He
has served as
editor-in-chief
of two of the
city's leading
magazines,*
City *and* San
Francisco
Focus, *was a*
Newsweek
*correspondent
and managing
editor of* Rolling
Stone, *and
currently edits
the quarterly*
American Kite.

There's never been any question whether or not there will be another earthquake in San Francisco. The question is how soon. Even the kids here grow up understanding that it's just a matter of time, and from grade school on, earthquake safety drills become routine. At the first rumble, duck under your desk or table or stand in a doorway, they are instructed. Get away from windows to avoid broken glass. When the shaking stops, walk—don't run—outdoors, as far away from buildings as possible.

Sure as there are hurricanes along the Gulf of Mexico and blizzards in Maine, San Francisco's earthquakes are inevitable. Nobody here is surprised when the rolling and tumbling begins—it happens all the time. Just in the six months following the jarring 1989 earthquake, for instance, seismologists reported hundreds of aftershocks, ranging from the scarcely perceptible to those strong enough to bring down buildings weakened by October's jolt.

The Bay Area itself was created in upheaval such as this. Eons ago, a restless geology of shifting plates deep in the earth gave birth to the Sierra Mountains and the Pacific Coast Range. Every spring when the snows melted, the runoff rushed down from the mile-high Sierra peaks westward across what would eventually be known as California. Here, the runoff ran up against the coastal range, and a vast inland lake was formed.

The rampaging waters from the yearly thaw eventually crashed through the quake-shattered Coast Range to meet the Pacific Ocean, creating the gap now spanned by the Golden Gate Bridge. This breakthrough created San Francisco Bay, one of the world's great natural harbors, its fertile delta larger than that of the Mississippi River. What a fabulous setting for the city-to-be—surrounded on three sides by water, set off by dramatic mountainscapes to the north and south, and blessed by cool ocean breezes.

All this and gold, too. The twisting and rolling of so-called terra firma exposed rich veins of gold at and near ground level that otherwise would have remained hidden deep underground. The great upheaval pushed the Mother Lode to the surface and set the scene for the Gold Rush. But before the '49 miners came the Europeans. In the late 15th century, the Spanish writer Garci Ordonez de Montalvo penned a fictional description of a place he called California, a faraway land ruled by Queen Califia, where gold and precious stones were so plentiful the streets were lined with them. Montalvo's vision of wealth without limit helped fuel the voyages of the great 15th- and 16th-century

European explorers in the new world. They never did hit pay dirt here, but the name California stuck nevertheless.

Northern California was eventually settled, and in 1848, the population of San Francisco was 832. The discovery of gold in the California hills brought sudden and unprecedented wealth to this coastal trading outpost and her population exploded; by the turn of the century San Francisco was home to 343,000 people.

En route to its destiny as a premier city of the West, San Francisco was visited by innumerable quakes. Yet while the city's very foundations shook, residents found that each new rattler helped to strengthen San Francisco's self-image of adaptability. Robert Louis Stevenson wrote of the quakes' alarming frequency: "The fear of them grows yearly in a resident; he begins with indifference and ends in sheer panic." The big shaker of 1865 inspired humorist Mark Twain to look at the quakes in a different light by writing an earthquake "almanac" for the following year, which advised:

Oct. 23—Mild, balmy earthquakes.
Oct. 26—About this time expect more earthquakes; but do not look for them . . .
Oct. 27—Universal despondency, indicative of approaching disaster. Abstain from smiling or indulgence in humorous conversation . . .
Oct. 29—Beware!
Oct. 31—Go slow!
Nov. 1—Terrific earthquake. This is the great earthquake month. More stars fall and more worlds are slathered around carelessly and destroyed in November than in any month of the twelve.
Nov. 2—Spasmodic but exhilarating earthquakes, accompanied by occasional showers of rain and churches and things.
Nov. 3—Make your will.
Nov. 4—Sell out.

On the whole, those who settled in San Francisco were more inclined toward Twain's devil-may-care attitude—those who succumbed to Stevenson's panic didn't stick around for long. Certainly the multitude of vices that saturated the metropolis were sufficient to distract many men from their fears; throughout Chinatown and the infamous Barbary Coast, opium dens, gin mills, and bordellos operated day and night.

Money flowed. Money tempted. Money corrupted. The city was built on graft, and city hall became synonymous with corruption under the influence of political crooks like Blind Chris Buckley and Boss Ruef. The very building itself was a scandal. Planned for completion in six months at a cost of half a million dollars, the city hall ultimately took 29 years to build at a graft-inflated cost of $8 million, an astronomical sum at the dawning of the 20th century. When the San Andreas Fault set loose the 1906 earthquake, the most devastating ever to hit an American city, city hall was one of the first buildings to come crashing down. Its ruins exposed the shoddiest of building materials, an ironic symbol of the city's crime-ridden past.

The 1906 earthquake and fire has come to define San Francisco both for itself and the outside world. In the immediate aftermath of the catastrophe, San Franciscans wondered whether they ought to believe the preachers and reformers who declared that this terrible devastation had been wrought upon their wicked city by the avenging hand of God. San Franciscans asked themselves whether, somehow, they had earned it.

But the city was quick to prove its character. Fifty years earlier, six separate fires had destroyed most of San Francisco—yet each time it was rebuilt by a citizenry not ready to give up on either the gold or the city that gold had built. Now, in 1906, heroic firefighters dynamited one of the city's main thoroughfares to prevent the inferno from spreading all the way to the Pacific. The mood of San Franciscans was almost eerily calm, their neighborliness both heartwarming and jaunty. "Eat, drink, and be merry," proclaimed signs about town, "for tomorrow we may have to go to Oakland." No sooner had the flames died than rebuilding began—true to San Francisco tradition. Forty thousand construction workers poured into town to assist the proud, amazingly resilient residents.

The 1906 earthquake provided a chance to rethink the hodgepodge, get-rich-quick cityscape that had risen in the heat of Gold Rush frenzy. City fathers imported the revered urban planner Daniel Burnham, architect of the magnificent 1893 Chicago World's Fair, to reinvent San Francisco. "Make no little plans," Burnham intoned. "They have no power to stir men's souls."

The city's new Civic Center, built under Burnham's direction, was raised to celebrate the city's comeback and is regarded as one of America's most stately works of civic architecture. Its city hall stands as a monument to the city's will to prevail—from its colonnaded granite exterior to its exuberant interior, once described by Tom Wolfe as resembling "some Central American opera house. Marble arches, domes, acanthus leaves . . . quirks and galleries and gilt filigrees . . . a veritable angels' choir of gold." The inscription found over the mayor's office seems to sum it all up: "San Francisco, O glorious city of our hearts that has been tried and not found wanting, go thou with like spirit to make the future thine."

In 1915, San Francisco dazzled the world with its Panama–Pacific Exposition, designed to prove not only that it was back, but that it was back bigger and better and badder than ever before. An architectural wonderland, the Expo was built on 70 acres of marshy landfill, which later became the residential neighborhood called the Marina District. When the October 1989 earthquake struck, this neighborhood was badly damaged, and became a focus as the entire nation tuned in to see how San Francisco and her people would fare this time around.

Like the gold that surfaced in the Mother Lode, the 1989 quake once again brought out the best in this region's people. Out at

Candlestick Park, 62,000 fans were waiting for the start of the World Series between the San Francisco Giants and the Oakland A's when everything started shaking. They cut loose with a big cheer after the temblor subsided. One San Francisco fan quickly hand-lettered a sign and held it aloft: "That was Nothing—Wait Til the Giants Bat." When it became apparent that there would be no ball played that night, the fans departed from the ballpark, just like in a grade school earthquake safety drill, quietly and in good order.

This was what millions of TV viewers across the nation first saw of the local response to this major (7.1) earthquake and, by and large, the combination of good humor and relative calm they observed was an accurate reflection of the prevailing mood around the city. San Franciscans were not about to panic. Minutes after the quake struck, a San Francisco couple spread a lace tablecloth over the hood of their BMW and, sitting in the driveway of their splintered home, toasted passersby with champagne. Simultaneously, across San Francisco Bay, courageous volunteers and rescue workers set to work digging through the pancaked rubble of an Oakland freeway in the search for survivors, heedless that they, too, could easily be crushed in an aftershock. Throughout the Bay Area, hundreds volunteered to fight the fires, clear away the mess, assist survivors, and donate food, money, and clothing.

San Francisco's city seal features the image of a phoenix rising from the flames of catastrophe, celebrating the city's fiery past and promising courage in the face of certain future calamity. The 1989 shake possessed only about one-fortieth the force of the legendary 1906 quake, and all projections point to the inevitability of another Big One, someday, on at least the scale of '06. Often people from other, more stable, parts of the world have trouble understanding how it is possible to live with such a certainty.

The *San Francisco Bay Guardian*, shortly after the 1989 quake, spoke for many Bay Area residents: "We live in earthquake country. Everybody knows that. It's a choice we've all made, a risk we're all more or less willing to accept as part of our lives. We're gambling against fate, and last week our luck ran out. It was inevitable—as the infamous bumper sticker says, 'Mother Nature bats last.' "

Former San Francisco Mayor Diane Feinstein explained it this way: "Californians seem undaunted. We [know] we'll never be a match for Mother Nature. But the principal thing that seems to arise from the ash and rubble of a quake is the strong resolve to rebuild and get on with life."

3 Exploring San Francisco

By Toni Chapman

Updated by Daniel Mangin

"You could live in San Francisco a month and ask no greater entertainment than walking through it," waxed Inez Hayes Irwin, the author of *The Californiacs*, an effusive 1921 homage to the state of California and the City by the Bay. Her claim remains as true as ever today, and, as in the '20s, touring on foot is the best way to experience this diverse metropolis.

San Francisco is a relatively small city, with fewer than 750,000 residents nested on a 46.6-square-mile tip of land between San Francisco Bay and the Pacific Ocean. San Franciscans cherish the city's colorful past, and many older buildings have been spared from demolition and nostalgically converted into modern offices and shops. Longtime locals rue the sites that got away— spectacular railroad and mining-boom-era residences lost in the '06 quake, the elegant Fox Theater, Playland at the Beach. But despite acts of God, the indifference of developers, and the at best mixed record of the city's Planning Commission, much of architectural and historical interest remains. Bernard Maybeck, Julia Morgan, Willis Polk, and Arthur Brown, Jr., are among the noted architects whose designs still grace the city's downtown and neighborhoods.

San Francisco's charms are both great and small. First-time visitors won't want to miss Golden Gate Park, the Palace of Fine Arts, the Golden Gate Bridge, or an exhilarating cable-car ride. A walk down the Filbert Steps or through Macondray Lane, though, or a peaceful hour gazing east from Ina Coolbrith Park, can be equally inspiring.

It's no accident that the San Francisco Bay Area has been a center for the environmental movement. An awareness of geographical setting permeates San Francisco life, with ever-present views of the surrounding mountains, ocean, and bay. Much of the city's neighborhood vitality comes from the distinct borders provided by its hills and valleys, and many areas are so named: Nob Hill, Twin Peaks, Eureka Valley, the East Bay. San Francisco neighborhoods are self-aware, and they retain strong cultural, political, and ethnic identities. Locals know this pluralism is the real life of the city. If you want to experience San Francisco, don't just stay downtown, visit the neighborhoods: the bustling Mission District, gay Castro, freaky Haight Street, serene Pacific Heights, historic Chinatown, still-exotic North Beach.

To do so you must navigate a maze of one-way streets and restricted parking zones. Public parking garages or lots tend to be expensive, as are the hotel parking spaces. The famed 40-plus hills can be a problem for drivers who are new to the terrain. Those museums on wheels—the cable cars—or the numerous buses or trolleys can take you to or near many of the area's attractions. In the exploring tours that follow, we have often included information on public transportation.

Highlights for First-time Visitors

Chinatown (*see* Tour 4)

Exploring San Francisco *(Boxes Refer to Detail Maps)*

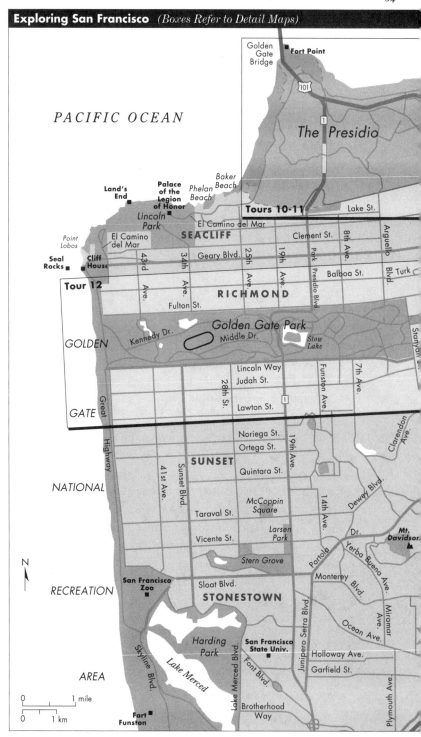

PACIFIC OCEAN

Golden Gate Bridge

Fort Point

The Presidio

Land's End

Palace of the Legion of Honor

Baker Beach

Phelan Beach

Lincoln Park

El Camino del Mar

Tours 10–11

Lake St.

Point Lobos

El Camino del Mar

SEACLIFF

Clement St.

8th Ave.

Arguello

Seal Rocks

Cliff House

43rd Ave.

34th Ave.

Geary Blvd.

25th Ave.

19th Ave.

Park Presidio Blvd.

Balboa St.

Turk

Tour 12

RICHMOND

Fulton St.

GOLDEN

Kennedy Dr.

Golden Gate Park

Middle Dr.

Stow Lake

Stanyan

GATE

Great

Lincoln Way

Judah St.

28th St.

Funston Ave.

7th Ave.

Lawton St.

Noriega St.

Ortega St.

19th Ave.

SUNSET

Quintara St.

14th Ave.

Clarendon Ave.

NATIONAL

41st Ave.

Sunset Blvd.

Taraval St.

McCoppin Square

Dewey Blvd.

Vicente St.

Larsen Park

Dr.

Mt. Davidson

Highway

Stern Grove

Portola

Yerba Buena Ave.

Miramar

RECREATION

San Francisco Zoo

Sloat Blvd.

STONESTOWN

Monterey Blvd.

Ave.

Junipero Serra Blvd

Ocean Ave.

Harding Park

San Francisco State Univ.

Holloway Ave.

Plymouth Ave.

AREA

Skyline Blvd.

Lake Merced

Lake Merced Blvd.

Font Blvd.

Garfield St.

N

0   1 mile

0   1 km

Fort Funston

Brotherhood Way

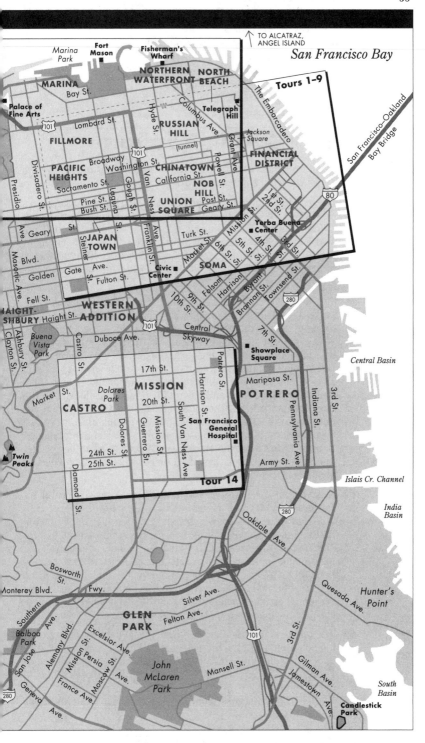

San Francisco Bay

TO ALCATRAZ, ANGEL ISLAND

Tours 1–9

Tour 14

The Cliff House (*see* Tour 13)
Coit Tower (*see* Tour 5)
Cruise to Alcatraz Island (*see* Tour 10)
Golden Gate Bridge (*see* Tour 11)
Hyde Street Cable Car (*see* Tour 10)
Japanese Tea Garden (*see* Tour 12)
Pacific Heights (*see* Tour 7)
Union Square (*see* Tour 1)

Tour 1: Union Square

Numbers in the margin correspond to points of interest on the Downtown San Francisco: Tours 1–9 map.

Since 1850 Union Square has been the heart of San Francisco's downtown. Its name derives from a series of violent pro-Union demonstrations staged in this hilly area just prior to the Civil War. This area is where you will find the city's finest department stores and its most elegant boutiques. There are 40 hotels within a three-block walk of the square, and the downtown theater district is nearby.

The square itself is a 2.6-acre oasis planted with palms, boxwood, and seasonal flowers, peopled with a kaleidoscope of characters: office workers sunning and brown-bagging, street musicians, always at least one mime, several vocal and determined preachers, and the ever-increasing parade of panhandlers. Throughout the year, the square hosts numerous public events: fashion shows, free noontime concerts, ethnic celebrations, and noisy demonstrations. Auto and bus traffic is often gridlocked on the four streets bordering the square. Post, Stockton, and Geary are one-way, while Powell runs in both directions until it crosses Geary, where it then becomes one-way to Market Street. Union Square covers a convenient but costly four-story underground garage. Close to 3,000 cars use it on busy holiday shopping and strolling days.

❶ Any visitor's first stop should be the **San Francisco Visitor Information Center** (tel. 415/391–2000) on the lower level of Hallidie Plaza at Powell and Market streets. It is open daily, and the multilingual staff will answer specific questions as well as provide maps, brochures, and information on daily events. You can pick up coupons for substantial savings on tourist attractions here, and if you're in need of a room for the night, most of the downtown area hotels leave pamphlets (and, depending on the season, discount vouchers) here. The office provides 24-hour recorded information (tel. 415/391–2001).

❷ The **cable-car terminus** at Powell and Market streets is the starting point for two of the three operating lines. The Powell-Mason line climbs up Nob Hill, then winds through North Beach to Fisherman's Wharf. The Powell-Hyde car also crosses Nob Hill, but then continues up Russian Hill and down Hyde Street to Victorian Park across from the Buena Vista Cafe and near Ghirardelli Square.

Andrew Hallidie introduced the system in 1873 when he demonstrated his first car on Clay Street. In 1964 the tramlike vehicles were designated national historic landmarks. Before 1900 there were 600 cable cars spanning a network of 100 miles. Today there are 39 cars in the three lines, and the network covers just 12 miles. Most of the cars date from the last century, although the cars and lines had a complete $58 million overhaul during the early 1980s. There are seats for about 30 passengers, with usually that number standing or strap-hanging. If possible, plan your cable-car ride for mid-morning or mid-afternoon during the week to avoid crowds. In summertime there are often long lines to board any of the three systems. Buy your ticket ($2, good in one direction) at nearby hotels or at the police/information booth near the turnaround. (*See* Getting Around by Cable Car in Chapter 1, Essential Information.)

Two helpful tips: The array of panhandlers, street preachers, and other regulars at this terminus can be daunting. Since you're going to stand in line anyway, you might want to do so at the Hyde Street end of the Powell-Hyde line, which affords views of the bay and Golden Gate Bridge while you wait, not to mention less racket. (*See* Tour 10: The Northern Waterfront, *below.*) Better yet, if it's just the experience of riding a cable car you're after (rather than a trip to the wharf or Nob Hill), try boarding the less-busy California line at Van Ness Avenue and ride it down to the Hyatt Regency. (*See* Tour 7: Pacific Heights, *below.*)

If you resist the urge to hop onto San Francisco's moving ❸ landmarks, you can head over to a stationary one, the **Old San Francisco Mint,** and get an instant immersion in San Francisco and California history. Walk one block south of the cable-car terminus past the 5th Street side of the San Francisco Shopping Centre. The old mint, at 5th and Mission streets, was built in 1873 and reopened as a museum in 1973. Its priceless collection of gold coins was removed in late 1993 for security reasons, but visitors can view an authentic re-creation of a miner's cabin and other historical exhibits, tour the mint's original vaults, and strike their own souvenir medal on an 1869 press. Several photos depict the sturdy building standing virtually alone amid the rubble of the 1906 earthquake and fire. "The Millionaire," a gigantic, old-fashioned calculator, and several Victrolas are among the other curiosities on display. *Tel. 415/744–6830. Admission free. Open weekdays 10–4:15.*

A two-block stroll, heading north of the cable-car terminus along ❹ bustling Powell Street, leads to **Union Square** itself. At center stage, the Victory Monument by Robert Ingersoll Aitken commemorates Commodore George Dewey's victory over the Spanish fleet at Manila in 1898. The 97-foot Corinthian column, topped by a bronze figure symbolizing naval conquest, was dedicated by Theodore Roosevelt in 1903 and withstood the 1906 earthquake.

After the earthquake and fire in 1906, the square was dubbed "Little St. Francis" because of the temporary shelter erected

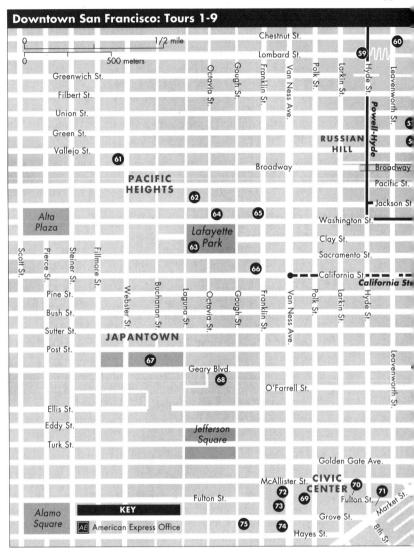

Downtown San Francisco: Tours 1-9

Ansel Adams
Center, **18**

Bank of America, **28**

Buddha's Universal
Church, **39**

Cable Car Museum, **55**

Cable-car terminus, **2**

Center for the Arts, **16**

Chinatown Gate, **32**

Chinese Cultural
Center, **36**

Chinese Historical
Society, **37**

Chinese Six
Companies, **41**

City Hall, **69**

City Lights
Bookstore, **46**

Coit Tower, **48**

Coleman House, **66**

Curran Theatre, **7**

Embarcadero
Center, **20**

Fairmont Hotel, **52**

Ferry Building, **22**

Feusier House, **57**

450 Sutter Street, **12**

Geary Theatre, **6**

Grace Cathedral, **50**

Haas-Lilienthal
Victorian, **65**

Hallidie Building, **24**

Hammersmith
Building, **11**

Ina Coolbrith Park, **56**

Jackson Square, **31**

Japan Center, **67**

Justin Herman
Plaza, **21**

Lafayette Park, **63**

Lombard Street, **59**

Louise M. Davies
Symphony Hall, **74**

Macondray Lane, **58**

Maiden Lane, **10**

Mark Hopkins Inter-
Continental Hotel, **53**

Masonic
Auditorium, **51**

Mills Building and
Tower, **25**

Moscone Convention
Center, **14**

Old Chinese Telephone
Exchange, **38**

San Francisco Bay

N

TELEGRAPH HILL

NORTH BEACH

NOB HILL

CHINATOWN

FINANCIAL DISTRICT

UNION SQUARE

YERBA BUENA

SOMA

Chestnut St.
Lombard St.
Greenwich St.
Filbert St.
Union St.
Green St.
Vallejo St.
Pine St.
Bush St.
utter St.
Post St.
O'Farrell St.
Ellis St.
Eddy St.
Turk St.
Maiden Ln.

Powell-Mason
Mason St.
Taylor St.
Columbus Ave.
Powell St.
Grant Ave.
Stockton St.
Kearny St.
Montgomery St.
Sansome St.
Battery St.
Front St.
Davis St.
The Embarcadero
Clay St.
Halleck St.
Davis St.
Front St.
Drumm St.
Spear St.
Steuart St.
Main St.
Beale St.
1st St.
Fremont St.
New Montgomery St.
2nd St.
Hawthorne St.
3rd St.
Mission St.
Market St.
Howard St.
Folsom St.
Harrison St.
Bryant St.
6th St.
5th St.
4th St.
Howard St.

for residents of the St. Francis Hotel. Actor John Barrymore was among the guests pressed into volunteering to stack bricks in the square. His uncle, thespian John Drew, remarked, "It took an act of God to get John out of bed and the United States government to get him to work."

5 The **Westin St. Francis Hotel,** on the southwest corner of Post and Powell, was built here in 1904 and was gutted by the 1906 disaster. The second-oldest hotel in the city was conceived by Charles Crocker and his associates as an elegant hostelry for their millionaire friends. Swift service and sumptuous surroundings were hallmarks of the property. A sybarite's dream, the hotel's Turkish baths had ocean water piped in. A new, larger, more luxurious residence was opened in 1907 to attract loyal clients from among the world's rich and powerful. The hotel has known its share of notoriety as well. Silent comedian Fatty Arbuckle's career plummeted faster than one of the St. Francis's glass-walled elevators after a wild 1921 party in one of the hotel's suites went awry. In 1975, Sara Jane Moore tried to shoot then-president Gerald Ford in front of the building. As might be imagined, plaques do not commemorate these events in the establishment's lobby. The ever-helpful staff will, however, gladly direct you to the traditional teatime ritual—or, if you prefer, to champagne and caviar—in the dramatic Art Deco Compass Rose lounge. Elaborate Chinese screens, secluded seating alcoves, and soothing background music make it an ideal time-out after frantic shopping or sightseeing.

Both the Geary and Curran theaters are a few blocks west on
6 Geary Street. The 1,300-seat **Geary** (415 Geary St., tel. 415/749–2228), built in 1910, is home of the American Conservatory Theatre, one of North America's leading repertory companies (*see* Chapter 8, The Arts and Nightlife). The building's serious neoclassical design is lightened somewhat by the colorful, carved terra-cotta columns depicting a cornucopia of fruits, that flank the theater's largest windows. The theater was closed as a result of the October 1989 earthquake, and currently productions are being run at the Stage Door theater (420 Mason St.) and elsewhere until repairs are complete, probably in time for the 1995–
7 96 season. Its main box office remains open. The **Curran** (445 Geary St., tel. 415/474–3800) is noted for showcasing traveling companies of Broadway shows. Farther up the street, and a must for film buffs, is the **Cinema Shop** (606 Geary St., tel. 415/885–6785), a tiny storefront jammed with posters, stills, lobby cards and rare videotapes of Hollywood classics and schlock films alike.

8 **TIX Bay Area,** formerly known as STBS, has a booth on the Stockton Street side of Union Square, opposite Maiden Lane. It provides day-of-performance tickets (cash or traveler's checks only) to all types of performing-arts events at half-price, as well as regular full-price box-office services. Telephone reservations are not accepted for half-price tickets. You can also buy $10 Golden Gate Park Cultural Passes here, which get you into all of the park's museums at a bargain rate. *Tel. 415/433–7827. Open Tues.–Thurs. 11–6, Fri. and Sat. 11–7.*

9 Just a dash up from TIX Bay Area, in front of the Grand Hyatt San Francisco (345 Stockton St.), is sculptor **Ruth Asawa's fantasy fountain** honoring the city's hills, bridges, and unusual architecture plus a wonder world of real and mythical creatures. Children and friends helped the artist shape the hundreds of tiny figures from baker's clay; these were assembled on 41 large panels from which molds were made for the bronze casting. Asawa's distinctive designs decorate many public areas in the city. You can see her famous mermaid fountain at Ghirardelli Square.

10 Directly across Stockton Street from TIX Bay Area is **Maiden Lane,** which runs from Stockton to Kearny streets. Known as Morton Street in the raffish Barbary Coast era, this red-light district reported at least one murder a week. But the 1906 fire destroyed the brothels and the street emerged as Maiden Lane. It has since become a chic and costly mall. The two blocks are closed to vehicles from 11 AM until 4 PM. During the day, take-out snacks can be enjoyed while resting under the gay, umbrella-shaded tables. Masses of daffodils and bright blossoms and balloons bedeck the lane during the annual spring festival. A carnival mood prevails, due to the throngs of zany street musicians, artsy-craftsy people, and spectators.

Note **140 Maiden Lane:** This handsome brick structure is the only Frank Lloyd Wright building in San Francisco. With its circular interior ramp and skylights, it is said to have been a model for his designs for the Guggenheim Museum in New York. It now houses the Circle Gallery, a showcase of contemporary artists. Be sure to examine the unique limited-edition art jewelry designed by internationally acclaimed Erté. *Tel. 415/989–2100. Open Mon.–Sat. 10–6, Sun. noon–5.*

Many of San Francisco's leading fine-arts galleries are around Union Square. Among them are **John Berggruen** (one of several establishments at 228 Grant Ave., tel. 415/781–4629; open weekdays 9:30–5:30, Sat. 10:30–5) and **Erika Meyerovich** (231 Grant Ave., tel. 415/421–9997; open weekdays 9–6, Sat. 10–5:30). At 49 Geary Street are **Fraenkel** (tel. 415/981–2661; open Tues.–Fri. 10:30–5:30, Sat. 11–5) and **Robert Koch** (tel. 415/421–0122; open Tues.–Sat. 11–5:30), both of which showcase contemporary and historic photographs.

11 At 301 Sutter Street, at the corner of Grant Avenue is the colorful **Hammersmith Building.** The small Beaux-Arts structure was completed in 1907. Its extensive use of glass is noteworthy, as is the playful design. Sutter Street is lined by prestigious art galleries, antiques dealers, smart hotels, and noted designer boutiques. Art Deco aficionados will want to head one block up Sutter Street for a peek at the striking medical/dental office **12** building at **450 Sutter Street.** Handsome Mayan-inspired designs are used on both exterior and interior surfaces of the 1930 terracotta skyscraper.

Tour 2: South of Market (SoMa) and the Embarcadero

The vast tract of downtown land **South of Market** Street along the waterfront and west to the Mission District is also known by the acronym SoMa (patterned after New York City's south-of-Houston SoHo). Formerly known as South of the Slot because of the cable-car slot that ran up Market Street, the area has a history of housing recent immigrants to the city—beginning with tents set up in 1848 by the gold-rush miners and continuing for decades. Except for a brief flowering of English-inspired elegance during the mid-19th century in the pockets of South Park and Rincon Hill, the area was reserved for newcomers who couldn't yet afford to move to another neighborhood. Industry took over most of the area when the big earthquake collapsed most of the homes into their quicksand bases.

For years the industrial South of Market area west of Fourth Street was a stomping ground for alternative artists and the gay leather set. A dozen bars frequented by the latter group existed alongside warehouses, small factories, and art studios. In the wake of the AIDS crisis, most of the area's gay bars have given way to trendy straight bars. Although many artists cleared out when urban renewal started in earnest, they still hang out in SoMa and show their work in several galleries on the cutting edge of San Francisco's art scene. Two important galleries are a bit of a walk up Folsom Street from the back side of Moscone Center. **New Langton Arts** (1246 Folsom St., tel. 415/626–5416) is one of the city's longest-surviving alternative mixed-media and performance spaces. **San Francisco Camerawork** (70 12th St., tel. 415/621–1001) exhibits the work of up-and-coming photographers.

⓭ The **San Francisco Museum of Modern Art** (SFMOMA) takes its place as the centerpiece of the SoMa arts scene in January 1995. The striking Modernist structure was designed by Swiss architect Mario Botta. It features a stepped-back burnt-sienna brick facade and a central tower constructed of alternating bands of black and white stone. Inside, natural light from the tower floods the central atrium and some of the museum's galleries. A grand staircase leads from the atrium up to four floors of galleries. *151 Third St., tel. 415/357–4000. Admission: $7 adults, $3.50 senior citizens and students over 12; free 1st Tues. of each month. Open daily 11–6, Thurs. until 9 (half-price admission 5–9). Closed major holidays.*

In the mid-1960s, the San Francisco Redevelopment Agency grabbed 87 acres of run-down downtown land, leveled anything that stood on them, and planned the largest building program in the city's history: **Yerba Buena Center.** The $1.5 billion project turned into something of a quagmire, proceeding in fits and starts throughout the '70s and '80s. After more than two decades, it has finally taken shape, although parts of it are still under construction and still other portions aren't past the blueprint stage.

⓮ **Moscone Convention Center,** on Howard Street between 3rd and 4th streets, was the first major Yerba Buena Center building to be completed. The site of the 1984 Democratic convention, it is distinguished by a contemporary glass-and-girder lobby at street level (most of the exhibit space is underground) and a monolithic, column-free interior. In 1992, the center finished a $150-million expansion project that doubled its size and incorporated a new building across Howard Street with underground exhibit space.

⓯ Above the new exhibit space is the **Yerba Buena Gardens** complex (in the block surrounded by 3rd, Mission, Howard, and 4th streets). A large expanse of green is surrounded by a circular walkway lined with benches and sculptures. A waterfall memorial to Martin Luther King, Jr. is the focal point of the gardens; above it are two cafes and an overhead walkway that traverses Howard Street to Moscone Center's main entrance. Retail shopping spaces and a multiplex cinema on the western side of the block are scheduled for completion in 1995. On the eastern side

⓰ of the block is the **Center for the Arts** (701 Mission St., tel. 415/978–2787), which opened in late 1993. The focus here is on the multicultural arts—dance, music, performance, theater, visual arts, film, video, and installations—from the community-based to the international. The center includes two theaters, three visual-arts galleries, a film and video screening room, and an outdoor performance esplanade.

Diagonally across Mission Street from the Center for the Arts,
⓱ you can't miss the main entrance to the **San Francisco Marriott at Moscone Center** (4th and Mission streets). Its 40-story ziggurat construction topped with reflecting glass pinwheels elicited gasps from newspaper columnists and passersby alike, earning it comparisons with a jukebox, a high-rise parking meter, and a giant rectal thermometer. In contrast, a bit of history has been preserved next door. The brick, Gothic Revival **St. Patrick's Church** (756 Mission St.) was completed in 1872 and rebuilt after the 1906 earthquake and fire destroyed its interior.

⓲ Just across 4th Street from the Moscone Center is the **Ansel Adams Center.** This gallery showcases historical and contemporary photography, and has an extensive permanent collection of Adams's work. *250 4th St., tel. 415/495–7000. Admission: $4 adults, $3 students, $2 youths 12–17 and senior citizens, free for children under 12 and for all on the first Tuesday of the month. Open Tues.–Sun. 11–5, first Thurs. of the month 11–8.*

One block north of SFMOMA on Third Street, at the traffic island where Third, Market, Kearny, and Geary streets come together, is **Lotta's Fountain.** This quirky monument, which now goes largely unnoticed by local passersby, was a gift to the city from singer Lotta Crabtree, a Madonna prototype. Her "brash music-hall exploits" so enthralled San Francisco's early population of miners that they were known to shower her with gold nuggets and silver dollars after her performances. The buxom Ms. Crabtree is depicted in one of the Anton Refregier murals in Rincon Center (*see below*).

Heading east on Market Street toward the waterfront, the venerable **Sheraton Palace Hotel** (at the corner of New Montgomery St., tel. 415/392–8600) has resumed its place among San Francisco's grandest. Opened in 1875, the hotel has a storied past, some of which is recounted in small cases off the main lobby; President Warren Harding died here while still in office in 1923. The original Palace was destroyed by fire following the 1906 earthquake, despite a 28,000-gallon reservoir fed by four artesian wells. The current building dates from 1909; late-1980s renovations included the restoration of the glass-domed Garden Court and the installation of original mosaic-tile floors in Oriental-rug designs. Maxfield Parrish's wall-size painting, *The Pied Piper,* graces the wall in the hotel's Pied Piper Room. The hotel offers interesting guided tours (tel. 415/546–5026; call a day or two in advance) Tuesday, Wednesday, and Saturday at 10:30 AM and Thursday at 2 PM.

Because it bisects the city at an angle, over the years, Market Street has consistently challenged San Francisco's architects. One of the most intriguing responses to the problem sits diagonally across Market Street from the Palace. The tower of the **Hobart Building** (582 Market St.) combines a flat facade and oval sides, and is considered to be among architect Willis Polk's best work in the city. It's worth the effort to walk south down Second Street (which runs right into the building) to get a full view of the tower. Farther east on Market Street between Sutter and Post is another classic solution, Charles Havens's triangular **Flatiron Building** (540–548 Market St.). At **388 Market** is a sleek, modern answer to the problem designed by Skidmore, Owings and Merrill.

Continue down Market Street's north side to Battery Street. The **Donahue Monument** holds its own against the skyscrapers that tower over this intersection. This homage to waterfront mechanics was designed by Douglas Tilden, a noted California sculptor who was deaf-mute. The plaque below it marks the spot as the location of the San Francisco Bay shoreline in 1848.

As you approach the Embarcadero, your attention is drawn to the **Hyatt Regency Hotel** (Embarcadero 5), part of the huge **Embarcadero Center** complex. The Hyatt, designed by John Portman, is noted for its spectacular lobby and 20-story hanging garden. On the waterfront side of the hotel is **Justin Herman Plaza.** There are arts and crafts shows, street musicians, and mimes here on weekends year-round. Kite flying is popular here. A huge concrete sculpture, the **Vaillancourt Fountain,** has had legions of critics since its installation in 1971; most of the time the fountain does not work, and many feel it is an eyesore.

A three-tier pedestrian mall connects the eight buildings that comprise Embarcadero Center. Frequently called "Rockefeller

Center West," the complex includes more than 100 shops, 40 restaurants, and two hotels, as well as office and residential space (*see* Chapter 4, Shopping). Louise Nevelson's dramatic 54-foot-high black-steel sculpture, *Sky Tree,* stands guard over Building 3.

Time Out On a sunny day, it's fun to grab something to go at one of Embarcadero Center's dozen or so take-out shops and enjoy the goings-on in Justin Herman Plaza. For something more substantial, **Splendido** (*see* Chapter 6, Dining) is a comfortable Mediterranean restaurant nestled amid the high rises.

In one instance, the 1989 Loma Prieta earthquake changed San Francisco for the better: The Embarcadero freeway had to be torn down, making the foot of Market Street clearly visible for the first time in 30 years. The trademark of the port is the quaint ㉒ **Ferry Building** that stands at the Embarcadero. The clock tower is 230 feet high and was modeled by Arthur Page Brown after the campanile of Seville's cathedral. The four great clock faces on the tower, powered by the swinging action of a 14-foot pendulum, stopped at 5:17 on the morning of April 18, 1906, and stayed that way for 12 months. The 1896 building survived the quake and is now the headquarters of the Port Commission and the World Trade Center. A waterfront promenade that extends from this point to the San Francisco–Oakland Bay Bridge is great for jogging, in-line skating, watching sailboats on the bay (if the day is not too windy), or enjoying a picnic. Check out the beautiful pedestrian pier adjacent to Pier 1, with its old-fashioned lamps, wrought-iron benches, and awe-inspiring views of the bay. Ferries from behind the Ferry Building sail to Sausalito, Larkspur, and Tiburon.

Walking south of the Ferry Building, you can't miss the initial section of the 5-foot-wide, 2½-mile-long glass-and-concrete Promenade Ribbon, construction of which began in 1994. Billed by the city as the "longest art form in the nation," upon its completion in 1997 the artwork will span the waterfront from the base of Telegraph Hill to China Basin.

As you continue down the promenade, notice the curiously styled Audiffred Building at the corner of Mission Street and the Embarcadero. It was built by a homesick gentleman who wanted a reminder of his native France. A few doors down, an old brick YMCA building is now the Harbor Court Hotel. Cross the Embarcadero at Howard Street, and turn right on Steuart Street.

Across Steuart Street from the main entrance to the hotel is the ㉓ new—and old—**Rincon Center.** Two modern office/apartment towers overlook a small shopping and restaurant mall behind an old post office built in the Streamline Moderne Style. A stunning five-story rain column draws immediate attention in the mall. In the "Historic Lobby" (which formerly housed the post office's walk-up windows) is a mural by Anton Refregier. One of the largest WPA-era art projects, its 27 panels depict California life from

the days when Indians were the state's sole inhabitants through
World War I. Completion of this significant work was interrupted by World War II and political infighting; the latter led to
some alteration in Refregier's "radical" historical interpreta-
tions. A permanent exhibit below the mural contains interesting
photographs and artifacts of life in the Rincon area in the 1800s.
Back in the mall, several new murals reflect San Francisco in
the '90s—office workers at computers, sporting events, and the
like.

Rincon Center represents the best aspects of the sometimes un-
easy tension between preservationist forces and developers
(and in this case the U.S. government). It took a fight to preserve
the murals and the architecturally important post office, which
now enhance what might otherwise be just another modern office space. The exhibit and the murals form a fascinating mini-
museum, a 15-minute cultural and historical interlude for
residents and tourists alike. The Historic Lobby is a modest example of something the city pioneered years ago: bringing art
and history "to the people." The most visible of these programs
are the large-scale permanent and temporary exhibits at the
airport, among the first of their kind in the nation.

Two blocks farther south on Steuart Street is the newly restored
Hills Brothers Coffee factory, now a retail and office complex.
"Brew pubs," establishments that make their own suds right on
the premises, are in vogue in San Francisco. The **Gordon Biersch
Brewing Co.** (2 Harrison St.), also a restaurant, was an instant
hit with local trendsetters. It's open for lunch and dinner.

Tour 3: The Financial District and Jackson Square

The heart of San Francisco's Financial District is Montgomery
Street. It was here in 1848 that Sam Brannan proclaimed the
historic gold discovery on the American River. At that time, all
the streets below Montgomery between California and Broadway were wharves. At least 100 ships were abandoned by frantic
crews and passengers all caught up in the '49 gold fever. Many
of the wrecks served as warehouses or were used as foundations
for new constructions.

The Financial District is roughly bordered by Kearny Street on
the west, Washington Street on the north, and Market Street on
the southeast. On workdays it is a congested canyon of soaring
skyscrapers, gridlock traffic, and bustling pedestrians. In the
evenings and on weekends the quiet streets allow walkers to
admire the distinctive architecture. Unfortunately, the museums in corporate headquarters are closed then.

Head down Sutter Street toward the Financial District to see
24 the **Hallidie Building** (130 Sutter St. between Kearny and Montgomery Sts.), named for cable-car inventor Andrew Hallidie.
The building, best viewed from across the street, is believed to
be the world's first all-glass curtain-wall structure. Willis Polk's

revolutionary design hangs a foot beyond the reinforced concrete of the frame. It dominates the block with its reflecting glass, decorative exterior fire escapes that appear to be metal balconies, the Venetian Gothic cornice, and horizontal ornamental bands of birds at feeders.

㉕ The **Mills Building and Tower** (220 Montgomery St.) was the outstanding prefire building in the Financial District. The 10-story all-steel construction had its own electric plant in the basement. The original Burnham and Root design of white marble and brick was erected in 1891–92. Damage from the 1906 fire was slight; its walls were somewhat scorched but were easily refurbished. Two compatible additions east on Bush Street were added in 1914 and 1918 by Willis Polk, and in 1931 a 22-story tower completed the design.

㉖ The **Russ Building** (235 Montgomery St.) was called "the skyscraper" when it was built in 1927. The Gothic design was modeled after the Chicago Tribune Tower, and until the 1960s was San Francisco's tallest—at just 31 stories. Prior to the 1906 earthquake and fire, the site was occupied by the Russ House, considered one of the finest hostelries in the city.

Ralph Stackpole's monumental 1930 granite sculptural groups, *Earth's Fruitfulness* and *Man's Inventive Genius*, flank another
㉗ imposing structure, the **Pacific Stock Exchange** (which dates from 1915), on the south side of Pine Street at Sansome Street. The Stock Exchange Tower around the corner at 155 Sansome Street, a 1930 modern classic by architects Miller and Pfleuger, features an Art Deco gold ceiling and black marble-walled entry. *301 Pine St., tel. 415/393–4000. Tours by 2-wk advance reservation; minimum 8 persons.*

㉘ The granite-and-marble **Bank of America** building dominates the territory bounded by California, Pine, Montgomery, and Kearny streets. The 52-story polished red granite complex is crowned by a chic cocktail lounge and restaurant. As in most corporate headquarters, the interiors display impressive original art, while outdoor plazas showcase avant-garde sculptures. In the mall, a massive abstract black granite sculpture designed by the Japanese artist Masayuki has been dubbed the "Banker's Heart" by local wags.

Soaring 52 stories above the Financial District, the Bank of America's **Carnelian Room** (tel. 415/433–7500) offers elegant and pricey dining with a nighttime view of the city lights. This is an excellent spot for a drink at sunset. By day, the room is the exclusive Banker's Club, open to members or by invitation.

Time Out   At lunchtime on weekdays you can rub elbows with power brokers and politicians in **Jack's Restaurant** (615 Sacramento St., tel. 415/986–9854). This venerable eatery opened in 1864 and survived the 1906 quake.

㉙ A quick but interesting stop is the **Wells Fargo Bank History Museum.** There were no formal banks in San Francisco during the early years of the gold rush, and miners often entrusted their gold dust to saloon keepers. In 1852, Wells Fargo opened its first bank in the city, and the company established banking offices in the Mother Lode camps using stagecoaches and pony express riders to service the burgeoning state. (California's population boomed from 15,000 to 200,000 between 1848 and 1852.) The History Museum displays samples of nuggets and gold dust from major mines, a mural-size map of the Mother Lode, original art by Western artists Charlie Russell and Maynard Dixon, mementos of the poet bandit Black Bart, and letters of credit and old bank drafts. The showpiece is the red, century-old Concord stagecoach that in the mid-1850s carried 15 passengers from St. Louis to San Francisco in three weeks. *420 Montgomery St., tel. 415/396–2619. Admission free. Open banking days 9–5.*

30 The city's most-photographed high rise is the 853-foot **Transamerica Pyramid** at 600 Montgomery Street, between Clay and Washington streets at the end of Columbus Avenue. Designed by William Pereira and Associates in 1972, the controversial $34 million symbol has become more acceptable to local purists over time. There is a public viewing area on the 27th floor (open weekdays 8–4). You can relax in a redwood grove along the east side of the building.

In the Gay Nineties San Francisco earned the title of "the Wickedest City in the World." The saloons, dance halls, cheap hotels, and brothels of its Barbary Coast attracted sailors and gold rushers. Most of this red-light district was destroyed in the 1906 **31** fire; what remains is now part of **Jackson Square**. A stroll through this district recalls some of the romance and rowdiness of early San Francisco.

Some of the city's earliest business buildings still stand in the blocks of Jackson Square between Montgomery and Sansome streets. By the end of World War II, most of the 1850 brick structures had fallen on hard times. In 1951, however, things changed. A group of talented, preservation-minded designers and furniture wholesale dealers selected the centrally located, depressed area for their showrooms. By the 1970s, the reclaimed two- and three-story renovated brick buildings were acclaimed nationwide. In 1972, the city officially designated the area—bordered by Columbus Avenue on the west, a line between Broadway and Pacific Avenue on the north, Washington on the south, and Sansome Street on the east—as San Francisco's first historic district. Seventeen buildings were given landmark status.

Jackson Square became the interior design center of the West. Unfortunately, property values soared, forcing many of the fabric and furniture outlets to move to the developing Potrero Hill section. Advertising agencies, attorneys, and antiques dealers now occupy the charming renovations.

Directly across Washington Street from the Transamerica redwood grove is Hotaling Place, a tiny alley east of and parallel to Montgomery Street. The alley is named for the head of the **A. P.**

Hotaling and Company whiskey distillery, which was located at 451 Jackson. This handsome brick building retains the iron shutters installed in 1866 to "fireproof" the house. A plaque on the side of the building repeats a famous query about its surviving the quake: "If, as they say, God spanked the town/for being over-frisky,/Why did He burn the churches down/and spare Hotaling's Whisky?"

The **Ghirardelli Chocolate Factory** was once housed at 415 Jackson. In 1857, Domenico Ghirardelli moved both his growing business and his family into this property. It was quite common for the upper floors of these buildings to be used as flats by either the building's owners or its tenants. By 1894, Ghirardelli had moved his expanding chocolate enterprise to Ghirardelli Square.

Head back up Jackson and turn left on Montgomery Street to see the much-photographed compound at **722–28 Montgomery Street.** For years this was the headquarters of Melvin Belli, the "King of Torts," one of the nation's most flamboyant attorneys. The site was originally a warehouse and later the **Melodeon Theater,** where the immortal Lotta Crabtree (*see* Lotta's Fountain in Tour 2: South of Market and the Embarcadero, *above*) performed.

The **Golden Era Building** at 732 Montgomery Street was the home of the most substantial literary periodical published locally during the 1850s and 1860s. Mark Twain and Bret Harte were two of its celebrated contributors.

Return to Union Square via Montgomery Street (turn right when you get to Post Street) or, if you're in the mood for more sightseeing, head up Columbus Avenue to North Beach. (*See* Tour 5: North Beach and Telegraph Hill, *below.*)

Tour 4: Chinatown

San Francisco is home to one of the largest Chinese communities outside Asia. While Chinese culture is visible throughout the city, this area, bordered roughly by Bush, Kearny, Powell and Broadway, remains the community's spiritual and political center. Recent immigrants from Southeast Asia have added new character and life to the neighborhood.

Visitors usually enter Chinatown through the green-tiled ③② dragon-crowned **Chinatown Gate** at Bush Street and Grant Avenue. To best savor this district, explore it on foot (it's not far from Union Square), even though you may find the bustling, noisy, colorful stretches of Grant and Stockton streets north of Bush difficult to navigate. Parking is extremely hard to find, and traffic is impossible. As in Hong Kong, most families shop daily for fresh meats, vegetables, and bakery products. This street world shines with much good-luck crimson and gold; giant beribboned floral wreaths mark the opening of new bakeries, bazaars, and banks. Note the dragon-entwined lampposts, the pagoda roofs, and street signs with Chinese calligraphy.

Merely strolling through Chinatown and its many bazaars, restaurants, and curio shops yields endless pleasures, but you also have an opportunity here to experience a bit of one of the world's oldest cultures. You needn't be shy about stepping into a temple or an herb shop. Chinatown has been a tourist stop for more than 100 years now and most of its residents welcome "foreign" guests.

Dragon House Oriental Fine Arts and Antiques (455 Grant Ave.), several doors up from the Chinatown gate, is an excellent place to start your Chinatown visit. Its collection of ivory carvings, ceramics, and jewelry dates back 2,000 years and beyond. The shop's display window is a history lesson in itself.

San Francisco pioneered the resurrection of Chinese regional cooking for American palates. Cantonese cuisine, with its familiar staples of chow mein and chop suey (said to be invented in San Francisco by gold rush–era Chinese cooks) now exists alongside spicier Szechuan, Hunan, and Mandarin specialties. With almost 100 restaurants squeezed into a 14-block area, Chinatown offers plenty of food. In the windows of markets on Stockton Street and Grant Avenue you can see roast ducks hanging, fresh fish and shellfish swimming in tanks, and strips of Chinese-style barbecued pork shining in pink glaze.

33 The handsome brick **Old St. Mary's Church** at Grant and California streets served as the city's Catholic cathedral until 1891. Granite quarried in China was used in the structure, which was **34** dedicated in 1854. Diagonally across the intersection is **St. Mary's Park,** a tranquil setting for local sculptor Beniamino (Benny) Bufano's heroic stainless-steel and rose-colored granite *Sun Yat-sen.* The 12-foot statue of the founder of the Republic of China was installed in 1937 on the site of the Chinese leader's favorite reading spot during his years of exile in San Francisco. Bufano was born in Rome on October 14, 1898, and died in San Francisco on August 16, 1970. His stainless-steel and mosaic statue of St. Francis welcomes guests at San Francisco International Airport.

The city's first house was built in 1836 at the corner of Grant Avenue and Clay Street; it was later destroyed in the 1906 earthquake. Turn right on Clay Street, continue one block to Kearny **35** Street, and turn left to reach **Portsmouth Square,** the potato patch that became the plaza for Yerba Buena. This is where Montgomery raised the American flag in 1846. Note the bronze galleon atop a 9-foot granite shaft. Designed by Bruce Porter, the sculpture was erected in 1919 in memory of Robert Louis Stevenson, who often visited the site during his 1879–80 residence. In the morning, the park is crowded with people performing solemn t'ai chi exercises. By noontime, dozens of men huddle around mah-jongg tables, engaged in not-always-legal competition. Occasionally, undercover police rush in to break things up, but this ritual, though as solemn as the t'ai chi, is hardly as productive.

㊱ From here you can walk to the **Chinese Cultural Center,** which frequently displays the work of Chinese-American artists as well as traveling exhibits of Chinese culture. The center also offers $15 Saturday-afternoon (2 PM) walking tours of historic points in Chinatown. *In the Holiday Inn, 750 Kearny St., tel. 415/986–1822. Admission free. Open Tues.–Sat. 10–4.*

In an alley parallel to and a half-block south of the side of the
㊲ Holiday Inn, the **Chinese Historical Society** traces the history of Chinese immigrants and their contributions to the state's rail, mining, and fishing industries. *650 Commercial St., parallel to Clay St. off Kearny, tel. 415/391–1188. Admission free. Open Tues.– Sat. noon–4.*

The original Chinatown burned down after the 1906 earthquake; the first building to set the style for the new Chinatown is near Portsmouth Square, at 743 Washington Street. The three-tier
㊳ pagoda called the **Old Chinese Telephone Exchange** (now the Bank of Canton) was built in 1909. The exchange's operators were renowned for their "tenacious memories," about which the San Francisco Chamber of Commerce boasted in 1914: "These girls respond all day with hardly a mistake to calls that are given (in English or one of five Chinese dialects) by the name of the subscriber instead of by his number—a mental feat that would be practically impossible to most high-schooled American misses."

㊴ **Buddha's Universal Church** is a five-story, hand-built temple decorated with murals and tile mosaics. The church is open the second and fourth Sunday of the month, 1–3, except from January to March, when it presents a bilingual costume play Saturdays and Sundays to celebrate the Chinese New Year. *720 Washington St., tel. 415/982–6116. Play tickets: $8–$10, reservations accepted.*

Time Out   Skip that Big Mac you've been craving; opt instead for dim sum, a variety of pastries filled with meat, fish, and vegetables, the Chinese version of a smorgasbord. In most places, stacked food-service carts patrol the premises; customers select from the varied offerings, and the final bill is tabulated by the number of different saucers on the table. A favorite on Pacific Avenue, two blocks north of Washington Street, is **New Asia.** *772 Pacific Ave., tel. 415/391–6666. Open for dim sum 8:30 AM–3 PM.*

Waverly Place is noted for ornate painted balconies and Chinese
㊵ temples. **Tien Hou Temple** was dedicated to the Queen of the Heavens and Goddess of the Seven Seas by Day Ju, one of the first three Chinese to arrive in San Francisco in 1852. A sign in Chinese welcomes visitors (now you know). Climb three flights of stairs—past two mah-jongg parlors whose patrons hope the spirits above will favor them. As you enter the temple, elderly ladies are often preparing "money" to be burned as offerings to various Buddhist gods. A (real) dollar placed in the donation box on their table will bring a smile. Notice the wood carving sus-

pended from the ceiling that depicts a number of gods at play. *125 Waverly Pl. Open daily 10 AM–4 PM.*

Throughout Chinatown you will notice herb shops that sell an array of Chinese medicines. The **Great China Herb Co.** (857 Washington St.), around the corner from the Tien Hou Temple, is one of the largest. All day, sellers fill prescriptions from local doctors, measuring exact amounts of tree roots, bark, flowers, and other ingredients with their hand scales, and add up the bill on an abacus (an ancient calculator). The shops also sell "over-the-counter" treatments for the common cold, heartburn, hangovers, and even impotence!

The other main thoroughfare in Chinatown, where locals shop for everyday needs, is Stockton Street, which parallels Grant Avenue. This is the real heart of Chinatown. Housewives jostle one another as they pick apart the sidewalk displays of Chinese vegetables. Double-parked trucks unloading crates of chickens or ducks add to the all-day traffic jams. You'll see excellent examples of Chinese architecture along this street. Most noteworthy is the elaborate **Chinese Six Companies** (843 Stockton St.), with its curved roof tiles and elaborate cornices. At 855 Stockton is **Kong Chow Temple,** established in 1851 and moved to this new building in 1977. Take the elevator up to the fourth floor. Again, a dollar bill is an appropriate gift from you or your group. The air at Kong Chow Temple is often thick with incense, a bit ironic what with the Chinese Community Smoke-Free Project but two floors below.

Around the corner at 965 Clay St. is the handsome, redbrick **Chinatown YWCA,** originally set up as a meeting place and residence for Chinese women in need of social services. It was designed by architect Julia Morgan, who was also responsible for the famous Hearst Castle at San Simeon, California. It's an easy 15-minute walk back downtown to Union Square via the **Stockton Street Tunnel,** which runs from Sacramento Street to Sutter Street. Completed in 1914, this was the city's first tunnel to accommodate vehicular and pedestrian traffic.

Tour 5: North Beach and Telegraph Hill

Like neighboring Chinatown, North Beach, centered on Columbus Avenue north of Broadway, is best explored on foot. In the early days there truly was a beach. At the time of the gold rush, the bay extended into the hollow between Telegraph and Russian hills. North Beach, less than a square mile, is the most densely populated district in the city and is truly cosmopolitan. Much of the old-world ambience still lingers in this easygoing and polyglot neighborhood. Novelist Herbert Gold, a North Beach resident, calls the area "the longest running, most glorious American bohemian operetta outside Greenwich Village."

Like Chinatown, this is a section of the city where you can eat and eat. Restaurants, cafés, delis, and bakeries abound. Many

Italian restaurants specialize in family-style full-course meals at reasonable prices. A local North Beach delicacy is focaccia—spongy pizzalike bread slathered with olive oil and chives or tomato sauce—sold fresh from the oven at quaint old **Liguria Bakery** at the corner of Stockton and Filbert streets. Eaten warm or cold, it is the perfect walking food.

Among the first immigrants to Yerba Buena during the early 1840s were young men from the northern provinces of Italy. By 1848, the village, renamed San Francisco, had become an overnight boomtown with the discovery of gold. Thousands more poured into the burgeoning area, seeking the golden dream. For many, the trail ended in San Francisco. The Genoese started the still-active fishing industry, as well as much-needed produce businesses. Later the Sicilians emerged as leaders of the fishing fleets and eventually as proprietors of the seafood restaurants lining Fisherman's Wharf. Meanwhile, their Genoese cousins established banking and manufacturing empires.

43 **Washington Square** may well be the daytime social heart of what was once considered "Little Italy." By mid-morning, groups of conservatively dressed elderly Italian men are sunning and sighing at the state of their immediate world. Nearby, laughing playmates of a half-dozen cultures race through the grass with Frisbees or colorful kites. Denim-clad mothers exchange shopping tips and ethnic recipes. Elderly Chinese matrons stare impassively at the passing parade. Camera-toting tourists focus **44** their lenses on the adjacent Romanesque splendor of **Sts. Peter and Paul,** often called the Italian Cathedral. Completed in 1924, its twin-turreted terra-cotta towers are local landmarks. On the first Sunday of October, the annual Blessing of the Fleet is celebrated with a mass followed by a parade to Fisherman's Wharf. Another popular annual event is the Columbus Day pageant.

The 1906 earthquake and fire devastated this area, and the park provided shelter for hundreds of the homeless. **Fior d'Italia,** facing the cathedral, is San Francisco's oldest Italian restaurant. The original opened in 1886 and continued to operate in a tent after the 1906 earthquake until new quarters were ready. Surrounding streets are packed with savory Italian delicatessens, bakeries, Chinese markets, coffeehouses, and ethnic restaurants. Wonderful aromas fill the air; coffee beans roasted at **Graffeo** at 735 Columbus Avenue are shipped to customers all over the United States. Stop by the **Panelli Brothers deli** (1419 Stockton St.) for a memorable, reasonably priced meat-and-cheese sandwich to go. **Florence Ravioli Factory** (1412 Stockton St.) features garlic sausages, prosciutto, and mortadella, as well as 75 tasty cheeses and sandwiches to go. **Victoria** (1362 Stockton St.) has heavenly cream puffs and eclairs. Around the corner on Columbus Avenue is **Molinari's,** noted for the best salami in town and a mouth-watering array of salads—there is usually a wait for service.

South of Washington Square and just off Columbus Avenue is **45** the **St. Francis of Assisi Church** (610 Vallejo St.). This 1860 Victorian Gothic building stands on the site of the frame parish church that served the gold-rush Catholic community.

Over the years, North Beach has attracted creative individualists. The Beat Renaissance of the 1950s was born, grew up, flourished, then faltered in this then-predominantly Italian enclave. The Beat gathering places are gone, and few of the original leaders remain. Poet Lawrence Ferlinghetti still holds court at his 46 **City Lights Bookstore** (261 Columbus Ave.). The face of North Beach is changing. The bohemian community has migrated up Grant Avenue above Columbus Avenue. Originally called Calle de la Fundacion, Grant Avenue is the oldest street in the city. Each June a street fair is held on the upper part of the avenue, where a cluster of cafés, boutiques, and galleries attract crowds.

The view from Columbus and Broadway characterizes the crossroads at which the area finds itself. Chinatown encroaches on Broadway west of Columbus; on the east side of the street the self-proclaimed "birthplace of topless dancing," the Condor, is now a coffee shop. Up Columbus, moving away from the Financial District, the traditional North Beach mix of Italian restaurants and cafés remains. Southward, it's a mixed bag: skyscrapers loom overhead; although one of the earliest and shortest examples, the triangular Sentinel Building (916 Kearny St.), owned by moviemaker Francis Ford Coppola, is the one that grabs the eye.

Time Out The richness of North Beach lifestyle is reflected in the neighborhood's numerous cafés. **Caffe Puccini** (411 Columbus Ave.) could be Italy: Few of the staff speak English. Their caffe latte (coffee, chocolate, cinnamon, and steamed milk) and strains of Italian operas recall *Roman Holiday.* A Saturday morning must is around the corner at **Caffe Trieste** (601 Vallejo St.). Get there at about 11; at noon, the Giotta family's weekly musical begins. The program ranges from Italian pop and folk music to favorite family operas. The Trieste opened in 1956 and became headquarters for the area's beatnik poets, artists, and writers.

47 **Telegraph Hill** rises from the east end of Lombard Street to about 300 feet and is capped with the landmark Coit Tower, dedicated as a monument to the city's volunteer firefighters. Early during the gold rush, an eight-year-old who would become one of the city's most memorable eccentrics, Lillie Hitchcock Coit, arrived on the scene. Legend relates that at age 17, "Miss Lil" deserted a wedding party and chased down the street after her favorite engine, Knickerbocker No. 5, clad in her bridesmaid finery. She was soon made an honorary member of the Knickerbocker Company, and after that always signed herself "Lillie Coit 5" in honor of her favorite fire engine. Lillie died in 1929 at the age of 86, leaving the city about $100,000 of her million-dollar-plus estate to "expend in an appropriate manner . . . to the beauty of San Francisco."

Telegraph Hill residents command some of the best views in the city, as well as the most difficult ascent to their aeries. The

Greenwich stairs lead up to Coit Tower from Filbert Street, and there are steps down to Filbert Street on the opposite side of Telegraph Hill. Views are superb en route, but most visitors should either taxi up to the tower or take the Muni bus No. 39-Coit at Washington Square. To catch the bus from Union Square, walk to Stockton and Sutter streets, board the Muni No. 30, and ask for a transfer to use at Washington Square (Columbus Ave. and Union St.) to board the No. 39-Coit. Public parking is very limited at the tower, and on holidays and weekends there are long lines of cars and buses winding up the narrow road.

⬤48 **Coit Tower** stands as a monument not only to Lillie Coit and the city's firefighters but also to the influence of the political and radical Mexican muralist Diego Rivera. Fresco was Rivera's medium, and it was his style that unified the work of most of the 25 artists who painted the murals in the tower. The murals were commissioned by the U.S. government as a Public Works of Art Project. The artists were paid $38 a week. Some were fresh from art schools; others found no market for art in the dark depression days of the early 1930s. An illustrated brochure for sale in the tiny gift shop explains the various murals dedicated to the workers of California.

Ride the elevator to the top to enjoy the panoramic view of both the Bay Bridge and Golden Gate Bridge; directly offshore is the famous Alcatraz and just behind it, Angel Island, a hikers' and campers' paradise. There are often artists at work in Pioneer Park, at the foot of the tower. Small paintings of the scene are frequently offered for sale at modest prices. *Discoverer of America*, the impressive bronze statue of Christopher Columbus, was a gift of the local Italian community.

Walk down the Greenwich Steps to Montgomery Street, and turn right. At the corner where the Filbert Steps intersect, you'll find the Art Deco masterpiece at 1360 Montgomery Street (*see* Off the Beaten Track, *below*). Its elegant etched-glass gazelle and palms counterpoint the silvered fresco of the heroic bridgeworker—echoed by an actual view of the Bay Bridge in the distance. Descend the Filbert Steps amid roses, fuchsias, irises, and trumpet flowers, courtesy of Grace Marchant, who labored for nearly 30 years to transform a dump into one of San Francisco's hidden treasures. At the last landing before the final descent to Sansome Street, pause and sit on the bench to breathe in the fragrance of roses as you gaze at the bridge and bay below. A small bronze plaque set into the bench reads: "I have a feeling we're not in Kansas anymore."

At the foot of the hill you will come to the Levi Strauss headquarters, a carefully landscaped $150 million complex that appears so collegial and serene it is affectionately known as LSU (Levi Strauss University). Fountains and grassy knolls complement the redbrick buildings and provide a perfect environment for brown-bag lunches; at **Uno Poco di Tutti** deli in Levi's Plaza (1265 Battery St., tel. 415/986–0646) you'll find everything you need.

Tour 6: Nob Hill and Russian Hill

If you don't mind climbing uphill, Nob Hill is within walking distance of Union Square. Once called the Hill of Golden Promise, it became Nob Hill during the 1870s when "the Big Four"—Charles Crocker, Leland Stanford, Mark Hopkins, and Collis Huntington—built their hilltop estates. It is still home to many of the city's elite as well as four of San Francisco's finest hotels.

In 1882 Robert Louis Stevenson called Nob Hill "the hill of palaces." But the 1906 earthquake and fire destroyed all the palatial mansions. The shell of one survived. The Flood brownstone (1000 California St.) was built by the Comstock silver baron in 1886 at a reputed cost of $1.5 million. In 1909 the property was

49 purchased by the prestigious **Pacific Union Club.** The 45-room exclusive club remains the bastion of the wealthy and powerful. Adjacent is a charming small park noted for its frequent art shows.

50 Neighboring **Grace Cathedral** (1051 Taylor St.) is the seat of the Episcopal church in San Francisco. The soaring Gothic structure, built on the site of Charles Crocker's mansion, took 53 years to build. The gilded bronze doors at the east entrance were taken from casts of Ghiberti's Gates of Paradise on the baptistery in Florence. The cathedral's original design called for the demolition of a four-story building to allow for a sweeping set of stairs leading up to the church, but the construction was delayed for decades, by which time preservationists began fighting to retain the structure. After what was described as "a civilized but passionate" planning commission debate, the building came down in late-1993 and architect Lewis Hobart's grand design was finally achieved in 1994. The cathedral's superb rose window is illuminated at night. There are often organ recitals on Sundays at 5 PM, as well as special programs during the holiday seasons.

51 The huge **Masonic Auditorium** (1111 California St.) is also the site of frequent musical events, including "Today's Artists," a concert series that highlights young classical musicians.

52 What sets the **Fairmont Hotel** (California and Mason Sts.) apart from other luxury hotels is its legendary history. Its dazzling opening was delayed a year by the 1906 quake, but since then the marble palace has hosted presidents, royalty, and local nabobs. Prices are up a bit, though: on the eve of World War I, you could get a room for as low as $2.50 per night—meals included! Nowadays, prices run as high as $6,000, which will get you a night in the eight-room penthouse suite that was showcased regularly in the TV series "Hotel." The apartment building on the corner of Sacramento Street across from the Fairmont is also a media star. In 1958 it was a major location in Alfred Hitchcock's *Vertigo* and was more recently (1993) featured in the BBC production of Armistead Maupin's homage to San Francisco in the wacky '70s, *Tales of the City.*

On the Fairmont's other flank at California and Mason streets
❸ is the **Mark Hopkins Inter-Continental Hotel,** which is remembered fondly by thousands of World War II veterans who jammed the Top of the Mark lounge (*see* Skyline Bars in Chapter 8, The Arts and Nightlife) before leaving for overseas duty.
❹ Down California at Powell Street stands the posh **Stouffer Stanford Court Hotel.** The structure is a remodeled 1909 apartment house.

❺ The **Cable Car Museum,** at the corner of Washington and Mason streets, exhibits photographs, old cars, and other memorabilia from the system's 115-year history. It's a brief but engaging stopover on the way to Russian Hill. An overlook allows you to observe the cables that haul the city's cars in action. *1201 Mason St., at Washington St., tel. 415/474–1887. Admission free. Open daily 10–5.*

Just nine blocks or so from downtown, **Russian Hill** has long been home to old San Francisco families and, during the 1890s, to a group of bohemian artists and writers that included Charles Norris, George Sterling, and Maynard Dixon. An old legend says that during San Francisco's early days the steep hill (294 feet high) was the site of a cemetery for Russian seal hunters and traders. Now the hills are covered with an astounding array of housing: simple studios, sumptuous pied-à-terre, Victorian flats, and costly boxlike condos.

From the Cable Car Museum, continue four blocks north on Mason Street to Vallejo Street. This will put you at an ideal spot from which to photograph Alcatraz Island and the bay. Slowly
❻ start climbing the Vallejo Steps up to attractive **Ina Coolbrith Park.** An Oakland librarian and poet, Ina introduced both Jack London and Isadora Duncan to the world of books. For years she entertained literary greats in her Macondray Lane home near the park. In 1915, she was named poet laureate of California.

A number of buildings in this neighborhood survived the 1906 earthquake and fire and still stand today. The house at **1652–56 Taylor Street** was saved by alert firefighters who spotted the American flag on the property and managed to quench the flames using seltzer water and wet sand. A number of brown-shingle structures on Vallejo Street designed by Willis Polk, one of the city's most famous architects, also survived. For years, the Polk family resided at **1013 Vallejo Street.** Stroll past **1034–1036 Vallejo**—both buildings, tucked in between million-dollar condominium neighbors, were designed by Polk.

At this point, two secluded alleys beckon: To the north, **Russian Hill Place** has a row of Mediterranean-style town houses designed by Polk in 1915. On **Florence Place** to the south, 1920s stucco survivors reign over more contemporary construction.

Follow Vallejo Street west to Jones Street, turn right, and continue on to Green Street. The 1000 block of Green, on one of the three crests of Russian Hill, is one of the most remarkable blocks in San Francisco. The **Feusier House** (1067 Green St.), built in 1857 and now a private residence, is one of two octagonal houses left in the city (*see* Sightseeing Checklists, *below;* for the other—Octagon House—which is open for tours on a limited basis). On the other side of the street (at 1088) is the **1907 firehouse.** Local art patron Mrs. Ralph K. Davies bought it from the city in 1956. There is a small museum, and the property is often used for charity benefits.

Continue west on Green Street to Hyde Street, where the Hyde-Powell cable car line runs. Turn right and stroll up to Union Street. (If you're tired of walking, stop at the original Swensen's for an ice-cream treat.) At this point you have two options: You can meander down Union Street to Jones Street, turn right and walk a few steps down to magical **Macondray Lane,** a quiet cobbled pedestrian street lined with Edwardian cottages. From a flight of steep wooden stairs that lead down to Taylor Street you'll get some spectacular views of the bay. From Taylor Street it is then a short walk downhill to North Beach.

Your other option is to keep walking north on Hyde Street three blocks to **Lombard Street.** Stretching the length of just one block, San Francisco's "crookedest street" drops down the east face of Russian Hill in eight switchbacks to Leavenworth Street. Few tourists with cars can resist the lure of the scary descent. Pedestrians should be alert while using the steep steps, especially when photographing the smashing views.

At the base of the steps, turn left on Leavenworth Street and then right on Chestnut Street. At 800 Chestnut Street is the **San Francisco Art Institute.** Established in 1871, it occupied the Mark Hopkins home at California and Mason streets from 1893 to 1906. The school carried on in temporary quarters until 1926, when the present Spanish Colonial building was erected on the top of Russian Hill. Be sure to see the impressive seven-section fresco painted in 1931 by the Mexican master Diego Rivera; it's in the gallery to the left as you enter the institute. There are also frequent exhibitions of student efforts.

From here you can walk back to Hyde Street and take the cable car back downtown or walk a few blocks north to Fisherman's Wharf. Hardy walkers will probably prefer to walk down to Columbus Avenue and then west on North Point or Beach streets to Ghirardelli Square, the Cannery, and Aquatic Park.

Tour 7: Pacific Heights

Pacific Heights forms an east–west ridge along the city's northern flank from Van Ness Avenue to the Presidio and from California Street to the bay. Some of the city's most expensive and dramatic real estate, including mansions and town houses priced at $1 million and up, are located here. Grand old Victorians, expensively face-lifted, grace tree-lined streets, although here and there glossy, glass-walled high-rise condos obstruct the view.

Old money and some new, trade and diplomatic personnel, personalities in the limelight, and those who prefer absolute media anonymity occupy the city's most prestigious residential enclave. Few visitors see anything other than the pleasing facades of Queen Anne charmers, English Tudor imports, and Baroque bastions, but strolling can still be rewarding. As you walk through Pacific Heights, you'll notice that few of the structures feature adjoining gardens. Space has always been at a premium in San Francisco; only the city's richest residents could afford to purchase a lot and then not build. Even in wealthy Pacific Heights, many of the structures stand close together, but extend in a vertical direction for two or more stories.

A good place to begin a tour of the neighborhood is at the corner of Webster Street and Pacific Avenue, deep in the heart of the Heights. You can get here from Union Square by taking Muni Bus 3 from Sutter and Stockton to Jackson and Fillmore streets. Head one block east on Jackson to Webster Street.

North on Webster Street, at 2550, is the massive Georgian brick mansion built in 1896 for William B. Bourn, who had inherited a Mother Lode gold mine. The architect, Willis Polk, was responsible for many of the most traditional and impressive commercial and private homes built from the prequake days until the early 1920s. (Be sure to see his 1917 Hallidie Building, 130 Sutter Street; *see* Tour 3: The Financial District and Jackson Square, *above*.) Polk also designed Bourn's palatial Peninsula estate, **Filoli** (*see* The San Francisco Peninsula in Chapter 9, Excursions from San Francisco).

61 Neighbors include a consulate and, on the northwest corner, two classic showplaces. **2222 Broadway** is the three-story Italian Renaissance palace built by Comstock mine heir James Flood. Broadway uptown, unlike its North Beach stretch, is big league socially. The former Flood residence was given to a religious order. Ten years later, the Convent of the Sacred Heart purchased the Baroque brick Grant house (2220 Broadway) and both serve as school quarters today. A second top-drawer school, the Hamlin (2120 Broadway), occupies another Flood property.

Movie buffs may want to make the effort to travel another block west on Broadway to Steiner Street for a gander at the handsome home (at the southeast corner) used in the movie hit *Mrs. Doubtfire*.

62 Return east on Broadway past the Hamlin School and turn right (south) on Buchanan Street, then left on Jackson Street to Laguna Street. The massive red sandstone **Whittier Mansion,** at 2090 Jackson Street, was one of the most elegant 19th-century houses in the state, built so solidly that only a chimney toppled over during the 1906 earthquake. One block south on **63** Laguna, at Washington Street, is **Lafayette Park,** a four-block-square oasis for sunbathers and dog-and-Frisbee teams. During the 1860s, a tenacious squatter, Sam Holladay, built himself a big wooden house in the center of the park. Holladay even instructed city gardeners as if the land were his own, and defied all attempts to remove him. The house was finally torn down in 1936.

Walking east on Washington street along the edge of Lafayette
64 Park, the most imposing residence is the formal French **Spreckels Mansion** (2080 Washington St.). Sugar heir Adolph Spreckels's wife, Alma, was so pleased with her house that she commissioned architect George Applegarth to design the city's European museum, the California Palace of the Legion of Honor in Lincoln Park. Alma, one of the city's great iconoclasts, is the model for the bronze figure atop the Victory Monument in Union Square.

Continue east on Washington Street two more blocks to Franklin Street and turn left. At 2007 Franklin is the handsome
65 **Haas-Lilienthal Victorian.** Built in 1886, at an original cost of $18,000, this grand Queen Anne survived the 1906 earthquake and fire and is the only fully furnished Victorian open to the public. The carefully kept rooms offer an intriguing glimpse into turn-of-the-century taste and lifestyle. A small display of photographs on the bottom floor proves that this elaborate house was modest compared with some of the giants that fell to the fire. It is operated by the Foundation for San Francisco's Architectural Heritage. Tours of the house are given by docent volunteers two days a week. The volunteers also conduct an informative two-hour tour of the eastern portion of Pacific Heights on Sunday afternoons. *Tel. 415/441–3004. Admission: $4 adults, $2 senior citizens and children under 12. Open Wed. noon–4 (last tour at 3:15), Sun. 11–5 (last tour at 4:15). Pacific Heights tours ($3 adults, $1 senior citizens and children) leave the house Sun. at 12:30 PM.*

Going south on Franklin Street, don't be fooled by the neoclassical **Golden Gate Church** at 1901—what at first looks like a stone facade is actually redwood painted white. At **1735 Franklin** is a stately brick Georgian that was built during the early 1900s for a coffee merchant. Looking east at the corner of Franklin Street and California is a "tapestry brick" **Christian Science church** built in the Tuscan Revival style. Its terra-cotta detailing is also noteworthy.

66 The **Coleman House** at 1701 Franklin Street is an impressive twin-turreted Queen Anne mansion built for a gold-rush mining and lumber baron. At 1818 and 1834 California are two stunning **Italianate Victorians.** A block farther at 1990 California is the Victorian-era **Atherton House,** perhaps the oddest combination of architectural elements—among them Queen Anne and Stick-Eastlake—in all of Pacific Heights.

To return to downtown, walk by the side of the Atherton House to Sacramento and catch the No. 1-California bus (get a transfer and change to the No. 30-Stockton bus on Stockton Street). If you haven't ridden a cable car yet, disembark the No. 1 at Van Ness Avenue and walk one block south to the California-line terminus. The wait here is much shorter than for the Powell-Hyde line.

If you'd like to see more Victorians, proceed west on California past the Atherton House another block to Laguna Street and turn left. The Italianate Victorians on the east side of the **1800 block** of Laguna Street cost only $2,000–$2,600 when they were built during the 1870s. This block is one of the most photographed rows of Victorians in the city.

Walk south on Laguna Street to Sutter and catch the No. 2, 3, or 4 bus to Union Square. If you still have some bounce in your step, proceed one block past Sutter to Post and walk west one block to Buchanan and begin the Japantown tour.

Tour 8: Japantown

Japanese-Americans began gravitating to the neighborhood known as the Western Addition prior to the 1906 earthquake. Early immigrants arrived about 1860, and they named San Francisco Soko. After the 1906 fire had destroyed wooden homes in other parts of the stricken city, many survivors settled in the Western Addition. By the 1930s the pioneers had opened shops, markets, meeting halls, and restaurants and established Shinto and Buddhist temples. Japantown was virtually disbanded during World War II when many of its residents, including second- and third-generation Americans, were "relocated" in camps.

Today **Japantown,** or "Nihonmachi," is centered on the slopes of Pacific Heights, north of Geary Boulevard, between Fillmore and Laguna streets. The Nihonmachi Cherry Blossom Festival is celebrated two weekends every April with a calendar of ethnic events. Walking in Nihonmachi is more than just a shopping and culinary treat; it is a cultural, sensory experience.

To reach Japantown from Union Square, take Muni bus No. 38-Geary or No. 2, 3, or 4 on Sutter Street, west-bound to Laguna. Remember to have exact change—fare is $1; paper money is accepted.

We recommend visiting Japantown and the Western Addition during the day. Though the hotel, restaurant, and Kabuki movie complex are relatively safe in the evenings, it is often difficult to avoid long waits at isolated bus stops or to find a cruising cab when you want to get back to the hotel. The proximity of the often-hostile street gangs in the Western Addition could cause unpleasant incidents.

The buildings around the traffic-free **Japan Center Mall** between Sutter and Post streets are of the shoji screen school of architecture, and Ruth Asawa's origami fountain sits in the middle. (*See* Tour 1: Union Square, *above,* for more information on Ms. Asawa.) The mall faces the three-block-long, 5-acre **Japan Center.** In 1968, the multimillion-dollar development created by noted American architect Minoru Yamasaki opened with a three-day folk festival. The three-block cluster includes an 800-

car public garage and shops and showrooms selling Japanese products: electronic products, cameras, tapes and records, porcelains, pearls, and paintings.

The center is dominated by its Peace Plaza and Pagoda located between the Tasamak Plaza and Kintetsu buildings. The original design of Professor Yoshiro Taniguchi of Tokyo, an authority on ancient Japanese buildings, has been altered greatly, mostly for the worse. Remaining from the original design are the graceful *yagura* (wooden drum tower) that spans the entrance to the mall and the copper-roofed *Heiwa Dori* (Peace Walkway) between the Tasamak Plaza and Kintetsu buildings. The five-tier, 100-foot Peace Pagoda overlooks the plaza, where seasonal festivals are held. The pagoda draws on the tradition of miniature round pagodas dedicated to eternal peace by Empress Koken in Nara more than 1,200 years ago. It was designed by the Japanese architect Yoshiro Taniguchi "to convey the friendship and goodwill of the Japanese to the people of the United States." A cultural bridge modeled after Florence's Ponte Vecchio spans Webster Street, connecting the Kintetsu and Kinokuniya buildings.

Some 40 restaurants in the neighborhood feature a choice of Japanese, Chinese, or Korean food. Most are found in the mall, a few are on side streets, and the rest are in the center itself, concentrated on the "street of restaurants" in the Kintetsu Building. Following the practice in Japan, plastic replicas of the various dishes are on view.

If touring has about done you in, we suggest a brief respite at the **Kabuki Hot Springs** (1750 Geary Blvd., tel. 415/922–6000). Open daily, the communal bath is open for men only on Monday, Tuesday, Thursday, and Saturday, and for women only on Wednesday, Friday, and Sunday. Private baths with sauna or steam are available daily. The spa offers a number of steam, sauna, and massage packages. One, the Shogun, includes an hour of shiatsu massage. This method concentrates on pressure points in the body and is guaranteed to get you back on the track.

Time Out   **Isobune** (tel. 415/563–1030), on the second floor of the Kintetsu Building, is unusual. The sushi chef prepares a variety of sushi, placing each small portion on a small wooden boat that floats on a "river" of water that circles the counter. The customer then fishes out a sampling. The inexpensive but superb **Mifune** (tel. 415/922–0337), diagonally across from Isobune, serves both hot and cold noodle dishes, either boiled and served in a broth or prepared toss-fried, with bits of greens and meat added for flavor.

Walk back east on Geary Boulevard's north side to Gough Street. This enclave of expensive high-rise residential towers is **68** known as Cathedral Hill. Dramatic **St. Mary's Cathedral,** on the south side of Geary, was dedicated in 1971 at a cost of $7 million. The impressive Catholic cathedral seats 2,500 people around the central altar. Above the altar is a spectacular cascade made of

7,000 aluminum ribs. Four magnificent stained-glass windows in the dome represent the four elements: the blue north window, water; the light-colored south window, the sun; the red west window, fire; and the green east window, earth. Designed by a team of local architects and Pier Nervi of Rome, the Italian travertine church is approached through spacious plazas.

You can catch the No. 38-Geary bus in front of the cathedral to return downtown, or get off at Van Ness Avenue. Transfer to the No. 42, 47, or 49 bus heading south and get off at McAllister Street. To walk takes less than 10 minutes.

Tour 9: Civic Center

San Francisco's Civic Center stands as one of the country's great city, state, and federal building complexes with handsome adjoining cultural institutions. It's the realization of the theories of turn-of-the-century proponents of the "City Beautiful." In early 1995 the center will close for three years of seismic upgrading.

69 Facing Polk Street, between Grove and McAllister streets, **City Hall** is a French Renaissance Revival masterpiece of granite and marble, modeled after the Capitol in Washington. Its dome is even higher than the Washington version, and it dominates the area. In front of the building are formal gardens with fountains, walkways, and seasonal flower beds. Brooks Exhibit Hall was constructed under this plaza in 1958 to add space for the frequent trade shows and other events based in the Bill Graham Civic Auditorium, recently renamed in honor of the late rock promoter, on Grove Street.

Across the plaza from City Hall on Larkin Street is the main
70 branch of the **San Francisco Public Library.** (A new library is being built directly across Fulton Street; when that is completed in early 1996, this site may become the new Asian Art Museum.) History buffs should visit the San Francisco History Room and Archives on the third floor. Historic photographs, maps, and other memorabilia are carefully displayed for the layman or research scholar. *Archives, tel. 415/557–4567. Open Tues., Wed., Fri. 1–6, Thurs. and Sat. 10–noon and 1–6.*

Just east of the new library, at the end of Fulton Street set on
71 an angle between Hyde and Market streets, is **United Nations Plaza,** the site of a farmers' market on Wednesday and Sunday. On the west side of City Hall, across Van Ness Avenue, are the Veterans Building, the Opera House, and Davies Symphony
72 Hall. The northernmost of the three is the **Veterans Building** (401 Van Ness Ave.), the third and fourth floors of which formerly housed the San Francisco Museum of Modern Art. Herbst Theatre, on the first floor, remains a popular venue for lectures and readings, classical ensembles, and dance performances. In 1995, celebrations are planned to commemorate the 50th anniversary of the signing of the United Nations Charter in the theater.

An ornate horseshoe carriage entrance on its south side separates the Veterans Building from the **War Memorial Opera House** (301 Van Ness Ave.), which opened in 1932. Modeled after European counterparts, the interior has a vaulted and coffered ceiling, a marble foyer, and two balconies. The San Francisco Opera (September–December) and the San Francisco Ballet (February–May, with December *Nutcracker* performances) perform here. (*See* Chapter 8: The Arts and Nightlife.)

Time Out For a quick pizza or a grilled chicken breast sandwich, dash over to the bustling bistro **Spuntino** (524 Van Ness Ave., tel. 415/861–7772). Open until midnight on Friday and Saturday, this is an excellent spot for an after-theater cappuccino. A bit down the alley that runs alongside Spuntino, celebrity chef Jeremiah Tower's **Stars** (*see* Chapter 6, Dining) offers exotic versions of California cuisine in an atmospheric room.

South of Grove Street, still on Van Ness, is the $27.5-million home of the San Francisco Symphony, the modern 3,000-plus-seat **Louise M. Davies Symphony Hall,** made of glass and granite. Tours are available of Davies Hall and the adjacent Performing Arts Center, which encompasses the Opera House and Herbst Theatre; architecture and art-history buffs will find the tours interesting. *201 Van Ness Ave., tel. 415/552–8338. Cost: $3 adults, $2 senior citizens and students. Tours of Davies Hall Wed. 1:30 and 2:30, Sat. 12:30 and 1:30. Tours of Davies Hall and the Performing Arts Center every half-hour Mon. 10–2.*

The **San Francisco Performing Arts Library and Museum,** also known as PALM, has a mission to collect, document, and preserve the San Francisco Bay Area's rich performing-arts legacy. It houses the largest collection of its kind on the West Coast. Exhibitions often include programs, photographs, manuscripts, newspaper clippings, and other memorabilia of historic performance events. *399 Grove St., at Gough St., tel. 415/255–4800. Admission free. Open Tues.–Fri. 10–5, Sat. noon–4.*

One block south of Grove Street, the renaissance of Hayes Street has expanded since a freeway ramp was dismantled after the Loma Prieta earthquake. From Franklin Street up to Laguna, there are some fine contemporary and ethnic art galleries, as well as boutiques and eateries. However, be careful not to stray past Gough Street after nightfall.

Tour 10: The Northern Waterfront

Numbers in the margin correspond to points of interest on the Northern Waterfront: Tours 10–11 map.

For the sight, sound, and smell of the sea, hop the Powell-Hyde cable car from Union Square to the end of the line. From the cable-car turnaround, Aquatic Park and the National Maritime Museum are immediately to the west; Fort Mason, with its several interesting museums, is just a bit farther west. If you want to explore the more commercial attractions, Ghirardelli Square is behind you and Fisherman's Wharf is to the east. We recommend casual clothes, good walking shoes, and a jacket or sweater for mid-afternoon breezes or foggy mists.

You could begin your day with one of the early-morning boat tours that depart from the Northern Waterfront piers. On a clear day (almost always), the morning light casts a warm glow on the colorful homes on Russian Hill, the weather-aged fishing boats cluttered at Fisherman's Wharf, rosy Ghirardelli Square and its fairy-tale clock tower, and the swelling seas beyond the entrance to the bay.

San Francisco is famous for the arts and crafts that flourish on the streets. Each day more than 200 of the city's innovative jewelers, painters, potters, photographers, and leather workers offer their wares for sale. You'll find them at Fisherman's Wharf, Union Square, Embarcadero Plaza, and Cliff House. Be wary: Some of the items are from foreign factories and may be overpriced. If you can't live without the item, try to bargain.

❶ The **National Maritime Museum** exhibits ship models, photographs, maps, and other artifacts chronicling the development of San Francisco and the West Coast through maritime history. *Aquatic Park, at the foot of Polk St., tel. 415/556–3002 (if no answer call 929–0202). Admission free. Open daily 10–5, until 6 in summer.*

❷ The museum also includes the **Hyde Street Pier** (two blocks east), where historic vessels are moored. The pier, one of the wharf area's best bargains, is always bustling with activity; depending on when you arrive, you might see boatbuilders at work or children manning a boat or ship as though it were still the early 1900s. The highlight of the pier is the *Balclutha,* an 1886 full-rigged, three-mast sailing vessel that sailed around Cape Horn 17 times. The *Eureka,* a side-wheel ferry, and the *C.A. Thayer,* a three-masted schooner, can also be boarded. *Tel. 415/929–0202. Admission: $3 adults, $1 children 12–18; children under 12 and senior citizens free. (Note: Travelers with a National Park Service Golden Eagle Pass enter the pier free.) Open fall–spring, daily 10–5; summer, daily 10–6.*

The ***Pampanito,*** at Pier 45, is a World War II submarine. An audio tour has been installed. *Tel. 415/929–0202. Admission: $4 adults, $2 senior citizens and students 12–18, $1 children 6–11 and active military. Open fall–spring, daily 9–6 ; summer, daily 9–9.*

❸ **Fort Mason,** originally a depot for the shipment of supplies to the Pacific during World War II, is a 10-minute walk west from the back of the Maritime Museum. Follow the railway tracks in back of the museum, turn right before they head into a (blocked) tunnel and then left up the fairly steep grade that leads to the complex. Fort Mason was converted into a cultural center in 1977. The immense, three-story, yellow-stucco buildings are nondescript. Four minimuseums merit mention, however.

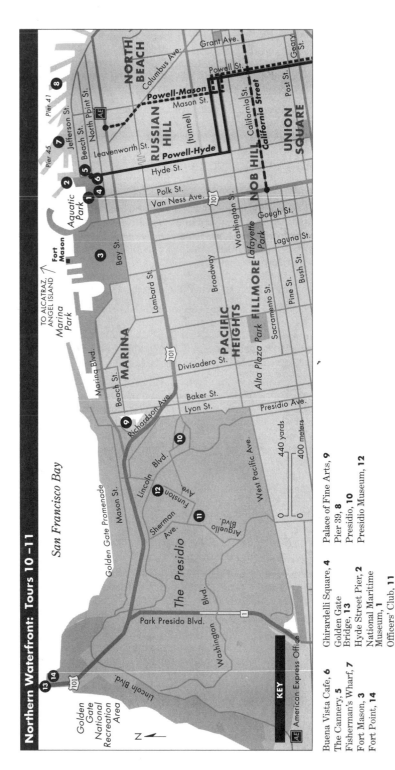

Northern Waterfront: Tours 10–11

San Francisco Bay

66

TO ALCATRAZ, ANGEL ISLAND

NORTH BEACH

RUSSIAN HILL

NOB HILL

UNION SQUARE

FILLMORE

PACIFIC HEIGHTS

MARINA

The Presidio

Golden Gate National Recreation Area

Grant Ave.
Columbus Ave.
Powell St.
Powell-Mason
Mason St. (tunnel)
Powell-Hyde
Leavenworth St.
Hyde St.
Beach St.
North Point St.
Jefferson St.
Pier 41
Pier 45
Polk St.
Van Ness Ave.
California St.
California Street
Post St.
Geary St.
Aquatic Park
Fort Mason
Bay St.
Marina Blvd.
Lombard St.
Broadway
Washington St.
Gough St.
Laguna St.
Lafayette Park
Sacramento St.
Pine St.
Bush St.
Alta Plaza Park
Divisadero St.
Baker St.
Lyon St.
Presidio Ave.
Richardson Ave.
Marina Park
Beach St.
West Pacific Ave.
Lincoln Blvd.
Funston Ave.
Sherman Ave.
Arguello Blvd.
Mason St.
Golden Gate Promenade
Park Presido Blvd.
Washington
Lincoln Blvd.

440 yards
400 meters

KEY

AE American Express Office

Buena Vista Cafe, **6**
The Cannery, **5**
Fisherman's Wharf, **7**
Fort Mason, **3**
Fort Point, **14**

Ghirardelli Square, **4**
Golden Gate Bridge, **13**
Hyde Street Pier, **2**
National Maritime Museum, **1**
Officers' Club, **11**

Palace of Fine Arts, **9**
Pier 39, **8**
Presidio, **10**
Presidio Museum, **12**

The **Mexican Museum** was the first American showcase to be devoted exclusively to Mexican and Mexican-American art. Plans are underway to build a larger modern building for the museum in the downtown Yerba Buena complex by the late 1990s. The museum's goal is to expose the vitality and scope of Mexican art from pre-Hispanic Indian terra-cotta figures and Spanish Colonial religious images to modern Mexican masters. Limited space allows only a fraction of the permanent collection, including a recent 500-piece folk-art collection (a gift from the Nelson A. Rockefeller estate), to be exhibited. The museum also mounts major special shows. One of the early, very successful exhibits displayed the work of Frida Kahlo, the Mexican surrealist and wife of Diego Rivera. The permanent collection includes such contemporary greats as Rivera, Tamayo, Orozco, Siquieros, and sculptor Francisco Zuniga. La Tienda, the museum shop, stocks colorful Mexican folk art, posters, books, and catalogues from museum exhibitions. *Fort Mason, Bldg. D, tel. 415/441-0404. Admission: $3 adults, $2 senior citizens and students, children under 10 free; free admission noon–8 PM on the first Wed. of the month. Open Wed.–Sun. noon–5.*

The **Museo Italo-Americano** has permanent exhibits of works of 19th- and 20th-century Italian-American artists. Shows include paintings, sculpture, etchings, and photographs. The museum presents special exhibits, lectures, and films. *Fort Mason, Bldg. C, tel. 415/673–2200. Admission: $2 adults, $1 senior citizens and students; admission free noon–8 PM on the 1st Wed. of the month. Open Wed.–Sun. noon–5.*

The **San Francisco African-American Historical and Cultural Society** maintains the only museum of black culture west of the Rockies. The permanent collection includes exhibits on black California and black Civil War history. Temporary exhibits showcase current black artists of California. *Fort Mason, Bldg. C, Room 165, tel. 415/979–6794. Admission: $2 adults, 50¢ senior citizens and children 6–17. Open Wed.–Sun. noon–5. Phone to verify schedules.*

The **San Francisco Craft and Folk Art Museum** features American folk art, tribal art, and contemporary crafts. *Fort Mason, Bldg. A, tel. 415/775–0990. Admission: $1 adults, 50¢ senior citizens and children; admission free Sat. 10–noon. Open Tues.–Sun. 11–5, Sat. 10–5. Occasionally open Mon.; call ahead.*

Several theater companies are housed at Fort Mason. Of particular note is the **Magic Theatre** (Fort Mason, Bldg. D, tel. 415/441–8822), known for producing the works of such contemporary playwrights as Sam Shepard and Michael McClure.

The **SS *Jeremiah O'Brien***, a World War II Liberty Ship freighter, returned to Fort Mason from Europe in October 1994, after participating in events commemorating the 50th anniversary of the D-Day landing at Normandy. The ship is staffed by volunteers, and there are special "steaming weekends," when the steam engine is in operation, the coal stove galley is open, and the "Slop Chest" store is set up. This is usually the third weekend of the month, but call to verify. *Fort Mason, Pier 3 East, Marina Blvd. and Buchanan St., tel. 415/441–3101. Summer admission: $4 adults, $3 senior citizens, $2 children 10–16, $1 children under 10, $6 per family. Subtract $1 for all but children under 10 during winter months. Open weekdays 9–3, weekends 9–4.*

Time Out   The San Francisco Zen Center operates a famous and beautiful restaurant at Fort Mason. **Greens** (Fort Mason, Bldg. A, tel. 415/771–6222) has won international acclaim for its innovative vegetarian menu. The room is decorated with contemporary art and offers some of the finest views (from down close to the water) across the bay to the Golden Gate Bridge. Reservations are essential, but you can stop by the bakery during the day and pick up some of their famous bread and pastries.

❹ Spend some time strolling through **Ghirardelli Square,** which is across Beach Street from the National Maritime Museum. This charming complex of 19th-century brick factory buildings has been transformed into specialty shops, cafés, restaurants, and galleries. Until the early 1960s, the Ghirardelli Chocolate Company's aromatic production perfumed the Northern Waterfront. Two unusual shops in the Cocoa Building deserve mention: **Xanadu Gallery** and **Folk Art International** display museum-quality tribal art from Asia, Africa, Oceania, and the Americas. Xanadu's array of antique and ethnic jewelry is peerless. Also of interest, on the Lower Plaza level of the Cocoa Building, is the **Creative Spirit Gallery** (tel. 415/441–1537), a space sponsored and run by the National Institute of Art and Disabilities to showcase works by artists with disabilities. Nearby, in Ghirardelli's Rose court, is the **California Crafts Museum** (tel. 415/771–1919), which honors the state's craft artists.

❺ Just east of the Hyde Street Pier, **The Cannery** is a three-story structure built in 1894 to house what became the Del Monte Fruit and Vegetable Cannery. Shops, art galleries, and unusual restaurants ring the courtyard today, and the new **Museum of the City of San Francisco** can be found on the third floor. The first independent museum on the history of the city displays a number of significant historical items, maps, and photographs, including the 8-ton head of the Goddess of Progress statue that toppled from City Hall just before the 1906 earthquake. *2801 Leavenworth St., tel. 415/928–0289. Admission free ($2 donation suggested). Open Wed.–Sun. 10–4.*

Just across the street, additional shopping and snacking choices are offered at the flag-festooned **Anchorage mall.**

❻ The mellow **Buena Vista Cafe** (2765 Hyde St., tel. 415/474–5044) claims to be the birthplace of Irish Coffee stateside; the late San Francisco columnist Stan Delaplane is credited with importing the Gaelic concoction. The BV opens at 9 AM weekdays, 8 AM weekends, and serves a great breakfast. It is always crowded, but try for a table overlooking nostalgic Victorian Park with its cable-car turntable.

❼ A bit farther west, at Taylor and Jefferson streets, is **Fisherman's Wharf.** Numerous seafood restaurants are located here, as well as sidewalk crab pots and counters that offer take-away shrimp and crab cocktails. Ships creak at their moorings; seagulls cry out for a handout. By mid-afternoon, the fishing fleet is back to port. T-shirts and sweats, gold chains galore, redwood furniture, acres of artwork—some original—beckon visitors. Wax museums, fast-food favorites, amusing street artists, and the animated robots at Lazermaze provide diversions for all ages.

Time Out   The swingin'est place on the wharf is the airy **Lou's Pier 47 Restaurant** and bar (300 Jefferson St., tel. 415/771–0377). You won't be able to miss this joint: the sounds of live jazz bands, many of them quite fine, flood the wharf, starting most days at noon. The food at Lou's—standard American fare—is not bad either. A good place for families is **Bobby Rubino's Place for Ribs** (245 Jefferson St., tel. 415/673–2266) across the street.

Cruises are an exhilarating way to see the bay. Among the cruises offered by the **Red and White Fleet,** berthed at Pier 41, are frequent 45-minute swings under the Golden Gate Bridge and along the Northern Waterfront. More interesting—and just as scenic—are the tours to Sausalito, Angel Island, Muir Woods, Marine World Africa USA, and the Napa Valley Wine Country. A real treat is the popular tour of **Alcatraz Island.** The boat ride to the island is brief (15 minutes), but affords beautiful views of the city, Marin County, and the East Bay. The audio tour, highly recommended, features observations of guards and prisoners about life in one of America's most notorious penal colonies. A separate, ranger-led tour surveys the island's ecology. Plan your schedule to include at least three hours for your visit and the boat rides to and from the island; you may even find yourself wanting to linger. Advanced reservations, even in the off-season, are strongly recommended. *Recorded information on all Red and White tours, tel. 415/546–2628. Alcatraz tours (including audio guide) are $8.75 adults and children 12–18, $7.75 senior citizens, $4.25 children 5-11; without audio, subtract $3 for adults and senior citizens, $1 for children 5–11. Add $2 per ticket to charge by phone at 415/546–2700.*

For a more natural adventure, consider a day at **Angel Island,** just north of Alcatraz. Picnics and hiking are the chief diversions here. The perimeter of the island is lined by a scenic bike path. Twenty-five bicycles are permitted on the regular ferry on a first-come, first-served basis. *Angel Island fares are $8 adults, $7 children 12–18, $4 children 5–11 (includes park admission). Weekends only during the off-season, daily during the summer months.*

The **Blue and Gold Fleet,** berthed at Pier 39, provides its passengers with validated parking across the street. The 1¼-hour tour sails under both the Bay and Golden Gate bridges. Friday and Saturday night dinner-dance cruises run April–mid-December. *Tel. 415/781–7877. Reservations not necessary. Bay Cruise: $15* *adults, $7 senior citizens, active military, and children 5–18, under 5 free. Summertime dinner-dance cruise: $35 per person (group rates available). Daily departures.*

❽ Pier 39 is the most popular of San Francisco's waterfront attractions, drawing millions of visitors each year to browse through its dozens of shops. Check out The Disney Store, with more Mickey Mouses than you can shake a stick at; Left Hand World, where left-handers will find all manner of gadgets designed with lefties in mind; and Only in San Francisco, the place for San Francisco memorabilia and the location of the Pier 39 information center. Ongoing free entertainment, accessible validated parking, and nearby public transportation ensure crowds most days. Opening in fall 1995 is a new attraction: Underwater World at Pier 39. Moving walkways will transport visitors through a space surrounded on three sides by water. The focus will be on indigenous San Francisco Bay marine life, from fish and plankton to sharks. Above water, don't miss the hundreds of sea lions that bask and play on the docks on the pier's north side. Bring a camera.

Tour 11: The Marina and the Presidio

❾ San Francisco's rosy and Rococo **Palace of Fine Arts** is at the very end of the Marina, near the intersection of Baker and Beach streets. The palace is the sole survivor of the 32 tinted plaster structures built for the 1915 Panama-Pacific Exposition. Bernard Maybeck designed the Roman Classic beauty, and in the ensuing 50 years the building fell into disrepair. It was reconstructed in concrete at a cost of $7 million and reopened in 1967, thanks to legions of sentimental citizens and a huge private donation that saved the palace from demolition. The massive columns, great rotunda, and swan-filled lagoon will be familiar from fashion layouts as well as from many recent films. Recently, travelers on package tours from Japan have been using it as a backdrop for wedding-party photos, with the brides wearing Western-style finery.

The interior houses a fascinating hands-on museum, the **Exploratorium,** which has been called the best science museum in the world. The curious of all ages flock here to try to use and understand some of the 600 exhibits. Be sure to include the pitch-black, crawl-through Tactile Dome in your visit. *Tel. 415/561–0360 for general information, 415/561–0362 for required reservations for Tactile Dome. Admission: $8 adults, $6 students over 18 with ID, $4 children 6–17, free 1st Wed. of every month. Open Tues.–Sun. 10–5, Wed. 10–9:30, legal Mon. holidays 10–5.*

If you have a car, now is the time to use it for a drive through
❿ the **Presidio.** (If not, Muni bus No. 38 from Union Square will take you to Park Presidio; from there use a free transfer to bus No. 28 into the Presidio.) A military post for more than 200 years, this headquarters of the U.S. Sixth Army is in the process

of becoming a public park. De Anza and a band of Spanish settlers claimed the area in 1776. It became a Mexican garrison in 1822 when Mexico gained its independence from Spain. U.S. troops forcibly occupied it in 1846.

The more than 1,500 acres of rolling hills, majestic woods, and attractive redbrick army barracks present an air of serenity in the middle of the city. There are two beaches, a golf course, and

⓫ picnic sites. The **Officers' Club,** a long, low adobe built around 1776, was the Spanish commandante's headquarters and is the oldest standing building in the city.

⓬ The **Presidio Museum,** housed in a former hospital built in 1857, focuses on the role played by the military in San Francisco's development. Behind the museum are two cabins that housed refugees from the 1906 earthquake and fire. Photos on the wall of one depict the rows and rows of temporary shelters at the Presidio and in Golden Gate Park following the disaster. *On the corner of Lincoln Blvd. and Funston Ave., tel. 415/556–0856. Admission free. Open Tues.–Sun. 10–4.*

⓭ Muni bus No. 28 will take you to the **Golden Gate Bridge** toll plaza. Nearly 2 miles long, connecting San Francisco with Marin County, its Art Deco design is powerful, serene, and tough, made to withstand winds of over 100 miles per hour. Though frequently gusty and misty (walkers should wear warm clothing), the bridge offers unparalleled views of the Bay Area. The east walkway offers a glimpse of the San Francisco skyline as well as the islands of the bay. On a sunny day sailboats dot the water, and brave windsurfers test the often treacherous tides beneath the bridge. The view west confronts you with the wild hills of the Marin headlands, the curving coast south to Land's End, and the majestic Pacific Ocean. There's a vista point on the Marin side, where you can contemplate the city and its spectacular setting.

⓮ **Fort Point** was constructed during the years 1853–1861 to protect San Francisco from sea attack during the Civil War. It was designed to mount 126 cannons with a range of up to 2 miles. Standing under the shadow of the Golden Gate Bridge, the national historic site is now a museum filled with military memorabilia. Guided group tours are offered by National Park Rangers, and there are cannon demonstrations. There is a superb view of the bay from the top floor. *Tel. 415/556–1693. Admission free. Open Wed.–Sun. 10–5.*

From here, hardy walkers may elect to stroll about 3½ miles (with bay views) along the Golden Gate Promenade to Aquatic Park and the Hyde Street cable-car terminus.

Tour 12: Golden Gate Park

Numbers in the margin correspond to points of interest on the Golden Gate Park: Tour 12 map.

It was a Scotsman, John McLaren, who became manager of Golden Gate Park in 1887 and transformed the brush and sand into the green civilized wilderness we enjoy today. Here you can attend a polo game or a Sunday band concert and rent a bike, boat, or roller skates. On Sundays, some park roads are closed to cars and come alive with joggers, bicyclists, skaters, museum goers, and picnickers. There are tennis courts, baseball diamonds, soccer fields, a buffalo paddock, and miles of trails for horseback riding in this 1,000-acre park.

Because it is so large, the best way for most visitors to see it is by car. Muni buses provide service, though on weekends there may be a long wait. On Market Street, board a westbound No. 5-Fulton or No. 21-Hayes bus and continue to Arguello and Fulton streets. Walk south about 500 feet to John F. Kennedy Drive.

From May through October, free guided walking tours of the park are offered every weekend by the Friends of Recreation and Parks (tel. 415/221–1311).

The oldest building in the park and perhaps San Francisco's
❶ most elaborate Victorian is the **Conservatory** (tel. 415/752–8080), a copy of London's famous Kew Gardens. The ornate greenhouse was originally brought around the Horn for the estate of James Lick in San Jose. The Conservatory was purchased from the Lick estate with public subscription funds and erected in the park. In addition to a tropical garden, there are seasonal displays of flowers and plants and a permanent exhibit of rare orchids. *Admission: $1.50 adults, 75¢ senior citizens and children 6–12, children under 6 and 1st and last half-hour free. Open daily 9–5.*

The eastern section of the park has three museums. Purchase of a $10 Golden Gate Park Cultural Pass gains you one-day admission to all three, plus the Japanese Tea Garden and the Conservatory, a substantial savings (for adults) if you are planning to visit all these attractions. Purchase your pass at any of
❷ the museums or at TIX Bay Area in Union Square. The **M. H. de Young Memorial Museum** was completely reorganized in 1989. It now features American art, with collections of paintings, sculpture, textiles, and decorative arts from Colonial times through the 20th century. Fifteen new galleries highlight the work of American masters, including Copley, Eakins, Bingham, and Sargent. Don't miss the room of landscapes, dominated by Frederic Church's moody, almost psychedelic *Rainy Season in the Tropics*. There is a wonderful gallery of American still-life and trompe l'oeil art and a small selection of classic Shaker furniture. The reorganization, in addition to acquisitions from Mr. and Mrs. John D. Rockefeller III, have resulted in what the museum rightly trumpets as one of the best survey collections of

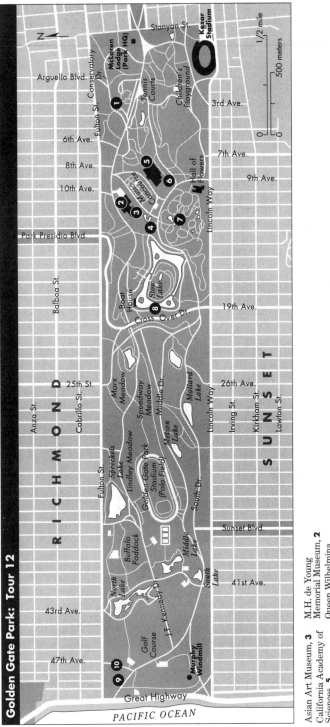

Golden Gate Park: Tour 12

Asian Art Museum, **3**
California Academy of Sciences, **5**
Conservatory, **1**
Dutch Windmill, **9**
Japanese Tea Garden, **4**

M.H. de Young Memorial Museum, **2**
Queen Wilhelmina Tulip Garden, **10**
Shakespeare Garden, **6**
Stow Lake, **8**
Strybing Arboretum, **7**

American art from colonial times to the mid-20th century. The de Young has also retained its dramatic collection of tribal art from Africa, Oceania, and the Americas, which includes pottery, basketry, sculpture, and ritual clothing and accessories. In 1993, the de Young opened a textiles gallery. An ongoing installation, *Unraveling Yarns: The Art of Everyday Life,* contains more than 60 samples of fiber art from around the world. In addition to its permanent collections, the museum hosts selected traveling shows—often blockbuster events for which there are long lines and additional admission charges. The museum has an outstanding shop with a wide selection of art objects. The **Cafe de Young,** which has outdoor seating in the Oakes Garden, serves a complete menu of light refreshments until 4 PM. *Tel. 415/863–3330 for 24-hr information. Admission: $5 adults, $3 senior citizens, $2 youths 12–17, under 12 free; free 1st Wed. (until 5) and Sat. (10–noon) of the month. Note: One admission charge admits you to the de Young, Asian Art, and Legion of Honor (when it reopens in fall of 1995) museums on the same day. Open Wed.–Sun. 10–5, 1st Wed. of the month only, 10–8:45; suggested admission after 5 PM that day is $1.*

❸ The **Asian Art Museum** is located in galleries that adjoin the de Young. This world-famous Avery Brundage collection consists of more than 10,000 sculptures, paintings, and ceramics that illustrate major periods of Asian art. Very special are the Magnin Jade Room and the Leventritt collection of blue and white porcelains. On the second floor are treasures from Iran, Turkey, Syria, India, Tibet, Nepal, Pakistan, Korea, Japan, Afghanistan, and Southeast Asia. Both the de Young and Asian Art museums have daily docent tours. *Tel. 415/668–8921. Admission collected when entering the de Young. Open Wed.–Sun. 10–5., 1st Wed. of the month 10–8:45.*

Time Out　The **Japanese Tea Garden,** next to the Asian Art Museum, is ideal
❹　for resting after museum touring. This charming 4-acre village was created for the 1894 Mid-Winter Exposition. Small ponds, streams, and flowering shrubs create a serene landscape. The cherry blossoms in spring are exquisite. The Tea House (tea, of course, and cookies are served) is popular and busy. *Tel. 415/752–1171. Admission: $2 adults and children 13–17, $1 senior citizens and children 6–12. Open daily 9–6 in the summer, daily 8:30–6 in the winter.*

❺ The **California Academy of Sciences** is directly opposite the de Young Museum. It is one of the top five natural history museums in the country, and has both an aquarium and a planetarium. Throngs of visitors enjoy its Steinhart Aquarium, with its dramatic 100,000-gallon Fish Roundabout, home to 14,000 creatures, and a living coral reef with colorful fish, giant clams, tropical sharks, and a rainbow of hard and soft corals. The Space and Earth Hall has an "earthquake floor" that enables visitors to experience a simulated California earthquake. The Wattis Hall of Man presents rotating natural history, art, and cultural exhibits. In the Wild California Hall are a 14,000-gallon aquarium tank showing underwater life at the Farallones (islands off the coast of northern California), life-size elephant-seal models, and video information on the wildlife of the state. The innovative Life Through Time Hall tells the story of evolution from the beginnings of life on earth through the age of dinosaurs to the age of mammals. A popular attraction at the Academy is the permanent display of cartoons by Far Side creator Gary Larson. There is an additional charge for Morrison Planetarium shows (depending on the show, up to $2.50 adults, $1.25 senior citizens and students, tel. 415/750–7141 for daily schedule). Laserium (tel. 415/750–7138 for schedule and fees) presents laser-light shows at Morrison Planetarium, accompanied by rock, classical, and other musical forms. Educational shows outline laser technology. A cafeteria is open daily until one hour before the museum closes, and the Academy Store offers a wide selection of books, posters, toys, and cultural artifacts. *Tel. 415/750–7145. Admission: $7 adults, $4 senior citizens and students 12–17, $1.50 children 6–11. $2 discount with Muni transfer. Free 1st Wed. of each month. Open July 4–Labor Day, daily 10–7; Labor Day–July 4, daily 10–5.*

A short stroll from the Academy of Sciences will take you to the **❻** free **Shakespeare Garden.** Two hundred flowers mentioned by the Bard, as well as bronze-engraved panels with floral quotations, are set throughout the garden.

❼ **Strybing Arboretum** specializes in plants from areas with climates similar to that of the Bay Area, such as the west coast of Australia, South Africa, and the Mediterranean. There are many gardens inside the grounds, with 6,000 plants and tree varieties blooming seasonally. *9th Ave. at Lincoln Way, tel. 415/661–0668. Admission free. Open weekdays 8–4:30, weekends and holidays 10–5. Tours leave the bookstore weekdays at 1:30 PM, weekends at 10:30 AM and 1:30 PM.*

The western half of Golden Gate Park offers miles of wooded greenery and open spaces for all types of spectator and partici-**❽** pant sports. Rent a paddleboat or stroll around **Stow Lake.** The Chinese Pavilion, a gift from the city of Taipei, was shipped in 6,000 pieces and assembled on the shore of Strawberry Hill Island in Stow Lake in 1981. At the very western end of the park, where Kennedy Drive meets the Great Highway, is the beauti-**❾ ❿** fully restored 1902 **Dutch Windmill** and the photogenic **Queen Wilhelmina Tulip Garden.**

Tour 13: Lincoln Park and the Western Shoreline

No other American city provides such close-up viewing of the power and fury of the surf attacking the shore. From Land's End in Lincoln Park you can look across the Golden Gate (the name was originally given to the opening of San Francisco Bay long before the bridge was built) to the Marin Headlands. From Cliff House south to the San Francisco Zoo, the Great Highway and Ocean Beach run along the western edge of the city.

The wind is often strong along the shoreline, summer fog can blanket the ocean beaches, and the water is cold and usually too rough for swimming. Carry a sweater or jacket and bring binoculars.

At the northwest corner of the San Francisco Peninsula is **Lincoln Park.** At one time all the city's cemeteries were here, segregated by nationality. Today there is an 18-hole golf course with large and well-formed Monterey cypresses lining the fairways. There are scenic walks throughout the 275-acre park, with particularly good views from **Land's End** (the parking lot is at the end of El Camino del Mar). The trails out to Land's End, however, are for skilled hikers only: There are frequent landslides, and danger lurks along the steep cliffs.

Also in Lincoln Park is the **California Palace of the Legion of Honor.** The building itself—modeled after the 18th-century Parisian original—is architecturally interesting and spectacularly situated on cliffs overlooking the ocean and the Golden Gate Bridge. The museum closed in 1992 for seismic and other renovations, and is set to reopen in late 1995.

The Cliff House (1066 Point Lobos Ave.), where the road turns south along the western shore, has existed in several incarnations. The original, built in 1863, and several later structures were destroyed by fire. The present building has restaurants, a pub, and a gift shop. The lower dining room overlooks Seal Rocks (the barking marine mammals sunning themselves are actually sea lions).

An adjacent attraction is the **Musée Mécanique,** a collection of antique mechanical contrivances, including peep shows and nickelodeons. The museum carries on the tradition of arcade amusement at the Cliff House. *Tel. 415/386–1170. Admission free. Open weekdays 11–7, weekends 10–8.*

Two flights below the Cliff House is a fine observation deck and the Golden Gate National Recreation Area **Visitors Center.** There are interesting and historic photographs of the Cliff House and the glass-roofed **Sutro Baths.** The baths covered 3 acres just north of the Cliff House and comprised six enormous baths, 500 dressing rooms, and several restaurants. The baths were closed in 1952 and burned in 1966. You can explore the ruins on your own or take ranger-led walks on weekends. The Visitors Center offers information on these and other trails. *Tel. 415/556–8642. Open daily 10–4:30.*

Because traffic is often heavy in summer and on weekends, you might want to take the Muni system from the Union Square area out to the Cliff House. On weekdays, take the Muni No. 38-Geary Limited to 48th Avenue and Point Lobos and walk down the hill. On weekends and during the evenings, the Muni No. 38 is marked "48th Avenue." Don't take the No. 38 bus marked "Ocean Beach," though, or you'll have to walk an extra 10 minutes to get to the Cliff House.

Time Out The Cliff House (tel. 415/386–3330) has several restaurants and a busy bar. **The Upstairs Room** features a light menu with a number of omelet suggestions. The lower dining room, the **Seafood & Beverage Co. Restaurant,** has a fabulous view of Seal Rocks. Reservations are recommended, but you may still have to wait for a table, especially at midday on Sunday.

Below the Cliff House are the **Great Highway** and **Ocean Beach.** Stretching for 3 miles along the western (Pacific) side of the city, this is a beautiful beach for walking, running, or lying in the sun—but not for swimming. Although dozens of surfers head to Ocean Beach each day, you'll notice they are dressed head-to-toe in wet suits, as the water here is extremely cold. Across the highway from the beach is a new path, which winds through landscaped sand dunes from Lincoln Avenue to Sloat Boulevard (near the zoo)—an ideal route for walking and bicycling.

At the Great Highway and Sloat Boulevard is the **San Francisco Zoo.** The zoo was begun in 1889 in Golden Gate Park. At its present home there are 1,000 species of birds and animals, more than 130 of which have been designated endangered species. Among the protected are the snow leopard, Sumatran tiger, jaguar, and the Asian elephant. A favorite attraction is the greater one-horned rhino, next to the African elephants.

Gorilla World, a $2-million exhibit, is one of the largest and most natural gorilla habitats in a zoo. The circular outer area is carpeted with natural African Kikuyu grass, while trees and shrubs create communal play areas. With the late-1993 birth of a lowland gorilla named Barney, three generations of the species now inhabit the zoo. The $5-million Primate Discovery Center houses 14 endangered species in atriumlike enclosures. One of the most popular zoo residents is Prince Charles, a rare white tiger and the first of its kind to be exhibited in the West.

There are 46 "storyboxes" throughout the zoo that, when turned on with blue and red keys ($2), recite animal facts and basic zoological concepts in four languages—English, Spanish, Cantonese, and Tagalog.

The children's zoo has a minipopulation of about 300 mammals, birds, and reptiles, plus an insect zoo, a baby-animal nursery, and a beautifully restored 1921 Dentzel Carousel. A ride astride one of the 52 hand-carved menagerie animals costs $1.

Zoo information, tel. 415/753–7083. Admission: $6.50 adults, $3 youths 12–15 and senior citizens, $1 children 6–12, under 5 free when accompanied by an adult; free first Wed. of the month. Open daily 10–5. Children's zoo admission: $1, under 3 free. Open daily 11–4.

Tour 14: Mission Dolores and Castro Street

Numbers in the margin correspond to points of interest on the Mission District and Castro Street: Tour 14 map.

During the 19th century the sunny weather of the then-rural Mission District made it a popular locale for resorts, racetracks, and gambling places. At 13th and Mission streets, where freeway traffic now roars overhead, stood Woodward's Gardens, a lush botanical garden with a zoo, playground, and pavilions featuring acrobatic performances.

1 **Mission Dolores,** on palm-lined Dolores Street, is the sixth of the 21 missions founded by Father Junipero Serra. The adobe building was begun in 1782 and was originally known as Mission San Francisco de Assisi. Completed in 1791, its ceiling depicts original Costanoan Indian basket designs, executed in vegetable dyes. There is a small museum, and the mission cemetery contains the graves of more than 5,000 Indians. *Dolores and 16th Sts., tel. 415/621–8203. Admission: $1. Open daily 9–4.*

Two blocks from Mission Dolores, the area around Valencia Street from 16th to 24th streets is developing its own neighborhood character. A mix of socialists, lesbian-feminists, new wavers, and traditional Hispanics has made it San Francisco's new

2 bohemia. The alternative **Roxie Cinema** (3117 16th St., tel. 415/863–1087 for daily schedule), the leftist **Modern Times Bookstore** (888 Valencia St.), **The Marsh** performance space (1062 Valencia St., tel. 415/641–0235), and a dozen-plus cafés all contribute to the idiosyncratic atmosphere. The cornerstone of the women-owned and -run businesses in the neighborhood is

3 the **Women's Building of the Bay Area** (3543 18th St., tel. 415/431–1180), which for more than a dozen years has held workshops and conferences of particular interest to women. It houses offices for many social and political organizations and sponsors talks and readings by such noted writers as Alice Walker and Angela Davis.

From the Women's Building, you can head east on 18th Street (the numbers get lower) to Mission Street or west to the Castro District.

All the Mission District's resident ethnic cultures are reflected in Mission Street's businesses: Spanish-language theaters, Italian restaurants, Arab-owned clothing stores, Vietnamese markets, and Filipino, Hispanic, and Chinese restaurants and groceries. The majority of Latinos here are from Central America. Most of them settled here during the late 1960s and early 1970s.

On 24th Street, the area takes on the flavor of another country, with small open-air groceries selling huge Mexican papayas and plantains, tiny restaurants serving *sopa de mariscos* (fish soup), and an abundance of religious shops. Bakeries, or *panaderias*

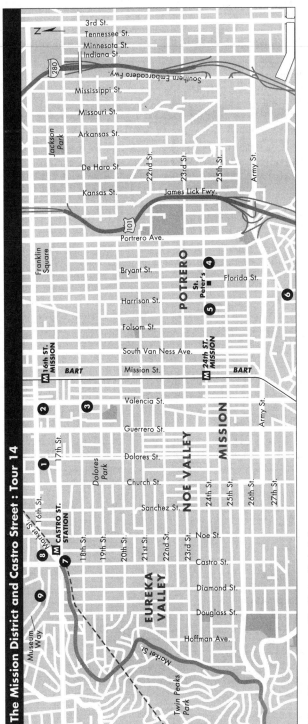

The Mission District and Castro Street : Tour 14

N

3rd St.
Tennessee St.
Minnesota St.
Indiana St.

I-280

Southern Embarcadero Fwy.

Mississippi St.
Missouri St.
Arkansas St.

Jackson Park

De Haro St.
Kansas St.

James Lick Fwy.

22nd St.
23rd St.
25th St.
Army St.

101

Portrero Ave.

Franklin Square

Bryant St.

Florida St.

POTRERO
St. Peter's

Harrison St.

Folsom St.

South Van Ness Ave.

M 16th ST. MISSION

BART

Mission St.

M 24th ST. MISSION

BART

Valencia St.

Guerrero St.

Dolores St.

Dolores Park

Church St.

Sanchez St.

MISSION

NOE VALLEY

Army St.

17th St.

16th St.

Market St.

M CASTRO ST. STATION

18th St.
19th St.
20th St.
21st St.
22nd St.
23rd St.
Noe St.
Castro St.
Diamond St.
Douglass St.
Hoffman Ave.

24th St.
25th St.
26th St.
27th St.

EUREKA VALLEY

Museum Way

Market St.

Twin Peaks Park

Balmy Alley, **5**
Castro Theatre, **7**
Galeria de la Raza, **4**
Josephine D. Randall
Junior Museum, **9**
Mission Dolores, **1**

The Names Project, **8**
Precita Eyes Mural
Arts Center, **6**
Roxie Cinema, **2**
Women's Building of
the Bay Area, **3**

are an essential stop. Two of the best places to sample these delicious, down-to-earth creations are **La Victoria** (2937 24th St.) and **Dominguez** (2951 24th St.), which has a most colorful exterior.

4 **Galeria de la Raza,** at the east end of the street, is an important showcase for Hispanic art. It shows local and international artists, sometimes mounting larger exhibits in conjunction with other Bay Area arts groups. *2855 24th St., tel. 415/826–8009. Open Tues.–Sat. noon–6.*

Next door to the Gallery is Studio 24 Galeria Shop, which sells handicrafts from Latin America. The studio specializes in figurines from *Dia de los Muertos*, the Latin American Halloween. The aim of the often brightly colored objects is to make death seem more familiar and less threatening; don't be surprised to see a skeleton calmly doing her ironing. *2857 24th St., tel. 415/826–8009. Open Tues.–Sat. noon–6.*

Art in the Mission District is not confined indoors. Keeping alive the tradition of the great muralist Diego Rivera, community artists have transformed the walls of their neighborhood with paintings. Two to watch for are those adorning the **St. Peter's Catholic Church** building at 24th and Florida streets and the **Mission Neighborhood Center** at 3013 24th Street. The center is **5** on the corner of **Balmy Alley** where a series of murals was begun in 1973 by a group of local children and continued by an affiliation of several dozen artists and community workers to promote peace in Central America. (Be careful in this area; the other end of the street adjoins the back of a somewhat danger- **6** ous housing project.) The **Precita Eyes Mural Arts Center** gives guided walks of the Mission District's murals. (*See* Sightseeing Checklists, *below.*)

The Mission District plays fiesta for two important occasions. There is a weekend of festivities around the *cinco de Mayo* (5th of May) holiday, but the neighborhood really erupts into celebration on a sunny weekend in late spring called *carnaval*. This Rio-like three-day extravaganza gets larger each year. Recent festivities closed Harrison Street between 16th and 20th streets, with four stages for live music and dancers, as well as crafts and food booths. A Grand Carnaval Parade along 24th Street caps the celebration.

Time Out Spanish, Latin American, and Caribbean *tapas* (appetizers) bars are all the rage in the Mission these days. The leader of the pack is **Esperpento,** where you can mix and match mild-to-spicy specialties to create a meal. The chicken croquettes are crispy outside, creamy inside, and not to be missed. *3295 22nd St., tel. 415/282–8867. Open weekdays 11–3 and 5–10, Sat. 11–3 and 5–10:30, Sun. noon–10.*

It's a bit of a walk (at least a half-hour) to the heart of the gay area of Castro Street from 24th Street in the Mission District. By foot or by car, go west on 24th Street to Castro Street, then turn right (north). Or, take the No. 48-Quintara bus west on 24th Street to Castro, and transfer to the No. 24-Divisadero bus.

Historians are still trying to discover what brought an estimated 100,000 to 250,000 gays and lesbians into the San Francisco area. Some point to the libertine tradition rooted in Barbary Coast piracy, prostitution, and gambling. Others note that as a huge military embarkation point during World War II, the city was occupied by tens of thousands of mostly single men. Whatever the cause, San Francisco became the city of choice for lesbians and gay men, and Castro Street, nestled at the base of Twin Peaks and just over Buena Vista hill from Haight Street, became its social, cultural, and political center.

The gay **Castro District** hosts two lively annual celebrations. In late September or early October, when San Francisco weather is at its warmest, the annual Castro Street Fair takes over several blocks of Castro and Market streets. Huge stages are erected for live music and comedy, alongside booths selling food and baubles. The weather inevitably brings off the men's shirts, and the Castro relives for a moment the permissive spirit of the 1970s. Each Halloween thousands of revelers (though most are just onlookers) converge on Castro Street from all over the city. Drag queens of all shapes and sizes intentionally reduce the crowd to laughter; the atmosphere is high and friendly. San Francisco's annual gay parade no longer originates in the Castro District. The late-June march, by far the city's largest, begins in the Civic Center and terminates at the Embarcadero.

Directly above the Castro Street Muni Metro station at 17th and Market streets (trains K, L, and M stop here) is **Harvey Milk Plaza,** named for the man who electrified the city in 1977 by being elected to its board of supervisors as an openly gay candidate. His high visibility accompanied demands by homosexuals for thorough inclusion in the city's life. San Francisco has responded with a tolerance found nowhere else in the United States: Gay people sit as municipal judges, police commissioners, and school board members. In the wake of Milk's assassination in 1978 by a fellow supervisor and the AIDS crisis, the Castro has become a little less flamboyant. It is still, however, the center of gay life. Gay bars abound, and gay-oriented boutiques line Castro, 18th, and Market streets.

Across the street from Harvey Milk Plaza is the great neon ❼ neighborhood landmark, the **Castro Theatre** marquee. Erected in 1922, the theater is the grandest of San Francisco's few remaining movie palaces. Its elaborate Spanish Baroque interior is well preserved, and a new pipe organ plays nightly, ending with a traditional chorus of the Jeanette McDonald standard, "San Francisco." The 1,500-capacity crowd can be enthusiastic and vocal, talking back to the screen as loudly as it talks to them. The Castro Theatre is the showcase for many community events, in particular the annual Gay and Lesbian Film Festival (tel. 415/703–8650) held each June.

A Different Light (489 Castro St., tel. 415/431–0891) features books by, for, and about lesbians and gay men. The store has become the unofficial Castro community center—residents regularly phone for nonbook info and a rack in the front is chock full of fliers for local events. Book signings and readings occur several times each week.

Time Out   There are several renowned gay chefs in San Francisco. Unfortunately, none of them work in the Castro, where a half-dozen greasy spoons do surprisingly well. Festive **Pozole,** which serves burritos, quesadillas, and other Mexican and Latin American specialties, is a welcome oasis of creative cuisine. *2337 Market St., tel. 415/626–2666. Open Mon.–Thurs. 4–11, Fri.–Sun. noon-midnight.*

8 Across Market Street, **The Names Project** (2362 Market St.) has its public workshop. A gigantic quilt made of more than 25,000 hand-sewn and -decorated panels has been pieced together by loved ones to serve as a memorial to those who have died of AIDS. People come from all over the country to work in this storefront as a labor of love and grief; others have sent panels here by mail. New additions to the quilt are always on display. **Under One Roof** (tel. 415/252–9430; open Sun.–Fri. 11–7, Sat. 10–8) is a store at the same address that sells T-shirts, posters, and other merchandise to raise funds for various AIDS organizations.

Just northwest of Castro and Market streets, an outcropping of rock provides one of the best viewing areas in the city. Walk north up Castro Street two blocks to 16th Street and turn left. This is a steep climb, and it gets steeper and a little more rugged, but it's worth the effort. Turn right at Flint Street; the hill to your left is variously known as Red Rock, Museum Hill, and, correctly, Corona Heights. Start climbing up the path by the tennis courts along the spine of the hill; the view downtown is increasingly superb.

9 At the base of Corona Heights is the **Josephine D. Randall Junior Museum.** Geared toward children by the Recreation and Park Department, the museum nevertheless has a variety of workshops and events for both young people and their parents. It includes a Mineral Hall, Animal Room, library, and an excellent woodworking studio. *199 Museum Way, tel. 415/554–9600. The museum is open Tues.–Sat. 10–5 and at night for workshops. The Animal Room is open 10:30–1 and 2–5.*

To get back downtown, walk down Roosevelt Way (which intersects Museum Way) to 14th Street and turn right on Castro Street. Muni Metro is three blocks away at 17th Street. Or, if you want to visit the Haight-Ashbury District, you're just seven blocks away. At Museum Way cross Roosevelt Way (watch out for the traffic on this curvy road), and head up the hill on the right side of the street, which turns into Masonic and veers off to the right after a block. Watch the signs to be sure you're still on Masonic, then head north down the street and turn left at Haight Street.

Tour 15: Haight-Ashbury

East of Golden Gate Park is the neighborhood known as "the Haight." Once home to large, middle-class families of European immigrants, the Haight began to change during the late 1950s and early 1960s. Families were fleeing to the suburbs; the big old Victorians were deteriorating or being chopped up into cheap housing. Young people found the neighborhood an affordable and exciting community in which to live according to new precepts.

The peak of the Haight as a youth scene came in 1966. It had become the home of many rock bands. The Grateful Dead moved into a big Victorian at 710 Ashbury Street, just a block off Haight Street. Jefferson Airplane had their grand mansion at 2400 Fulton Street. By 1967, 200,000 young people with flowers in their hair were heading for the Haight. The peace and civil rights movements had made "freedom" their generation's password.

Sharing the late-1980s fascination with things of the 1960s, many visitors to San Francisco want to see the setting of the "Summer of Love." Back in 1967, Gray Lines instituted their "Hippie-Hop," advertising it as "the only foreign tour within the continental limits of the United States," piloted by a driver "especially trained in the sociological significance of the Haight." Today's explorers can walk from Union Square to Market Street and hop aboard Muni's No. 7-Haight.

Haight Street has once again emerged as the center of youth culture in San Francisco, though this time it is an amalgam of punkers, neo-hippies, and suburbanites out to spend their cash. The street has become the city's prime shopping district for "vintage" merchandise.

Time Out Island cuisine—a mix of Cajun, Southwest, and Caribbean influences—is served at **Cha Cha Cha,** which is informal and inexpensive. The decor is technicolor tropical plastic, and the food is hot and spicy. Try the spicy fried calamari or chili-spiked shrimp. *1801 Haight St., tel. 415/386-5758. No reservations; expect to wait. No credit cards. Open daily for lunch and dinner.*

Golden Gate Park provides the Haight with a variety of opportunities for recreation and entertainment. You can rent roller skates, in-line skates, and skateboards at **Skates on Haight** (1818 Haight St.) and roll through the park—it's partially closed to traffic for skaters on Sundays—or you can take the more genteel route and rent bicycles at several shops along Stanyan Street, right by the park's entrance.

The Haight's famous political spirit (it was the first neighborhood in the United States to lead a freeway revolt, and it continues to feature regular boycotts against chain stores said to ruin the street's local character) exists alongside some of the finest

Victorian-lined streets in the city; more than 1,000 such houses occupy the Panhandle and Ashbury Heights streets.

Great city views can be had from **Buena Vista Park** at Haight and Lyon streets. One landmark is the **Spreckels Mansion** at 737 Buena Vista West, several blocks south of Haight Street. The house was built for sugar baron Richard Spreckels in 1887, and later tenants included Jack London and Ambrose Bierce.

San Francisco for Free

This is not a cheap city to live in or visit. Hotels and restaurants are expensive; museums, shopping, the opera, or a nightclub may set you back a bit. It is possible, however, to do much of your sightseeing very cheaply. Walking is often the best way to get around, and it's not very expensive to use the cable cars and buses. Exploring most of Golden Gate Park is absolutely free, and so is walking across the Golden Gate Bridge.

The **Golden Gate National Recreation Area** (GGNRA), comprising most of San Francisco's shoreline, Alcatraz and Angel islands, and the headlands of Marin County, is the largest urban park in the world. The Golden Gate Promenade's 3½-mile footpath runs from Fort Point at the base of the bridge along the shore to Hyde Street Pier. There's also a new 8-mile-long bicycle path along Ocean Beach from Cliff House south to Fort Funston, hugging sand dunes and providing constant ocean views. The GGNRA is San Francisco at its natural best.

From May through September, there are several popular neighborhood fairs held on weekends throughout the city. Among them are the Union Street Festival, the Fillmore Art and Jazz Festival, and the Grant Street Fair in North Beach. All are free and feature booths selling ethnic food, crafts from local artists, and stages with musical performances. Check the Sunday Datebook section in the *San Francisco Examiner and Chronicle* to find out what's happening during your stay.

There are also free band concerts on Sunday and holiday afternoons at 1 PM, April through October, in the music concourse in Golden Gate Park (tel. 415/666–7035, opposite the de Young Museum and California Academy of Sciences).

What to See and Do with Children

The attractions described in the exploring sections, above, offer a great deal of entertainment for children as well as their families. We suggest, for example, visiting the ships at the **Hyde Street Pier** and spending some time at **Pier 39**, where there is a double-decker Venetian carousel. (*See* Tour 10: The Northern Waterfront, *above.*)

Children will find much to amuse themselves with at **Golden Gate Park,** from the old-fashioned conservatory to the expansive lawns and trails. There is another vintage carousel (1912) at the children's playground. The **Steinhart Aquarium** at the California Academy of Sciences has a "Touching Tide Pool," from which docents will pull starfish and hermit crabs for children or adults to feel. The winding paths and high, humpbacked bridges in the **Japanese Tea Garden** are fun for children to explore. (*See* Tour 12: Golden Gate Park, *above.*)

It is also possible to walk across the **Golden Gate Bridge.** The view is thrilling and the wind invigorating, if the children (and adults) are not overwhelmed by the height of the bridge and the nearby automobile traffic. (*See* Tour 11: The Marina and the Presidio, *above.*)

Many children may enjoy walking along crowded **Grant Avenue** and browsing in the many souvenir shops. Unfortunately, nothing—not even straw finger wrestlers, wooden contraptions to make coins "disappear," shells that open in water to release tissue paper flowers, and other true junk—is as cheap as it once was. (*See* Tour 4: Chinatown, *above.*)

The **San Francisco Zoo,** with a children's zoo, playground, and carousel, is always a good choice and is not far from Ocean Beach. The weather and the currents do not allow swimming there, but it's a good place for walking and playing in the surf. (*See* Tour 13: Lincoln Park and the Western Shoreline, *above.*)

The **Exploratorium** at the Palace of Fine Arts is a preeminent children's museum and is very highly recommended. (*See* Tour 11: The Marina and the Presidio, *above.*)

If you're ready to spend a day outside of the city, consider a trip to Vallejo's **Marine World Africa USA.** (*See* Chapter 9, Excursions from San Francisco.)

Off the Beaten Track

Dark Passage Do you remember Lauren Bacall's fantastic Art Deco apartment in the 1947 movie *Dark Passage*? Do you remember Humphrey Bogart climbing those unending stairs? In this film, Bogart plays a man who has been convicted of murdering his wife; with the help of Bacall, he escapes from prison and has plastic surgery to disguise himself (and ends up looking like Bogart!). You can take a look at these sites if, after visiting Coit Tower on Telegraph Hill, you turn right, cross the street, and walk down the brick- and ivy-lined Greenwich Steps, ending up on Montgomery Street. The famous apartment house is number 1360. A little to the left you can pick up the Filbert Steps or walk down Union Street to Grant Avenue and the North Beach attractions.

Showplace Square A 12-block complex of renovated brick warehouses south of Market Street at the foot of Potrero Hill, Showplace Square is where more than 300 furniture wholesalers display some of the most elegant furnishings and accessories in the country. The showrooms are generally closed to the public, but you can tour scme of them with Showplace Tours, which leave from the complex's headquarters in the Galleria Design Center every Thursday from noon to 2; call 415/864–1500 24 hours ahead to reserve a space. Showplace Square is at the corner of Kansas Street (called Henry Adams St. here, in honor of the developer) and 15th Street and has what is so sorely needed elsewhere in the city—a large parking lot.

Orchids If you are an orchid fancier or if you ever thought you might like to try your hand at growing these exotic flowers, we recommend that you visit **Rod McLellan's Acres of Orchids** in South San Francisco. The McLellan Company runs the largest orchid nursery in the world. Two daily (free) tours lead guests through the large facility and brief them on the propagation of orchids as well as on the history of the company (which led a nationwide fad for gardenias when refrigerated railroad cars made transportation of the delicate blossoms possible). There is also a large showroom and a gift shop with hundreds of plants from which to choose. Not all orchids are difficult to grow at home, even if you must do without a greenhouse and gardener. A cymbidium large enough to produce three sprays of orchids costs about $30–$40. The staff will give you plenty of instructions and pack your plant carefully for transportation home. *1450 El Camino Real, South San Francisco 94080, tel. 415/871–5655. Take I–280 south to the Hickey exit; then go east to El Camino and south (right). Showroom open daily 9–6. Free tours 10:30 and 1:30.*

Sightseeing Checklists

Historic Buildings and Sites

This list of San Francisco's principal buildings and sites includes both attractions that were covered in the preceding tours and additional attractions that are described here for the first time.

Bank of America. The polished red-granite headquarters of this corporate giant is one of the city's most eye-catching buildings. The chic Carnelian Room on the 52nd floor offers a sweeping view of the city. *California St. at Kearny St.* (*See* Tour 3: The Financial District and Jackson Square.)

The Cannery. What was once a bustling fruit and vegetable cannery now houses shops, restaurants, and the Museum of the City of San Francisco. Street artists provide entertainment for young and old in the complex's courtyard. *2801 Leavenworth St., near Fisherman's Wharf.* (*See* Tour 10: The Northern Waterfront.)

Chinese Six Companies. This elaborately decorated building is an example of the Chinese influence on San Francisco architecture. *843 Stockton St.* (*See* Tour 4: Chinatown.)

City Hall. This stunning French Renaissance Revival building is actually San Francisco's fourth city hall in the town's 150-year existence. *Entrance: Polk St. at McAllister St.* (*See* Tour 9: Civic Center.)

The Cliff House. From this historic site you can view the Pacific Ocean, Seal Rocks, and, on a clear day, the Farralon Islands, more than 30 miles away. Nearby are the ruins of the Sutro

Baths. *1066 Point Lobos at the end of Geary Blvd. (See* Tour 13: Lincoln Park and the Western Shoreline.)

Coit Tower. A gift from Lillie Hitchcock Coit, one of the city's more eccentric residents, this building showcases a series of murals painted by local artists under the influence of Mexican painter Diego Rivera. *Greenwich St. at Kearny St. (See* Tour 5: North Beach and Telegraph Hill.)

The Conservatory. Perhaps San Francisco's most elaborate Victorian, this copy of a similar structure in London's Kew Gardens has a tropical garden plus seasonal plants and floral displays. *John F. Kennedy Dr. (See* Tour 12: Golden Gate Park.)

Davies Hall. Home to the San Francisco Symphony, the glass-and-granite Louise M. Davies Hall is open for tours Monday, Wednesday, and Saturday. *Grove St. and Van Ness Ave. (See* Tour 9: Civic Center.)

Embarcadero Center. Offices, shops, restaurants, and two hotels are all contained in this eight-building complex. Justin Herman Plaza, near Embarcadero 5, offers views of the waterfront and East Bay. *Off the Embarcadero between California and Clay Sts. (See* Tour 2: South of Market (SoMa) and the Embarcadero.)

Fairmont Hotel. This Nob Hill landmark, under construction during the '06 earthquake, survived the catastrophe. It remains one of the city's finest hostelries. *Mason St. at California St. (See* Tour 6: Nob Hill and Russian Hill.)

Ferry Building. Another earthquake survivor, this building houses the San Francisco Port Commission. A scenic waterfront promenade extends south to the Bay Bridge. *The Embarcadero at the foot of Market St. (See* Tour 2: South of Market (SoMa) and the Embarcadero.)

Fort Mason. A former military installation is now home to theaters, restaurants, galleries, small museums, and the World War II freighter, the SS *Jeremiah O'Brien. Entrance: Marina Blvd. at Buchanan St. (See* Tour 10: The Northern Waterfront.)

450 Sutter Street. Handsome Mayan-inspired designs are used in both exterior and interior surfaces of this 1930 terra-cotta skyscraper. (*See* Tour 1: Union Square.)

Ghirardelli Square. The famed chocolate was once made here; now the brick factory buildings house shops, galleries, cafés, and restaurants. *Beach St. at Polk St. (See* Tour 10: The Northern Waterfront.)

Golden Gate Bridge. The city's most famous landmark offers unparalleled views of the Bay Area. A walk across the bridge to the Marin side takes about a half-hour each way. *Doyle Dr. above Fort Point. (See* Tour 11: The Marina and the Presidio.)

Grace Cathedral. This 20th-century Gothic structure was designed by Lewis Hobart. The gilded-bronze doors at its east entrance were taken from casts of Ghiberti's *Gates of Paradise* on the baptistery in Florence. *1051 Taylor St. at California St. (See* Tour 6: Nob Hill and Russian Hill.)

Haas-Lilienthal House. One of the few Pacific Heights homes open to public view, the period-furnished rooms of this Queen Anne mansion offer a glimpse into turn-of-the-century taste and lifestyle. *2007 Franklin St. at Jackson St. (See* Tour 7: Pacific Heights.)

Hallidie Building. One of a number of Willis Polk-designed buildings in the city, this is believed to be the world's first all-glass-curtain-wall structure. *130 Sutter St. (See* Tour 3: The Financial District and Jackson Square.)

Hammersmith Building. The small Beaux-Arts structure was completed in 1907. Its extensive use of glass is noteworthy, as is the highly playful design. *301 Sutter St. (See* Tour 1: Union Square.)

Hobart Building. This Willis Polk skyscraper, one of the architect's best, is noteworthy for its unique combination of a flat facade and oval sides. *582 Market St. (See* Tour 2: South of Market (SoMa) and the Embarcadero.)

Hyde Street Pier. Three historic vessels are moored here. The highlight is the *Balclutha,* an 1886, full-rigged, three-mast sailing vessel. *The end of Hyde St., at Beach St. (See* Tour 10: The Northern Waterfront.)

Jackson Square. Some of the city's oldest buildings survive in this district, just below North Beach. Walk east on Jackson from Columbus to see the original Ghirardelli Chocolate Factory and A. P. Hotaling's whiskey distillery, immortalized in verse after the '06 earthquake. (*See* Tour 3: The Financial District and Jackson Square.)

Japan Center Mall. Folk crafts, antiques, kimonos, and the best udon (noodles) this side of Tokyo can all be found at this complex in the heart of Japantown. *Post St. between Laguna and Fillmore Sts. (See* Tour 8: Japantown.)

Land's End. Beautiful views of the Golden Gate can be had from here. The rocky trails that lead to the shoreline are for skilled hikers only. *At the end of El Camino del Mar. (See* Tour 13: Lincoln Park and the Western Shoreline.)

Maiden Lane. What was once a notorious red-light district is now a chic shopping area. The Circle Gallery at 140 Maiden Lane, said to be a prototype for the Guggenheim Museum in New York, is the only Frank Lloyd Wright–designed building in San Francisco. *Off Stockton St. at Union Sq. (See* Tour 1: Union Square.)

Mills Building and Tower. One of the city's outstanding prefire buildings was erected in 1891–92 and is a rare remaining example of the Chicago School of architecture. *At 220 Montgomery St. and 220 Bush St. (See* Tour 3: The Financial District and Jackson Square.)

Mission Dolores. Originally known as the Mission San Francisco de Assisi, this historic adobe building was completed in 1791. *Dolores and 16th Sts. (See* Tour 14: Mission Dolores and Castro Street.)

Old St. Mary's Church. This brick church in Chinatown served as the city's Catholic cathedral until 1891. *Grant Ave. and California St. (See* Tour 4: Chinatown.)

Pacific Stock Exchange. Ralph Stackpole's monumental sculptural groups, *Earth's Fruitfulness* and *Man's Inventive Genius,* flank this imposing building. Don't miss the marble Art Deco lobby at the Stock Exchange Tower around the corner. *301*

Pine St. at Sansome St. (*See* Tour 3: The Financial District and Jackson Square.)

Pacific Union Club. Also known as the Flood Mansion, this residence and the Fairmont Hotel, across the street, were among the few Nob Hill survivors of the 1906 quake and fire. *California St. at Mason St.* (*See* Tour 6: Nob Hill and Russian Hill.)

Palace of Fine Arts. A remnant of San Francisco's 1915 Panama-Pacific International Exposition, this beautiful edifice and surrounding lagoon form one of the city's signature images. *Baker and Beach Sts.* (*See* Tour 11: The Marina and the Presidio.)

Precita Eyes Mural Arts Center. The center gives guided walks of the Mission District's murals. The tour starts with a half-hour slide presentation, and the walk takes about an hour, visiting over 40 murals in the area. *348 Precita Ave., tel. 415/285–2287. $3 adults, $1 students under 18. Tours every Sat. at 1:30 PM. Walks can also be arranged by appointment for groups of 10 or more.*

Presidio. This 200-year-old army installation in the process of becoming a public park. Its adobe Officer's Club is the oldest standing structure in the city. (*See* Tour 11: The Marina and the Presidio.)

Russ Building. Its intriguing Gothic design, modeled after the Chicago Tribune Tower, distinguishes what was San Francisco's tallest building from 1927 until the early 1960s. *235 Montgomery St.* (*See* Tour 3: The Financial District and Jackson Square.)

St. Francis Hotel. The city's second-oldest hotel anchors Union Square. A ride up to the tower in a glass-walled, exterior elevator yields spectacular views of the square and beyond. *Powell St. at Union Sq.* (*See* Tour 1: Union Square.)

St. Mary's Cathedral. The third church to bear this name is a dramatic piece of modern architecture. Above the altar is a spectacular cascade made of 7,000 aluminum ribs. *Geary Blvd. at Gough St.* (*See* Tour 8: Japantown.)

Sheraton Palace Hotel. One of the city's oldest and finest hotels has recently been restored. It's worth a trip to see the stunning Garden Court. Maxfield Parrish's *The Pied Piper* hangs in the bar of the same name. *2 New Montgomery St. at Market St.* (*See* Tour 2: South of Market (SoMa) and the Embarcadero.)

Spreckels Mansion. Alma Spreckels, one of San Francisco's most iconoclastic residents, lived with husband Adolph in this palatial Pacific Heights home. Novelist Danielle Steele and husband John Traina reside here now. *2080 Washington St.* (*See* Tour 7: Pacific Heights.)

Sutro Baths. Even the ruins of this famous landmark—100 yards north of the Cliff House—are arresting. Photographs at the site recall the glory of what was once a 3-acre entertainment complex. *Point Lobos at the end of Geary Blvd.* (*See* Tour 13: Lincoln Park and the Western Shoreline.)

Union Square. The heart of San Francisco's downtown, this urban park hosts numerous public events: fashion shows, free noontime concerts, and ethnic celebrations. *Surrounded by Stockton, Geary, Powell, and Post Sts.* (*See* Tour 1: Union Square.)

Vedanta Society Headquarters. This 1905 architectural cocktail may be the most unusual structure in San Francisco: It's a pastiche of Colonial, Queen Anne, Moorish, and Hindu opulence. Vedanta is the highest of the six Hindu systems of religious philosophy. One of its basic tenets is that all religions are paths to one goal. *2963 Webster St., at Filbert St., tel. 415/922–2323.*

Victory Monument. The centerpiece of Union Square was designed by Robert Ingersoll Aitken to commemorate Commodore George Dewey's victory over the Spanish fleet in Manila in 1898. (*See* Tour 1: Union Square.)

Wedding Houses. These structures were built during the late 1870s or 1880s. The romantic history of one of the houses recounts that its builder sold the property to a father as wedding presents for his two daughters. *1980 Union St., at Buchanan St.*

Museums and Galleries

Ansel Adams Center. One of the best small museums in town features the works of one of America's masters, plus works of other historical and contemporary photographers. (*See* Tour 2: South of Market (SoMa) and the Embarcadero.)

Asian Art Museum. The world-famous Avery Brundage Collection consists of more than 10,000 sculptures, paintings, and ceramics that illustrate the major periods of Asian Art. (*See* Tour 12: Golden Gate Park.)

Cable Car Museum. Here you can view the cables that run San Francisco's cable cars in action, sit in vintage cars, and learn about the history of this form of transportation. (*See* Tour 6: Nob Hill and Russian Hill.)

California Academy of Sciences. A natural history museum, an aquarium, and a planetarium all share space here. The Fish Roundabout is a favorite with children. (*See* Tour 12: Golden Gate Park.)

Cartoon Art Museum. Here's a place that takes the funnies seriously. Rotating exhibits include comic books, plates and sketches from comic strips, film animation cels, and computer-generated imagery. At press time, the museum was planning a move to a site near Yerba Buena Center. *Tel. 415/546–3922. Admission: $3 adults, $2 students, $1 senior citizens. Open Wed.–Fri. 11–5, Sat. 10–5. Sun. 1–5.*

Chevron: A World of Oil. Exhibits and an audiovisual show explore the history of the oil industry. The museum is a five-minute walk from the Market-Powell Street cable-car terminus. *555 Market St., lobby level, tel. 415/894–7700. Admission free. Open weekdays 9–4.*

Chinese Cultural Center. The center displays the works of Chinese and Chinese-American artists and traveling exhibits of Chinese culture. A $15 walking tour of Chinatown begins at 2 PM each Saturday. (*See* Tour 4: Chinatown.)

Chinese Historical Society. The society boasts the largest collection of Chinese-American artifacts in the country. Its mission is to trace the history of Chinese immigrants and their contributions to California (and American) history. (*See* Tour 4: Chinatown.)

De Young Memorial Museum, M.H. One of the city's premier museums showcases American art from Colonial times through the 20th century, and houses a dramatic collection of tribal art from Africa, Oceania, and the Americas. (*See* Tour 12: Golden Gate Park.)

Exploratorium. Inside the Palace of Fine Arts is a fascinating hands-on museum that is fun for kids and intriguing to adults. There are 600 exhibits and a pitch-black, crawl-through Tactile Dome. (*See* Tour 11: The Marina and the Presidio.)

Fort Point National Historic Site. This Civil War–era fortress is now a museum filled with military memorabilia. National Park Rangers offer guided group tours. (*See* Tour 11: The Marina and the Presidio.)

Galeria de la Raza. This Mission District gallery, which shows local and international artists, is an important showcase for Hispanic art. *2855 24th St., at Hampshire St.* (*See* Tour 14: Mission Dolores and Castro Street.)

Jewish Community Museum. Revolving exhibits in this small, handsome museum trace important moments in Jewish history. *121 Steuart St., tel. 415/543–8880. Admission: $3 adults, $1.50 students, children, and senior citizens. Hours can vary depending on the exhibit, so it's wise to check ahead. Open (generally) Sun.–Wed. 11–5, Thurs. 11–7. Closed Fri. and Sat.*

Mexican Museum. The first American showcase devoted exclusively to Mexican and Mexican-American art has a marvelous collection of art from pre-Hispanic Indian figures to modern Mexican masters. (*See* Tour 10: The Northern Waterfront.)

Museo Italo-Americano. This pleasant museum features permanent exhibits of works of l9th- and 20th-century Italian-American artists. Shows include paintings, sculpture, etchings, and photographs. The museum presents special exhibits, lectures, and films. (*See* Tour 10: The Northern Waterfront.)

Museum of the City of San Francisco. Odd bits of San Franciscana can be viewed at this new museum in the Cannery. The centerpiece here is the 8-ton Goddess of Progress's head, which she lost just before the '06 quake. (*See* Tour 10: The Northern Waterfront.)

National Maritime Museum. This two-floor facility exhibits ship models, photographs, maps, and other artifacts chronicling the development of San Francisco and the West Coast. (*See* Tour 10: The Northern Waterfront.)

Octagon House. Eight-sided homes were once thought to be good luck. This is one of the two remaining examples in the city of this mid-19th-century architectural form. The house sits across the street from its original site on Gough Street. It is a treasure trove of American antique furniture and accessories from the 18th and 19th centuries. *2645 Gough St. at Union St., tel. 415/441–7512. Admission free. Open Feb.–Dec., 2nd Sun. and 2nd and 4th Thurs. of each month noon–3.*

Old San Francisco Mint. Home for a time to the world's largest coin-minting operation, this sturdy Greek Revival building is now a museum. (*See* Tour 1: Union Square.)

Ripley's Believe It or Not. There are 200 exhibits, many of them newly installed interactive displays, some of which actually are amazing. *175 Jefferson St., tel. 415/771–6188. Admission: $7.75* *adults, $6.75 senior citizens and children 13–17, $4.50 children 5–12. Open Mon.–Thurs. 10 AM–10 PM, Fri. and Sat. 10 AM–midnight, Sun. 10 AM–11 PM.*

San Francisco Art Institute. A seven-section fresco by Diego Rivera adorns one of the galleries here. Exhibits at the Walter McBean Gallery most often feature student and alumni work. (*See* Tour 6: Nob Hill and Russian Hill.)

San Francisco Craft and Folk Art Museum. American folk art, tribal art, and contemporary crafts are on display in this pleasant museum. Its gift shop offers handmade items at reasonable prices. (*See* Tour 10: The Northern Waterfront.)

San Francisco Fire Department Museum. More than 100 years of fire department history are documented with photographs and other memorabilia. *655 Presidio Ave. at Bush St. Take Muni Bus No. 38 on Geary St. to Presidio Ave.; walk 3 blocks north to Bush. Admission free. Open Thurs.–Sun. 1–4.*

San Francisco History Room and Archives. Historic photographs, maps, and other memorabilia of the city are carefully documented for the layman or research scholar on the third floor of the city's main library. (*See* Tour 9: Civic Center.)

San Francisco Museum of Modern Art. The Bay Area's preeminent showcase for modern painting, sculpture, graphics, photographs, and multimedia installations moves to its new home in Yerba Buena Center in early 1995. (*See* Tour 2: South of Market (SoMa) and the Embarcadero.)

San Francisco Performing Arts Library and Museum. Also known as PALM, this organization collects, documents, and preserves the San Francisco Bay Area's rich performing arts legacy. It houses the largest collection of its kind on the West Coast. (*See* Tour 9: Civic Center.)

Wax Museum. Visit with almost 300 wax figures of film stars, U.S. presidents, and world celebrities. Other attractions (separate admission) include a medieval dungeon and Lasermaze, a walk-in video game. *145 Jefferson St., near Fisherman's Wharf, tel. 415/885–4975. Admission: $8.95 adults; $6.95 children 13–17, military, and senior citizens; $4.95 children 6–12, under 6 free. Open Sun.–Thurs. 9 AM–10 PM, Fri. and Sat. 9 AM–11 PM.*

Wells Fargo Bank History Museum. Original Western art, samples of nuggets and gold dust from major mines, and a century-old Concord stagecoach are among the attractions at this storefront museum. (*See* Tour 3: The Financial District and Jackson Square.)

World of Economics. Economics is explained through videotapes, computer games, and electronic displays. Tours of the Federal Reserve Bank are given by appointment only. *101 Market St., tel. 415/974–3252. Take Muni Bus 8 from Market and Powell Sts. to Main and Market Sts. Open weekdays 9–4:30.*

Parks and Gardens

Alta Plaza Park. Look north to Marin, east to downtown, south to Twin Peaks, and west to Golden Gate Park from this Pacific Heights park. *Bordered by Clay, Steiner, Jackson and Scott Sts.*

Buena Vista Park. This hilly park rises above Haight Street between Baker and Central streets. It offers splendid views of the city's north side and the Golden Gate Bridge. *Off Haight St., encircled by Buena Vista East and Buena Vista West Sts.*

Coolbrith Park, Ina. The Bay Bridge and Alcatraz are among the views from this restful site. *Taylor St., between Vallejo and Green Sts.* (*See* Tour 6: Nob Hill and Russian Hill.)

Dolores Park. Several blocks long, this graceful grassy knoll faces downtown San Francisco. *Dolores and Church Sts., between 18th and 20th Sts.*

Dutch Windmill. Built to supply water for Golden Gate Park, this restored windmill is now powered by electric motors. It retains its charm if not its function. *Make a right turn at the end of John F. Kennedy Dr.* (*See* Tour 12: Golden Gate Park.)

Golden Gate Park. Among the options here are the Japanese Tea Garden, three museums, the Conservatory, an arboretum, lawn bowling, a carousel, Stow Lake, riding stables, numerous playing fields, and a bison paddock. (*See* Tour 12: Golden Gate Park.)

Japanese Tea Garden. Small ponds, streams, and flowering shrubs create a serene landscape. The Tea House serves a variety of teas. *Tea Garden Dr. and South Dr.* (*See* Tour 12: Golden Gate Park.)

Lafayette Park. Sunbathers love the western slope of this Pacific Heights spot. Benches offer views of the neighborhood and beyond. A small playground diverts the kids. *Sacramento and Washington Sts., between Gough and Laguna Sts.* (*See* Tour 7: Pacific Heights.)

Lake Merced. It's a 6-mile jog (or, if you prefer, drive) around this Sunset District lake. Along the way you'll see a golf course and a shooting range, among other things. *Bordered by Lake Merced Blvd., John Muir Dr., and Skyline Blvd.*

Lincoln Park. This 275-acre park in the city's northwest section includes the Palace of the Legion of Honor museum, a golf course, and steep cliffs that swoop down to the Golden Gate. *Entrance at 34th St. and Clement St.* (*See* Tour 13: Lincoln Park and the Western Shoreline.)

Mt. Davidson Park. A huge cross that has been the subject of several court battles marks this Sunset District spot with views (on sunny days) to the Farralon Islands. *Hillcrest Dr., off Myra Way in the Sunset District.*

Pioneer Park. At the base of Coit Tower, this park, which is filled with eucalyptus, offers views exceeded only by those of the tower itself. *Above Kearny St., near Filbert St.* (*See* Tour 5: North Beach and Telegraph Hill.)

Portsmouth Square. This park, now mostly cement and blacktop, dates back to the days when San Francisco was called Yerba Buena. A spot for repose in bustling Chinatown, it hosts community events. *Kearny St. and Walter U. Lum Pl., between Clay and Washington Sts.* (*See* Tour 4: Chinatown.)

Queen Wilhelmina Tulip Garden. This beautiful garden surrounds the base of the Dutch Windmill at the far end of Golden Gate Park. *Make a right turn at the end of John F. Kennedy Dr.* (*See* Tour 12: Golden Gate Park.)

St. Mary's Park. Beniamino Bufano's 12-foot statue of Chinese leader Sun Yat-sen anchors this small Chinatown park. *Grant Ave. and California St. (See* Tour 4: Chinatown.)

Sigmund Stern Grove. This park encompasses a small valley that forms a kind of natural amphitheater. From mid-June through August, free outdoor Sunday programs feature opera, ballet, jazz, symphony, and ethnic dance. Bring a sweater, in case ocean breezes and fog roll in. *19th Ave. and Sloat Blvd., in the Sunset District. Take the Muni light rail system (M or K cars) from Powell and Market Sts. to Sloat Blvd. and West Portal. Walk 3 blocks west on Sloat.*

Strybing Arboretum. Six thousand plants and tree varieties create calm, not cacophony, in the groves and gardens here. (*See* Tour 12: Golden Gate Park.)

Washington Square. A great mix of people and cultures can be found at this bustling North Beach park. The church of Saints Peter and Paul overlooks the proceedings. *Columbus and Union Sts. (See* Tour 5: North Beach and Telegraph Hill.)

4 Shopping

By Sheila Gadsden

Updated by Daniel Mangin

San Francisco is a shopper's dream—major department stores, fine fashion, discount outlets, art galleries, and crafts stores are among the many offerings. Most accept at least Visa and MasterCard charge cards, and many also accept American Express and Diners Club. A very few accept cash only. Ask about traveler's checks; policies vary. The *San Francisco Chronicle* and *Examiner* advertise sales; for smaller innovative shops, check the San Francisco *Bay Guardian.* Store hours are slightly different everywhere, but a generally trusted rule is to shop between 10 AM and 5 or 6 PM Monday–Wednesday, Friday, and Saturday; between 10 AM and 8 or 9 PM on Thursday; and from noon until 5 PM on Sunday. Stores on and around Fisherman's Wharf often have longer summer hours.

Major Shopping Districts

Fisherman's Wharf

San Francisco's Fisherman's Wharf is host to a number of shopping and sightseeing attractions: **Pier 39,** the **Anchorage, Ghirardelli Square,** and **The Cannery.** Each offers shops, restaurants, and a festive atmosphere as well as such outdoor entertainment as musicians, mimes, and magicians. Pier 39 includes an amusement area and a double-decked Venetian carousel. One attraction shared by all the centers is the view of the bay and the proximity of the cable car lines, which can take shoppers directly to Union Square.

Union Square

Serious shoppers will find the entire Union Square area richly rewarding. Bordering the square itself are leading department and specialty stores. **I. Magnin & Co.,** on the south side of Union Square at Stockton Street, is noted for its designer fashions, magnificent fur salon, and precious jewelry salon. Just across Stockton Street is the checkerboard-faced **Neiman Marcus,** opened in 1982. Philip Johnson's controversial design replaced an old San Francisco favorite, the City of Paris; all that remains is the great glass dome. **Macy's,** with entrances on Geary, Stockton, and O'Farrell streets, has huge selections of clothing, plus extensive furniture and household accessories departments. The men's department—one of the world's largest—occupies its own building across Stockton Street. Opposite is the new **FAO Schwarz** children's store, with its extravagant assortment of life-size stuffed animals, animated displays, and steep prices. A half block down Stockton Street from FAO Schwarz is the new **Virgin Megastore** (scheduled to open in late 1994), four floors of music, entertainment, and software in a building also housing a **Planet Hollywood** restaurant (whose owners include Demi Moore, Danny Glover, Arnold Schwarzenegger, Bruce Willis, and Sylvester Stallone). Also livening up the already lively Union Square area: a huge new **Disney Store** (to open in November 1994), selling memorabilia and other merchandise from the famous movie studio. The Disney space, across Post Street from the St. Francis Hotel, also includes a 45,000-square-foot **Borders Books and Music** store. Across Powell Street from Disney, **Saks Fifth Avenue** still caters to the upscale shopper. Nearby are the pricey international boutiques of Hermès of Paris, Gucci, Celine of Paris, Alfred Dunhill, Louis Vuitton, and Cartier.

Across from the cable-car turntable at Powell and Market streets is the **San Francisco Shopping Centre,** with the fashionable **Nordstrom** department store and more than 35 other shops. A big hit since the day it opened in 1992 is the two-floor **Warner Bros.** shop, which carries T-shirts, posters, and other momentos of the studio's past and present. And underneath a glass dome at Post and Kearny streets is **Crocker Galleria,** a complex of 50 shops and restaurants topped by two rooftop parks.

Embar-cadero Center Five modern towers of shops, restaurants, and offices plus the Hyatt Regency Hotel make up the downtown Embarcadero Center at the end of Market Street. Like most malls, the center is a little sterile and falls short in the character department. What it lacks in charm, however, it makes up for in sheer quantity. The center's 175 stores and services include such nationally known stores as **The Limited, B. Dalton Bookseller,** and **Ann Taylor,** as well as more local or West Coast–based businesses such as the **Nature Company** and **Lotus Designer Earrings.** Each tower occupies one block, and parking garages are available.

Jackson Square Jackson Square is where a dozen or so of San Francisco's finest retail antiques dealers are located. If your passion is 19th-century English furniture, for example, there's a good chance that something here will suit. Knowledgeable store owners and staffs can direct you to other places in the city for your special interests. The shops are along Jackson Street in the Financial District, so a visit there will put you very close to the Embarcadero Center and Chinatown.

Chinatown The intersection of Grant Avenue and Bush Street marks "the Gateway" to Chinatown; here shoppers and tourists are introduced to 24 blocks of shops, restaurants, markets, and temples. There are daily "sales" on gems of all sorts—especially jade and pearls—alongside stalls of bok choy and gingerroot. Chinese silks and toy trinkets are also commonplace in the shops, as are selections of colorful pottery, baskets, and large figures of soapstone, ivory, and jade.

North Beach The once largely Italian enclave of North Beach gets smaller each year as Chinatown spreads northward. It has been called the city's answer to New York City's Greenwich Village, although it's much smaller. Many of the businesses here tend to be small clothing stores, antiques shops, or such eccentric specialty shops as **Quantity Postcard** (1441 Grant Ave.), which has an inventory of 15,000 different postcards. If you get tired of poking around in the bookstores, a number of cafés dot the streets and there are lots of Italian restaurants.

Union Street Out-of-towners sometimes confuse Union Street—a popular stretch of shops and restaurants five blocks south of the Golden Gate National Recreation Area—with downtown's Union Square (*see above*). Nestled at the foot of a hill between Pacific Heights and the Marina District, Union Street shines with contemporary fashion and custom jewelry. Union Street's feel is

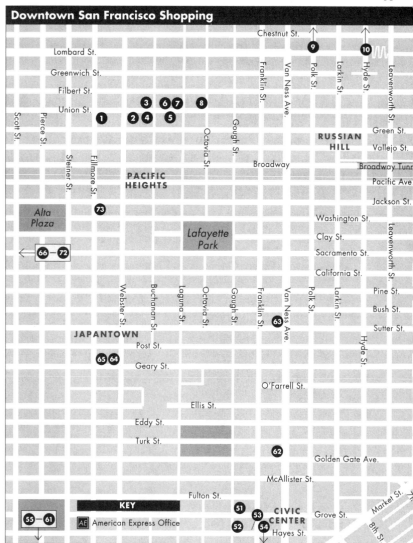

98

Downtown San Francisco Shopping

A Clean, Well-lighted Place for Books, **62**
Abitare, **11**
American Rag, **63**
Another Time, **54**
Apacci Paris, **35**
Biordi, **14**
Body Time, **3**
Brava Strada, **66**
Britex, **34**
Buffalo Exchange, **56**
City Lights, **16**

The Coach Store, **33**
Cottonwood, **68**
Crabtree & Evelyn, **32**
Designers Too, **58**
Dottie Doolittle, **71**
Edward's Unusual Fabrics, **31**
Esprit, **49**
Eileen West, **40**
Emporium, **43**
Evelyne Conquaret Antiques, **50**

FAO Schwarz Fifth Avenue, **42**
Far East Fashion, **20**
F. Dorian, **52**
Folk Art International Gallery, **9**
Forma, **60**
Fumiki, **4**
Harcourts Gallery, **21**
Held Over, **57**
Hunt Antiques, **18**
Images, **53**

Jade Empire, **19**
Japonesque, **17**
Jeanne Marc, **23**
Justine, **67**
Kids Only, **55**
Kinokuniya Bookstores, **64**
Krazy Kaps, **12**
Kris Kelly, **39**
Lang Antiques and Estate Jewelry, **24**
Loehmann's, **27**

San Francisco Bay

Ma-Shi'-Ko Folk Craft, **56**	Patagonia, **10**	Shige Antiques, **65**	Walker McIntyre, **70**
Macy's, **37**	Patronik Designs, **5**	Shreve & Co., **29**	Whittler's Mother, **12**
Malm Luggage, **22, 32**	Peluche, **69**	Simply Cotton, **47**	Wholesale Jewelers Exchange, **38**
Nordstrom, **44**	Polo/Ralph Lauren, **32**	Six Sixty Center, **48**	Yankee Doodle Dandy, **6**
North Beach Leather, **36**	Rainbeau Bodywear Factory Store, **46**	Smile: A Gallery, **25**	Yerba Buena Square, **45**
The North Face, **30**	Revival of the Fittest, **59**	Spellbound, **58**	Yountville, **73**
Old and New Estates, **1**	Santa Fe, **70**	Stacey's, **41**	Z Gallerie, **2**
Origins, **61**	Scheuer Linen, **26**	Sy Aal, **8**	
Paris 1925, **7**	The Sharper Image, **15, 28**	Telegraph Hill Antiques, **13**	
		Virginia Breier, **72**	
		Vorpal Gallery, **51**	

largely new and upscale, although there are a few antiques shops and some long-term storekeepers. Here are some local favorites: **Arte Forma** (1775 Union St.), which sells wild, yet elegant, contemporary art furniture; the magical, mystical **Enchanted Crystal** (1771 Union St.); **Armani Exchange** (2090 Union St.) clothing boutique; and **Yankee Doodle Dandy** (1974 Union St.), with its delightful collection of teddy bears and antique American quilts. The main shopping area runs from Laguna Street to Steiner Street, and also north on Fillmore (don't miss these fine shops) to Lombard Street and the edge of the Marina District shopping area.

The Marina District One block north of Lombard Street, Chestnut Street caters to the shopping needs of Marina District residents. It offers more of a neighborhood feeling than do other well-touristed shopping areas. Banks and well-known stores, including **Waldenbooks, The Gap,** and **Lucca Delicatessen Goods,** are interspersed with such unique gift shops as the **Red Rose Gallerie,** which specializes in "tools for personal growth," including body scents, exotic clothing, and audiotapes for rejuvenating the mind. Shops start at Fillmore Street and end at Broderick Street.

Pacific Heights When Pacific Heights residents look for practical services, they look toward Fillmore and Sacramento streets. Both streets feel more like neighborhood streets than upscale shopping areas, and that is exactly their appeal to tourists and natives—easygoing and personal with good bookstores, fine clothing shops, gift shops, thrift stores, and furniture and art galleries. **Sue Fisher King Company** (3067 Sacramento St.) is an eclectic collection of home accessories, and **Yountville** (2416 Fillmore St.) has lovely children's clothing from local and European designers. The Fillmore Street shopping area runs from Post Street to Pacific Avenue. Most shops on the western end of Sacramento Street are between Lyon and Maple streets.

Japantown Unlike Chinatown, North Beach, or the Mission, the 5-acre **Japan Center** (between Laguna and Fillmore Sts., and between Geary Blvd. and Post St.) is contained under one roof. The three-block cluster includes an 800-car public garage and shops and showrooms selling Japanese products: cameras, tapes and records, new and old porcelains, pearls, antique kimonos, beautiful tansu chests, and paintings. The center always feels a little empty, but the good shops here are well worth a visit, as are the adjoining ones on Post and Buchanan streets. Among the favorites: **Soko Hardware** (1698 Post St.), which has been run by the Ashizawa merchant family since 1925, specializes in beautifully crafted Japanese tools for gardening and carpentry; **Nichi Bei Bussan** (1715 Buchanan St.) has a collector's choice of quilts covered with fabulous Japanese designs; **Kinokuniya** (on the second floor of the center's western-most Kinokuniya Building) may have the finest selection of English-language books on Japanese subjects in the United States. The shops in the **Tasamak Plaza Building,** east of the Peace Plaza, are a paradise for souvenir shoppers. Colorful flying-fish kites and delicate floral-patterned cocktail napkins are popular choices.

The Haight Haight Street is always an attraction for visitors, if only to see the sign at Haight and Ashbury streets—the geographic center of flower power during the 1960s. These days, in addition to renascent tie-dyed shirts, you'll find good-quality vintage clothing, funky jewelry, art from Mexico, and reproductions of Art Deco accessories (*see* Vintage Fashion *and* Vintage Furniture and Accessories, *below*). The street also boasts several used-book stores and some of the best used-record stores in the city: **Recycled Records** (1377 Haight St.), **Reckless Records** (1401 Haight St.), and **Rough Trade** (1529 Haight St.) focus on classic rock-and-roll, obscure independent labels, and hard-to-find imports.

Civic Center The shops and galleries that have sprung up around the Civic Center reflect the cultural offerings of Davies Symphony Hall, Herbst Theatre, the Opera House, and (until its pending move to Yerba Buena) the Museum of Modern Art. The area is a little sparse compared with other tightly packed shopping streets in the city, but is still well worth a visit. The **San Francisco Opera Shop** (199 Grove St.), across Van Ness Avenue from Davies Hall, is packed with recordings, books, posters, and gift items associated with the performing arts. The tree-lined block of Hayes Street between Gough and Franklin streets includes art galleries, crafts shops, and pleasant cafés. This area includes Hayes and Grove streets from Polk Street and extends to Laguna Street.

South of Market In keeping with SoMa's tradition of being the underside of the city, the area now offers you the underside of shopping: discount outlets. Dozens, most of them open seven days a week, have sprung up along the streets and alleyways bordered by 2nd, Townsend, Howard, and 10th streets. A good place to start is the **Six Sixty Center** (660 3rd St.), two floors of shops offering everything from designer fashions to Icelandic sweaters. For other outlet listings, *see* Outlets, *below.*

Department Stores

Emporium (835 Market St., tel. 415/764–2222). This full-service department store carries a complete line of clothing and home furnishings. The prices are reasonable compared with those you'll find at many downtown department stores.

Macy's (Stockton and O'Farrell Sts., tel. 415/397–3333). Designer fashions, an extensive array of shoes, household wares, furniture, food, and even a post office and foreign-currency exchange.

Nordstrom (865 Market St., tel. 415/243–8500). This large downtown store is known for providing excellent service to customers. The building's stunning interior design features spiral escalators circling a four-story atrium. Designer fashions, shoes, accessories, and cosmetics are specialties.

Three other large stores that offer high-quality merchandise are **I. Magnin, Neiman Marcus,** and **Saks Fifth Avenue** (all are on Union Sq.). Venerable **Gump's,** after 85 years at the same Union

Square location, lost its lease. It is scheduled to reopen one block away (135 Post St.) in the fall of 1994.

Outlets

A number of clothing factory outlets in San Francisco offer goods at quite reasonable prices. Here are a few of the more popular ones. Outlet maps are available at some of these locations for a nominal fee.

Esprit (499 Illinois St. at 16th St., south of China Basin, tel. 415/957–2550). Hip sportswear for the young and the young-at-heart at this San Francisco–based company. Savings are 30%–70% off retail prices.

Loehmann's (222 Sutter St., near Union Sq., tel. 415/982–3215). Many fashionably dressed women swear by Loehmann's, where designer labels such as Karl Lagerfeld and Krizia are sold at drastically reduced prices. It helps to know designers, however, as labels are often removed.

Rainbeau Bodywear Factory Store (300 4th St., tel. 415/777–9786). Excellent-quality exercise gear and dancewear in a wide variety of colors, sizes, and styles.

Simply Cotton (610 3rd St., tel. 415/543–2058). This outlet sells sensible cottonwear—dresses, jackets, tops, vests, and T-shirts.

Six Sixty Center (660 3rd St. at Townsend St., tel. 415/227–0464). There are nearly two dozen outlet stores here, offering apparel, accessories, and shoes for men, women, and children. Open daily.

Yerba Buena Square (899 Howard St. at 5th St., tel. 415/974–5136). The Burlington Coat Factory (tel. 415/495–7234), with a full range of clothing, is the anchor in this center for apparel, shoes, and toys. It is only two blocks from Market Street, and most of the shops are open daily.

Specialty Stores

Antique Furniture **Evelyne Conquaret Antiques** (Showplace Sq. W, 550 15th St., tel. 415/552–6100). This showroom specializes in 18th- and 19th-century French antique furniture and has a large selection of lamps and accessories. As you enter the Showplace Square West interior design center, it may seem this is "only for the trade," but don't be shy; Evelyne Conquaret and its neighbor, the Ginsberg Collection, are open to the public.

Fumiki (2001 Union St., tel. 415/922–0573). This store offers a fine selection of Asian arts, including antiques, art, fine jewelry, Chinese silk paintings, and Korean and Japanese furniture. Two specialties here are obis (sashes worn with kimonos) and antique Japanese baskets. **A Touch of Asia,** two blocks east on Union Street, is another good source for Asian antiques.

Hunt Antiques (478 Jackson St., tel. 415/989–9531). Fine 17th- to 19th-century period English furniture as well as porcelains, Staffordshire pottery, prints, clocks, and paintings in a gracious country-house setting can be found here. This is only one of a dozen or so shops in the Jackson Square area. Others, such as **Foster-Gwin Antiques, Carpets of the Inner Circle,** and the **Antiques Gallery,** are also fine bets.

Origins (637 Townsend St., tel. 415/252–7089). This large Asian-antiques store—part of the Baker Hamilton Square complex in the South of Market area—imports unusual collector's items, Chinese furniture, porcelain, silk, and jade. It's not unheard of to find a piece up to 400 years old here. The complex houses more than a dozen other antique furniture shops, which, among them, cover quite a few different periods and styles, ranging from Thai to Art Deco to 19th-century French and English pieces.

Shige Antiques (Japan Center, 1825 Webster St., on Webster Street Bridge between Kinokuniya and Kintetsu Bldgs.). This shop is frequented by collectors of art-to-wear for its antique, handpainted, silk-embroidered kimonos. The shop also sells Arita porcelains, silk calligraphy scrolls, tea-ceremony utensils, and dazzling lacquerware boxes. Downstairs in the Kinokuniya Building, at **Asakichi Japanese Antiques,** are antique blue-and-white Imari porcelains and handsome tansu chests.

Telegraph Hill Antiques (580 Union St., tel. 415/982–7055). A very mixed but fine selection is available in this little North Beach shop: fine china and porcelain, crystal, cut glass, Oriental objects, Victoriana, bronzes, and paintings. **Walker McIntyre** (3419 Sacramento St., tel. 415/563–8024). This shop specializes in pieces from the Georgian period, but it also offers 19th-century Japanese Imari cloisonné, lamps custom-made from antique vases, and Oriental rugs. Other very fine antiques stores on this street include **Jasper Byron, La Madeleine,** and **Les Poisson.**

Antique Jewelry **Lang Antiques and Estate Jewelry** (323 Sutter St., tel. 415/982–2213). This is another good source for both jewelry and small antique objects, particularly fine glass, amber, and silver.

Old and New Estates (2181-A Union St., tel. 415/346–7525). This shop offers both antique and modern jewelry, crystal, and silver. It is generally open on weekdays and Saturdays 11–6, but the hours vary, so it's best to call first.

Paris 1925 (1954 Union St., tel. 415/567–1925) specializes in estate jewelry and vintage watches.

Art Galleries There are dozens of art galleries scattered throughout the city. Most surround downtown Union Square, although in recent years some of the interest has shifted to the newly thriving Hayes Valley area near the Civic Center and South of Market. Pick up a copy of the free *San Francisco Arts Monthly* at the TIX Bay Area booth in Union Square (Stockton St. at Geary St.) for listings of other galleries in the area and elsewhere in the city.

Harcourts Gallery (460 Bush St., tel. 415/421–3428). One of the city's best-known galleries, Harcourts exhibits paintings, sculpture, and graphics by 19th- and 20th-century artists, including Picasso, Chagall, Renoir, and Miró, as well as works by contemporary artists such as Robert Rauschenberg, Sylvia Glass, and Roland Petersen. Open Tuesday–Saturday.

Images (372 Hayes St., tel. 415/626–2284) specializes in oil paintings and watercolors by northern California realist and impressionist artists. Crafts and jewelry are also on display. Open Tuesday–Saturday.

Vorpal Gallery (393 Grove St., tel. 415/397–9200). A premier gallery that focuses on postmodern painting, drawing, and sculpture, Vorpal also has an excellent collection of graphic arts.

Books **City Lights** (261 Columbus Ave., tel. 415/362–8193). The city's most famous bookstore—and possibly the most comfortable bookstore for browsing—this was a major center for poetry readings during the 1960s. City Lights publishes books as well. The store is particularly well stocked in poetry, contemporary literature and music, and translations of third-world literature. There is also an interesting selection of books on nature, the outdoors, and travel. Open daily 10 AM–midnight.

A Clean Well-lighted Place for Books (601 Van Ness Ave., tel. 415/441–6670). You'll find "a large selection of paperbacks and hardbacks in all fields for all ages," particularly books on opera, and San Francisco history.

Kinokuniya Bookstores (Kinokuniya Bldg., 1581 Webster St., 2nd Floor, tel. 415/567–7625). This Japan Center store offers all sorts of books and periodicals in Japanese and English, but a major attraction is the collection of beautifully produced graphics and art books. Closed first Tuesday of every month.

Stacey's (581 Market St., tel. 415/421–4687). Come here for professional books such as computer, medical, business, travel, and reference texts.

Other excellent bookstores in the city include **Solar Light Books** (general needs), **The Sierra Club Bookstore** (California and the West), and **William Stout Architectural Books** (for interiors, exteriors, graphics, and landscape design).

Fabrics **Britex** (146 Geary St., tel. 415/392–2910). Here is one of the city's largest collections of fabrics and notions: There are four floors of colors and patterns.
Edward's Unusual Fabrics (80 Geary St., tel. 415/397–5625). This store offers another fine selection of fabrics, especially good silks.
Far East Fashion (953 Grant Ave., tel. 415/362–8171 or 415/362–0986). This store has one of Chinatown's better selections of Chinese embossed silks and lace.

Fine Gifts and Specialty Items **Biordi** (412 Columbus Ave., tel. 415/392–8096). In the heart of North Beach, this small colorful store sells Majolica dinnerware and other imported Italian handicrafts and ceramics.
Whittler's Mother (Pier 39, Embarcadero, tel. 415/433–3010). Handcrafted wood reigns here, including carousel animals—both small and full-size—created and painted on the premises.

Other good specialty stores are **Yone** in North Beach (for beads), the **Sharper Image** downtown (gadgets), and **Waterford Wedgwood** on Union Square (crystal and china).

Clothing for Children **Dottie Doolittle** (3680 Sacramento St., tel. 415/563–3244). This store offers domestic and imported clothing sized from infant to 14 years, as well as baby furniture.

Yountville (2416 Fillmore St., tel. 415/922–5050). California and European designs are the draw here, from infant to eight years.

Clothing for Men and Women **Apacci Paris** (50 Grant Ave., tel. 415/982–7222). This exclusive store sells a collection of menswear from Italy, France, and Switzerland. It is known for its unique ties.

Brava Strada (3247 Sacramento St., tel. 415/567–5757). Featured here are designer knitwear and accessories; Italian and other European leather goods; and one-of-a-kind jewelry from American and European artists. Also on Sacramento Street is **Button Down,** carrying "updated traditional" clothing and accessories.

Designers Too (3899 24th St., tel. 415/648–1057). The natural fiber creations of local designer Cia Van Orden and jewelry by Audrey Daniels are the chief draws at this charming Noe Valley shop.

Eileen West (33 Grant Ave., tel. 415/982–2275). San Francisco designer Eileen West displays her lovely dresses, sleepwear, lingerie, linens, and more in this cozy boutique.

Jeanne Marc (262 Sutter St., tel. 415/362–1121). This boutique sells sportswear and more formal clothes in the striking prints that have become the hallmark of this San Francisco designer.

Justine (3263 Sacramento St., tel. 415/921–8548). Women's clothes by French designers Dorothee Bis, George Rech, and Ventilo are the draw here, as well as shoes by Charles Kammer.

Krazy Kaps (Pier 39, tel. 415/296–8930). Here you'll find silly hats as well as top hats, Stetsons, and Greek fishermen's caps—a good assortment for personal use and gift giving.

Peluche (3366 Sacramento St., tel. 415/346–6361). This shop specializes in one-of-a-kind, hand-knit sweaters, mostly from Italy, and European fashions for women.

Polo/Ralph Lauren (Crocker Galleria, Post and Kearny Sts., tel. 415/567–7656). This store offers designer apparel and accessories as well as home furnishings.

Sy Aal (1864 Union St., tel. 415/929–1864). Offering "men's fashion with a woman's point of view," Sy Aal carries a full line of fine clothing, including hand-knits, and specializes in ties.

Other good places for women's clothing stores are Union Square; Crocker Galleria, which has such internationally known shops as **Gianni Versace**; Fillmore Street between Post and Clay streets; and the Embarcadero Center, whose selection includes **Ann Taylor, The Limited,** and **Banana Republic.**

Handicrafts and Folk Art **Cottonwood** (3461 Sacramento St., tel. 415/346–6020). Fine handcrafted home furnishings and decorative objects, including flatware, dinnerware, leather boxes, sculpture, and baskets abound in this store.

F. Dorian (388 Hayes St., tel. 415/861–3191). Cards, jewelry, and other crafts from Mexico, Japan, Italy, Peru, Indonesia, Philippines, and Sri Lanka as well as items from local crafts-people are the specialties here.

Folk Art International Gallery (Ghirardelli Sq., 900 North Point St., tel. 415/441–6100). This gallery, with shops on two levels of the Cocoa Building at Ghirardelli, features an extensive contemporary folk-art collection from Mexico, China, Ecuador, France, Sri Lanka, Peru, Haiti, and other countries—masks, boxes, sculpture, baskets, toys, and textiles. Adjoining the Folk Art's upper-level gallery, **Xanadu** (tel. 415/441–5211) offers artifacts and tribal art from Asia, Africa, Oceania, and the Americas.

Japonesque (824 Montgomery St., tel. 415/398–8577). Here you'll find handcrafted wooden boxes, sculpture, paintings, and handmade glass from Japan and the United States.

Ma-Shi'-Ko Folk Craft (Japan Center, Kinokuniya Bldg., 1581 Webster St., 2nd Floor, tel. 415/346–0748). This store carries handcrafted pottery from Japan, including Mashiko, the style that has been in production longer than any other. There are also masks and other handcrafted goods, all from Japan.

Santa Fe (3571 Sacramento St., tel. 415/346–0180). This is where you'll find old Navajo rugs, ranch furniture, old silver and turquoise jewelry, Indian pots and baskets, and cowboy relics.

Smile: A Gallery (500 Sutter St., tel. 415/362–3436). A whimsical, colorful collection of folk art, jewelry, and mobiles, including extraordinary life-size soft sculptures of people, created by an artist in Marin.

Virginia Breier (3091 Sacramento St., tel. 415/929–7173). A colorful gallery of contemporary and ethnic crafts from Mexico, Indonesia, Korea, Japan, Brazil, and the United States, especially the West Coast; includes decorative and functional items, antiques.

Yankee Doodle Dandy (1974 Union St., tel. 415/346–0346). A large selection of American antique quilts, carvings, handmade stuffed animals, woven throws.

Other shops to look at are **Oggetti** on Union Street, which carries Italian marbleized papers and gifts; **Designs in Motion** at Pier 39; **Images of the North** on Union Street; **Artifacts** on Fillmore Street; **Planetweavers Treasure Store** on Haight Street; and **Xela** on 24th Street.

Jewelry   **Jade Empire** (832 Grant Ave., tel. 415/982–4498). One of the many fine jewelry stores in Chinatown, this one has good jade, diamonds, and other gems. **Patronik Designs** (1949 Union St., tel. 415/922–9716). Innovative contemporary and custom jewelry. Other good stores on Union are **Union Street Goldsmith** and **David Clay.**

Shreve & Co. (Post St. and Grant Ave., tel. 415/421–2600). One of the city's most elegant jewelers, and the oldest retail store in San Francisco, is near Union Square.

Wholesale Jewelers Exchange (121 O'Farrell St., tel. 415/788–2365). This is a source for fine gems and finished jewelry at less than retail prices.

Leather   **The Coach Store** (190 Post St., tel. 415/392–1772). A branch of the nationally known purveyor of classically designed leather goods, the inventory here includes purses, briefcases, silk scarves, and belts and wallets of all sizes, colors, and weights.

Malm Luggage (Crocker Galleria, Post and Kearny Sts., tel. 415/391–5222; 222 Grant Ave., tel. 415/392–0417). Fine luggage, leather goods, and accessories.

North Beach Leather (190 Geary St., tel. 415/362–8300). One of the best sources for high-quality leather garments—skirts, jackets, pants, dresses, accessories. With its sculpted walls, the store itself is a work of art. The original store is still in business at Fisherman's Wharf (1365 Columbus Ave., tel. 415/441–3208).

Linens **Kris Kelly** (174 Geary St., tel. 415/986–8822). This lovely store sells imported and domestic handcrafted tablecloths, bed linens, and bath accessories.

Scheuer Linen (318 Stockton St., tel. 415/392–2813). Luxurious linens for the bed, the bath, and the dining table abound here, including European linens and special designs.

Miscella- **Abitare** (522 Columbus St., tel. 415/392–5800). This popular
neous North Beach shop features an eclectic mix of goods—soaps and bath supplies, candleholders, artsy picture frames, and one-of-a-kind furniture, artworks, and decorations.

Z Gallerie (2071 Union St., tel. 415/346–9000; Stonestown Galleria, 19th Ave. at Winston Dr., tel. 415/664–7891). Home furnishings in black—butterfly chairs, dinnerware, desks, chairs, lamps, and a variety of high-tech accessories—are the specialties here; also posters, both black-and-white and color. There are other stores in the San Francisco Shopping Centre on Market Street and on Haight Street.

Sporting **The North Face** (180 Post St., tel. 415/433–3223; and 1325
Goods Howard St. [outlet], tel. 415/626–6444). This Bay Area–based company is famous for its top-of-the-line tents, sleeping bags, backpacks, skis, and outdoor apparel, including stylish Gore-Tex jackets and pants.

Patagonia (770 North Point St., near Fisherman's Wharf, tel. 415/771–2050). The outdoorsy set will want to check out Patagonia's signature parkas and jackets.

Toiletries **Body Time** (2072 Union St., tel. 415/922–4076). These are some of the best concoctions around for the face and body—locally produced soaps, lotions, creams, perfumes, and body oils.

Crabtree & Evelyn (Crocker Galleria, Post and Kearny Sts., tel. 415/392–6111; Stonestown Galleria, 19th Ave. and Winston Dr., tel. 415/753–8015). English and French soaps, shampoos, lotions, creams, shaving supplies, and grooming implements; also jams, assorted condiments, and specialty gifts. Also at the Embarcadero Center and Ghirardelli Square.

Toys and **FAO Schwarz Fifth Avenue** (48 Stockton St., tel. 415/394–8700).
Gadgets The San Francisco branch of an American tradition, this store features a little of everything, from games and stuffed toys to motorized cars and trains.

Forma (1715 Haight St., tel. 415/751–0545) is one of the most imaginative shops in the city, with items ranging from design accessories by artists to 1950s-style lava lamps and toy animals inspired by Japanese monster movies.

Kids Only (1415 Haight St., tel. 415/552–5445). A children's emporium, this store has a little bit of everything.

The Sharper Image (532 Market St., tel. 415/398–6472; 680 Davis St. at Broadway, tel. 415/445–6100). This paradise for gadget lovers features everything from five-language translators and super-shock-absorbent tennis rackets to state-of-the-art speaker systems and Walkman-size computers. Also at Ghirardelli Square.

Vintage Fashion

American Rag (1305 Van Ness Ave., tel. 415/474–5214). Stocked here is a large, department-store-like selection of men's and women's clothes from the United States and Europe, all in excellent shape. They also carry shoes and accessories such as sunglasses, hats, belts, and scarves.

Buffalo Exchange (1555 Haight St., tel. 415/431–7733). One of five stores in the Bay Area and in Arizona, the Haight Street store sells both new and recycled clothing and will also trade items. Also at 1800 Polk Street.

Held Over (1543 Haight St., tel. 415/864–0818). An extensive collection of clothing from the 1940s, '50s, and '60s.

Spellbound (1670 Haight St., tel. 415/863–4930). Fine fashions from decades past—including bugle-beaded dresses, silk scarves, and suits—are offered here. Some of the inventory comes from estate sales.

Vintage Furniture and Accessories

Another Time (1586 Market St, tel. 415/553–8900). This shop, near several other shops with vintage collectibles, is an Art Deco–lover's delight, with furniture and accessories by Heywood Wakefield, and others.

Revival of the Fittest (1701 Haight St., tel. 415/751–8857). Telephones, dishes, assorted collectibles, as well as vintage and reproduction jewelry, clocks, lamps, vases, and furniture can be found here.

5 Sports, Fitness, Beaches

Participant Sports and the Outdoors

By Casey Tefertiller

Updated by Daniel Mangin

One great attraction of the Bay Area is the abundance of activities. Joggers, bicyclists, and aficionados of virtually all sports can find their favorite pastimes within driving distance, and often within walking distance, from downtown hotels. Golden Gate Park has numerous paths for runners and cyclists. Lake Merced in San Francisco and Lake Merritt in Oakland are among the most popular areas for joggers.

For information on running races, tennis tournaments, bicycle races, and other participant sports, check the monthly issues of *City Sports* magazine, available free at sporting goods stores, tennis centers, and other recreational sites. The most important running event of the year is the *Examiner* Bay-to-Breakers race on the third Sunday in May. For information on this race, call 415/512–5000, cat. 2222.

Bicycling Two bike routes are maintained by the San Francisco Recreation and Park Department (tel. 415/666–7201). One route goes through Golden Gate Park to Lake Merced; the other goes from the south end of the city to the Golden Gate Bridge and beyond. Many shops along Stanyan Street rent bikes.

Boating and Sailing **Stow Lake** (tel. 415/752–0347) in Golden Gate Park has rowboat, pedal boat, and electric boat rentals. The lake is open daily for boating, but call for seasonal hours. San Francisco Bay offers year-round sailing, but tricky currents make the bay hazardous for inexperienced navigators. Boat rentals and charters are available throughout the Bay Area and are listed under "boat rentals" in the Yellow Pages. A selected charter is **A Day on the Bay** (tel. 415/922–0227). **Cass' Marina** (tel. 415/332–6789) in Sausalito has a variety of sailboats that can be rented or hired with a licensed skipper. Local sailing information can be obtained at **The Eagle Cafe** on Pier 39.

Fishing Numerous fishing boats leave from San Francisco, Sausalito, Berkeley, Emeryville, and Point San Pablo. They go for salmon outside the bay or striped bass and giant sturgeon within the bay. Temporary licenses are available on the charters. In San Francisco, lines can be cast from San Francisco Municipal Pier, Fisherman's Wharf, or Aquatic Park. Trout fishing is available at Lake Merced. Licenses can be bought at sporting goods stores. The cost of fishing licenses ranges from $5.50 for one day to $23.25 for a complete state license. For charters, reservations are suggested. Some selected sportfishing charters are listed below. Mailing addresses are given, but you're more likely to get a response if you call.
Capt. Fred Morini (Fisherman's Wharf. Write to 138 Harvard Dr., Larkspur, CA 94939, tel. 415/924–5575).
Muny Sport Fishing (156 Linden Ave., San Bruno, CA 94066, tel. 415/871–4445). Leaves daily from Fisherman's Wharf.

Sea Breeze Sportfishing (Box 713, Mill Valley, CA 94942, tel. 415/474–7748). Departs daily from Fisherman's Wharf.

Wacky Jacky (Fisherman's Wharf. Write Jacky Douglas at 473 Bella Vista Way, San Francisco, CA 94127, tel. 415/586–9800).

Fitness   Physical fitness activities continue to be popular, but most clubs are private and visitors could have trouble finding a workout location. Several hotels have arrangements with neighborhood health clubs. A number of hotels have large health facilities of their own, including the Fairmont, Hotel Nikko, San Francisco Marriott, the Mark Hopkins Inter-Continental, the Ritz-Carlton, and the Sheraton Palace Hotel. Of these, two are open to the public: the Marriott charges a $10 drop-in fee and the Nikko $20.

The **24-hour Nautilus** centers downtown (1335 Sutter, tel. 415/776–2200) and at Fisherman's Wharf (350 Bay St., tel. 415/395–9595) are open to the public for a $10 drop-in fee. The clubs offer aerobics and other classes and complete lines of fitness equipment. The **Embarcadero YMCA** (169 Steuart St., tel. 415/957–9622) reopened in 1991 after a massive renovation, and is now one of the finest facilities in San Francisco. For $12, visitors can exercise and use the sauna, whirlpool, and swimming pool, all while enjoying a view of the bay.

Golf   San Francisco has four public golf courses; visitors should call for tee times: **Harding Park** (Lake Merced Blvd. and Skyline Blvd., tel. 415/664–4690), an 18-hole, par 72 course; **Lincoln Park** (34th and Clement Sts., tel. 415/221–9911), 18 holes, par 69; **Golden Gate Park** (47th Ave. at Fulton St., tel. 415/751–8987), a "pitch and putt" 9-holer; **Glen Eagles Golf Course** (2100 Sunnydale Ave., tel. 415/587–2425), a full-size 9-holer in McLaren Park. Another municipal course, the 18-hole, par 72 **Sharp Park** (tel. 415/355–8546), is south of the city in Pacifica.

Horseback Riding   Western-style horseback riding is available throughout the Bay Area. Two stables in Half Moon Bay have rentals for beach rides: **Friendly Acres** (2150 N. Cabrillo Hwy., tel. 415/726–8550) and **Sea Horse Ranch** (1828 N. Cabrillo Hwy., tel. 415/726–2362). Other selected stables include **Sonoma Cattle Co.** (tel. 707/996–8566), which offers rides through Jack London State Park and Sugar Loaf Ridge in Sonoma County; **Five Brooks** (tel. 415/663–1570) in Marin County; and **Miwok Livery** in Mill Valley (tel. 415/383–8048).

Ice Skating   The venerable San Francisco Ice Rink closed in 1991, but in the Bay Area you'll still find **Berkeley Iceland** (2727 Milvia St., 4 blocks from the Ashby BART station, tel. 510/843–8800) and **Belmont Iceland** (815 Old County Rd., tel. 415/592–0532).

In-Line Skating   **Golden Gate Park** is one of the best places in the country for in-line skating, with smooth surfaces, manageable hills, and lush scenery. There's vehicular traffic during the week and on Saturdays, but the JFK Drive, which extends almost to the ocean, is closed to cars on Sundays. Within the park is a large, flat area between the Conservatory and the de Young Museum, where beginners practice stopping and artistic skaters perform their newest moves to music. Nearby, the flashiest pros strut their stuff on the area by the 6th Avenue and Fulton Street pedestrian entrance to the park; watch 'em or join in—if you dare. **Skates on Haight** (1818 Haight St., tel. 415/752–8376), near the Stanyan Street entrance to the park, rents recreational and speed skates, as well as the essential protective gear.

For beginners, the paved path along the **Marina** offers a 1½-mile (round-trip) easy route on flat, well-paved surface and glorious views of San Francisco Bay. **SportsTech/FTC Sports** (1586 Bush St., tel. 415/673–8363) rents and sells in-line skates and protective gear. Advanced skaters will likely want to experience the challenge and take in the brilliant views offered at **Tilden Regional Park** (follow signs from South Park Dr., tel. 510/843–2137), in the Berkeley Hills (*see* Oakland in Chapter 9). Follow signs to the parking lot at Inspiration Point and the trailhead for Nimitz Way, a nicely paved 8-mile (round-trip) recreational path that stretches along a ridge overlooking San Francisco Bay and the East Bay Mudlands and Mt. Diablo. The difficult terrain, with hairpin turns and steep inclines, is sure to test your mettle at points, but it will all seem worth it as you coast through cow pastures, woods, and seemingly endless fields of wildflowers and brush.

Racquetball The San Francisco Recreation and Park Department maintains a racquetball facility at the **Mission Recreation Center** (2450 Harrison St., tel. 415/695–5012).

Swimming The San Francisco Recreation and Park Department manages one outdoor swimming pool and eight indoor pools throughout the city. Popular choices are the **Sava Pool** (19th Ave. and Wawona St.) and **Rossi Pool** (Arguello Blvd. and Anza St.).The outdoor **Mission Pool** (19th St. at Linda St.) is open summers only.

Tennis The San Francisco Recreation and Park Department maintains 130 free tennis courts throughout the city. The largest set of free courts is at **Dolores Park** (18th and Dolores Sts.), with six courts available on a first-come, first-served basis. There are 21 public courts in **Golden Gate Park**; reservations and fee information can be obtained by calling 415/753–7101.

Windsurfing and Gliding Windsurfing is becoming increasingly popular in the Bay Area, with participants taking advantage of the brisk bay breezes to improve their skills. **San Francisco School of Windsurfing** (40A Loyola Terr., tel. 415/750–0412) offers rentals, lessons for beginners on mild Lake Merced, and lessons for more advanced surfers at Candlestick Point. For adventurous types, **Airtime of San Francisco** (3620 Wawona St., tel. 415/759–1177) offers hang-gliding lessons, para-gliding lessons, and rentals off the Marin coastline.

Spectator Sports

For the sports fan, the Bay Area offers a vast selection of events—from yacht races to rodeo to baseball.

Auto Racing **Sears Point International Raceway** (tel. 707/938–8448), in Sonoma at Highways 37 and 121, offers a variety of motor sports events. The track is also the home of the Bondurant High Performance Driving School. There are motor-sports events at various locations around the Bay Area. Check local papers for details.

Baseball A local investment group saved the **San Francisco Giants** from a move to Tampa/St. Petersburg in 1993, and San Francisco city officials hope to build a new stadium for the team. In the meantime the Giants will continue to play at chilly Candlestick Park (tel. 415/467–8000). The **Oakland A's** play at the Oakland Coliseum (tel. 510/638–0500). Game-day tickets are usually available at the stadiums. Premium seats, however, often do sell out in advance. City shuttle buses marked Ballpark Special run from numerous bus stops. Candlestick Park is often windy and cold, so take along extra layers of clothing. The Oakland Coliseum can be reached by taking BART trains to the Coliseum stop.

Basketball The **Golden State Warriors** play NBA basketball at the Oakland Coliseum Arena from October through April. Tickets are available through BASS (tel. 510/762–2277). Again, BART trains to the Coliseum stop are the easiest method of travel.

College Sports Major college football, basketball, and baseball are played at the University of California in Berkeley, at Stanford University on the peninsula in Palo Alto, and at San Jose State. Stanford won the College World Series in the not-so-distant past, and home baseball games at sunny Sunken Diamond often sell out.

Football The **San Francisco 49ers** play at Candlestick Park, but the games are almost always sold out far in advance, so call first (tel. 415/468–2249).

Hockey The Bay Area welcomed the **San Jose Sharks** as its first National Hockey League team in 1991. Their popular home games can be seen at the new arena in downtown San Jose, where they began playing in the 1993–94 season. The team has been a wild success, and though many of their games sell out, try calling BASS (tel. 510/762–2277) for tickets.

Horse Racing Depending on the season, there is racing at **Golden Gate Fields** in Albany, at **Bay Meadows** in San Mateo, or on the Northern California fair circuit. Check local papers for post time and place.

Rodeo and Horse Shows San Francisco relives its western heritage each October with the **Grand National Rodeo and Livestock Show** at the Cow Palace (tel. 415/469–6000) just south of the city limits in Daly City. The 15-Third bus will take you there. In August, the Cow Palace hosts the **San Francisco Equestrian Festival,** featuring such events as dressage and vaulting.

Tennis   The Civic Auditorium (999 Grove St.) is the site of the **Volvo Tennis/San Francisco tournament** in early February (tel. 415/239–4800). The **Virginia Slims women's tennis tour** visits the Oakland Coliseum Arena in October.

Yacht Racing   There are frequent yacht races on the bay. The local papers will give you details, or you can be an uninformed but appreciative spectator from the Golden Gate Bridge or other vantage points around town.

Beaches

San Francisco's beaches are perfect for romantic sunset strolls, but don't make the mistake of expecting to find Waikiki-by-the-Metropolis. The water is cold, and the beach areas are often foggy and usually jammed on sunny days. They can be satisfactory for afternoon sunning, but treacherous currents make most areas dangerous for swimming. During stormy months, beachcombers can stroll along the sand and discover a variety of ocean treasures: glossy agates and jade pebbles, sea-sculptured roots and branches, and—rarely—glass floats.

Baker Beach   Baker Beach is not recommended for swimming: Watch for larger-than-usual waves. In recent years, the north end of the beach has become popular with nude sunbathers. This is not legal, but such laws are seldom enforced. The beach is in the southwest corner of the Presidio and begins at the end of Gibson Road, which turns off Bowley Street. Weather is typical for the bay shoreline: summer fog, usually breezy, and occasionally warm. Picnic tables, grills, day-camp areas, and trails are available. The mile-long shoreline is ideal for jogging, fishing, and building sand castles.

China Beach   From April through October, China Beach, south of Baker Beach, offers a lifeguard, gentler water, changing rooms, and showers. It is also listed on maps as Phelan Beach.

Half Moon Bay   The San Mateo County coast has several beaches and some nice ocean views, most notably at Half Moon Bay State Beach. A drive south on Highway 1 is scenic and will provide access to this and other county beaches. You can take Highway 92 east over the mountains to I–280 for a faster but still scenic route back to the city.

Marin Beaches   The Marin headlands beaches are not safe for swimming. The cliffs are steep and unstable, making falls a constant danger. The Marin coast, however, offers two beaches for picnics and sunning: Muir and Stinson beaches. Swimming is recommended only at Stinson Beach, and only from late May to mid-September, when lifeguard services are provided. If possible, visit these areas during the week; both beaches are crowded on weekends.

Ocean Beach   South of Cliff House, Ocean Beach stretches along the western (ocean) side of San Francisco. It has a wide beach with scenic views and is perfect for walking, running, or lying in the sun—but not for swimming.

6 Dining

By Jacqueline Killeen

Jacqueline Killeen has been writing about San Francisco restaurants for over 25 years. She is a restaurant critic for San Francisco Focus magazine.

San Francisco probably has more restaurants per capita than any other city in the United States, including New York. Practically every ethnic cuisine is represented. That makes selecting some 90 restaurants to list here from the vast number available a very difficult task indeed. We have chosen several restaurants to represent each popular style of dining in various price ranges, in most cases because of the superiority of the food, but in some instances because of the view or ambience.

Because we have covered those areas of town most frequented by visitors, this meant leaving out some great places in outlying districts such as Sunset and Richmond. The outlying restaurants we *have* recommended were chosen because they offer a type of experience not available elsewhere. All listed restaurants serve dinner and are open for lunch unless otherwise specified; restaurants are not open for breakfast unless the morning meal is specifically mentioned.

Parking accommodations are mentioned only when a restaurant has made special arrangements; otherwise you're on your own. There is usually a charge for valet parking. Validated parking is not necessarily free and unlimited; often there is a nominal charge and a restriction on the length of time.

Restaurants do change their policies about hours, credit cards, and the like. It is always best to make inquiries in advance.

The most highly recommended restaurants are indicated by a star ★.

The price ranges listed below are for an average three-course meal. A significant trend among more expensive restaurants is the bar menu, which provides light snacks—hot dogs, chili, pizza, and appetizers—in the bar for a cost that is often less than $10 for two.

Category	Cost*
$$$$	over $45
$$$	$30–$45
$$	$18–$30
$	under $18

per person, excluding drinks, service, and 8¹/₂% sales tax

The following credit card abbreviations are used: AE, American Express; DC, Diners Club; MC, MasterCard; V, Visa. Many restaurants accept cards other than those listed here, and some will accept personal checks if you carry a major credit card.

American

Before the 1980s, it was hard to find a decent "American" restaurant in the Bay Area. In recent years, however, the offerings have grown and diversified, with fare that includes barbecue,

Southwestern, all-American diner food, and that mix of Mediterranean-Asian-Latino known as California cuisine.

Civic Center
★

Stars. This is the culinary temple of Jeremiah Tower, the superchef who claims to have invented California cuisine. Stars is a must on every traveling gourmet's itinerary, but it's also where many of the local movers and shakers hang out, a popular place for post-theater dining, and open till the wee hours. The dining room has a clublike ambience, and the food ranges from grills to ragouts to sautés—some daringly creative and some classical. Dinners here are pricey, but if you're on a budget, you can have a hot dog at the bar. *150 Redwood Alley, tel. 415/861–7827. Reservations accepted up to 2 wks in advance, some tables reserved for walk-ins. Dress: informal. AE, DC, MC, V. No lunch weekends. Valet parking at night. $$$*

Stars Cafe. For some years, a casual café adjacent to Stars offered a taste of Jeremiah Tower's renowned cuisine at down-to-earth prices. Now the satellite café has moved into its own orbit in much larger quarters around the corner. Both bar and table seating is available. Highlights are pizzas from the wood-burning oven and desserts by Stars' noted pastry chef Emily Luchetti. *500 Van Ness Ave., tel. 415/861–4344. Reservations accepted for 5 or more. Dress: informal. AE, DC, MC, V. $–$$*

Embarcadero North
★

Fog City Diner. This is where the diner and grazing crazes began in San Francisco, and the popularity of this spot knows no end. The long, narrow dining room emulates a luxurious railroad car with dark wood paneling, huge windows, and comfortable booths. The cooking is innovative, drawing its inspiration from regional cooking throughout the United States. The sharable "small plates" are a fun way to go. *1300 Battery St., tel. 415/982–2000. Reservations advised. Dress: informal. DC, MC, V. $$*

MacArthur Park. Year after year San Franciscans acclaim this as their favorite spot for ribs, but the oakwood smoker and mesquite grill also turn out a wide variety of all-American fare, from steaks, hamburgers, and chili to seafood. Takeout is also available at this handsomely renovated pre-earthquake warehouse. *607 Front St., tel. 415/398–5700. Reservations advised. Dress: informal. AE, DC, MC, V. No lunch weekends and major holidays. Valet parking at night. $$*

Embarcadero South

Boulevard. Two of San Francisco's top restaurant talents teamed up in 1993 in one of the city's most magnificent landmark buildings. The culinary half of the team is chef Nancy Oakes, who received national acclaim for her sophisticated French-accented American cooking at her tiny L'Avenue bistro (now closed). The design partner is Pat Kuleto, creator of numerous award-winning restaurant interiors in the Bay Area and abroad. The setting is the 1889 Audiffred Building, a Parisian look-alike that was one of the few to survive the 1906 earthquake and fire. Oake's menu is seasonally in flux, but you can be certain to find her signature juxtaposition of aristocratic fare—foie gras is a favorite—with homey comfort foods like pot roast with mashed potatoes. There will be a long wait for a reservation, but you can always drop in for a bite from the bar menu. *1 Mission St., tel.*

Downtown San Francisco Dining

415/543–6084. Reservations advised 3 wks in advance. Jacket and tie suggested at night. AE, MC, V. No lunch weekends. Valet parking. $$–$$$

Harry Denton's. Every night's a party at this new waterfront hangout, where singles congregate in a Barbary Coast–style bar and the rugs are rolled up at 10:30 on Thursday, Friday, and Saturday nights for dancing in the dining room. Sometimes Harry himself—the city's best-known saloon keeper—dances on the bar. But at lunchtime the place is quieter, attracting diners with its fine bay view and earthy saloon food: cheesy onion soup, burgers, oyster loaf, pot roast, and the like. Breakfast is served daily and extends to brunch on weekends. *161 Steuart St., tel. 415/882–1333. Reservations advised. Dress: informal. AE, DC, MC, V. Valet parking nights, except Sun. $$*

One Market. A giant among American chefs, Bradley Ogden gained fame at Campton Place and later at his Lark Creek Inn in Marin County. In 1993, he and partner Mike Dellar opened this huge, bustling brasserie across from the Ferry Building. The two-tier dining room seats 170 and a large bar-café serves snacks from noon on. With his move back to the city, Odgen's cuisine has acquired a slight Italian accent. Polenta and pasta now share the spotlight with pot roast and garlic mashed potatoes. One large table next to the kitchen is reserved for singles to eat community style, and there's a table for seven smack in the middle of the kitchen. There's a jazz brunch on Sunday. *1 Market St., tel. 415/777–5577. Reservations advised for dining room 2 wks in advance; open seating in bar-café. Dress: informal. AE, DC, MC, V. No lunch Sat. Valet parking. $$*

Financial District **Cypress Club.** Fans of John Cunin have flocked here since 1990 when Masa's long-time maître d' opened his own place, which he calls a "San Francisco brasserie." This categorizes the contemporary American cooking somewhat, but the decor defies description. It could be interpreted as anything from a parody of an ancient temple to a futuristic space war. *500 Jackson St., tel. 415/296–8555. Reservations advised. Dress: informal. AE, DC, MC, V. No lunch. Valet parking at night. $$$*

Nob Hill **Ritz-Carlton Restaurant and Dining Room.** There are two ★ distinctly different places to eat in this neoclassical Nob Hill showplace. The Restaurant, a cheerful, informal spot with a large patio for outdoor dining, serves breakfast, lunch, dinner, and a Sunday jazz brunch. The Dining Room, formal and elegant with a harpist playing, serves only two- to five-course dinners, which are uniquely priced by the course, not by the item. Except for the chef's five-course tasting menu, there's a wide selection of choices at the Dining Room. Both rooms present a superb version of Northern California cooking that is basically American utilizing local products and adding Mediterranean and Asian overtones. The culinary master behind this is chef Gary Danko, who developed the menu for the Restaurant and then went on to win four-star reviews as executive chef of the Dining Room. *600 Stockton St., tel. 415/296–7465. Reservations advised. Dress: informal in the Restaurant, jacket and tie requested in the Dining*

Room. AE, DC, MC, V. The Dining Room closed Sun. Valet parking. $$–$$$

North Beach **Bix.** The owners of Fog City Diner have re-created a '40s supper club in a historic building that was an assay office in gold-rush days. The place resembles a theater, with a bustling bar and dining tables downstairs and banquettes on the balcony. Opt for the lower level; the acoustics upstairs are dreadful. The menu offers contemporary renditions of 1940s fare; there's piano music in the evenings. *56 Gold St., tel. 415/433–6300. Reservations advised. Dress: informal. AE, DC, MC, V. No lunch weekends. Valet parking at night. $$*

Pacific **Pacific Heights Bar & Grill.** This popular neighborhood hangout
Heights on chic upper Fillmore built its reputation on its terrific oyster bar, and knowledgeable shuckers find that's still the best reason for going there. But the menu in the small dining room has recently departed from a seafood theme to include an eclectic range of meat, poultry, shellfish, pasta dishes, and sandwiches. *2001 Fillmore St., tel. 415/567–3337. Reservations advised. Dress: informal. AE, DC, MC, V. No lunch Mon. and Tues. $$*

Perry's. The West Coast equivalent of P.J. Clarke's in Manhattan, this popular watering hole and meeting place for the button-down singles set serves good, honest saloon food—London broil, corned-beef hash, one of the best hamburgers in town, and a great breakfast. Brunch is served on weekends. *1944 Union St., tel. 415/922–9022. Reservations accepted. Dress: informal. AE, MC, V. $$*

Union **Postrio.** This is the place for those who want to see and be seen;
Square there's always a chance to catch a glimpse of some celebrity,
★ including Postrio's owner, superchef Wolfgang Puck, who periodically commutes from Los Angeles to make an appearance in the restaurant's open kitchen. A stunning three-level bar and dining area is highlighted by palm trees and museum-quality contemporary paintings. The food is Puckish Californian with Mediterranean and Asian overtones, emphasizing pastas, grilled seafood, and house-baked breads. A substantial breakfast and bar menu (with great pizza) are served here, too. *545 Post St., tel. 415/776–7825. Reservations advised. Jacket and tie suggested. AE, DC, MC, V. Valet parking. $$$–$$$$*

★ **Campton Place.** This elegant, ultrasophisticated small hotel put new American cooking on the local culinary map. Chef Todd Humphries carries on the innovative traditions of opening chef Bradley Ogden with great aplomb and has added his own touches, such as embellishing traditional American dishes with ethnic flavors from recent immigrations. You might find cilantro and Szechuan peppers, for example, in his Nantucket Bay scallops. Breakfast and brunch are major events. A bar menu offers some samplings of appetizers, plus a caviar extravaganza. *340 Stockton St., tel. 415/955–5555. Reservations suggested, 2 wks in advance on weekends. Jacket required at dinner; tie requested. AE, DC, MC, V. Valet parking. $$$*

La Scene Café & Bar. This sleek little gem in the Warwick St. Regis Hotel provides an elegant and sophisticated setting for pre- or post-theater dining. Drawings of theatrical luminaries line the walls, and light classics or show tunes are played on a baby grand. The restaurant is owned by a French hotel group, but the cuisine shows more Asian and Latin-American influences than you might expect. A sure winner is the house-cured salmon, sometimes served with corn cakes, crème fraîche, and salmon caviar. The bar menu is available until midnight, and the café is open for breakfast. *490 Geary St., tel. 415/292–6430. Reservations advised. Dress: informal. AE, DC, MC, V. No lunch. No dinner Sun. and Mon. Valet parking at night. $$*

Chinese

For nearly a century, Chinese restaurants in San Francisco were confined to Chinatown and the cooking was largely an Americanized version of peasant-style Cantonese. The past few decades, however, have seen an influx of restaurants representing the wide spectrum of Chinese cuisine: the subtly seasoned fare of Canton, the hot and spicy cooking of Hunan and Szechuan, the northern style of Peking, where meat and dumplings replace seafood and rice as staples, and, more recently, some more esoteric cooking, such as Hakka and Chao Chow. The current rage seems to be the high-style influence of Hong Kong. These restaurants are now scattered throughout the city, leaving Chinatown for the most part to tourists.

Embarcadero North ★ **Harbor Village.** Classic Cantonese cooking, dim-sum lunches, and fresh seafood from the restaurant's own tanks are the hallmarks of this 400-seat branch of a Hong Kong establishment, which sent five of its master chefs to San Francisco to supervise the kitchen. The setting is opulent, with Chinese antiques and teak furnishings. *4 Embarcadero Center, tel. 415/781–8833. Reservations not accepted for lunch on weekends. Dress: informal. AE, DC, MC, V. Validated parking in Embarcadero Center Garage. $$*

Embarcadero South **Wu Kong.** Tucked away in the splashy Art Deco Rincon Center, Wu Kong features the cuisine of Shanghai and Canton. Specialties include dim sum; braised yellow fish; and the incredible vegetarian goose, one of Shanghai's famous mock dishes, created from paper-thin layers of dried bean-curd sheets and mushrooms. *101 Spear St., tel. 415/957–9300. Reservations advised. Dress: informal. AE, DC, MC, V. Validated parking at Rincon Center garage. $$*

Financial District **Yank Sing.** This tea house has grown by leaps and branches with the popularity of dim sum. The Battery Street location seats 300 and the older, smaller Stevenson Street site has recently been rebuilt in high-tech style. *427 Battery St., tel. 415/362–1640; 49 Stevenson St., tel. 415/495–4510. Reservations advised. Dress: informal. AE, MC, V. No dinner. Stevenson site closed weekends. $*

North Beach **Fortune.** The Chao Chow tradition of the southern coast of China is well represented in this small restaurant on the edge of Chinatown. Among the complexly seasoned dishes for which Chao Chow cooking is noted are braised duck with a garlicky vinegar sauce and an eggy oyster cake. *675 Broadway, tel. 415/421–8130. Reservations advised. Dress: informal. MC, V. $*

Hunan. Henry Chung's first café on Kearny Street had only six tables, but his Hunanese cooking merited six stars from critics nationwide. He has now opened this larger place on Sansome Street; it's equally plain but has 250 seats. Smoked dishes are a specialty, and Henry guarantees no MSG. *924 Sansome St., tel. 415/956–7727. Reservations advised. Dress: informal. AE, DC, MC, V. $*

Richmond District ★
Hong Kong Flower Lounge. Many Chinaphiles swear that this outpost of a famous Asian restaurant chain serves the best Cantonese food in town. The seafood is spectacular, as is the dim sum. *5322 Geary Blvd., tel. 415/668–8998. Reservations advised. Dress: informal. AE, DC, MC, V. $$*

Ton Kiang. The lightly seasoned Hakka cuisine of south China, rarely found in this country, was introduced to San Francisco here with regional specialties like salt-baked chicken and casseroles of meat and seafood cooked in clay pots. But the menu has grown to more than 150 items, including many Szechuan dishes and over 50 choices of seafood. There are two branches on Geary Boulevard. The newest, at 5821, is more stylish, and has a dim-sum menu. *3148 Geary Blvd., tel. 415/752–4440; 5821 Geary Blvd., tel. 415/387–8273. Reservations advised. Dress: informal. MC, V. $*

French

French cooking has gone in and out of vogue in San Francisco since the extravagant days of the Bonanza Kings. A renaissance of the classic haute cuisine occurred during the 1960s, but recently a number of these restaurants closed. Meanwhile, nouvelle cuisine went in and out of fashion, and the big draw now is the bistro or brasserie.

vic Center
California Culinary Academy. This historic theater houses one of the most highly regarded professional cooking schools in the United States. Watch the student chefs at work on the double-tier stage while you dine on classic French cooking. Prix-fixe meals and bountiful buffets are served in the main dining room, and there's an informal grill on the lower level. *625 Polk St., tel. 415/771–3500. Reservations advised (2–4 wks for Fri. night buffet). Jacket and tie requested. AE, DC, MC, V. Closed weekends. $$–$$$*

Embarcadero South
Bistro Roti. Tables in the rear of this waterfront café overlook the bay and bridge, while those at the front surround a boisterous bar. A giant rotisserie and grill turn out succulent chops and roasts, but don't overlook that bistro classic: French onion soup. *155 Steuart St., tel. 415/495–6500. Reservations advised. Dress: informal. AE, DC, MC, V. No lunch weekends. $$*

Financial District
Le Central. This is the quintessential bistro: noisy and crowded, with nothing subtle about the cooking. But the garlicky pâtés, leeks vinaigrette, cassoulet, and grilled blood sausage with crisp french fries keep the crowds coming. *453 Bush St., tel. 415/391–2233. Reservations advised. Dress: informal. AE, DC, MC, V. Closed Sun. $$*

Midtown
★

La Folie. This pretty storefront café showcases the nouvelle cuisine of Roland Passot, a former sous-chef at Illinois's famous Le Français. Much of the food is edible art—whimsical presentations that recall palm trees or peacocks; even a soup garnish that looks like a giant ladybug. The fun spirit of the place matches the cuisine, with Passot's wife Jamie acting as hostess in the best *mere-pere* tradition. *2316 Polk St., tel. 415/776–5577. Reservations advised. Dress: informal. AE, DC, MC, V. No lunch. Closed Sun. $$$*

North Beach

Ernie's. This famous old-timer recently had a face-lift and now conjures up innovative light versions of French classics. Even so, Ernie's is still steeped with the aura of Gay Nineties San Francisco and is about the only place in town that offers tableside service. *847 Montgomery St., tel. 415/397–5969. Reservations advised. Jacket required. AE, DC, MC, V. No lunch. Valet parking. $$$$*

Des Alpes. Basque dinners are offered here, with soup, salad, *two* entrées—sweetbreads on puff pastry and rare roast beef are a typical pair—ice cream, and coffee included in the budget price. This haven for trenchermen is a pleasant spot, with wood-paneled walls and bright, embroidered cloths on the tables. Service is family style. *732 Broadway, tel. 415/788–9900. Reservations advised on weekends. Dress: informal. MC, V. No lunch. Closed Mon. $*

Pacific Heights

The Sherman House. Cloistered in a 19th-century mansion, the intimate, candlelit dining room of the city's most exclusive small hotel is a favorite special-occasion destination for San Franciscans. Dinners are either à la carte or prix-fixe. Breakfast and a lovely Sunday brunch are served in the solarium with a partial view of the bay. *2160 Green St., tel. 415/563–3600. Reservations required. Jacket required at dinner. AE, DC, MC, V. Valet parking at dinner. $$$$*

Richmond District
★

Alain Rondelli. A career beginning at a legendary three-star kitchen in Burgundy (L'Esperance) and leading to a modest block in San Francisco's Richmond District may sound like it's headed down, but for Paris-born chef Alain Rondelli—and his loyal clientele—it's a dream come true. After a three-year stint at Ernie's (*see above*), this enormously talented young Frenchman opened his own beguiling little restaurant in 1993. The cuisine adapts Rondelli's background in classic-yet-contemporary French cooking to the agricultural abundance and Asian and Hispanic influences of his adopted state. A zap of jalapeño chili here, a bit of star anise there; a Rondelli signature is his two-part entrée, such as a breast of chicken, followed up with a confit of the leg in a custard tart. Desserts range from homey to exquisite. *126 Clement St., tel. 415/387–0408. Reservations advised. Dress: informal. MC, V. Closed Mon. $$–$$$*

South of Market
★

Fringale. The bright-yellow paint on this dazzling bistro stands out like a beacon on an otherwise bleak industrial street, attracting a Pacific Heights–Montgomery Street clientele. They come for the French Basque-inspired creations of Biarritz-born chef Gerald Hirigoyen—at remarkably reasonable prices. Hallmarks include Roquefort ravioli, rare ahi (tuna) with onion marmalade, and the ultimate crème brûlée. *570 Fourth St., tel. 415/543-0573. Reservations required. Dress: informal. AE, MC, V. No lunch Sat. Closed Sun. $$*

Union **Fleur de Lys.** The creative cooking of chef-partner Hubert
Square Keller is drawing rave reviews for this romantic spot that some
★ consider the best French restaurant in town. The menu changes
constantly, but such dishes as lobster soup with lemongrass are
a signature. The intimate dining room, like a sheikh's tent, is
encased with hundreds of yards of paisley. *777 Sutter St., tel.
415/673-7779. Weekend reservations advised 2 wks in advance.
Jacket required. AE, DC, MC, V. No lunch. Closed Sun. Valet parking. $$$$*

★ **Masa's.** Chef Julian Serrano carries on the tradition of the late
Masa Kobayashi. In fact, some Masa regulars even say the cooking is better. The artistry of the presentation is as important as
the food itself in this pretty, flower-filled dining spot in the Vintage Court Hotel. *648 Bush St., tel. 415/989-7154. Reservations
accepted up to 2 months in advance. Jacket and tie required. AE,
DC, MC, V. No lunch. Closed Sun., Mon., and several weeks in late
Dec. and early Jan. Valet parking. $$$$*

Brasserie Savoy. This lively theater-district eaterie takes its cues
from Parisian brasseries with a long bar, an open kitchen, and
adaptations on French bourgeois cuisine, but the end result is
an ambience that recalls old San Francisco. A signature is the
seafood extravaganza, a pedestaled platter of assorted shellfish
heaped on ice. An oyster bar and late-supper menu are also available. *580 Geary St., tel. 415/474-8686. Reservations advised. Dress:
informal. AE, DC, MC, V. No lunch. Closed Mon. Valet parking.
$$*

City of Paris. In this new bistro smack in the middle of theater
row, every effort was made to replicate a typical Parisian bistro—jammed-together tables, an open kitchen where plump
chickens slowly turn on an ornate cast-iron and brass rotisserie,
and such bistro classics as *petit salé* (pork pickled in brine), *gîte
gîte* (skirt steak with frites), and French onion soup. But unlike
prices in the City of Lights, the prices here (same at lunch and
dinner) are remarkably low. *101 Shannon Alley (off Geary St.
between Jones and Taylor), tel. 415/441-4442. Reservations advised. Dress: informal. AE, MC, V. Valet parking. $–$$*

Greek and Middle Eastern

The foods of Greece and the Middle East have much in common:
a preponderance of lamb and eggplant dishes, a widespread use
of phyllo pastry, and an abundance of pilaf.

North Beach **Maykadeh.** Here you'll find authentic Persian cooking in a setting so elegant that the modest check comes as a great surprise.
Lamb dishes with rice are the specialties. *470 Green St., tel.
415/362-8286. Reservations advised. Dress: informal. AE, MC, V.
Valet parking at night. $–$$*

Helmand. Don't be put off by its location on a rather scruffy
block of Broadway. The Helmand offers authentic cooking of Af-

ghanistan, elegant surroundings with white napery and rich Afghan carpets, and amazingly low prices. Don't miss the *aushak* (leek-filled ravioli served with yogurt and ground beef). The lamb dishes are also exceptional. *430 Broadway, tel. 415/362–0641. Reservations advised. Dress: informal. AE, MC, V. No lunch weekends. Free validated parking at night at 468 Broadway. $*

South of Market **S. Asimakopoulos Cafe.** Terrific Greek food at reasonable prices keeps the crowds waiting for seats at the counter or at bare-topped tables in this storefront café. The menu is large and varied, but lamb dishes are the stars. Convenient to Showplace Square. *288 Connecticut St., Potrero Hill, tel. 415/552–8789. No reservations. Dress: informal. AE, MC, V. No lunch weekends. $–$$*

Sunset District **Ya-Ya Cuisine.** Yahya Salih has brought the culinary treasures of Iraqi cuisine to a delightful storefront café and embellished them with Mediterranean and Californian touches. Of note are the charcoal-grilled river fish and dishes based on Basmati rice, which is indigenous to Iraq. *1220 Ninth Ave., tel. 415/566–6966. Dress: informal. AE, MC, V. No lunch weekends. Closed Mon. $$*

Indian

The following restaurants serve the cuisine of northern India, which is more subtly seasoned and not as hot as its southern counterparts. They also specialize in succulent meats and crispy breads from the clay-lined tandoori oven.

Marina **North India.** Small and cozy, this restaurant has a more limited menu and hotter seasoning than Gaylord's. Both tandoori dishes and curries are served, plus a range of breads and appetizers. Everything is cooked to order. *3131 Webster St., tel. 415/931–1556. Reservations advised. Dress: informal. AE, DC, MC, V. No lunch weekends. Parking behind restaurant. $$*

Northern Waterfront and Embarcadero **Gaylord's.** A vast selection of mildly spiced northern Indian food is offered here, along with meats and breads from the tandoori ovens and a wide range of vegetarian dishes. The dining rooms are elegantly appointed with Indian paintings and gleaming silver service. The Ghirardelli Square location offers bay views. *Ghirardelli Sq., tel. 415/771–8822; Embarcadero 1, tel. 415/397–7775. Reservations advised. Dress: informal. AE, DC, MC, V. No lunch Sun. at Embarcadero. Validated parking at Ghirardelli Sq. garage and Embarcadero Center garage. $$*

Italian

Italian food in San Francisco spans the "boot" from the mild cooking of northern Italy to the spicy cuisine of the south. Then there is the style indigenous to San Francisco, known as North Beach Italian—such dishes as *cioppino* (a fisherman's stew) and Joe's special (a mélange of eggs, spinach, and ground beef).

Embarcadero North **Il Fornaio.** An offshoot of the Il Fornaio bakeries, this handsome tile-floored, wood-paneled complex combines a café, bakery, and upscale trattoria with outdoor seating. The cooking is Tuscan, featuring pizzas from a wood-burning oven, superb house-made pastas and gnocchi, and grilled poultry and seafood. Anticipate a wait for a table, but once seated you won't be disappointed— only surprised by the moderate prices. *Levi's Plaza, 1265 Battery St., tel. 415/986–0100. Reservations advised. Dress: informal. AE, DC, MC, V. Valet parking. $$*

Financial District **Palio d'Asti.** This moderately priced venture of restaurateur Gianni Fassio draws a lively Financial District lunch crowd. Some specialties are Piedmontese, and a good show is provided by the open kitchen and pizza oven, as well as the rolling carts of antipasti. *640 Sacramento St., tel. 415/395–9800. Reservations advised. Dress: informal. AE, DC, MC. No lunch Sat. Closed Sun. $$*

Marina **Ristorante Parma.** This is a warm, wonderfully honest trattoria with excellent food at modest prices. The antipasti tray, with a dozen unusual items, is one of the best in town, and the pastas and veal are exceptional. Don't pass up the spinach gnocchi when it is offered. *3314 Steiner St., tel. 415/567–0500. Reservations advised. Dress: informal. AE, MC, V. No lunch Sat. Closed Sun. $$*

Midtown **Acquarello.** This exquisite restaurant is one of the most roman-
★ tic spots in town. The service and food are exemplary, and the menu covers the full range of Italian cuisine, from northern Italy to the tip of the boot. Desserts are exceptional. *1722 Sacramento St., tel. 415/567–5432. Reservations advised. Dress: informal. AE, DC, MC, V. No lunch. Closed Sun. and Mon. $$–$$$*

North Beach **Buca Giovanni.** Giovanni Leoni showcases the dishes of his
★ birthplace, the Serchio Valley in Tuscany, and grows many of the vegetables and herbs used in his recipes at his Mendocino County ranch. Pastas made on the premises are a specialty, and the calamari salad is one of the best around. The subterranean dining room is cozy and romantic. *800 Greenwich St., tel. 415/776– 7766. Reservations advised. Dress: informal. AE, DC, MC, V. No lunch. Closed Sun and Mon. $$*

Capp's Corner. At one of the last of the family-style trattorias, diners sit elbow to elbow at long oilcloth-covered tables to feast on bountiful, well-prepared five-course dinners. For calorie-counters or the budget-minded, a shorter dinner includes a tureen of minestrone, salad, and pasta. *1600 Powell St., tel. 415/989–2589. Reservations advised. Dress: informal. AE, DC, MC, V. No lunch weekends. Credit toward meal check for parking in garage across the street. $*

Russian Hill **Hyde Street Bistro.** The ambience says quintessential neighbor-hood bistro, but the food is part *gasthaus*, part trattoria, and closely in line with the Austro-Italian tradition of Italy's north-eastern Frioli region. Strudels and spaetzles are served along-side pastas and polentas, potato dumplings are paired with a gorgonzola sauce, and the pastries belie the chef-owner's Aus-trian roots. *1521 Hyde St., tel. 415/441–7778. Reservations advised. Dress: informal. MC, V. No lunch. $$*

South of Market **Ristorante Ecco.** Hidden within a labyrinth of industrial sprawl is South Park, one of the city's most fashionable addresses in the 1850s. Now the tree-filled square is being gentrified with lofts of artists and designers and one of the city's best new Italian cafés—Ecco. The cooking is robust; select from zesty antipasti like deep-fried polenta. The kitchen performs best with hearty main dishes like osso buco and braised rabbit. Ask for a seat in the main dining room, which overlooks the square. *101 South Park, tel. 415/495–3291. Reservations advised. Dress: informal. AE, MC, V. No lunch Sat. Closed Sun. $$*

Ruby's. The local pizza lovers' cult claims that Ruby's cornmeal crust is the best in town, and toppings like gorgonzola with roasted garlic, walnuts, and tomatoes keep things lively. But pizza is only part of the story here: There's also a host of creative small plates and a range of unusual pastas, fish, poultry, and meats to choose from. Save room for a memorable dessert. *489 Third St., tel. 415/541–0795. Reservations accepted for 6 or more. Dress: informal. AE, DC, MC, V. No lunch weekends. $$*

Union Square

Emporio Armani Express. Designer Giorgio Armani is best known for his clothing, but with little fanfare he has also designed some smart little cafés within his boutiques in London, Costa Mesa, Seoul—and now San Francisco. Here, under the Pantheon-like dome of a former bank building, tables and banquettes are set on a mezzanine overlooking the store's main floor. The food is exquisite northern Italian fare uncluttered by clichés. For antipasti, try the *breseaoloa* (paper-thin slices of air-dried beef) tossed with baby greens and artichoke hearts, or the grilled polenta, crowned with sautéed wild mushrooms. The pastas are also recommended, and the desserts—often the weak spot of an Italian meal—are superb. *1 Grant Ave., tel. 415/677–9010. Reservations advised. Dress: informal. AE, DC, MC, V. Closed Sun. $$*

Kuleto's. The contemporary cooking of northern Italy, the atmosphere of old San Francisco, and an antipasti bar have made this spot off Union Square a hit since it opened in the 1980s. Publike booths and a long, open kitchen fill one side of the restaurant; a gardenlike setting with light splashed from skylights lies beyond. Grilled seafood dishes are among the specialties. Breakfast is served, too. *221 Powell St., tel. 415/397–7720. Reservations advised. Dress: informal. AE, DC, MC, V. $$*

Japanese

To understand a Japanese menu, you should be familiar with the basic types of cooking: *yaki*, marinated and grilled foods; *tempura*, fish and vegetables deep-fried in a light batter; *udon* and *soba*, noodle dishes; *domburi*, meats and vegetables served over rice; *ramen*, noodles served in broth; and *nabemono*, meals cooked in one pot, often at the table. Sushi bars are extremely popular in San Francisco; most offer a selection of *sushi*, vinegared rice with fish or vegetables, and *sashimi*, raw fish. Western seating refers to conventional tables and chairs; *tatami* seating is on mats at low tables.

Chinatown

Yamato. The city's oldest Japanese restaurant is by far its most beautiful, with inlaid wood, painted panels, a meditation garden, and a pool. Both Western and tatami seating, in private shoji-screened rooms, are offered, along with a fine sushi bar. Come primarily for the atmosphere; the menu is somewhat limited, and more adventurous dining can be found elsewhere. *717 California St., tel. 415/397–3456. Reservations advised. Dress: informal. AE, DC, MC, V. No lunch weekends. Closed Mon. $$*

Financial District ★ **Kyo-ya.** Rarely replicated outside Japan, the refined experience of dining in a fine Japanese restaurant has been introduced with extraordinary authenticity at this new showplace within the Sheraton Palace Hotel. In Japan, a *kyo-ya* is a nonspecialized restaurant that serves a wide range of food types. And, at this Kyo-ya, the range is spectacular—encompassing tempuras, one-pot dishes, deep-fried and grilled meats, not to mention a choice of some three dozen sushi selections. The lunch menu is more limited than dinner, but does offer a *shokado*, a sampler of four classic dishes encased in a handsome lacquered lunch box. *Sheraton Palace Hotel, 2 New Montgomery St., at Market St., tel. 415/546–5000. Reservations advised. Dress: informal. AE, DC, MC, V. Closed weekends. $$–$$$*

Japantown **Sanppo.** This small place has an enormous selection of almost every type of Japanese food: yakis, nabemono dishes, domburi, udon, and soba, not to mention feather-light tempura and interesting side dishes. Western seating only. *1702 Post St., tel. 415/346–3486. No reservations. Dress: informal. MC, V. Closed Mon. Validated parking in Japan Center garage. $*

Richmond **Kabuto Sushi.** For one of the most spectacular acts in town, head out Geary Boulevard past Japantown to tiny Kabuto. Here, behind his black-lacquered counter, master chef Sachio Kojima flashes his knives with the grace of a samurai warrior to prepare sushi and sashimi of exceptional quality. Traditional Japanese dinners are also served in the adjoining dining room with both Western seating and, in a shoji-screened area, *tatami* seating. *5116 Geary Blvd., tel. 415/752–5652. Reservations advised for dinner. Dress: informal. MC, V. No lunch. Closed Mon. $$*

Mediterranean

In its climate and topography, its agriculture and viticulture, and the orientation of many of its early settlers, northern California resembles the Mediterranean region. But until quite recently no restaurant billed itself as "Mediterranean." Those that do so now primarily offer a mix of southern French and northern Italian food, but some include accents from Spain, Greece, and more distant ports of call.

Civic Center ★ **Zuni Cafe Grill.** Zuni's Italian-Mediterranean menu and its unpretentious atmosphere pack in the crowds from early morning to late evening. A balcony dining area overlooks the large bar, where shellfish, one of the best oyster selections in town, and drinks are dispensed. A second dining room houses the giant pizza oven and grill. Even the hamburgers have an Italian accent—they're served on herbed focaccia buns. *1658 Market St.,* *tel. 415/552–2522. Reservations advised. Dress: informal. AE, MC, V. Closed Mon. $$–$$$*

Embarca- **Square One.** Chef Joyce Goldstein introduces an ambitious new
dero North menu daily, with dishes based on the classic cooking of the Medi-
★ terranean countries, although she sometimes strays to Asia and
Latin America. The dining room, with its views of the open
kitchen and the Golden Gateway commons, is an understated
setting for some of the finest food in town—and an award-winning wine list. A bar menu is available. *190 Pacific Ave., tel.
415/788–1110. Reservations advised. Dress: informal. AE, DC,
MC, V. No lunch weekends. Valet parking in evenings. $$–$$$*

Splendido. Mediterranean cooking is the focus at this handsome
new restaurant. Diners here are transported to the coast of
southern France or northern Italy by the pleasant decor; only
the bay view reminds you that you are in San Francisco. Among
the many winners are the shellfish soup and warm goat-cheese
and ratatouille salad. Desserts are truly *splendido.* A bar menu
is available. *Embarcadero 4, tel. 415/986–3222. Reservations advised. Dress: informal. AE, DC, MC, V. Validated parking at Em-
barcadero Center garage. $$*

North Beach **Moose's.** Longtime San Francisco restauranteur Ed Moose's
★ restaurant was destined to become a top celebrity hangout from
the moment it opened in 1992. Politicians and media types have
followed him from his former digs at Washington Square Bar &
Grill just across the large, tree-shaded plaza. Along with a host
of local luminaries, Tom Brokaw, Walter Cronkite, Tom Wolfe,
and Senator Dianne Feinstein head for Moose's when they're in
town. And the food impresses as much as the clientele: A Medi-
terranean-inspired menu highlights innovative appetizers, pas-
tas, seafood, and grills. The surroundings are classic and
comfortable, with views of Washington Square and Russian Hill
from a front café area and, in the rear facing the open kitchen,
counter seats for singles. There's live music at night and a fine
Sunday brunch. *1652 Stockton St., tel. 415/989–7800. Reservations
advised several wks in advance. Dress: informal. AE, DC, MC, V.
Valet parking. $$*

South of **LuLu.** Since opening day in 1993, a seat at this boisterous café
Market has been about the hottest ticket in town. Chef Reed Hearon has
★ brought a touch of the French-Italian Riviera to a spacious and
stunningly renovated San Francisco warehouse. Under the
high, barrel-vaulted ceiling, beside a large open kitchen, diners
feast on sizzling mussels roasted in an iron skillet, pizza with
calamari and aioli, ricotta gnocchi with butternut squash, and
wood-roasted Dungeness crab. Sharing dishes family-style is
the custom here. For those who like a quieter ambience, Hearon
has opened a little bistro, LuLu Bis, just next door, and offers
four-course prix-fixe dinners at communal tables. *816 Folsom
St., tel. 415/495–5775. Reservations advised. Dress: informal. AE,
MC, V. $–$$*

Union **Aioli.** The food and decor of this tiny bistro is a sunny potpourri
Square derived from the exotic locales in chef Sebastien Urbain's background, ranging from his birthplace on the French island of

Réunion in the Indian Ocean to cities in Africa, France, and the Middle East in which he served as chef for Méridien hotels. These culinary influences are bound together with a passion for garlic, as the name of the restaurant suggests. The garlicky sauce of Provence embellishes an extraordinary platter of mixed seafood. Sample the oysters baked in their shells with caramelized onions and a pungent puree of garlic. The soups are robust, and the pastas are outstanding. *469 Bush St., tel. 415/249–0900. Reservations advised. Dress: informal. AE, MC, V. $$*

Lascaux. Despite its Gallic name (after the primitive caves in France), the menu at this smart restaurant is primarily Mediterranean. Recently taken over by celebrity chef Elka Gilmore, the cuisine now has an appropriate French twist. A huge fireplace cheers the romantically lighted subterranean dining room. Live jazz is offered at night. *248 Sutter St., tel. 415/391–1555. Reservations advised. Dress: informal. AE, DC, MC, V. No lunch weekends. $$*

Mexican/Latin American

In spite of San Francisco's Mexican heritage, until recently most south-of-the-border eateries were locked into the Cal-Mex taco-enchilada-beans syndrome. But now some newer places offer a broader spectrum of Mexican and Latin American cooking.

Civic Center **Bahia.** An evening at this festive Brazilian café is like a quick trip to the tropics. Amid lush foliage, bold paintings, and the beat of the samba, you can feast on all the great Brazilian classics like *feijoada* (pork and black-bean stew), *bobo de camarão* (shrimp in coconut milk), and creamy chicken croquettes. In the early evening, there's a tapas bar. On Thursday, Friday, and Saturday nights, the music is live. And just down the street is Bahia's nightclub, which gyrates with the lambada until the wee hours. *41 Franklin St., tel. 415/626–3306. Reservations advised. Dress: informal. MC, V. $–$$*

Marina **Café Marimba.** Chef Reed Hearon struck gold in 1993. First he
★ and partner Louise Clement opened the sensationally popular LuLu (*see above*). Later that year, they launched this casual café as a showplace for their contemporary renditions of regional specialties. The colorful Mexican folk art that adorns the walls was collected during Hearon's numerous trips south of the border—as were the recipes: a silken *mole negro* from Oaxaca that appears in tamales and other dishes, shrimp prepared with roasted onions and tomatoes in the style of Zihuatenejo, chicken with a marinade from Yucatán stuffed into one of the world's greatest tacos. Though he imparts his own imaginative touches, Hearon is fanatic about the authenticity of preparation—onions, tomatoes, and chilies are dry-roasted in the ancient tradition of the *comal,* and the guacamole is made to order in a *molcajete* (the three-legged version of a pestle). And he has such a repertoire of salsas, he wrote a book on the subject—another hit of 1993! *2317 Chestnut St., tel. 415/776–1506. Reservations advised. Dress: informal. MC, V. $$*

South of **Chevy's.** Just across from Moscone center, this branch of a
Market popular Mexican minichain is decked with funky neon signs and
"El Machino" turning out flour tortillas. "Stop gringo food" is
the motto here, and the emphasis is on the freshest ingredients
and sauces. Of note are the fabulous fajitas and the grilled quail
and seafood. *4th and Howard Sts., tel. 415/543–8060. Reservations
accepted for parties of 8 or more. Dress: informal. AE, MC, V. Validated parking at garage under building (enter from Minna St.).*
$

Moroccan

San Francisco's Moroccan restaurants share a similarity of
decor, menu, and ritual. Diners are seated on pillows or hassocks
at low round tables for a sumptuous multicourse feast: spicy len-
til-based soup; platters of vegetables scooped up with Arabic
bread; *bastilla,* slivers of chicken, hard-boiled eggs, and almonds
layered with honey and cinnamon in paper-thin pastry; and a
choice of more than a dozen entrées. Most of the main dishes are
chicken or lamb stewed with various combinations of fruits and
vegetables. The finale is sweet Moroccan pastries washed down
with mint tea. The following restaurants, both in the Richmond
District, offer these banquets at quite moderate prices, considering the abundance of food.

Richmond **El Mansour.** *3123 Clement St., tel. 415/751–2312. Reservations ad-
District vised. Dress: informal. AE, DC, MC, V. No lunch. $*
Mamounia. *4411 Balboa St., tel. 415/752–6566. Reservations ad-
vised. Dress: informal. AE, MC, V. No lunch. Closed Mon. $*

Old San Francisco

Several of the city's landmark restaurants don't fit neatly into
any ethnic category. Some might call them Continental or
French or even American. But dating back to the turn of the
century or earlier, these places all exude the traditions and aura
of old San Francisco. The oldest one of them all, Tadich Grill, is
listed under Seafood.

Financial **Garden Court.** After a massive, two-year, multimillion-dollar
District renovation, the Garden Court of the Sheraton Palace hotel has
★ reemerged as the ultimate old San Francisco experience. From
breakfast through lunch, teatime, and the early dinner hours,
light splashes through the $7 million stained-glass ceiling
against the towering Ionic columns and crystal chandeliers. The
classic European menu highlights some famous dishes devised
by Palace chefs early this century, such as Green Goddess salad,
and the extravagant Sunday buffet brunch again takes center
stage as one of the city's great traditions. *Market and New Montgomery Sts., tel. 415/546–5000. Reservations advised. Jacket and
tie required at dinner. AE, DC, MC, V. $$$*
Jack's. Little has changed in more than 100 years at this bankers'
and brokers' favorite. The menu is extensive, but regulars opt
for the simple fare—steaks, chops, seafood, and stews. The din-
ing room, like the food, has an old-fashioned, no-nonsense aura,

and private upstairs rooms are available for top-secret meetings. *615 Sacramento St., tel. 415/986–9854. Reservations advised. Jacket requested. AE. No lunch Sat. Closed Sun.* $$

Union Square **Bardelli's.** Founded in 1906 as Charles' Oyster House, this turn-of-the-century showplace boasts vaulted ceilings, massive marble columns, and stained glass. The traditional menu mixes French, Italian, and American fare with superb fresh seafood. *243 O'Farrell St., tel. 415/982–0243. Reservations accepted. Dress: informal. AE, DC, MC, V. No lunch Sat. Closed Sun. Validated parking at Downtown Center garage.* $$

Seafood

Like all port cities, San Francisco takes pride in its seafood, even though less than half the fish served here is from local waters. In winter and spring look for the fresh Dungeness crab, best served cracked with mayonnaise. In summer, feast on Pacific salmon, even though imported varieties are available year-round. A recent development is the abundance of unusual oysters from West Coast beds and an outburst of oyster bars.

Civic Center ★ **Hayes Street Grill.** Eight to 15 different kinds of seafood are chalked on the blackboard each night at this extremely popular restaurant. The fish is served simply grilled, with a choice of sauces ranging from tartar to a spicy Szechuan peanut concoction. Appetizers are unusual, and desserts are lavish. *320 Hayes St., tel. 415/863–5545. Reservations should be made precisely 3 wks in advance. Dress: informal. AE, DC, MC, V. No lunch weekends.* $$

Financial District ★ **Aqua.** This quietly elegant and ultrafashionable spot is possibly the city's most important seafood restaurant ever. Chef-owner George Morrone has a supremely original talent for creating contemporary versions of French, Italian, and American classics: Expect mussel, crab, or lobster soufflés; lobster gnocchi with lobster sauce; shrimp and corn madeleines strewn in a salad; and ultrarare ahi paired with foie gras. Desserts are miniature museum pieces. *252 California St., tel. 415/956–9662. Reservations essential. Dress: informal. AE, DC, MC, V. No lunch Sat. Closed Sun. Valet parking at night.* $$$

Sam's Grill. Sam's and Tadich (*see below*) are two of the city's oldest restaurants and so popular for lunch that you must arrive before noon to get a table. No frills here. The aura is starkly old-fashioned; some booths are enclosed and curtained. Although the menu is extensive and varied, those in the know stick with the fresh local seafood and East Coast shellfish. *374 Bush St., tel. 415/421–0594. Reservations accepted only for parties of 6 or more. Dress: informal. AE, DC, MC, V. Closed weekends.* $$

Tadich Grill. Owners and locations have changed many times since this old-timer opened during the gold-rush era, but the 19th-century atmosphere remains, as does the kitchen's special way with seafood. Simple sautés are the best choices, or the cioppino during crab season. There is seating at both the counter and in private booths, but expect long lines for a table at lunchtime. *240 California St., tel. 415/391–2373. No reservations. Dress: informal. MC, V. Closed Sun. $$*

Japantown **Elka.** One of the most talked-about chefs in town nowadays is Elka Gilmore. Her innovative East-meets-West seafood cuisine has had the critics turning cartwheels since 1992 when she arrived at the Miyako Hotel, which rechristened its handsome multilevel dining room in her honor. For a starter, Elka's "Japanese box filled with small seafood dishes" is a must. It's a small wooden cabinet with nooks and crannies that conceal the changing whims of the chef—perhaps a dab of sturgeon mousse, a scallop garnished with foie gras, or a crab cake with corn relish. For desserts, Elka looks to the West with the likes of apple pie and ice cream. *1611 Post St., tel. 415/922–7788. Reservations advised. Dress: informal. AE, MC, V. $$–$$$*

Northern Waterfront **McCormick & Kuleto's.** This seafood emporium in Ghirardelli Square is a visitor's dream come true: a fabulous view of the bay from every seat in the house; an old San Francisco atmosphere; and some 30 varieties of fish and shellfish prepared in some 70 globe-circling ways, from tacos, pot stickers, and fish cakes to grills, pastas, and stew. The food has its ups and downs, but even on foggy days you can count on the view. *Ghirardelli Sq., tel. 415/929–1730. Reservations advised. Dress: informal. AE, DC, MC, V. Validated parking in Ghirardelli Sq. garage. $$*

Union Square **Bentley's Oyster Bar & Restaurant.** The bustling bar downstairs dispenses at least 10 different types of oysters. An upstairs dining room offers the eclectic seafood concoctions of chef Amey Shaw, who mixes and matches the hot-and-spicy flavors of Southeast Asia, the American Southwest, and the Mediterranean. *185 Sutter St., tel. 415/989–6895. Reservations advised. Dress: informal. AE, DC, MC, V. No lunch Sun. Validated parking at downstairs garage in the evening. $$*

Southeast Asian

In recent years San Franciscans have seen tremendous growth in the numbers of restaurants specializing in the foods of Thailand, Vietnam, and, most recently, Cambodia. The cuisines of these countries share many features, and one characteristic in particular: The cooking is highly spiced, and often very hot.

Civic Center **Thepin.** It seems as if there's a Thai restaurant on every block now, but this is the jewel in the crown. The stylish dining room sparkles with linen napery, fresh flowers, Thai artworks, and a wine list that surpasses the Asian norm. Notable are the duck dishes and the curries, each prepared with its own mixture of freshly blended spices. *298 Gough St., tel. 415/863–9335. Reservations advised. Dress: informal. AE, MC, V. No lunch weekends. $–$$*

Marina **Angkor Palace.** This is one of the loveliest Cambodian restaurants in town and also the most conveniently located for visitors. The extensive family-style menu offers such exotic fare as fish-and-coconut mousse baked in banana leaves. You'll have questions, of course, but you'll find the staff eager to explain the contents of the menu. *1769 Lombard St., tel. 415/931–2830. Reservations advised. Dress: informal. AE, MC, V. No lunch.* $

Midtown **Crustacean.** Vietnamese butter-roasted crab is the signature of this smart restaurant opened in 1991 by the An family, who have been preparing this treat in a Sunset hole-in-the-wall for some 20 years. But other crustaceans with a French-Vietnamese twist are offered here too: grilled tiger prawns tossed with garlicky buttered noodles, fried baguette slices spread with shrimp paste, stuffed squid, crab farci, and more. *1475 Polk St., tel. 415/776–2722. Reservations advised. Dress: informal. AE, DC, MC. V. No lunch. Valet parking at night.* $$

Richmond **Khan Toke Thai House.** The city's first Thai restaurant has a
District lovely dining room furnished with low tables and cushions, and
★ a garden view. The six-course dinners, with two entrées from an extensive choice, provide a delicious introduction to Thai cooking. The seasoning will be mild, unless you request it hot. Classical Thai dancing on Sunday. *5937 Geary Blvd., tel. 415/668–6654. Reservations advised. Dress: informal. AE, DC, MC, V. No lunch.* $–$$

South of **Manora.** When this homey Thai café way out on Mission Street
Market first opened, crowds from all over town were lined up for a table to try the extensive selection of carefully prepared dishes. Now there is a more conveniently located Manora, not far from the Performing Arts Center, with the same great food. Good choices are the fish cakes and the exemplary curries. *3226 Mission St., tel. 415/550–0856; 1600 Folsom St., tel. 415/861–6224. Dress: informal. MC, V. No lunch and closed Mon. at Mission St.; no lunch weekends at Folsom St.* $

Steak Houses

Although San Francisco traditionally has not been a meat-and-potatoes town, the popularity of steak is on the rise. Following are some of the best steak houses, but you can also get a good piece of beef at most of the better French, Italian, and American restaurants.

Marina **Izzy's Steak & Chop House.** Izzy Gomez was a legendary San Francisco saloonkeeper, and his namesake eatery carries on the tradition with terrific steaks, chops, and seafood, plus all the trimmings—such as cheesy scalloped potatoes and creamed spinach. A collection of Izzy memorabilia and antique advertising art covers almost every inch of wall space. *3345 Steiner St., tel. 415/563–0487. Reservations accepted. Dress: informal. AE, DC, MC, V. No lunch. Validated parking at Lombard Garage.* $$

Midtown **Harris'.** Ann Harris knows her beef. She grew up on a Texas
★ cattle ranch and was married to the late Jack Harris of Harris Ranch fame. In her own elegant restaurant she serves some of the best dry-aged steaks in town, but don't overlook the grilled seafood or poultry. There is also an extensive bar menu. *2100 Van Ness Ave., tel. 415/673–1888. Reservations recommended. Dress: informal. AE, DC, MC, V. No lunch. Valet parking.* $$$

Vegetarian

Aside from the restaurant mentioned below, vegetarians should also consider Gaylord's (*see* Indian restaurants, *above*), which offers a wide variety of meatless dishes from the Hindu cuisine.

Marina **Greens at Fort Mason.** This beautiful restaurant with its bay
★ views is a favorite with carnivores as well as vegetarians. Owned and operated by the Tassajara Zen Center of Carmel Valley, the restaurant offers a wide, eclectic, and creative spectrum of meatless cooking, and the bread promises nirvana. Dinners are à la carte on weeknights, but only a five-course prix-fixe dinner is served on Friday and Saturday. *Bldg. A, Fort Mason, tel. 415/771–6222. Reservations advised. Dress: informal. MC, V. No dinner Sun. Closed Mon. Public parking at Fort Mason Center. $$*

American Express offers Travelers Cheques built for two.

Cheques *for Two*^{SM} from American Express are the Travelers Cheques that allow either of you to use them because both of you have signed them. And only one of you needs to be present to purchase them.

Cheques *for Two* are accepted anywhere regular American Express Travelers Cheques are, which is just about everywhere. So stop by your bank, AAA* or any American Express Travel Service Office and ask for Cheques *for Two*.

Pack light.

Take the one number you need for any kind of call, anywhere you travel.

Checking in with your family back home? Calling for a tow truck? When you're on the road, the phone you use might not accept your calling card. Or you might get overcharged by an unknown telephone company. Here's the solution: dial 1 800 CALL ATT.[sm] You'll get flawless AT&T service, competitive calling card prices, and the lowest prices for collect calls from any phone, anywhere. Travel light. Just bring along this one simple number: 1 800 CALL ATT.

7 Lodging

By Laura Del Rosso and Patrick Hoctel

Patrick Hoctel is an Assistant Editor at the Bay Area Reporter *and writes arts features for several Bay Area publications.*

Few cities in the United States can rival San Francisco's variety in lodging. There are plush hotels ranked among the finest in the world, renovated older buildings that have the charm of Europe, bed-and-breakfasts in the city's Victorian "Painted Ladies," and the popular chain hotels found in most cities in the United States.

One of the brightest spots in the lodging picture is the transformation of handsome early 20th-century downtown high rises into small, distinctive hotels that offer personal service and European ambience. Another is the recent addition of ultradeluxe modern hotels such as the Nikko, Pan Pacific, ANA, and Mandarin Oriental, which promote their attentive Asian-style hospitality. On top of those offerings are the dozens of popular chain hotels that continually undergo face-lifts and additions to keep up with the competition.

The **San Francisco Convention and Visitors Bureau** (tel. 415/391–2001) publishes a free lodging guide with a map and listing of all hotels. Send $2 for postage and handling to Box 429097, San Francisco 94142-9097.

Because San Francisco is one of the top destinations in the United States for tourists as well as business travelers and convention goers, reservations are always advised, especially during the May–October peak season.

San Francisco's geography makes it conveniently compact. No matter what their location, the hotels listed below are on or close to public transportation lines. Some properties on Lombard Street and in the Civic Center area have free parking, but a car is more a hindrance than an asset in San Francisco.

Although not as high as the rates in New York, San Francisco hotel prices may come as a surprise to travelers from less urban areas. Average rates for double rooms downtown and at the wharf are in the $120 range. Adding to the expense is the city's 12% transient occupancy tax, which can significantly boost the cost of a lengthy stay. The good news is that because of the hotel building boom of the late 1980s, there is now an oversupply of rooms, which has led to much discounting of prices. Check for special rates and packages when making reservations.

If you are looking for truly budget accommodations (under $50), consider the Adelaide Inn (*see* Union Square/Downtown, *below*) and the **YMCA Central Branch.** *220 Golden Gate Ave., 94102, tel. 415/885–0460. 102 rooms, 3 with bath. Facilities: health club, pool, sauna. MC, V.*

An alternative to hotels and motels is staying in private homes and apartments, available through **American Family Inn/Bed & Breakfast San Francisco** (Box 420009, San Francisco 94142, tel. 415/931–3083), **Bed & Breakfast International–San Francisco** (Box 282910, San Francisco 94128–2910, tel. 415/696–1690 or 800/872–4500, fax 415/696–1699), and **American Property Exchange** (170 Page St., San Francisco 94102, tel. 415/863–8484 or 800/747–7784).

Home Exchange

This is obviously an inexpensive solution to the lodging problem, because house-swapping means living rent-free. You find a house, apartment, or other vacation property to exchange for your own by becoming a member of a home-exchange organization, which then sends you its annual directories listing available exchanges and includes your own listing in at least one of them. Arrangements for the actual exchange are made by the two parties to it, not by the organization. Principal clearinghouses include **Intervac U. S. /International Home Exchange** (Box 590504, San Francisco, CA 94159, tel. 415/435–3497), the oldest, with thousands of foreign and domestic homes for exchange in its three annual directories; membership is $62, or $72 if you want to receive the directories but remain unlisted. The **Vacation Exchange Club** (Box 650, Key West, FL 33041, tel. 800/638–3841), also with thousands of foreign and domestic listings, publishes four annual directories plus updates; the $50 membership includes your listing in one book. **Loan-a-Home** (2 Park La., Apt. 6E, Mount Vernon, NY 10552, tel. 914/664–7640) specializes in long-term exchanges; there is no charge to list your home, but the directories cost $35 or $45 depending on the number you receive.

Apartment and Villa Rentals

If you want a home base that's roomy enough for a family and comes with cooking facilities, a furnished rental may be the solution. It's generally cost-wise, too, although not always—some rentals are luxury properties (economical only when your party is large). Home-exchange directories do list rentals—often second homes owned by prospective house swappers—and there are services that can not only look for a house or apartment for you (even a castle if that's your fancy) but also handle the paperwork. Some send an illustrated catalogue and others send photographs of specific properties, sometimes at a charge; upfront registration fees may apply.

Among the companies are **Interhome Inc.** (124 Little Falls Rd., Fairfield, NJ 07004, tel. 201/882–6864) and **Rent a Home International** (7200 34th Ave. NW, Seattle, WA 98117, tel. 206/789–9377 or 800/488–7368). **Hideaways International** (767 Islington St., Box 4433, Portsmouth, NH 03802-4433, tel. 603/430–4433 or 800/843–4433, fax 603/430–4444) functions as a travel club. Membership ($99 yearly per person or family at the same address) includes two annual guides plus quarterly newsletters; rentals are arranged directly between members, not by the club staff.

The most highly recommended hotels are indicated by a star ★.

Category	Cost*
$$$$	over $175
$$$	$120–$175
$$	$80–$120
$	under $80

All prices are for a standard double room, excluding 12% tax.

The following credit card abbreviations are used: AE, American Express; DC, Diners Club; MC, MasterCard; V, Visa.

Union Square/Downtown

The largest variety and greatest concentration of hotels are in the city's downtown hub, Union Square, where hotel guests can find the best shopping, the theater district, and convenient transportation to every spot in San Francisco.

$$$$ **Campton Place Kempinski.** Behind a simple brownstone facade
★ with white awning, quiet reigns. Highly attentive, personal service—from assistance with unpacking to nightly turndown—begins the moment uniformed doormen greet guests outside the marble-floored lobby. The rooms are done with Asian touches in subtle tones of gold and brown and are relatively small but well appointed, with double-pane windows, Chinese armoires, and good-size writing desks. From the ninth floor up, there are only four rooms to a floor. They overlook an atrium, which lends a cozy, residential feel. The hotel is a 10-minute walk from the Moscone Center and the new Yerba Buena Center complex. The Anjou Restaurant, famed for its French cuisine, is on Campton Place, beside the hotel. *340 Stockton St., 94108, tel. 415/781–5555 or 800/426–3135, fax 415/955–5536. 126 rooms. Facilities: restaurant, bar. AE, DC, MC, V.*

★ **Four Seasons Clift.** The Clift towers over San Francisco's theater district. Its crisp, forest-green awnings and formal door service give hint of the elegance inside. In the busy lobby, dominated by dark paneling and four enormous chandeliers, everything runs smoothly. The Clift is noted for its swift personalized service; a phone call will get you everything from an interpreter to a chocolate cake. Color schemes differ from room to room: from dark woods, burgundies, and reds, to lighter palettes. The furniture includes a large writing desk, and plants and flowers are scattered throughout. Be sure to sample a cocktail in the famous Redwood Room lounge; it's an art-deco lover's dream, with chandeliers and a sweeping redwood bar. *495 Geary St., 94102, tel. 415/775–4700 or 800/332–3442, fax 415/441–4621. 329 rooms. Facilities: restaurant, lounge, exercise room, meeting rooms, complimentary morning limousine downtown. AE, DC, MC, V.*

Westin St. Francis. Host to the likes of Emperor Hirohito, Queen Elizabeth II, and many presidents, the St. Francis, with its imposing, immediately recognizable facade, black marble lobby, and gold-topped columns, looks more like a great public building than a hotel. However, the effect is softened by the columns and exquisite woodwork of the Compass Rose bar and restaurant; since its inception, this has been a retreat from the bustle of Union Square, especially for those in a romantic frame of mind. The guest rooms in the original building are rather small by modern standards and retain some of the 1904, Victorian-style moldings and bathroom tiles. The rooms in the modern tower are larger and have brighter, lacquered furniture. *335 Powell St., 94102, tel. 415/397–7000 or 800/228–3000, fax 415/774–0124. 1,200* *rooms. Facilities: 5 restaurants, 5 lounges, 24-hr room service, fitness center; shopping arcade. AE, DC, MC, V.*

$$$ **Galleria Park.** This hotel a few blocks east of Union Square is
★   close to the Chinatown gate and the Crocker Galleria, one of San
Francisco's most elegant shopping areas. The staff is remarkably pleasant and helpful. The rooms are done in a simple
French-country style, with floral bedspreads and white furniture that includes a writing desk. Guests can often be found sitting around the lobby's inviting fireplace or in the adjacent
Bentley's Seafood Grill. *191 Sutter St., 94104, tel. 415/781–3060 or
800/792–9639, fax 415/433–4409. 162 rooms, 15 suites. Facilities: 2
restaurants, rooftop park and jogging track, 3 floors of nonsmoking rooms. AE, DC, MC, V.*
Holiday Inn–Union Square. Given the rather undistinguished,
'60s-style facade of this convention-oriented hotel right on the
cable-car line, you probably wouldn't expect the rooms to be
done in charming, 19th-century English decor. Back rooms on
upper floors have commanding views of the bay; from the front
rooms, you can see west all the way to the Avenues. Every room
has a large writing desk and two phones. For an evening of intimacy, try the Sherlock Holmes lounge on the 30th floor—great
views, two fireplaces, and the lights are kept low. *480 Sutter St.,
94108, tel. 415/398–8900 or 800/465–4329, fax 415/989–8823. 400
rooms. Facilities: restaurant, lounge, health club. AE, DC, MC, V.*
Inn at Union Square. When you step through the dark-timber
double doors of this inn, you may feel like you're stepping into
the foyer of someone's home. The tiny but captivating lobby, with
trompe l'oeil bookshelves painted on the walls, adds to the illusion. Comfortable, Georgian-style rooms promote indolence
with goosedown pillows and four-poster beds; brass lion's-head
door knockers are a unique touch. Complimentary Continental
breakfast and afternoon tea are served in front of a fireplace in
a sitting area on each floor. *440 Post St., 04102, tel. 415/397–3510
or 800/288–4346, fax 415/989–0529. 30 rooms. No smoking. AE, DC,
MC, V.*
Petite Auberge. "The Teddy Bears' Picnic" might be an alternate
name for this whimsical recreation of a French country inn a
couple of blocks uphill from Union Square. The lobby, festooned
with teddies of all shapes, sizes, and costumes, sets the tone of
this B&B; the country kitchen and side garden create a pastoral
atmosphere despite the downtown location. The rooms are
rather small, but each has a teddy bear, bright flowered wallpaper, an old-fashioned writing desk, and a much-needed armoire—there's little or no closet space. Some rooms have
wood-burning fireplaces. The atmosphere borders on precious
but doesn't stray past the mark. Next door, at 845 Bush Street,
is a sister hotel, the 27-room **White Swan,** similar in style but
with an English-country flavor and larger rooms. *863 Bush St.,
94108, tel. 415/928–6000, fax 415/775–5717. 26 rooms. Facilities:
breakfast rooms, parlors. AE, MC, V.*
Prescott Hotel. A gourmet's delight might be the best way to
describe this plush hotel, thanks to the presence of Wolfgang
Puck's Postrio (*see* Chapter 6, Dining), which consistently

Downtown San Francisco Lodging

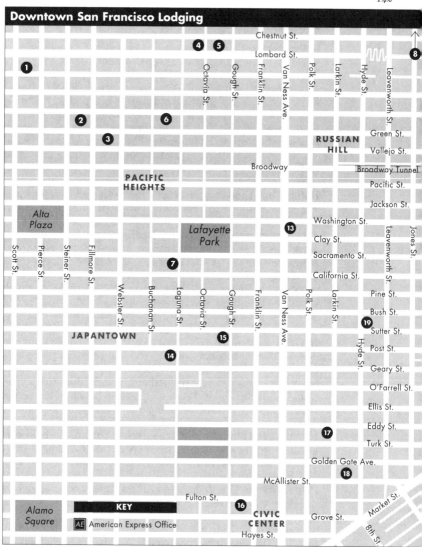

Abigail Hotel, **18**
Adelaide Inn, **20**
Bed and Breakfast Inn, **6**
Campton Place Kempinski, **39**
The Cartwright, **28**
Chancellor Hotel, **36**
Clarion Hotel, **53**
Crown Sterling Suites–Burlingame, **49**
Days Inn, **55**
Edward II Inn, **1**
Fairmont Hotel and Tower, **25**
Four Seasons Clift, **32**

Galleria Park, **42**
Grant Plaza, **45**
Harbor Court, **48**
Holiday Inn–Union Square, **38**
Holiday Lodge and Garden Hotel, **13**
Hotel Diva, **30**
Hotel Sofitel–San Francisco Bay, **50**
Huntington Hotel, **23**
Hyatt-Fisherman's Wharf, **8**
Hyatt Regency, **47**
Inn at the Opera, **16**
Inn at Union Square, **35**

King George, **33**
La Quinta Motor Inn, **56**
Majestic Hotel, **15**
Mandarin Oriental, **46**
The Mansion, **7**
Marina Inn, **4**
Mark Hopkins Inter–Continental, **24**
Miyako Hotel, **14**
Nob Hill Lambourne, **43**
Petite Auberge, **21**
Phoenix Inn, **17**
Prescott Hotel, **29**
Radisson Hotel, **54**

The Raphael, **34**
Ritz–Carlton San Francisco, **44**
San Francisco Airport Hilton, **51**
San Francisco Marriott-Fisherman's Wharf, **9**
San Remo Hotel, **10**
Sheraton Palace, **41**
Sherman House, **3**
Sir Francis Drake, **37**
Stouffer Stanford Court Hotel, **26**
Town House Motel, **5**
TraveLodge at the

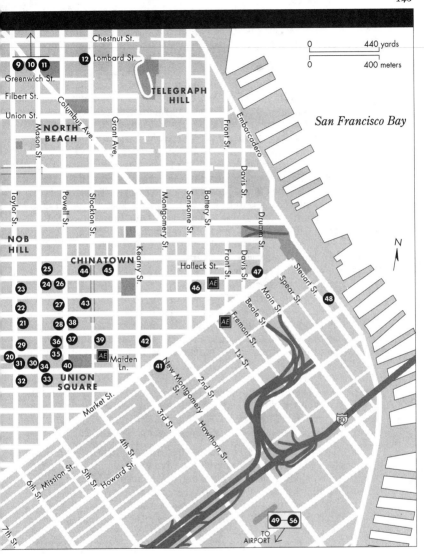

Chestnut St.

12 Lombard St.

9 **10** **11**

Greenwich St.

Filbert St.

TELEGRAPH HILL

Union St.

Columbus Ave.

Grant Ave.

NORTH BEACH

Mason St.

Front St.

Embarcadero

Davis St.

San Francisco Bay

Taylor St.

Powell St.

Stockton St.

Montgomery St.

Sansome St.

Battery St.

Davis St.

Drumm St.

Front St.

NOB HILL

CHINATOWN

44 **45**

Kearny St.

Halleck St.

47

N

25

46 AE

48

Stewart St.

23 **24** **26**

Main St.

Spear St.

22 **27** **43**

Beale St.

21 **28** **38**

AE

29 **36** **37** **39**

Fremont St.

1st St.

42

20 **31** **30** **34** **35** **40**

AE Maiden Ln.

41

New Montgomery St.

2nd St.

32 **33**

UNION SQUARE

Market St.

3rd St.

Hawthorn St.

80

4th St.

Mission St.

5th St.

Howard St.

6th St.

7th St.

49 **56**

TO AIRPORT

0 — 440 yards
0 — 400 meters

Wharf, **11**
Tuscan Inn, **12**
Union Street Inn, **2**
Vintage Court, **27**
Warwick Regis
Hotel, **31**
Westin Hotel, **52**
Westin
St. Francis, **40**
White Swan, **22**
York Hotel, **19**

hovers near the top of San Francisco's best-restaurant lists. Cuisine-conscious guests can order room service—from Postrio—and avoid trying to make a reservation. The rooms, which vary only in size and shape, are traditional in style, with dark, rich color schemes. Each bed is backed by a partially mirrored wall and has a boldly patterned spread; the bathrooms have marble-top sinks and gold fixtures. The Prescott's personalized service includes complimentary limousine service to the Financial District. *545 Post St., tel. 415/563–0303 or 800/283–7322, fax 415/563–6831. 166 rooms. Facilities: restaurant, lounge, health club next door at Press Club. AE, DC, MC, V.*

Sir Francis Drake. Although Beefeater-costumed doormen and dramatic red theater curtains still grace the front of the Drake, the inside has undergone a profound change. The lobby is still opulent, with wrought-iron lion balustrades, chandeliers, and Italian marble, but guest rooms now have the flavor of a B&B, with California mission-style furnishings and floral-print fabrics. The decor seems designed to appeal to pleasure travelers, but business travelers will appreciate the modem hookups and voice mail. Party-giver extraordinaire Harry Denton will soon run the renowned Starlite Roof supper club here. *450 Powell St., 94102, tel. 415/392–7755 or 800/227–5480, fax 415/677–9341. 417 rooms. Facilities: 2 restaurants, meeting room. AE, DC, MC, V.*

Warwick Regis Hotel. The cherubs outside and the frescoes and columns inside lend a postmodern, neoclassical look to the facade and lobby of the Warwick, one of the finest examples of the new generation of small hotels. The large, elegant rooms, some with fireplaces, are done in the Louis XVI style with French and Asian antiques and canopy beds; baths are decorated with Italian black marble. Continental breakfast is complimentary. *490 Geary St., 94102, tel. 415/928–7900 or 800/827–3447, fax 415/441–8788. 74 rooms. Facilities: restaurant, lounge. AE, DC, MC, V.*

$$ The Cartwright. A block or so northwest of Union Square and just off the cable-car line, this family-owned hotel's motto is "It's like being at home." This is only true, however, if your home is filled with authentic European antiques, fresh-cut flowers, and floral-print bedspreads and curtains and serves an English tea from 4 to 6. Guests may choose rooms with old-fashioned carved-wood or brass beds. *524 Sutter St., 94102, tel. and fax 415/421–2865 or 800/227–3844. 114 rooms. Facilities: coffee shop. AE, DC, MC, V.*

Chancellor Hotel. The three almost-floor-to-ceiling windows of the modest Chancellor Hotel lobby overlook cable cars passing by on Powell Street en route to nearby Union Square or Fisherman's Wharf. This family-owned and -oriented hotel, although not as grand as some of its neighbors, more than lives up to its promise of comfort without extravagance—it's one of the best buys on Union Square. All rooms are of moderate size, have high ceilings, and are done in an Edwardian style with a peach, green, and rose color scheme; the ceiling fans and deep bathtubs are a treat. Connecting rooms are available for couples with children. *433 Powell St., 94102, tel. 415/362–2004 or 800/428–4748, fax*

415/362–1403. 140 rooms. Facilities: restaurant, lounge. AE, DC, MC, V.

Hotel Diva. A black awning and beaten-and-burnished silver facade give this hotel a slick, high-tech look that sets it apart from all other hotels in San Francisco. The clientele is mostly theater folk—the Diva is directly across from the landmark Curran—and others of an artistic bent. The black-and-silver color scheme with touches of gray extends to the nightclub-esque lobby and to the rooms, which vary in size and are comfortable but not fussy. The black-lacquered armoires, writing desks, and headboards are set off by gray pin-striped bedspreads and gray carpeting. *440 Geary St., 94102, tel. 415/885–0200 or 800/553–1900, fax 415/346–6613. 125 rooms. Facilities: restaurant, lounge, small fitness center. AE, DC, MC, V.*

King George. The staff at the King George more than upholds this hotel's well-deserved 80-year reputation for hospitality; the desk clerks are especially adept at catering to their guests' every whim—they'll book anything from a Fisherman's Wharf tour to a dinner reservation. Behind the George's white-and-green Victorian facade, the rooms are a bit compact but nicely furnished in classic English style, with walnut furniture and a pastel-and-earthtone color scheme. British and Japanese tourists and suburban couples seeking a weekend getaway frequent this adult-oriented hotel. *334 Mason St., 94102, tel. 415/781–5050 or 800/288–6005, fax 415/391–6976. 144 rooms. Facilities: tearoom. AE, DC, MC, V.*

The Raphael. With its own marquee proclaiming it San Francisco's "little elegant hotel," the Raphael has few pretensions to grandeur, preferring to focus its efforts on service: tour bookings, limousine service, same-day laundry, and valet service. The moderate-size rooms are austere, with simple, dark furnishings; each has a unique hand-painted door. *386 Geary St., 94102, tel. 415/986–2000 or 800/821–5343, fax 415/397–2447. 152 rooms. Facilities: restaurant, lounge. AE, DC, MC, V.*

Vintage Court. This bit of the Napa Valley right off Union Square has lavish rooms decorated in a Wine Country theme, and each afternoon complimentary wine is served in front of a crackling fire in the lobby. For fine food, guests need go no farther than Masa's (*see* Chapter 6, Dining), one of the city's most celebrated French restaurants. *650 Bush St., 94108, tel. 415/392–4666 or 800/362–1100, fax 415/433–4065. 106 rooms. Facilities: restaurant, lounge, affiliated health club 1 block away. AE, DC, MC, V.*

York Hotel. This hotel several blocks west of Union Square is probably the most gay-friendly of San Francisco's more elegant hotels; it's also popular with businesspeople and European tourists. The gray stone facade and ornate, high-ceiling lobby give the hotel a touch of elegance. The moderate-size rooms are a mix of contemporary and Victorian styles with a dark gray and rose color scheme. The Plush Room cabaret, where you can catch such entertainers as Dixie Carter, Michael Feinstein, and Andrea Marcovicci, is the York's drawing card. *940 Sutter St., 94109, tel. 415/885–6800 or 800/227–3608, fax 415/885–2115. 96 rooms. Facilities: nightclub, fitness center, complimentary chauffeured limousine. AE, DC, MC, V.*

$ **Adelaide Inn.** The bedspreads at this quiet retreat may not match the drapes or carpets, and the floors may creak, but the rooms are clean and cheap ($48–$58 for a double) and get bright sunlight. Tucked away in an alley, this funky European-style pension hosts primarily guests from Germany, France, and Italy. *5 Isadora Duncan Ct. (off Taylor between Geary and Post Sts.), 94102, tel. 415/441-2474 or 415/441-2261, fax 415/441-0161. 18 rooms share baths. Facilities: sitting room, refrigerator for guest use. AE, MC, V.*

★ **Grant Plaza.** Serious Asian-cuisine aficionados take note—this bargain-price hotel in the shadow of the Chinatown gate has small but clean, attractively furnished rooms from $39. The Grant stands midway between the shopping options of Union Square and the Italian cafés and restaurants of North Beach. *465 Grant Ave., 94108, tel. 415/434-3883 or 800/472-6899, fax 415/434-3886. 72 rooms. AE, MC, V.*

Financial District

High-rise growth in San Francisco's Financial District has turned it into a mini-Manhattan and a spectacular sight by night.

$$$$ **Hyatt Regency.** The gray concrete, bunkerlike exterior of the Hyatt Regency at the foot of Market Street doesn't prepare the traveler for the spectacular 17-story atrium lobby inside. A favorite convention site, this hotel is a good place to work and play. Besides the Hyatt's plethora of meeting spaces, Embarcadero Center (with its 125 shops) is right next door, and the Equinox, San Francisco's only revolving rooftop restaurant, sits atop the hotel like a crown jewel. The rooms, some of which have bay-view balconies, come in two slightly different styles. Both styles have cherry-wood furniture, but one strikes a decidedly more masculine tone with a black-and-brown color scheme; the other has soft rose-and-plum combinations. *5 Embarcadero Center, 94111, tel. 415/788-1234 or 800/233-1234, fax 415/398-2567. 803 rooms. Facilities: 2 restaurants, coffee shop, lounge, affiliated health club 1 block away, 24-hr room service, gift shop. AE, DC, MC, V.*

Mandarin Oriental. The Mandarin comprises the top 11 floors (38–48) of San Francisco's third-tallest building, the California Center, so no matter what room you're in, you'll get some of the most panoramic vistas of the city and beyond. The front and back towers of this structure are connected by a sky bridge. Rooms in the front tower are reserved most quickly because of their dramatic, sweeping view of the ocean all the way to Angel Island; the Mandarin Rooms in each tower are favorites because their bathtubs are flanked by windows. The extremely appealing rooms are done in California style with Asian touches—a light, creamy yellow with black accents and wood tones. *222 Sansome St., 94104, tel. 415/885-0999 or 800/622-0404, fax 415/433-0289. 154 rooms, 4 suites. Facilities: restaurant, lounge, in-room fitness equipment available. AE, DC, MC, V.*

Sheraton Palace. One of the city's grand old hotels—with a guest list that has included Enrico Caruso, Woodrow Wilson, and Al Jolson—the Palace has a pool with skylight, a health club, and a business center. The famous Golden Court restaurant has been resurrected, and its leaded-glass, domed ceiling is more breathtaking than ever. With their 14-foot ceilings, the rooms are splendid on a smaller scale. Modern amenities are carefully integrated into the classic decor, from the TV inside the mahogany armoire to the telephone in the marble bathroom. Service is the only element that is not quite up to par. *2 New Montgomery St., 94105, tel. 415/392–8600 or 800/325–3535, fax 415/543–0671. 550 rooms. Facilities: 3 restaurants, 2 lounges, fitness center with sauna and whirlpool, 24-hr room service. AE, DC, MC, V.*

$$$ **Harbor Court Hotel.** Within shouting distance of the Bay Bridge,
★ the hot South of Market area, and new waterfront districts with their plentiful nightclubs and restaurants, this boutique-style hotel, formerly a YMCA, is noted for the exemplary service of its warm, friendly staff. The small rooms, some with exciting bay views, have a sage-green color scheme and partial canopy beds resting on wood casements. The adult-oriented Harbor Court attracts corporate types (especially on weekdays) as well as the average traveler. Guests have the use of YMCA facilities to one side of the hotel, and Harry Denton's Bar and Grill is on the other side. *165 Steuart St., tel. 415/882–1300 or 800/346–0555, fax 415/882–1313. 131 rooms. Facilities: adjacent health club, business center, complimentary limousine to Financial District. AE, DC. MC, V.*

Nob Hill

Synonymous with San Francisco's high society, Nob Hill contains some of the city's best-known luxury hotels. All offer spectacular city and bay views and noted gourmet restaurants. Cable-car lines that cross Nob Hill make transportation a cinch.

$$$$ **Fairmont Hotel and Tower.** Perched atop Nob Hill and queen of all she surveys, the Fairmont, which served as the model for the St. Gregory in the TV series "Hotel," has the most awe-inspiring lobby in the city, with a soaring, vaulted ceiling; towering, hand-painted, faux-marble columns; gilt mirrors; red-velvet upholstered chairs; and a memorable staircase. The tower rooms reflect a more modern style than their smaller Victorian counterparts in the older building. Done in a beige scheme, the tower rooms are often preferred because of their city and bay views. *950 Mason St., 94108, tel. 415/772–5000 or 800/527–4727, fax 415/772–5013. 596 rooms. Facilities: 5 restaurants, 5 lounges, health club and spa, gift shops, 24-hr room service. AE, DC, MC, V.*

★ **Huntington Hotel.** Across from Grace Cathedral and the small but captivating Huntington Park, the redbrick, ivy-covered Huntington provides a quiet alternative to the larger, more famous hotels down the street. The crowd here is mostly regulars who return year after year for the attentive personal service that is the hallmark of this hotel; the concierge calls each guest to offer complimentary sherry or formal tea. The management style is impeccably British in preserving the privacy of its celebrated guests. Each of the rooms and suites is appointed with traditional English furnishings, and color schemes range from chocolate brown—as in velvet walls designed for the late Princess Grace of Monaco—to sky-blue damask. *1075 California St., 94108, tel. 415/474–5400, 800/227–4683, or 800/652–1539 in CA, fax 415/474–6227. 143 rooms. Facilities: restaurant, lounge with entertainment, health club available across street at Fairmont. AE, DC, MC, V.*

Mark Hopkins Inter-Continental. The circular drive to this Nob Hill landmark across from the Fairmont leads to a lobby with floor-to-ceiling mirrors and marble floors. The rooms, with dramatic neoclassical furnishings of gray, silver, and khaki and bold leaf-print bedspreads, are lovingly maintained. The bathrooms are lined with Italian marble. Even-number rooms on high floors have views of the Golden Gate Bridge. No visit would be complete without a gander at the panoramic views from the Top of the Mark, *the* rooftop lounge in San Francisco since 1939. *999 California St., 94108, tel. 415/392–3434 or 800/327–0200, fax 415/616–6907. 392 rooms. Facilities: restaurant, 2 lounges, workout room, gift shops. AE, DC, MC, V.*

★ **Ritz-Carlton San Francisco.** Rated one of the top three hotels in the world by *Condé Nast Traveler,* the Ritz-Carlton is a stunning tribute to beauty, grandeur, and warm, attentive service. Beyond the neoclassical facade, crystal chandeliers and museum-quality 18th-century oil paintings grace a fabulous lobby. The rooms are elegant and spacious, and every bath is appointed with double sinks, hair dryers, and vanity tables. There is maid service twice a day, and guests staying on the butler level enjoy the added luxury of their own butler. The hotel's dining room, presided over by renowned chef Gary Danko, is a worthy destination in its own right. *600 Stockton St., at California St., 94108, tel. 415/296–7465 or 800/241–3333, fax 415/291–0288. 336 rooms. Facilities: 2 restaurants, 3 lounges, health club with indoor pool, retail stores. AE, DC, MC, V.*

Stouffer Stanford Court Hotel. Despite its relatively large size, the Stanford Court has a distinctly residential feeling. It's hidden from the street by a low archway that leads to an inner parking area covered by a stained-glass dome. The lobby is dominated by a similar stained-glass dome and a dramatic mural depicting scenes of early San Francisco. The moderate-size rooms are of varying shapes and come in four styles: Montana (Southwestern), Florentine (Italian), Bentley (English), and Coulter (floral with Asian accents). The hotel's restaurant, Fournou's Ovens—famed for its Provençal decor, 54-square-foot roasting oven, and California cuisine—is usually packed. *905 California St., 94108, tel. 415/989–3500, 800/227–4736, or 800/622–0957 in CA, fax 415/391–0513. 402 rooms. Facilities: restaurant, lounge, free access to Nob Hill Health Club across street, complimentary drop-off limousine, gift shops. AE, DC, MC, V.*

$$$ **Nob Hill Lambourne.** This urban retreat designed with the traveling executive in mind takes pride in taking care of business while offering stress-reducing pleasures. Personal computers, fax machines, personalized voice mail, laser printers, and a fully equipped boardroom help you maintain your edge, and the on-

site spa, with massages, body scrubs, herbal wraps, manicures, and pedicures, helps you take it off. Except for the two winged horses joined at the tail on the awning, you might miss this rather squat hotel, dwarfed by taller buildings on either side. The rooms have queen-size beds and contemporary furnishings in Mediterranean colors. A deluxe Continental breakfast is complimentary. *725 Pine St., at Stockton, 94108, tel. 415/433–2287 or 800/274–8466, fax 415/433–0975. 20 rooms. Facilities: kitchenettes in every room. AE, DC, MC, V.*

Fisherman's Wharf/North Beach

Fisherman's Wharf, San Francisco's top tourist attraction, is also the most popular area for lodging. All accommodations are within a couple of blocks of restaurants, shops, and cable-car lines. Because of city ordinances, none of the hotels exceeds four stories; thus, this is not the area for fantastic views of the city or bay. Reservations are always necessary, sometimes weeks in advance during peak summer months (when hotel rates rise by as much as 30%). Some street-side rooms can be noisy.

$$$$ **Hyatt Fisherman's Wharf.** Location is the key to this hotel's popularity with business travelers and families: It's within walking distance of Ghirardelli Square, the Cannery, Pier 39, Aquatic Park, and docks for ferries and bay cruises. It's also across the street from the cable-car turnaround and bus stop. The moderate-size guest rooms are done in greens and burgundies with dark woods, brass fixtures, and double-pane windows to keep out the often considerable street noise. Each floor has a laundry room. The hotel's conference-center area contains the North Point Lounge, with a fireplace and fountain beneath a domed Tiffany skylight, and a small, expensive café—a banana will run you $1.36. The Marble Works Restaurant, which still has the original facade of the 1906 Musto Marble Works, is next door and has a children's menu. *555 North Point St., 94133, tel. 415/563–1234 or 800/233–1234, fax 415/563–2218. 313 rooms. Facilities: restaurant, sports bar, outdoor pool and whirlpool, small gym and sauna, valet parking. AE, DC, MC, V.*

$$$ **San Francisco Marriott–Fisherman's Wharf.** Behind an unremarkable sand-color facade, the Marriott strikes a grand note in its lavish, albeit low-ceiling, lobby with marble floors and English club-style furniture. With the Transamerica Pyramid downtown to its left and the Cannery nearby on its right, the hotel is well situated for business and pleasure. The recently renovated rooms have dark natural wood, Asian art touches, and a king-size bed or two double beds and follow a turquoise, blue, and white color scheme. *1250 Columbus Ave., 94133, tel. 415/775–7555 or 800/228–9290, fax 415/474–2099. 256 rooms. Facilities: restaurant, lounge, health club, gift shop. AE, DC, MC, V.*

Tuscan Inn. The major attraction of this beautifully maintained hotel is its friendly, attentive staff. The concierge is particularly helpful—if she doesn't know the answer to your question, she'll find someone who does. The condo-like exterior of the inn is made of reddish brick with white concrete and gives little indication of the charm of the relatively small, Italian-influenced guest rooms, with their white-pine furniture and floral bedspreads and curtains. Room service is provided by Cafe Pescatore, the Italian seafood restaurant off the lobby. *425 North Point St., 94133, tel. 415/561–1100 or 800/648–4626, fax 415/561–1199. 220 rooms. Facilities: restaurant, valet parking, complimentary limousine to Financial District, meeting rooms, nonsmoking rooms. AE, DC, MC, V.*

$$ **Travelodge at the Wharf.** Taking up an entire city block, the Travelodge is the only bayfront hotel at Fisherman's Wharf and is known for its reasonable rates. The higher-price rooms (third and fourth floors) have balconies that provide unobstructed views of Alcatraz and overlook a landscaped courtyard and pool. The rooms at this family-oriented hotel have either a king-size bed or two double beds and are simply and brightly furnished with blond, lacquered-wood furniture, lime-green leather chairs, and curtains and bedspreads of vaguely Southwestern hues and designs. The '50s-style Johnny Rockets diner is popular for burgers and fries. *250 Beach St., 94133, tel. 415/392–6700 or 800/255–3050, fax 415/986–7853. 250 rooms. Facilities: 3 restaurants, heated outdoor pool, free parking. AE, DC, MC, V.*

$ **San Remo Hotel.** A guest recently described a sojourn at the San
★ Remo as being "like staying at Grandma's house." This three-story, blue-and-white Italianate Victorian just a couple of blocks from Fisherman's Wharf has reasonably priced rooms and a down-home, slightly tatty elegance. The somewhat cramped rooms are crowded with furniture: vanities, rag rugs, pedestal sinks, ceiling fans, antique armoires, and brass, iron, or wooden beds. The rooms share six black-and-white tiled shower rooms, one bathtub chamber, and six scrupulously clean toilets with brass pull chains and oak tanks. Daily and weekly rates are available. *2237 Mason St., 94133, tel. 415/776–8688 or 800/352–7366, fax 415/776–2811. 62 rooms, 61 with shared baths. AE, DC, MC, V.*

Lombard Street/Cow Hollow

Lombard Street, a major traffic corridor leading to the Golden Gate Bridge, stretches through San Francisco's poshest neighborhoods: Pacific Heights, Cow Hollow, and the Marina District.

$$$$ **Sherman House.** This magnificent landmark mansion on a low
★ hill in residential Pacific Heights is the most luxurious small hotel in San Francisco. Each room is individually decorated with Biedermeier, English Jacobean, or French Second Empire antiques. Tapestrylike canopies over four-poster beds, wood-burning fireplaces with marble mantels, and black-granite bathrooms with whirlpool baths complete the picture. The six romantic suites attract honeymooners from around the world, and the in-house restaurant is superb. *2160 Green St., 94123, tel. 415/563–3600 or 800/424–5777, fax 415/563–1882. 14 rooms. Facilities: dining room, sitting rooms, valet parking. AE, DC, MC, V.*

$$$ **Bed and Breakfast Inn.** This ivy-covered, dark-green-and-white Victorian with black trim lays claim to being San Francisco's

first B&B and is hidden in an alleyway off Union Street between Buchanan and Laguna. The English-country-style rooms are done in florals and pastels—Pierre Deux and Laura Ashley are the inspirations—with antiques, plants, and floral paintings by the owner placed throughout. The Mayfair, a private apartment above the main house, with a living room, kitchen, latticed balcony, and spiral staircase leading to a sleeping loft, is a new addition. *4 Charlton Ct., 94123, tel. 415/921–9784. 7 rooms with bath, 4 rooms share baths, apartment. Facilities: breakfast room. No credit cards.*

$$ Edward II Inn. Banners of the English king and the state of California fly from the rooftop of this picturesque B&B. A variety of English-country style accommodations is available, including rather small pension rooms with shared bath; six suites with one or two bedrooms, whirlpool baths, living rooms, kitchens, and wet bars; a carriage-house annex with apartment suites; and a three-bedroom, one-bath, cottage suite perfect for traveling families. Two junior suites in the main building are especially popular, as is the pub. *3155 Scott St., at Lombard St., 94123, tel. 415/922–3000 or 800/473–2846, fax 415/931–5784. 31 rooms, 19 with bath. Facilities: limited reserved parking nearby. AE, MC, V.*

★ Union Street Inn. A retired schoolteacher has transformed this ivy-draped, Edwardian, 1902 home into a delightful B&B filled with antiques and fresh flowers. The small size of the inn affords a cozy intimacy that has made it popular with honeymooners and other romantics. Two of the six rooms, all of which are strikingly decorated, are particular favorites: The Wildrose, with its king-size brass bed and persimmon-and-mauve decor, has a garden view that can be seen from the Jacuzzi. The Carriage House, separated from the main house by an old-fashioned English garden complete with lemon trees, a flagstone path, and a white picket fence, also has a Jacuzzi and lots of privacy. A Continental breakfast is served to guests in the parlor, in the garden, or in their rooms, and next door to the inn are two fine restaurants, Ristorante Bonta and Doidge's. *2229 Union St., 94123, tel. 415/346–0424. 6 rooms with bath. Facilities: breakfast room. AE, MC, V.*

$ Holiday Lodge and Garden Hotel. This three-story, split-level hotel with a redwood-and-stone facade has a California air about it. The rooms either overlook or open onto landscaped grounds with palm trees and a small, heated swimming pool. The decor has a '50s feel, with white beamed ceilings, beige wood paneling, and floral bedspreads. The lodge is two blocks from the Hard Rock Cafe, three blocks from the cable car, and within walking distance of Pacific Heights and Union Street shopping and restaurants. Its low-key atmosphere endears it to older couples, who enjoy the Holiday's laid-back, West Coast style. *1901 Van Ness Ave., 94109, tel. 415/776–4469 or 800/367–8504, fax 415/474–7046. 77 rooms. Facilities: free parking, kitchenettes in some rooms. AE, MC, V.*

Marina Inn. This inn five blocks from the marina offers B&B-style accommodations at motel prices. Rooms are sparsely appointed with a queen-size four-poster bed and private bath and are done in English-country style, with small pine-wood writing desks, nightstands, and armoires; the wallpaper and bedspreads are aggressively floral. Some of the rooms facing Octavia and Lombard streets have bay windows. A complimentary Continental breakfast is served in the central sitting room, and a barbershop and beauty salon are on the premises. *3110 Octavia St., at Lombard St., 94123, tel. 415/928–1000 or 800/274–1420. 40 rooms. Facilities: lounge. AE, MC, V.*

Town House Motel. What this family-oriented motel lacks in luxury and ambience it makes up for in value: The rooms are simply furnished and well-kept. Like its grander neighbor, the Marina Inn, this motel is convenient to many sights of interest, although its blaring blue facade may put off some visitors. The modest, medium-size rooms have a pastel, Southwestern color scheme, lacquered-wood furnishings, and either a king-size bed or two doubles. Continental breakfast is complimentary. *1650 Lombard St., 94123, tel. 415/885–5163 or 800/255–1516, fax 415/771–9889. 24 rooms. Facilities: free parking. AE, DC, MC, V.*

Civic Center/Van Ness

The governmental heart of San Francisco, flanked by a boulevard of cultural institutions, is enjoying a renaissance that has engendered fine restaurants, fashionable night spots, and well-situated small hotels.

$$$ **Inn at the Opera.** This seven-story hotel a block or so from City
★ Hall, Davies Hall, the War Memorial Opera Building, the War Memorial Veterans Building, Civic Auditorium, and Stars Restaurant hosts the likes of Pavarotti and Baryshnikov, as well as lesser lights of the music, dance, and opera worlds. Behind the yellow faux-marble front and red carpet are rooms of various sizes, decorated with creamy pastels and dark wood furnishings. Even the smallest singles have queen-size beds. The bureau drawers are lined with sheet music, and every room is outfitted with terry-cloth robes, microwave ovens, minibars, fresh flowers, and a basket of apples. Those in the know say the back rooms are preferable because the front ones get street noise. A major attraction here is the sumptuous, dimly lighted Act IV restaurant; stars congregate in its mahogany-and-green-velvet interior before and after performances. *333 Fulton St., 94102, tel. 415/863–8400, 800/325–2708, or 800/423–9610 in CA, fax 415/861–0821. 48 rooms. Facilities: restaurant, lounge. AE, DC, MC, V.*

★ **Majestic Hotel.** The Majestic is one of San Francisco's original grand hotels. The gingerbread and scrollwork on this five-story, yellow-and-white Edwardian are so ornate that the building bears a strong resemblance to a wedding cake. Stepping through the portals of the immaculate, gay-friendly hotel is like stepping into an earlier, more gracious era. The lobby, with its black marble stairs, antique chandeliers, plush Victorian chairs, white marble fireplace, and red velvet sofa, manages to appear simultaneously awesome and comfy. Most rooms contain a fireplace and either a large, hand-painted, four-poster, canopied bed or two-poster bonnet twin beds, and most have a mix of French

Empire and English antiques and custom furniture. Some have original claw-foot bathtubs. The hotel's Cafe Majestic evokes turn-of-the-century San Francisco and is "San Francisco's most romantic restaurant," according to *San Francisco Focus Magazine*; the menu blends California and French cuisines. *1500 Sutter St., 94109, tel. 415/441–1100 or 800/869–8966, fax 415/673–7331. 57 rooms. Facilities: restaurant, lounge. AE, DC, MC, V.*

Miyako Hotel. The Japanese ambience at this pagoda-style hotel is established by the greeting from the kimono-clad concierge. Next to the Japantown complex and near Fillmore Street, this hotel is frequented by Asian travelers and others who appreciate a taste of the East. The guest rooms are in either the tower building or the garden wing, which has traditional seasonal gardens. The rooms are done in Western or Japanese style, the major difference being that the former have a traditional Western bed with a mattress, and the latter have futon beds with tatami mats. Both room styles are strikingly decorated with Japanese touches such as shojis; most have their own soaking rooms with a bucket and stool and a Japanese tub (1 foot deeper than Western tubs). Chocolates set by the bedside on top of a haiku await each guest. The hotel's Elka restaurant (*see* Chapter 6, Dining) is nationally known for its French- and Japanese-influenced seafood dishes. *1625 Post St., at Laguna St., 94115, tel. 415/922–3200 or 800/533–4567, fax 415/921–0417. 218 rooms. Facilities: restaurant, lounge, Japanese baths, saunas. AE, DC, MC, V.*

$$ **The Mansion.** This twin-turreted Queen Anne was built in 1887 and today houses one of the most unusual hotels in the city. Rooms contain an odd collection of furnishings and vary from the tiny Tom Thumb Room to the opulent Josephine Suite, the favorite of such celebrities as Barbra Streisand. Owner Bob Pritikin's pig paintings and other "porkabilia" are everywhere. Full breakfast is included. *2220 Sacramento St., 94115, tel. 415/929–9444, fax 415/567–9391. 21 rooms. Facilities: dining room, nightly concerts, sculpture and flower garden. AE, DC, MC, V.*

Phoenix Inn. Dubbed the "hippest hotel" in San Francisco by *People* magazine, this turquoise-and-coral hideaway on the fringes of the Tenderloin district is a little bit south-of-the-equator and a little bit *Gilligan's Island*—probably not the place for a traveling executive. The Phoenix bills itself as an urban retreat in a resortlike environment. Its bungalow-style rooms, decorated with casual, handmade, bamboo furniture and original art by San Francisco artists, have white beamed ceilings, white wooden walls and vivid tropical-print bedspreads. All rooms face a pool (with a mural by Francis Forlenza on its bottom) adjacent to a courtyard and sculpture garden. An in-house cable channel plays films made in San Francisco and films about bands on the road. Miss Pearl's Jam House restaurant and bar is a good place to hear reggae; the Chef Delicious Jerked Chicken should not be missed. *601 Eddy St., 94109, tel. 415/776–1380, 415/861–1560, or 800/248–9466, fax 415/885–3109. 44 rooms. Facilities: restaurant, bar, lounge, free parking, heated pool. AE, DC, MC, V.*

$ **Abigail Hotel.** This hotel, a former B&B, retains its distinctive atmosphere with an eclectic mix of faux-stone walls, a faux-marble front desk, and an old-fashioned telephone booth in the lobby. Hissing steam radiators, sleigh beds, and antiques set the mood. Room 211—the hotel's only suite—is the most elegant and spacious. Try the grilled pizzas and gingerbread cookies at the Mama Justice City Kitchen off the lobby. *246 McAllister St., 94102, tel. 415/861-9728, 415/861-1560, or 800/243-6510. 60 rooms. Facilities: restaurant. AE, DC, MC, V.*

The Airport

A construction boom near San Francisco International Airport during the mid-'80s added several luxury-class hotels. Rates are about 20% less those than at in-town counterparts. Airport shuttle buses are provided by all of the following hotels. Because they cater primarily to midweek business travelers, the airport hotels often cut weekend prices drastically; be sure to inquire.

$$$ **Crown Sterling Suites–Burlingame.** This California Mission–
★ style hostelry is arguably the most lavish in the airport area. On the bay with views of planes taking off and landing, this all-suite hotel has a spectacular setting and impressive service. A black-marble, stone-floor lobby with burnt-orange roof tiles leads into a nine-story atrium and tropical garden replete with ducks, parrots, fish, and a waterfall. Suites are pink and turquoise and open onto the atrium; they have moderate-size bedrooms with either a king-size or two double beds. The suites' living rooms include a work area with a dual-line telephone and voice mail; a sleeper sofa; and a wet bar, microwave, and refrigerator. Among the other amenities are a putting green, complimentary evening beverages and cooked-to-order breakfast, and an executive business center with a meeting and catering staff to help you arrange any event. *150 Anza Blvd., Burlingame 94010, tel. 415/342-4600 or 800/433-4600, fax 415/343-8137. 339 suites. Facilities: restaurant and lounge with live entertainment, jogging path, indoor pool, steam room and sauna, transportation to nearby health club, in-room movies, gift shop. AE, DC, MC, V.*

Hotel Sofitel–San Francisco Bay. Parisian-boulevard lampposts, a Métro sign, and a kiosk covered with posters bring an unexpected bit of Paris to this bayside hotel. The French-themed public spaces—the Gigi Brasserie, Baccarat restaurant, and La Terrasse bar—have a light, open, airy feeling that extends to the room decor of light woods and pastel floral prints. In addition to the minibar, large writing desk, king or two double beds, and turndown service, you'll find pleasant extras like a makeup mirror, complimentary Nina Ricci toiletries, a second telephone, and a rose in the bathroom. The Sofitel is tucked away in the Redwood Shores industrial park south of the airport and backs up to a lagoon. The Gigi and the Baccarat are famous locally for their joint Sunday brunches. *223 Twin Dolphin Dr., Redwood City 94065, tel. 415/598-9000 or 800/763-4835, fax 415/598-0459. 319 rooms, 28 suites. Facilities: 2 restaurants, lounge, concierge, valet/laundry service, outdoor heated pool, health club, spa. AE, DC, MC, V.*

San Francisco Airport Hilton. The only airport hotel located on airport property—right off Highway 101—the Hilton provides 24-hour shuttle service to the terminal, though you could probably walk. The rooms are simply furnished with a king, a queen, or two double beds and minibars and are done in pastels. Continental breakfast is complimentary. The courtyard and poolside area provide respite for the weary traveler. *San Francisco International Airport, Box 8355, 94128, tel. 415/589–0770 or 800/445–8667, fax 415/589–4696. 529 rooms. Facilities: 2 restaurants, lounge, outdoor heated Olympic-size pool, Jacuzzi, fitness center, landscaped grounds. AE, DC, MC, V.*

Westin Hotel. This bayfront hotel, with an elegant, palm-tree-lined entrance and sparkling fountain, is geared toward business travelers and conventioneers. There are 27 meeting rooms, which run the gamut from a grand ballroom for 700 to a lovely pool-atrium area where luncheons are sometimes held; on-site meeting managers, a catering staff, and an in-house audiovisual company are available to help. The medium-size rooms have blond-wood furnishings with Asian touches and are done in muted pink, blue, peach, and beige pastels. Be sure to request a room with a bay view so you can watch the planes. Right next door is the black-and-white tiled Bayshore Diner, with weekly burger specials, and around the corner is the rich, darkly paneled Benchmark bar and grill, known for its steaks. *1 Old Bayshore Hwy., Millbrae 94030, tel. 415/692–3500 or 800/228–3000, fax 415/872–8104. 388 rooms. Facilities: 2 restaurants, 2 lounges, concierge floor, health club, indoor pool, United Airlines ticket counter. AE, DC, MC, V.*

$$ **Clarion Hotel.** This busy hotel west of the Westin, toward the freeway, is a favorite of airline personnel. Respite from the bustle in the gigantic, glass-fronted, deco-style lobby can be found in an adjoining garden area; wrought-iron benches, a heated pool, and a Jacuzzi are set among fragrant pine trees. Although the styles and furnishings of the rooms vary—some are in dark woods and brass, and others are more floral—all are spacious, comfortable, and have either a king-size or two double beds. *401 E. Millbrae Ave., Millbrae 94030, tel. 415/692–6363 or 800/223–7111, fax 415/697–8735. 435 rooms. Facilities: 2 restaurants, lounge, in-room movies, health club, heated pool, spa. AE, DC, MC, V.*

Radisson Hotel. Although the '60s-style tinted-glass-and-aluminum facade and the scuffed marble floors in the lobby have seen better days, an amusing "waterfall" adds a cheery note—the water flows out of small spigots. The rather charmless guest rooms on the second and eighth floors are drably decorated in subdued shades of gray and brown; furnishings include a king, queen, or two double beds, plus a small table with two chairs. The executive-level rooms on the ninth and tenth floors have been upgraded with black, lacquered furnishings and lighter colors and accents. Freeway noise can be heard in rooms on both sides of the hotel. *1177 Airport Blvd., Burlingame 94010, tel. 415/342–9200 or 800/333–3333, fax 415/342–1655. 301 rooms. Facili-*

ties: restaurant, lounge, indoor and outdoor pools, fitness center, shuttle service to and from airport, free parking. AE, DC, MC, V.

$ **Days Inn.** This five-story, redbrick hotel, which attracts families and business travelers, has undergone a recent renovation; unfortunately, so have its prices. The regular rate for a room with either a queen or two double beds is $72; a king-size bed commands $82 a night. The guest rooms with double beds are modest but pleasant and extremely clean; they have light wood furnishings, white walls, floral-and-striped bedspreads, and a small circular table with two chairs. The fancier king and queen rooms are done in green, pink, and burgundy with ersatz mahogany furnishings, dark green carpeting, and a midsize writing desk. Amenities are limited, but there is a vending area on each floor. *777 Airport Blvd., Burlingame 94010, tel. 415/342–7772 or 800/325–2525, fax 415/342–2635. 200 rooms. Facilities: 24-hr restaurant, heated outdoor pool, nonsmoking rooms, in-room movies. AE, DC, MC, V.*

La Quinta Motor Inn. Literally a stone's throw from Highway 101, this Mission-style inn nonetheless provides quiet, well-insulated accommodations for the tired visitor. Weathered wood balconies and a red tile roof betray the decor inside: guest rooms have stucco walls, Southwestern-print bedspreads and curtains, and sturdy blond-wood furniture. Each room is designated smoking or nonsmoking and comes with a king-size or two double beds; king-size rooms also have a recliner. A complimentary Continental breakfast with juice bar is served in the lobby until 10 AM daily. Complimentary van service to and from the airport is provided. Prices are from $58 up. *20 Airport Blvd., South San Francisco 94080, tel. 415/583–2223 or 800/531–5900, fax 415/589–6770. 174 rooms. Facilities: adjacent 24-hr restaurant, heated outdoor pool, exercise room, Jacuzzi, laundry facilities. AE, DC, MC, V.*

8 The Arts and Nightlife

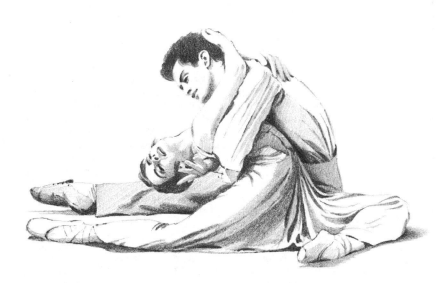

The Arts

By Robert Taylor

Robert Taylor is a longtime San Francisco arts and entertainment writer.

The best guide to arts and entertainment events in San Francisco is the "Datebook" section, printed on pink paper, in the Sunday *Examiner and Chronicle.* The *Bay Guardian* and *S.F. Weekly,* free and available in racks around the city, list more neighborhood, avant-garde, and budget-priced events. For up-to-date information about cultural and musical events, call the Convention and Visitors Bureau's *Cultural Events Calendar* (tel. 415/391–2001).

Half-price tickets to many local and touring stage shows go on sale (cash only) at 11 AM, Tuesday–Saturday, at the TIX Bay Area booth on the Stockton Street side of Union Square, between Geary and Post streets. TIX is also a full-service ticket agency for theater and music events around the Bay Area (open until 6 PM Tuesday–Thursday, 7 PM Friday–Saturday). While the city's major commercial theaters are concentrated downtown, the opera, symphony, and ballet perform at the Civic Center. For recorded information about TIX tickets, call 415/433–7827.

The city's charge-by-phone ticket service is **BASS** (tel. 510/762–2277 or 415/776–1999), with one of its centers in the TIX booth mentioned above and another at **Tower Records** (Bay St. at Columbus Ave.), near Fisherman's Wharf. Other agencies downtown are the **City Box Office,** 141 Kearny Street in the Sherman Clay store (tel. 415/392–4400) and **Downtown Center Box Office** in the parking garage at 320 Mason Street (tel. 415/775–2021). The opera, symphony, the ballet's *Nutcracker,* and touring hit musicals are often sold out in advance; tickets are usually available within a day of performance for other shows.

Theater

San Francisco's "theater row" is a single block of Geary Street west of Union Square, but a number of commercial theaters are located within walking distance, along with resident companies that enrich the city's theatrical scene. The three major commercial theaters are operated by the Shorenstein-Nederlander organization, which books touring plays and musicals, some of them before they open on Broadway. The most venerable is the **Curran** (445 Geary St., tel. 415/474–3800). A production of Andrew Lloyd Webber's *The Phantom of the Opera* opened there in December 1993 and is expected to run as long as two years. The **Golden Gate** is a stylishly refurbished movie theater (Golden Gate Ave. at Taylor St., tel. 415/474–3800), now primarily a musical house. The 2,500-seat **Orpheum** (1192 Market St. near the Civic Center, tel. 415/474–3800) is used for the biggest touring shows.

The smaller commercial theaters, offering touring shows and a few that are locally produced, are the **Marines Memorial Theatre** (Sutter and Mason Sts., tel. 415/441–7444) and **Theatre on the Square** (450 Post St., tel. 415/433–9500). For commercial and popular success, nothing beats *Beach Blanket Babylon,* the zany revue that has been running for years at **Club Fugazi** (678 Green St. in North Beach, tel. 415/421–4222). Conceived by imaginative San Francisco director Steve Silver, it is a lively, colorful musical mix of cabaret, show-biz parodies, and tributes to local landmarks. (*See* Cabarets in Nightlife, *below.*)

The city's major theater company is the **American Conservatory Theatre (ACT),** which was founded in the mid-1960s and quickly became one of the nation's leading regional theaters. It presents a season of approximately eight plays in rotating repertory from October through late spring. ACT's ticket office is at 405 Geary Street (tel. 415/749–2228), next door to its **Geary Theatre,** closed since the 1989 earthquake. During reconstruction, ACT is performing at the nearby **Stage Door Theater** (420 Mason St.) and the **Marines Memorial Theatre** (Sutter and Mason Sts.).

The leading producer of new plays is the **Magic Theatre** (Bldg. D, Fort Mason Center, Laguna St. at Marina Blvd., tel. 415/441–8822).

The city boasts a wide variety of specialized and ethnic theaters that work with dedicated local actors and some professionals. Among the most interesting are **The Lamplighters,** the delightful Gilbert and Sullivan troupe that often gets better reviews than touring productions of musicals, performing at **Presentation Theater** (2350 Turk St., tel. 415/752–7755); the **Lorraine Hansberry Theatre,** which specializes in plays by black writers (620 Sutter St., tel. 415/474–8800); the **Asian American Theatre** (405 Arguello Blvd., tel. 415/751–2600); and two stages that showcase gay and lesbian performers: **Theatre Rhinoceros** (2926 16th St., tel. 415/861–5079) and **Josie's Cabaret & Juice Joint** (3583 16th St., tel. 415/861–7933). The **San Francisco Shakespeare Festival** offers free performances on summer weekends in Golden Gate Park (tel. 415/666–2222).

Avant-garde theater, dance, opera, and "performance art" turn up in a variety of locations, not all of them theaters. The major presenting organization is the **Theater Artaud** (499 Alabama St. in the Mission District, tel. 415/621–7797), which is situated in a huge, converted machine shop. Some contemporary theater events, in addition to dance and music, are scheduled at the theater in the **Center for the Arts at Yerba Buena Gardens** (3rd and Howard Sts., tel. 415/978–2787).

Berkeley Repertory Theatre (tel. 510/845–4700), across the bay, is the American Conservatory Theatre's major rival for leadership among the region's resident professional companies. It performs a more adventurous mix of classics and new plays in a more modern, intimate theater at 2025 Addison Street near BART's downtown Berkeley station. It's a fully professional theater, with a fall–spring season. Tickets are available at the TIX booth in San Francisco's Union Square. The Bay Area's most professional outdoor summer theater, **California Shakespeare Festival,** performs in an amphitheater east of Oakland, on Gateway Boulevard just off state Highway 24 (tel. 510/548–3422).

Music

The completion of Davies Symphony Hall at Van Ness Avenue and Grove Street finally gave the San Francisco Symphony a home of its own. It solidified the base of the city's three major performing arts organizations—symphony, opera, and ballet—in the Civic Center. The symphony and other musical groups also perform in the smaller, 928-seat Herbst Theatre in the Opera's "twin" at Van Ness Avenue and McAllister Street, the War Memorial Building. Otherwise the city's musical ensembles can be found all over the map: in churches and museums, in restaurants and parks, and in outreach series in Berkeley and on the peninsula.

San Francisco Symphony (Davies Symphony Hall, Van Ness Ave. at Grove St., tel. 415/431–5400. Tickets, $8–$65, at the box office or through BASS, tel. 510/762–2277). The city's most stable performing-arts organization plays from September through May, with music director Herbert Blomstedt conducting for about two-thirds of the season. Michael Tilson Thomas, who is California-born and relatively young for a conductor of a major orchestra, takes over as music director in September 1995. He is expected to offer innovative programming and more performances of 20th-century and American works. Guest conductors often include Edo de Waart and Riccardo Muti. Soloists include artists of the caliber of Andre Watts, Peter Serkin, and Pinchas Zukerman. Special events include a summer festival built around a particular composer, nation or musical period, and summer Pops Concerts in the nearby Civic Auditorium. Throughout the season, the symphony presents a Great Performers Series of guest soloists and orchestras.
Philharmonia Baroque (Herbst Theatre, Van Ness Ave. at McAllister St., tel. 415/391–5252. Tickets also at the TIX booth). This stylish ensemble has been called the local baroque orchestra with the national reputation, and the nation's preeminent group for performances of early music. Its season of concerts, fall–spring, celebrates composers of the 17th and 18th centuries, including Handel, Vivaldi, and Mozart.
San Francisco Chamber Symphony (various locations, tel. 415/495–2919). This group has become known for the variety of its programming, which can include composers from Handel to VillaLobos.
Kronos Quartet (Herbst Theatre and other locations, tel. 415/731–3533). Twentieth-century works and a number of premieres make up the programs for this group, which goes as far as possible to prove that string quartets are not stodgy.
Midsummer Mozart (Herbst Theatre and occasionally at Davies Symphony Hall, tel. 415/781–5931). This is one of the few Mozart festivals that hasn't filled programs with works by other composers. It performs in July and August under conductor George Cleve.
Old First Concerts (Old First Church, Van Ness Ave. at Sacramento St., tel. 415/474–1608. Tickets also at TIX booth, Union Square). This is a well-respected Friday evening and Sunday

afternoon series of chamber music, vocal soloists, new music, and jazz.

Pops Concerts (Polk and Grove Sts., tel. 415/431–5400). Many members of the symphony perform in the July Pops series in the 7,000-seat Civic Auditorium. The schedule includes light classics, Broadway, country, and movie music. Tickets cost as little as a few dollars.

Stern Grove (Sloat Blvd. at 19th Ave., tel. 415/252–6252). This is the nation's oldest continual free summer music festival, offering 10 Sunday afternoons of symphony, opera, jazz, pop music, and dance. The amphitheater is in a eucalyptus grove below street level; remember that summer in this area near the ocean can be cool.

There are also free band concerts on Sunday and holiday afternoons in the **Golden Gate Park** music concourse (tel. 415/666–7024) opposite the de Young Museum.

Opera

San Francisco Opera (Van Ness Ave. at Grove St., tel. 415/864–3330). Founded in 1923, and the resident company at the War Memorial Opera House in the Civic Center since it was built in 1932, the Opera has expanded to a fall season of 13 weeks. Approximately 70 performances of 10 operas are given, beginning on the first Friday after Labor Day. The Opera uses "supertitles": Translations are projected above the stage during almost all the operas not sung in English. For many years the Opera has been considered a major international company and the most artistically successful operatic organization in the United States outside New York. International competition and management changes have made recent seasons uneven; the company has revitalized under general director Lofti Mansouri, formerly head of Toronto's Canadian Opera Company. International opera stars frequently sing major roles here, and the Opera is well known for presenting the American debuts of singers who have made their names in Europe.

In addition to the fall season, the Opera schedules occasional summer festivals. Ticket prices range from about $35 to $100. Standing-room tickets (less than $10) are always sold at 10 AM for same-day performances, and patrons often sell extra tickets on the Opera House steps just before curtain time. Note that the Opera House will be closed in 1996 for repairs; performances will take place at the Civic Auditorium a block east at Grove and Polk Streets.

Pocket Opera (tel. 415/989–1853). This lively, modestly priced alternative to "grand" opera gives concert performances, mostly in English, of rarely heard works. Offenbach's operettas are frequently on the bill during the winter–spring season. Concerts are held at various locations.

Another operatic alternative is the **Lamplighters** (*see* Theater, *above*), which specializes in Gilbert and Sullivan but presents other light operas as well.

Dance

San Francisco Ballet (War Memorial Opera House, Van Ness Ave. at Grove St., tel. 415/703–9400). The ballet has regained much of its luster under artistic director Helgi Tomasson, and both classical and contemporary works have won admiring reviews. The company's primary season runs February–May; its repertoire includes such full-length ballets as *Swan Lake* and a new production of *Sleeping Beauty.* The company is also intent on reaching new audiences with bold new dances, what it likes to call "cutting-edge works that will make you take a second look." Like many dance companies in the nation, the ballet presents the *Nutcracker* in December, and its recent production is one of the most spectacular.

Oakland Ballet (Paramount Theatre, 2025 Broadway, Oakland, near BART's 19th St. Station, tel. 510/465–6400). Founded in 1965, this company is not simply an imitation of the larger San Francisco Ballet across the bay. It has earned an outstanding reputation for reviving and preserving ballet masterworks from the early 20th century and presenting innovative contemporary choreography. It has re-created historic dances by such choreographers as Diaghilev, Bronislava Nininska, and Mikhail Fokine. The company also presents its own *Nutcracker* in December; its season begins in September.

Margaret Jenkins Dance Company (Theater Artaud, 450 Florida St., tel. 415/863–1173). This is one of the most reliable of the city's modern experimental dance troupes, in which the dancers themselves help shape the choreography.

Ethnic Dance Festival (Palace of Fine Arts Theatre, Bay and Lyon Sts., tel. 415/474–3914). Approximately 30 of the Bay Area's estimated 200 ethnic dance companies and soloists perform on several programs in June. Prices are modest for the city-sponsored event.

San Francisco and the Bay Area support innumerable experimental and ethnic dance groups. Among them are ODC/San Francisco (tel. 415/863–6606), performing at Herbst Theatre (Van Ness Ave.); the **Joe Goode Performance Group** (tel. 415/648–4848); and **Rosa Montoya Bailes Flamenco** (tel. 415/931–7374), which often performs at Herbst Theatre. The **Footworks Studio** (3221 22nd St., tel. 415/824–5044) gives many more local dancers a chance to perform.

Film

The San Francisco Bay Area, including Berkeley and San Jose, is considered one of the nation's most important movie markets. Films of all sorts can find an audience here. The Bay Area is also a filmmaking center: Documentaries and experimental works are being produced on modest budgets, feature films and television programs are shot on location, and some of Hollywood's biggest directors live here, particularly in Marin County. In San Francisco, about a third of the theaters regularly show foreign and independent films. The city is also one of the last strongholds of "repertory cinema," showing older American and foreign films on bills that change daily.

While Market Street has a large number of movie theaters, most of them have gone over to screening only sex and action movies. First-run commercial movie theaters are now scattered throughout the city and are concentrated along Van Ness Avenue, near Japantown, and in the Marina District. All are accessible on major Muni bus routes, as are the art-revival houses. Several of the most respected and popular independent theaters have been taken over by chains recently, so their programming might change. The San Francisco International Film Festival (*see below*), the oldest in the country, continues to provide an extensive selection of foreign films each spring. The Pacific Film Archive in Berkeley (*see below*) is an incomparable source for rare American and foreign films.

Foreign and Independent Films
The most reliable theaters for foreign and independent films are **Opera Plaza Cinemas** (Van Ness Ave. at Golden Gate Ave., tel. 415/771–0102); **Lumiere** (California St. near Polk St., tel. 415/885–3200); **Clay** (Fillmore and Clay Sts., tel. 415/346–1123); **Gateway** (215 Jackson St. at Battery St., tel. 415/421–3353); **Castro** (Castro St. near Market St., tel. 415/621–6120), the last remaining 1920s movie palace that is still showing movies, including an extensive schedule of revivals; and **Bridge** (3013 Geary Blvd. near Masonic Ave., tel. 415/751–3212).

Festivals
The San Francisco International Film Festival (tel. 415/931–3456) takes over several theaters for two weeks in late April at the AMC Kabuki complex at Post and Fillmore streets. The festival schedules about 75 films from abroad, many of them American premieres, along with a variety of independent American documentaries. In recent years there has been an emphasis on films from Africa and Asia.

Other showcases for films out of the commercial mainstream include the **Roxie Cinema** (3116 16th St., tel. 415/863–1087), which specializes in social and political documentaries; the **Cinematheque** at the San Francisco Art Institute (800 Chestnut St., tel. 415/558–8129), which often features films and personal appearances by avant-garde artists; and **Eye Gallery** (1151 Mission St., tel. 415/431–6911), which offers experimental videos and films.

The most extensive screening schedule for both American and foreign, old and new films is the **Pacific Film Archive** (2625 Durant Ave., Berkeley, tel. 510/642–1124). It often shows films from New York's Museum of Modern Art collection.

Nightlife

By Daniel Mangin

A longtime Bay Area resident, Daniel Mangin writes on the arts for several local papers. He is an instructor of film history at City College of San Francisco.

San Francisco provides a tremendous potpourri of evening entertainment ranging from ultrasophisticated cabarets to bawdy bistros that reflect the city's gold-rush past. With the exception of the hotel lounges and discos noted below, the accent is on casual dress—call ahead if you are uncertain.

For information on who is performing where, check the following sources: The Sunday San Francisco *Examiner and Chronicle*'s pink "Datebook" insert lists major events and cultural happenings. The free alternative weeklies, the *Bay Guardian* and *SF Weekly,* are terrific sources for current music clubs and comedy. Another handy reference for San Francisco nightlife is *Key* magazine, offered free in most major hotel lobbies. For a phone update on sports and musical events, call the Convention and Visitor Bureau's *Events Hotline* (tel. 415/391–2001). Those seeking weekly jazz headliners should dial the KJAZ *Jazz Line* (tel. 510/769–4818).

Although San Francisco is a compact city with the prevailing influences of some neighborhoods spilling into others, the following generalizations should help you find the kind of entertainment you're looking for. **Nob Hill** is noted for its plush piano bars and panoramic skyline lounges. **North Beach,** infamous for its topless and bottomless bistros, also maintains a sense of its beatnik past and this legacy lives on in atmospheric bars and coffeehouses. **Fisherman's Wharf,** while touristy, is great for people watching and provides plenty of impromptu entertainment from street performers. **Union Street** is home away from home for singles in search of company. South of Market (**SoMa,** for short) has become a hub of nightlife, with a bevy of highly popular nightclubs, bars, and lounges in renovated warehouses and auto shops. Gay men will find the **Castro** and **Polk Street** scenes of infinite variety.

No-Fault Night Spots

In a hurry or just don't want to think about where to go? There's rarely a bad night at any of the clubs below. Detailed descriptions can be found within listings for each category.

Rock/Pop/Folk/Blues: Slim's, which books the top artists in each of these areas, is almost risk-free; for rock, **Bottom of the Hill** is hot with the locals right now.

Jazz: The best bargain is **Jazz at Pearl's**; supermodel Christy Turlington bought into the already hoppin' **Up and Down Club,** and it has become superhip.

Cabaret: Club Fugazi's *Beach Blanket Babylon* revue has been going strong for nearly 20 years—they must be doing something right.

Comedy: Go where your favorite comics are; if it's ambience you're after, try **Cobb's Comedy Club.**

Dancing Emporiums: Salsa weekends are hot at **Cesar's Latin Palace**; the trendy young and restless love **Harry Denton's**; get (way) down at the ultrafunky **Kennel Club.**

Piano Bars: The **Redwood Room** is plush; featuring top talent, **Club 36** is an entertainment bargain—with a view.

Skyline Bars: The **Carnelian Room** is the classiest; **Top of the Mark** is regaining its reputation as a lively yet romantic room with a view.

Singles Bars: Johnny Love's, without question.

Rock, Pop, Folk, and Blues

The hip SoMa scene of a few years ago has mellowed a bit of late; the clubs still feature fine music, but the trendies have bailed out. Musical offerings in this part of town and elsewhere run from mainstream to way, way out.

The Blue Lamp. An aura of faded opulence permeates this downtown "hole in the wall," where the fare ranges from '20s blues to original rock-and-roll. *561 Geary St., tel. 415/885–1464. Shows begin at 10 PM Mon.–Sat., Sun. blues jam 7–midnight. Cover: $3, Fri. and Sat. only.*

Bottom of the Hill. This great little club "two minutes south of SoMa" in the Potrero Hill District showcases some of the best local alternative rock and blues in the city. The atmosphere is ultra low-key, though even these cool folks start a-buzzin' when the occasional rock or pop star drops in to check out the scene. *1233 17th St. at Texas St., tel. 415/626–4455. Shows begin 9:30–10 PM. Cover: $3–$7.*

Brave New World. Hot with the underground set, BNW lures a fancifully garbed, heavily pierced clientele. Bands like Jack Killed Jill and the Mental Pigmies (sic) enthrall the assembled youngsters. *1751 Masonic St. at Fulton St., tel. 415/441–1751. Cover: none–$5, depending on the act. No credit cards.*

DNA Lounge. Alternative independent rock, funk, and rap are the usual fare at this longtime SoMa haunt. Live bands are on most nights at 10 PM; other nights the club is open for dancing to recorded music. *375 11th St. near Harrison St., tel. 415/626–1409. Cover: none–$6 weeknights, from $6 up Fri. and Sat.. No credit cards.*

The Fillmore. San Francisco's famous rock music hall, closed for several years, was refurbished and retrofitted in 1994. It serves up a varied menu of national and local acts: rock, reggae, grunge, jazz, comedy, folk, acid house, and more. On the empty lot nearby was another famous landmark, Jim Jones's People's Temple. *1805 Geary Blvd. at Fillmore St., tel. 415/346–6000. Doors open at 8, shows at 9. Tickets: $12.50–$22.50. Credit cards not taken for tickets; for food and beverages, AE, MC, and V.*

Freight and Salvage Coffee House. This is one of the finest folk houses in the country; it's worth a trip across the bay. Some of the most talented practitioners of folk, blues, Cajun, and bluegrass perform at the Freight, among them U. Utah Phillips and Rosalie Sorrels. *1111 Addison St., Berkeley, tel. 510/548–1761. Tickets also available through BASS, tel. 510/762–2277. Shows: Sun. and Tues.–Thurs. 8 PM, Fri. and Sat. 8:30. Cover: $6–$12. No credit cards (except through BASS).*

Great American Music Hall. This is one of the great eclectic nightclubs, not only in San Francisco but in the entire country. Here you will find truly top-drawer entertainment, running the gamut from the best in blues, folk, and jazz to rock with a sprinkling of outstanding comedians. This colorful marble-pillared emporium will also accommodate dancing to popular bands. Past headliners here include Carmen McCrae, B.B. King, Billy Bragg, NRBQ, and Doc Watson. *859 O'Farrell St. between Polk and Larkin Sts., tel. 415/885–0750. Shows usually at 8 PM, but this may vary, so call. Cover: $5–$20. No credit cards.*

Jack's Bar. This smoky R&B dive (in every sense of the word) has been serving up hot music since 1932. There's dancing seven nights a week in a soulful atmosphere. The club's Sunday and Monday jam sessions are legendary. It's best to take a cab to and from this place. *1601 Fillmore St., tel. 415/567–3227. Shows begin at 9 PM. Cover: $3 Sun.–Thurs., $5 Fri. and Sat. nights. AE.*

Last Day Saloon. In an attractive setting of wooden tables and potted plants, this club offers some major entertainers and a varied schedule of blues, Cajun, rock, and jazz. Some of the illustrious performers who have appeared here are Taj Mahal, the Zazu Pitts Memorial Orchestra, Maria Muldaur, and Pride and Joy. *406 Clement St., between 5th and 6th Aves. in the Richmond District, tel. 415/387–6343. Shows begin at 9 PM Sun.–Thurs., and 9:30 PM Fri. and Sat. Cover: $4–$20. No credit cards.*

Lou's Pier 47. This Wharf restaurant features cool music and hot food on the waterfront. *300 Jefferson St., Fisherman's Wharf, tel. 414/771–0377. Shows Mon.–Thurs. at 4 and 9PM, Fri.–Sun. noon, 4 and 9 PM, but music's apt to be pouring out of the place other times as well. Cover only for 9 PM shows: $4 Mon.–Thurs., $5 Fri. and Sun., $6 Sat. AE, MC, V.*

Paradise Lounge. This quirky lounge has two stages for eclectic live music and dancing, plus an upstairs cabaret featuring offbeat performers. *1501 Folsom St., tel. 415/861–6906. Live music 10 PM nightly. Cover: none–$5, depending on the night and the act. No credit cards.*

Pier 23. A waterfront restaurant by day, this spot turns into a packed club by night, with a musical spectrum ranging from Caribbean, salsa, and jazz to Cajun zydeco. Get here early in the evening for dinner and you can keep your table after the music starts. *At Embarcadero and Pier 23, across from Fog City Diner, tel. 415/362–5125. Shows 9:30 PM Tues.–Sun. Cover: none–$8, depending on the night and act. MC, V.*

The Saloon. Some locals consider the historic Saloon the best spot in San Francisco for the blues. Headliners here include local R&B favorites Johnny Nitro and the Doorslammers. *1232 Grant*

St., near Columbus Ave. in North Beach, tel. 415/989–7666. Shows begin at 9 or 9:30 PM nightly. Cover: $5–$8 Fri. and Sat. No credit cards.

Slim's. One of the most popular nightclubs on the SoMa scene, Slim's specializes in what it labels "American roots music"— blues, jazz, classic rock, and the like. The club has expanded its repertoire in recent years with national touring acts playing alternative rock-and-roll and a series of "spoken word" concerts. Co-owner Boz Scaggs helps bring in the crowds and famous headliners. *333 11th St., tel. 415/621–3330. Shows nightly 9 PM. Cover: none–$20, depending on the night and act. AE, MC, V.*

The Warfield. One of the city's movie palaces was renovated as a showcase for mainstream rock-and-roll. There are tables and chairs downstairs, and theater seating upstairs. Such contemporary acts as the the Neville Brothers, Los Lobos, and k.d. lang have played here recently. *982 Market St. tel. 415/775–7722. Shows most nights at 8 PM. Tickets $15–$30. No credit cards (except through BASS).*

Jazz

Your jazz options run the gamut from a mellow restaurant cocktail lounge to hip SoMa venues to stylish showcases for top acts.

Cafe du Nord. What was once a Basque restaurant now hosts some of the liveliest jam sessions in town. The atmosphere in this basement poolroom/bar is decidedly casual, but the music, provided mostly by local talent, is strictly top-notch. *2170 Market St. at Sanchez St., tel. 415/861–5016. Open daily 4 PM–2 AM (the "tapas-inspired" kitchen serves food 6:30–11 Wed.–Sat.), with live music nightly at 9. Cover: $2, no drink minimum.*

Jazz at Pearl's. This club is one of the few reminders of North Beach's days as a hot spot for cool tunes. Sophisticated and romantic, the club's picture windows overlook City Lights Bookstore across the street. The talent level is remarkably high, especially considering that there is rarely a cover. *256 Columbus Ave., near Broadway, tel. 415/291–8255. Live music Sun.–Thurs. 9 PM–1 AM, Fri.–Sat. 9–1:30. Cover: none, except for special shows, 2-drink minimum every night.*

Kimball's East. This club in a shopping complex in Emeryville, just off Highway 80 near Oakland, hosts jazz greats such as Wynton Marsalis and Hugh Masekela and popular vocalists such as Lou Rawls and Patti Austin. With an elegant interior and fine food, this is one of most luxurious supper clubs in the Bay Area. *5800 Shellmound St., Emeryville, tel. 510/658–2555. Shows Wed.–Sun. at 8 and 10. Cover: $12–$24 with $5 minimum. Advance ticket purchase advised for big-name shows. MC, V.*

Moose's. One of the city's hottest new restaurants also features great sounds in its small but stylish bar area. *1652 Stockton St., in North Beach, tel. 415/989–7800. First set begins after 8 PM; music continues until midnight. No cover.*

New Orleans Room. This attractive room in the Fairmont Hotel is quickly gaining popularity, with such draws as Stanley Turrentine, Joe Williams, and others. *Mason and California Sts., tel. 415/772–5259. Showtimes vary, but generally are Thurs. and Sun. (and Mon.–Wed. on some occasions) 8 and 10, Fri. and Sat. 9 and 11. Cover: $18–$32. No drink minimum.*

Pasand Lounge. Jazz and R&B are the main attractions here. *1875 Union St., Pacific Heights, tel. 415/922–4498. Shows nightly, 8 PM–1 AM. No cover. 2-drink minimum. AE, MC, V.*

Up and Down Club. This hip restaurant and club, whose owners include supermodel Christy Turlington, books up-and-coming jazz artists downstairs Monday through Saturday. There's a bar and dancing to a DJ upstairs Wednesday through Saturday. *1151 Folsom St., tel. 415/626–2388. Downstairs shows begin at 9:30 PM. Cover: $3–$5 (admits you to either bar). AE, MC, V.*

Yoshi's. At press time, Yoshi's, one of the best jazz venues in the Bay Area, was moving to a location that should have been determined by the time you read this. Wherever the club lands, it will continue to book the biggest and best names in jazz—such as Betty Carter, local favorite Kenny Burrell, and Cecil Taylor. Check the *Chronicle's* Pink Section or phone the KJAZ *Jazz Line* at 510/769–4818.

Cabarets

Traditional cabaret is in short supply in San Francisco, but two longtime favorite spots and a couple of alternative venues offer a range of entertainment.

Club Fugazi. *Beach Blanket Babylon* is a wacky musical revue that has become the longest-running show of its genre in the history of the theater. A send-up of San Francisco moods and mores, *Beach Blanket* has now run for two decades, outstripping the Ziegfeld Follies by years. While the choreography is colorful and the songs witty, the real stars of the show are the exotic costumes—worth the price of admission in themselves. Order tickets as far in advance as possible; the revue has been sold out up to a month in advance. *678 Green St., 94133, tel. 415/421–4222 (for an order form, fax 415/421–4817). Shows Wed. and Thurs. 8 PM, Fri. and Sat. 7 and 10 PM, Sun. 3 and 7 PM. Cover: $17–$40, depending upon date and seating location. Note: those under 21 are admitted only to the Sun. matinee performance. MC, V.*

Finocchio's. The female impersonators at this amiable, world-famous club have been generating confusion for 56 years now. The scene at Finocchio's is decidedly retro, which for the most part only adds to its charm. *506 Broadway, North Beach, tel. 415/982–9388. Note: those under 21 not admitted. Shows Wed.–Sun. at 8:30, 10, and 11:30 (open Thurs.–Sat. in the off-season). Cover: $12, 2-drink minimum. MC, V.*

Josie's Cabaret and Juice Joint. This small stylish café and cabaret in the predominantly gay Castro District books performers who reflect the countercultural feel of the neighborhood. National talents stopping through have included Lypsinka and transsexual performance artist Kate Bornstein. *3583 16th St., at Market St., tel. 415/861–7933. Shows nightly, times vary. Cover: $6–$10. No credit cards.*

The Marsh. This Mission District venue books an eclectic mix of alternative/avant-garde theater, performance, comedy, and musical acts. *1062 Valencia St., tel. 415/641–0235. Most shows begin at 8 PM; often a different performer or event is scheduled at 10:30 PM.*

Comedy Clubs

In the '80s it seemed like every class clown or life-of-the-party type was cutting it up at a comedy club. The stand-up boom, like others from the decade, has gone bust, except for the two fine clubs listed below.

Cobb's Comedy Club. Bobby Slayton, Paula Poundstone, and Dr. Gonzo are among the super stand-up comics who perform here. *In the Cannery, 2801 Leavenworth St. at the corner of Beach St., tel. 415/928–4320. Shows Mon. 8 PM, Tues.–Thurs. 9 PM, Fri.–Sat. 9 and 11 PM. Cover: $8 weeknights, $10 and 2-drink minimum Fri. and Sat. MC, V.*

The Punch Line. A launching pad for the likes of Jay Leno and Whoopi Goldberg, the Punch Line features some of the top talents around—several of whom are certain to make a national impact. Note that weekend shows often sell out, and it is best to buy tickets in advance at BASS outlets (tel. 510/762–2277). *444-A Battery St. between Clay and Washington Sts., tel. 415/397–PLSF. Shows Sun.–Thurs. 9 PM, Fri.–Sat. 9 and 11 PM. Cover: $8 Tues.– Thurs., $10 Fri. and Sat.; special $5 showcases Mon. and Sun. 2-drink minimum. MC, V.*

Other comedy possibilities: Josie's and the Marsh (*see* Cabarets, *above*) often book, respectively, gay and avant-garde comics. The Fillmore and the Great American Music Hall (*see* Rock, Pop, Folk, and Blues, *above*) are also apt to have a favorite comic onstage.

Dancing Emporiums

Some of the rock, blues, and jazz clubs listed above sport active dance floors. Some also feature DJ dancing when live acts aren't on the stage. Below are eight spots devoted solely to folks out to shake a tail feather.

Bahia Tropical. Here's a truly international club. Dance to Salsa, Caribbean, African, Latin, Brazilian, and reggae music (sometimes in the same night) at this always-jumping joint. Cover includes lambada dance lessons Saturday nights. Some nights are given over to reggae, rap, deep house, and hip hop; live bands perform occasionally. The crowd is young and casual. *1600 Market St., tel. 415/861–8657. Dancing Tues.–Sun. 9:30 PM–1:30 AM. Cover: $3–$10.*

Cesar's Latin Palace. Salsa-style Latin music attracts all kinds of dancers to this popular club in the city's Mission District. Latin dance lessons from 9 to 10 PM are included in the price of admission Friday and Saturday nights. Note: no alcohol is served here. *3140 Mission St., tel. 415/648–6611. Open Sun. and*

Thurs. 8 PM–2 AM, Fri. and Sat. 9 PM–5 AM. Cover: $5–$7, which includes nearby parking and coat check.

Club DV8. One of SoMa's largest clubs, DV8 has two huge dance floors with DJs mixing up funk, flashback, Euro HiNRG, house, and techno. *540 Howard St., tel. 415/957–1730. Open Thurs. and Sun. 9 PM–5 AM, Fri. and Sat. 9 PM–4 AM. Cover: none 1st ½ hr Thurs.–Sat. and all day Sun., $5 Thurs., $10 Fri. and Sat.*

The Kennel Club. Alternative rock and funk rule in this small, steamy room. Monday, Wednesday, and Friday are live music nights, with bands from Zulu Spear or Sister Double Happiness to esoteric talents from around the world taking the stage. On Sundays DJs spin worldbeat and reggae; the Saturday menu varies from week to week. *628 Divisadero St., tel. 415/931–1914. Open nightly 9 PM–2 AM. Cover: $3–$10.*

Metronome Ballroom. Weekend nights are lively yet mellow at this smoke- and alcohol-free spot for ballroom dancing. Brush up on your steps on your own, or take the beginners' lessons early in the evening. *1830 17th St., tel. 415/252–9000. Open Fri. 9:30–midnight, Sat. 9–midnight, Sun. 7:30–11. Cover: $10 (includes dance lessons, which begin at 7:30 Fri. and Sat., 6:30 on Sun.).*

Oz. Take the St. Francis Hotel's glass elevator way up(scale) to the land of Oz. Surrounded by a splendid panorama of the city, you dance on marble floors and recharge on cushy sofas and bamboo chairs. The fine sound system belts out oldies, disco, Motown, and new wave. *335 Powell St., between Geary and Post Sts. on the top floor of the Westin St. Francis Hotel, tel. 415/397–7000. Open Sun.–Thurs. 9 PM–1:30 AM, Fri. and Sat. 9–2:30. Cover: $8 Sun.–Thurs.; $15 Fri.–Sat.*

Sound Factory. This south of Market club became an instant hit when it opened in 1993. Musical styles change with the night and sometimes the hour. Depending on who's up in the DJ booth, you're likely to hear anything from garage and deep house to '70s disco. Live bands also perform at special events. Some nights the venue becomes an alcohol-free, after-hours club. *525 Harrison St., tel. 415/543–1300. Hours and cover vary; call ahead.*

Up and Down Club. The upstairs bar here (there's live jazz downstairs) is given over to DJ dancing five nights a week. The dance floor isn't large, but it's always crammed on weekends with the beautiful people. *1151 Folsom St., tel. 415/626–2388. Open Mon. and Wed.–Sat. beginning at 9:30 PM. Cover: $3–$5 (admits you to both bars).*

If none of the above tickles your fancy, give the events hotline of one of these clubs a jingle: **Miss Pearl's Jam House** (tel. 415/775–JAMS); **El Rio** (tel. 415/282–3325); **The Upper Room** (tel. 415/861–0594; no smoking, no alcohol); **Avenue Ballroom** (tel. 415/681–2882; no smoking, no alcohol).

Piano Bars

You only have eyes for her. Or him. Six quiet spots with talented tinklers provide the perfect atmosphere for holding hands and making plans.

Act IV Lounge. A popular spot for a romantic rendezvous, the focal point of this tastefully appointed lounge is a crackling fireplace. *At the Inn at the Opera, 333 Fulton St. near Franklin St., tel. 415/553-8100. Pianist nightly 6-9. No cover.*

Club 36. Relax to piano music or jazz combos while overlooking Union Square from the top floor of the Grand Hyatt. *345 Stockton St., tel. 415/398-1234. Piano Mon.-Thurs., jazz Fri.-Sat., 9 PM- 1 AM. Cover: none Mon.-Thurs. or for hotel guests, $7 Fri.-Sat. for nonguests.*

Masons. Fine local talents play pop and show standards at this elegant restaurant in the Fairmont Hotel. *California and Mason Sts., tel. 415/392-0113. Piano Tues.-Thurs. and Sun. 7-11, Fri. and Sat. 8-midnight. No cover.*

Redwood Room. The atmosphere is low-key but sensuous in this classy Art Deco lounge. Klimt reproductions grace the walls, mellow sounds fill the air. *In the Four Seasons Clift Hotel, Taylor and Geary Sts., tel. 415/775-4700. Piano Sun.-Thurs. 5:30-11:30, Fri.-Sat. until 1:30 AM. No cover.*

Ritz-Carlton Hotel. The tastefully appointed Lobby Lounge features a harpist for high tea daily from 2:30 to 5 PM. The lounge shifts to piano (with occasional vocal accompaniment) for cocktails until 11:30 weeknights and 1:30 AM weekends. *600 Stockton St., tel. 415/296-7465. No cover.*

Washington Square Bar and Grill. A favorite of San Francisco politicians and newspaper folk, the "Washbag," as it is affectionately known, hosts pianists performing jazz and popular standards. *On North Beach's Washington Sq., 1707 Powell St., tel. 415/982-8123. Music Sun.-Tues. 6-10, Wed. 7-11, Thurs. 7-11:30, Fri. and Sat. 8:30-12:30. No cover.*

Skyline Bars

San Francisco is a city of spectacular vistas. Enjoy drinks, music, and sometimes dinner with 360-degree views at any of the bars below.

Carnelian Room. At 781 feet above the ground, enjoy dinner or cocktails here on the 52nd floor, where you may drink from the loftiest view of San Francisco's magnificent skyline. Reservations are a must for dinner here. *Top of the Bank of America Building, 555 California St., tel. 415/433-7500. Open Mon.-Thurs. 3-11:30 PM, Fri. 3 PM-12:30 AM, Sat. 4 PM-12:30 AM, Sun. 10 AM- 11:30 PM.*

Cityscape. At the top of the Hilton's tower, dance to Top 40, rock, and pop spun by a DJ nightly from 10 to 1. *In the Hilton Hotel, Mason and O'Farrell Sts., tel. 415/771-1400. Open nightly 5 PM-1 AM.*

Club 36. (*See* Piano Bars, *above.*)

Crown Room. Just ascending to the well-named Crown Room is a drama in itself as you take the Fairmont's glass-enclosed Skylift elevator to the top. Some San Franciscans maintain that this lounge is the most luxurious of the city's skyline bars. Lunch, dinner, and Sunday brunch are also served. *29th floor of the Fair-*

mont Hotel, California and Mason Sts., tel. 415/772–5131. Open daily 11 AM–1 AM.

Equinox. What's distinctive about the Hyatt Regency's skyline-view bar is its capacity to revolve atop its 22nd-floor perch, offering 360-degree views to guests from their seats. *At the Hyatt Regency, 5 Embarcadero Center, tel. 415/788–1234. Open Mon.–Thurs. 4 PM–1:30 AM, Fri. and Sat. 11 AM–1:30 AM, Sun. 10 AM–1:30 AM.*

Phineas T. Barnacle. This bar offers a unique panorama with views not of rooftops but of seal rocks and the horizon of the Pacific Ocean. *In the Cliff House, 1090 Point Lobos Ave., tel. 415/386–3330. Open daily 10 AM–2 AM.*

Top of the Mark. A famous magazine photograph immortalized this rooftop bar as a hotspot for World War II service people on leave or about to ship out; now folks can dance to the sounds of that era on weekends. There's live music Wednesday through Saturday nights, and dancing to standards from the '20s, '30s, and '40s Fridays and Saturdays. The view is superb seven nights a week. *In the Mark Hopkins Hotel, California and Mason Sts., tel. 415/392–3434. Open nightly 4 PM–12:30 AM.*

View Lounge. Found on the 39th floor of the San Francisco Marriott, one of the newest and loveliest of the city's skyline lounges features live piano music Monday–Saturday. *777 Market St., tel. 415/896–1600. Open noon–2 AM daily.*

Singles Bars

Ever notice how everyone looks so much better when you visit another town? That same sleight of eye happens here, too. If you're young, single, and free—and like that extra edge potential romance lends to a night spot—don your best duds and head to:

Balboa Cafe. A jam-packed hangout for the young, upwardly mobile crowd, this bar/restaurant is famous for its burgers and single clientele. *3199 Fillmore St., tel. 415/921–3944. Open nightly until 2 AM.*

Gordon Biersch Brewery and Restaurant. The great brew and its airy, Embarcadero setting have made this a favorite of the swinging twentysomething set. *2 Harrison St., in the old Hills Bros. coffee factory, tel. 415/243–8246. Bar opens daily at 11 AM and closes at 11:30 PM Mon.–Wed., 12:45 AM Thurs.–Sat., and 10 PM Sun.*

Hard Rock Cafe. Part of the famous chain of youth-oriented bars, this crowded saloon is filled with a collection of rock-and-roll memorabilia that won't disappoint fans. *1699 Van Ness Ave., tel. 415/885–1699. Open Sun.–Thurs. until midnight, Fri.–Sat. until 1 AM (kitchen closes 1 hr earlier).*

Harry Denton's. One of San Francisco's liveliest, most upscale saloons, Denton's is packed with well-dressed young professionals. There are live bands and dancing after 10 PM nightly except Sunday. Its location on the Embarcadero, where the freeway came down after the '89 quake, affords stunning views of the bay from the back bar. *161 Steuart St., tel. 415/882–1333. Open daily 5:30 PM–1 AM (kitchen closes at 10).*

The Holding Company. This is one of the most popular weeknight Financial District watering holes, where scores of office workers gather to enjoy friendly libations. *In 2 Embarcadero Center, tel. 415/986–0797. Open Mon.–Tues. until midnight, Wed.–Fri. until 2 AM. Closed weekends.*

Johnny Love's. The popular Mr. Love, formerly of Harry Denton's, opened his own place at the base of Russian Hill. It became an instant hit, and one of *the* places to be seen. Live music (heavy on the R&B) nightly. *1500 Broadway, at Polk St., tel. 415/931–8021. Bar is open Mon.–Sat. 5 PM–2 AM, Sun. 8PM–2 AM (dinner Mon.–Sat. 6–10).*

Perry's. Usually jam-packed, Perry's is the most famous of San Francisco's singles bars. You can dine here on great hamburgers as well as more substantial fare. *1944 Union St. at Buchanan St., tel. 415/922–9022. Open daily 9 AM–midnight.*

San Francisco's Favorite Bars

Locals patronize all of the places listed above, but there are several joints they hold near and dear:

Buena Vista. Even though the Buena Vista's claim of having introduced Irish coffee to the New World may be dubious, this is the Wharf area's most popular bar. It's usually packed with tourists and has a fine view of the waterfront. *2765 Hyde St., near Fisherman's Wharf, tel. 415/474–5044.*

Cypress Club. Sensual, '20s opulence clashes with Fellini/Dali frivolity in this San Francisco favorite. The decor alone is worth a visit, but this is a fine spot for a before-dinner or after-theater chat. Dashiell Hammett's *The Big Sleep* inspired the club's name. *500 Jackson St., off Columbus Ave., tel. 415/296–8555.*

Edinburgh Castle. Scots all over town went into mourning when this cherished watering hole closed in 1993. After several dark months, the Castle doors reopened, and its jukebox again pours out happy and sometimes baleful Scottish folk tunes the likes of which can be heard nowhere else in town; Fridays feature bagpipe performances. There are plenty of Scottish brews from which to choose. You can work off the fish-and-chips variety fare with a turn at the dart board. *950 Geary St. near Polk St., tel. 415/885–4074.*

Harrington's. This Irish drinking saloon is the place to be on St. Patrick's Day. *245 Front St., tel. 415/392–7595. Closed Sun.*

House of Shields. For a taste of an authentic old-time San Francisco saloon, try this bar, which attracts an older, Financial District crowd after work. It closes at 8 PM weekdays, 6 PM Saturday. *39 New Montgomery St., tel. 415/392–7732.*

John's Grill. Located on the fringe of the Tenderloin, this bar was featured in *The Maltese Falcon*, and mystery fans will revel in its Hammett memorabilia. *63 Ellis St., tel. 415/986–0069.*

Peer Inn. If you want to get away from the tourist scene while at the waterfront, this is a good place in which to imbibe; it also has an adjacent restaurant. *Pier 33 at the Embarcadero at the end of Bay St., tel. 415/788–1411.*

Spec's. It's worth looking for this somewhat hard-to-find hangout for artists, poets, and seamen. Spec's is a wonderful watering hole hideaway, reflecting a sense of the North Beach of days gone by. *12 Adler Pl., just south of Broadway on the east side of Columbus Ave., tel. 415/421–4112.*

Tosca Café. Like Spec's and Vesuvio nearby, Tosca holds a special place in San Francisco lore. There is some Italian flavor, with opera and Italian standards on the jukebox and an antique espresso/cappuccino machine that is nothing less than a work of art. Known as a hangout for filmmaker Francis Ford Coppola, playwright/actor Sam Shepard, and ballet star Mikhail Baryshnikov (when they're in town), this place positively breathes a film noir atmosphere. *242 Columbus Ave., tel. 415/391–1244.*

Vesuvio Cafe. Near the legendary City Lights Bookstore, this quintessentially North Beach bar is little altered since its heyday as a haven for the Beat poets. *255 Columbus Ave. between Broadway and Pacific Ave., tel. 415/362–3370.*

Gay and Lesbian Nightlife

In the days before the gay liberation movement, bars were more than mere watering holes. They also served as community centers where members of a mostly undercover minority could network and socialize. In the 1960s, they became hotbeds of political activity. The Tavern Guild of San Francisco, comprising the town's major gay establishments, achieved several of the community's first political victories, waging and winning a legal and public relations battle to end police harassment. Even teetotaling gays benefited from the confrontation. By the 1970s, other social opportunities became available to gay men and lesbians, and the bars' importance as centers of activity decreased. Old-timers wax nostalgic about the vibrancy of pre-AIDS, '70s bar life, but plenty of fun is still to be had today. There's one difference, though: some of the best clubs operate only one night per week at a location that may have a completely different (sometimes straight) clientele on other nights. A currently popular one-nighter for gay men happens every Friday night at the **End Up** (*see below*) at Sixth and Harrison, which on other nights is a lesbian hot spot (Saturday) or home to all-day dancing Saturdays and Sundays starting at 6 AM (really!).

The one-night-a-week clubs tend to come and go, so it's best to pick up one of the two main gay papers: the *Bay Area Reporter* (tel. 415/861–5019 to find out where to pick up a copy) or the *San Francisco Bay Times* (tel. 415/626–8121). Both, plus *Odyssey,* a club-info and gossip sheet, are usually available at the clubs listed below.

The papers reveal something else: there's more to gay nightlife than the bars. Most nights, **Theatre Rhinoceros** (tel. 415/861–5079) offers plays or solo shows on two stages and **Josie's Cabaret** features work by cutting-edge performance, comedy, and theater artists. Members of the Tavern Guild (tel. 415/752–2366) and Japantown Bowling (tel. 415/921–6200) leagues compete Monday–Thursday nights. City College's Gay and Lesbian Studies Department (tel. 415/239–3383) holds Monday–Thursday classes (6:30–9:30 PM) in film, literature, and other topics at Everett Middle School, 17th Street at Church (it's almost always OK to drop in for a session). Check the gay papers' extensive calendar listings for other activities.

Lesbian Bars Surprisingly, for a place known as a "gay" mecca, at present there are only two seven-days-a-week women's bars and a few reliable one-nighters (call ahead to be sure they are still operating). Younger lesbians and gays, some of whom prefer to call themselves "queers," don't segregate themselves quite as much as the older set; you'll find mixed crowds at a number of the bars listed under Gay Male Bars, below.

The Box. This long-running one-nighter moved to new digs in 1994, but "Mixtress" Page Hodel still keeps the crowd here in constant motion with house, hip-hop, and funk sounds. *City Nights, 715 Harrison St., tel. 415/647–8258 for Box info. Open 8 PM–2 AM. Cover: $4. Thurs. nights only.*

The Café. Formerly Café San Marcos, this bar in the heart of the gay Castro district is always comfortable and often crowded. Chat quietly at one end or cut the rug at the other. *2367 Market St. at 17th St., tel. 415/861–3846. Open noon–2 AM. No cover.*

Faster Pussycat. A fun-loving crowd engages in "shedonism in all its glory," with popular DJ Downtown Donna and others. This long-running club has survived several moves and changes of day. It's presently at: *The Pit, 201 9th St. at Howard St., tel. 415/863–2548. Starts at 9:30 PM. Cover: $4–$5.*

Girlspot. The best place for a lesbian to be on Saturday night, this hot spot (aka G-Spot) features good dance music, mostly pop (Whitney Houston, etc.,) with a bit of techno-beat. *At the End Up, 6th and Harrison Sts., tel. 415/543–7700. Doors open at 9 PM. Sat. only. Cover: $5.*

Red Dora's Bearded Lady Café and Cabaret. This neighborhood venue serves a predominantly lesbian and gay clientele. It's also a gallery (mostly women's work) and music outlet for local independent labels. *485 14th St., at Guerrero St., tel. 415/626–2805. Open weekdays 7 AM–7 PM, Sat. and Sun. 9 AM–7 PM. Irregularly scheduled weekend performances begin at 8 PM (cover varies). Call ahead or check gay papers. No alcohol served.*

The Wild Side West. Its name notwithstanding, mellow is the word for this neighborhood bar, way off the beaten path in Bernal Heights. *429 Cortland St., tel. 415/647–3099. Open daily 1 PM–2 AM. No cover.*

Gay Male "A bar for every taste, that's the ticket," was how the curious
Bars "documentary" *Gay San Francisco* described late-'60s nightlife here. Leather bars, drag-queen hangouts, piano bars, and bohemian cafés were among the many options for gay men back then. The scene remains just as versatile today. Unless otherwise noted, there is no cover charge at these establishments.

The SoMa Scene

The End Up. Patrons here cruise and carouse in the open-air courtyard or work up a sweat on two dance floors. From night to night, the bar attracts a highly eclectic crowd, from preppies and "baby dykes" to outrageous drag queens and multiple-pierced, leather-clad lesbians. *6th and Harrison Sts., tel. 415/543–7700. Open nightly until 2 AM, after hours (no alcohol) some weekends. Cover: variable on weekends.*

Esta Noche. Latino gays, including some of the city's wildest drag queens, dance and hang out at this longtime Mission District establishment. *3079 16th St., below Valencia St., tel. 415/861–5757. Open 1 PM–2 AM. Cover: weeknights none, $4 Fri.–Sun.*

Rawhide II. A favorite spot among gay C&W fans, the Rawhide offers dance lessons most nights and a convivial atmosphere every night. *280 7th St., tel. 415/621–1197. Open daily noon–2 AM. Cover: none Sun.–Thurs., $5 Fri.–Sat. (includes 2 drink tickets).*

SF-Eagle. In the days before AIDS and gentrification, SoMa was the headquarters for the gay leather set, with a dozen or so bars along Folsom and Harrison streets. Of the few that remain, the SF-Eagle is by far the most popular. International leather legend Mister Marcus (to you) drops by to judge the Mr. SF Leather, Mr. Leather Calendar, and innumerable other contests, most of which are AIDS benefits. *12th and Harrison Sts., tel. 415/626–0880. Open weekdays 4 PM–2 AM, weekends 2 PM–2 AM.*

The Stud. Still going strong after 29 years, the Stud's always-groovin' DJs mix up-to-the-minute music with carefully chosen highlights from the glory days of gay disco. *Harrison and 9th Sts., tel. 415/863–6623. Open daily 5 PM–2 AM. Dancing continues (without alcohol) on weekends as long as the crowd remains frisky. Cover: none–$3.*

In the Castro

Café Flore. Poets, punks, and poseurs mingle day and night at open-air tables or inside the glass walls of this bohemian bistro, which serves beer, wine, coffee, and tea. A separate concessionaire serves surprisingly tasty food until 10 PM, though most people come only for drinks or dessert. *2298 Market St., tel. 415/621–8579. Open daily 7:30 AM–11:30 PM.*

Detour. The crowd here is youngish and a bit surly (in a sexy sort of way). The music is loud but well selected. *2348 Market St., tel. 415/861–6053. Open daily 2 PM–2 AM.*

The Elephant Walk. One of the Castro's cozier bars, this is among the few (along with Moby Dick, at 18th and Hartford streets, and Twin Peaks, at 17th and Castro streets) where the music level allows for easy conversation. *Castro St., at 18th St., no phone. Open 11 AM–2 AM.*

The Metro. Just down Market Street from the Detour is the more upscale Metro, whose balcony overlooks the intersection of Noe, 16th, and Market streets. "Guppies" (gay yuppies) love this place, which has a fairly good restaurant adjoining the bar. *3600 16th St., at Market St., tel. 415/703–9750. Open Mon.–Thurs. 2:30 PM–2 AM, weekends 1 PM–2 AM.*

The Midnight Sun. This is one of the Castro's longest-standing and most popular bars, with giant video screens riotously programmed. Don't expect to hear yourself think. *4067 18th St., tel. 415/861–4186. Open noon–2 AM.*

On/Near **The Cinch.** Country-western music rules in this neighborhood
Polk Street bar, one of several in the city that hosts the gay San Francisco
Pool Association's weekly matches. *1723 Polk St., tel. 415/776–4162. Open 6 AM–2 AM.*

Giraffe Video Lounge. This lively bar has multiple TV screens
playing the latest music videos. *1131 Polk St., tel. 415/474–1702.
Open 11 AM–2 AM.*

Kimo's. Floor-to-ceiling windows provide a great view of Polk
Street action from this laid-back club. *1551 Polk St., tel. 415/885–4535. Open 8 AM–2 AM.*

N Touch. This tiny dance bar has long been popular with Asian-
Pacific Islander gay men. Video screens alternately play mildly
erotic videos and MTV fare. *1548 Polk St., tel. 415/441–8413. Open
3 PM–2 AM. Cover: none Sun.–Wed., $2 Thurs.–Sat.*

Around Town **The Lion Pub.** One of the community's older enterprises, the
Lion is a cozy neighborhood bar with an ever-changing but always singular decor. *2062 Divisadero St., at Sacramento St., tel.
415/567–6565. Open 3 PM–2 AM.*

Sutter's Mill. A longtime favorite with the gay Financial District
set, this bar is usually packed for lunch (served 11:30–3) and
right after work. *10 Mark La., off Bush St. between Grant Ave.
and Kearny St., tel. 415/788–8377. Open weekdays 10:30–10.*

9 Excursions from San Francisco

Sausalito

*By Robert
Taylor*

The San Francisco Convention and Visitors Bureau describes Sausalito's location as "the Mediterranean side of the Golden Gate." With its relatively sheltered site on the bay in Marin County, just 8 miles from San Francisco, it appeals to Bay Area residents and visitors for the same reason: It is so near and yet so far. As a hillside town with superb views, an expansive yacht harbor, the aura of an artist's colony, and ferry service, Sausalito might be a resort within commuting distance of the city. It is certainly the primary excursion for visitors to San Francisco, especially those with limited time to explore the Bay Area. Mild weather encourages strolling and outdoor dining, although afternoon winds and fog can roll over the hills from the ocean, funneling through the central part of town once known as Hurricane Gulch.

There are substantial homes, including Victorian mansions, in Sausalito's heights, but the town has long had a more colorful and raffish reputation. Discovered in 1775 by Spanish explorers and named Saucelito (Little Willow) for the trees growing around its springs, Sausalito was a port for whaling ships during the 19th century. In 1875, the railroad from the north connected with ferryboats to San Francisco and the town became an attraction for the fun-loving. Even the chamber of commerce recalls the time when Sausalito sported 25 saloons, gambling dens, and bordellos. Bootleggers flourished during Prohibition in the 1920s, and shipyard workers swelled the town's population during the 1940s, when tour guides divided the residents into "wharf rats" and "hill snobs."

Ensuing decades brought a bohemian element with the development of an artists' colony and a houseboat community. Sausalito has also become a major yachting center, and restaurants attract visitors for the fresh seafood as well as the spectacular views. Sausalito remains a friendly and casual small town, although summer traffic jams can fray nerves. If possible, visit Sausalito on a weekday—and take the ferry.

Arriving and Departing

By Car Cross the Golden Gate Bridge and go north on U.S. 101 to the Sausalito exit, then go south on Bridgeway to municipal parking near the center of town. The trip takes 30 to 45 minutes one-way. (You will need change for the parking lots' meters.)

By Bus **Golden Gate Transit** (tel. 415/332–6600) travels to Sausalito from 1st and Mission streets and other points in the city.

By Ferry **Golden Gate Ferry** (tel. 415/332–6600) crosses the bay from the Ferry Building at Market Street and the Embarcadero; **Red and White Fleet** (tel. 415/546–2896) leaves from Pier 41 at Fisherman's Wharf. The trip takes 15–30 minutes.

The Bay Area

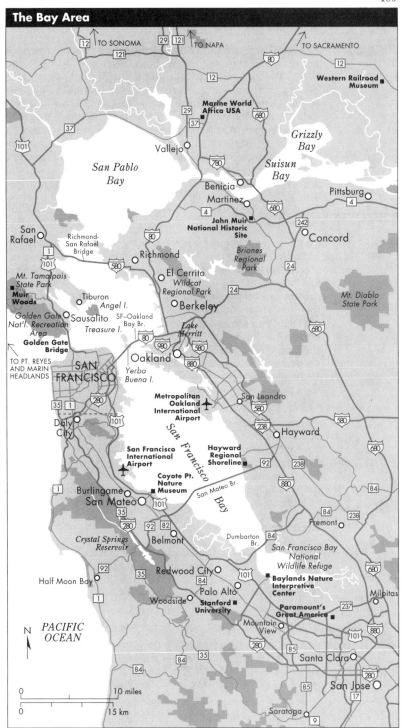

TO SONOMA 12

29 121 TO NAPA

TO SACRAMENTO 80

12

12

Western Railroad Museum

101

37

Marine World Africa USA

29

37

Vallejo

780

680

Grizzly Bay

San Pablo Bay

Suisun Bay

Benicia

Martinez

4

Pittsburg

4

680

242

Concord

San Rafael

101

Richmond-San Rafael Bridge

580

Richmond

80

John Muir National Historic Site

Briones Regional Park

24

Mt. Diablo State Park

1

Mt. Tamalpais State Park

Muir Woods

Tiburon

Angel I.

El Cerrito

Wildcat Regional Park

Berkeley

24

680

Golden Gate Nat'l. Recreation Area

Sausalito

Treasure I.

SF-Oakland Bay Br.

Lake Merritt

80

980

580

Golden Gate Bridge

TO PT. REYES AND MARIN HEADLANDS

SAN FRANCISCO

Yerba Buena I.

Oakland

880

35 1

280

Metropolitan Oakland International Airport

San Leandro

580

Daly City

101

238

Hayward

580

680

San Francisco International Airport

San Francisco Bay

Hayward Regional Shoreline

92

238

880

84

Coyote Pt. Nature Museum

1

Burlingame

San Mateo

35

101

San Mateo Br.

84

238

92

82

280

Belmont

Dumbarton Br.

84

Fremont

680

Crystal Springs Reservoir

35

San Francisco Bay National Wildlife Refuge

Half Moon Bay

92

Redwood City

84

101

Baylands Nature Interpretive Center

Milpitas

1

Woodside

Stanford University

Paramount's Great America

237

880

N

PACIFIC OCEAN

Mountain View

280

85

Santa Clara

280

35

84

84

85

17

San Jose

9

Saratoga

0 _____ 10 miles

0 _____ 15 km

Guided Tours

Most tour companies include Sausalito on excursions north to Muir Woods and the Napa Valley Wine Country. Among them are **Gray Line** (tel. 415/558–9400) and **Great Pacific Tour Co.** (tel. 415/626–4499).

Exploring

Numbers in the margin correspond to points of interest on the Sausalito map.

Bridgeway is Sausalito's main thoroughfare and prime destination, with the bay, yacht harbor, and waterfront restaurants on one side, and more restaurants, shops, hillside homes, and hotels on the other. It is only a few steps from the ferry terminal to the

1 tiny landmark park in the center of town: the **Plaza Vina del Mar,** named for Sausalito's sister city in Chile. The park features a fountain and two 14-foot-tall statues of elephants created for the 1915 Panama-Pacific International Exposition in San Francisco.

2 Across the street to the south is the Spanish-style **Sausalito Hotel,** which has been refurbished and filled with Victorian an-

3 tiques. Between the hotel and the **Sausalito Yacht Club** is another unusual historic landmark, a drinking fountain with the invitation Have a Drink on Sally. It's in remembrance of Sally Stanford, the former San Francisco madam who later ran Sausalito's Valhalla restaurant and became the town's mayor. Actually, the monument is also in remembrance of her dog. There is a sidewalk-level bowl that suggests Have a Drink on Leland.

South on Bridgeway, toward San Francisco, there is an esplanade along the water with picture-perfect views. Farther south are a number of restaurants on piers, including—near the end

4 of Bridgeway at Richardson Street—what was the **Valhalla** and is the oldest restaurant in Sausalito. Built in 1893 as "Walhalla," it was one of the settings for the film *The Lady from Shanghai* in the 1940s, Sally Stanford's place in the 1950s, and most recently a Chart House restaurant.

North on Bridgeway from the ferry terminal are yacht harbors and, parallel to Bridgeway a block to the west, the quieter Caledonia Street, with its own share of cafés and shops. There is a pleasant, grassy park with a children's playground at Caledonia and Litho streets, with a food shop nearby for picnic provisions.

Here and there along the west side of Bridgeway are flights of steps that climb the hill to Sausalito's wooded, sometimes rustic and sometimes lavish residential neighborhoods. The stairway just across the street from Vina del Mar Park is named Excel-

5 sior, and it leads to the **Alta Mira,** a popular Spanish-style hotel and restaurant with a spectacular view (*see* Dining, *below*). However, there are vistas of the bay from all these streets.

Where there isn't a hillside house or a restaurant or a yacht in Sausalito, there is a shop. Most are along Bridgeway and Prin-

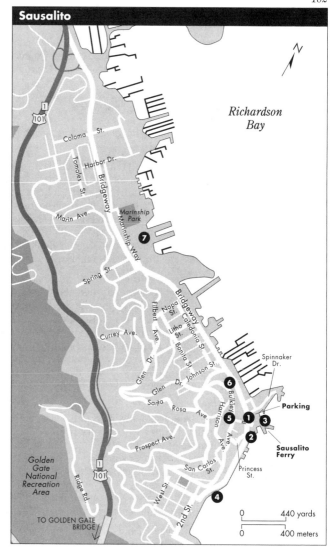

cess Street, and they offer a wide assortment of casual and sophisticated clothing, posters and paintings, imported and hand-crafted gifts, and the expected variety of T-shirts, ice cream, cookies, and pastries. The **Village Fair** (777 Bridgeway) is a four-story former warehouse that has been converted into a warren of clothing, craft, and gift boutiques. Crafts workers often demonstrate their talents in the shops, and a winding brick path—Little Lombard Street—connects various levels. The shopping complex is a haven during wet weather.

Sausalito's reputation as an art colony is enhanced by the **Art Festival** held during the three-day Labor Day weekend in September. It attracts more than 35,000 visitors to the waterfront area, and ferry service is extended to the site during the festival. Details are available from the Sausalito Chamber of Commerce (333 Caledonia St., 94965, tel. 415/332–0505).

⑦ North on Bridgeway, within a few minutes' drive, is the **Bay Model,** a re-creation in miniature of the entire San Francisco Bay and the San Joaquin–Sacramento River delta. It is actually nearly 400 feet square and is used by the U.S. Army Corps of Engineers to reproduce the rise and fall of tides, the flow of currents, and the other physical forces at work on the bay. It is housed in a former World War II shipyard building, and there is a display of shipbuilding history. At the same site is the Wapama, a World War I–era steam freighter being restored by volunteers. *2100 Bridgeway, tel. 415/332–3871. Open Tues.–Fri. 9–4, weekends 10–6. Closed Sun. in winter.*

Along the shore of Richardson Bay, between the Bay Model and U.S. 101, are some of the 400 houseboats that make up Sausalito's "floating homes community." In the shallow tidelands, most of them float only about half the time, but they are always a fanciful collection of the rustic, the eccentric, the flamboyant, and the elegant.

Just south of Sausalito, facing a cove beneath the Golden Gate Bridge, the **Bay Area Discovery Museum** fills five former military buildings with entertaining and enlightening hands-on exhibits. Youngsters and their families can crew on a boat, explore in and under a house, and make multitrack recordings. From San Francisco take the Alexander Avenue exit from U.S. 101 and follow signs to East Fort Baker. *Tel. 415/332–7674. Admission $4. Open Wed.–Sun. 1–5, and Tues. 10–5 in summer. Closed major holidays.*

Dining

Dining listings revised and updated by Catherine McEver

Restaurants by the bay or perched on Sausalito's hillside feature prime views and fare that covers the waterfront. The town's unique cholesterol-free ordinance means you'll find at least one heart-healthy pick on every menu. Casual dress is acceptable everywhere.

Restaurants are listed according to price category.

Category	Cost*
$$$$	over $30
$$$	$20–$30
$$	$10–$20
$	under $10

per person, excluding drinks, service, and 7¹/₄% sales tax

$$$ **Casa Madrona.** Part of a hotel complex that includes a classic Victorian, a cluster of cottages, and terraced gardens stepping down the hillside, this upscale dining scenario serves up fine

American cuisine and all-star views of the bay. The light, airy dining terrace with retractable roof and sliding glass walls is a great spot to splurge on a Sunday brunch buffet. *801 Bridgeway, tel. 415/331–5888. AE, D, DC, MC, V. No lunch Sat.*

$$–$$$ **Alta Mira.** This Sausalito landmark, in a Spanish-style hotel a block above Bridgeway, has spectacular views of the bay from the front terrace and the windowed dining room. It's a favored destination Bay Area–wide for Sunday brunch (try the famed eggs Benedict), an alfresco lunch, or cocktails at sunset. The California-Continental cuisine created here includes succulent rack of lamb, duckling, seafood salad, and a stellar Caesar salad. *125 Bulkley Ave., tel. 415/332–1350. Reservations advised. AE, DC, MC, V.*

$$ **The Spinnaker.** Spectacular bay views, homemade pastas, and seafood specialties like fresh grilled salmon are the prime attractions in a contemporary building on a point beyond the harbor, near the yacht club. You may see a pelican perched on one of the pilings just outside. *100 Spinnaker Dr., tel. 415/332–1500. Reservations advised. Sunday brunch. AE, DC, MC, V.*

$–$$ **Margaritaville.** Exotic drinks and every Mexican favorite you'd ever crave from fajitas and enchiladas to *camarones ranchero* (fresh Pacific prawns sautéed in a flavorful red sauce) are on the bill of fare in a tropically hip setting with views of the marina and the bay. *1200 Bridgeway, tel. 415/331–3226. Reservations accepted for 8 or more. AE, DC, MC, V.*

$ **Lighthouse Coffee Shop.** This budget-priced coffee shop serves breakfast and lunch (omelets, sandwiches, and burgers) every day starting at dawn. Most find the down-to-earth atmosphere and simple fare a relief from tourist traps and seafood extravaganzas. *1311 Bridgeway, tel. 415/331–3034. No reservations. No credit cards. No alcohol.*

Tiburon

Located on a peninsula called Punta de Tiburon (Shark Point) by the Spanish explorers, this Marin County community has maintained its village atmosphere. The harbor faces Angel Island across Raccoon Strait, and San Francisco is directly south, 6 miles across the bay. The view from the decks of restaurants on the harbor may be the town's major attraction to visitors. No matter how crowded it gets on weekends, Tiburon remains more low-key than Sausalito. Tiburon has always been a waterfront settlement, beginning in 1884 when ferryboats from San Francisco connected here with a railroad to San Rafael. Whenever there's pleasant weather, and particularly during the summer, the ferry is the most relaxing way to visit and avoid traffic and parking problems.

Arriving and Departing

By Car   Take U.S. 101 north to the Tiburon Boulevard exit. The trip takes about 45 minutes to one hour one-way.

By Ferry   **Red and White Fleet** (tel. 415/546–2896) ferries depart weekdays in the early morning, late afternoon, and evening from the Ferry Building. Ferries also depart midday on weekdays and all day on weekends from Pier 41. The trip takes a half-hour. Ferry service is available across the strait from Tiburon to Angel Island (tel. 415/435–2131).

By Bus   **Golden Gate Transit** (tel. 415/332–6600) sends buses to Tiburon from First and Mission streets and other points in San Francisco and also from Sausalito.

Exploring

Tiburon's main street is indeed called **Main Street.** It's lined on the bay side with restaurants that overlook the harbor and offer views of San Francisco from outdoor decks. Sunday brunch is especially popular. On the other side of the narrow street are shops and galleries that sell casual clothing, gifts, jewelry, posters, and paintings. One gallery is devoted to a visual celebration of food. West along Main Street is **Ark Row.** During the 19th century these buildings were houseboats on the bay. Later they were beached and transformed into shops; now they are antiques and specialty stores along a tree-lined walk. On a hill above town is **Old St. Hilary's Historic Preserve,** a Victorian-era church operated by the Landmarks Society as a historical and botanical museum. The surrounding area is a wildflower preserve. *Esperanza and Alemany Sts., tel. 415/435–1853. Admission free. Open Wed. and Sun. 1–4.*

Between Tiburon Boulevard and Richardson Bay, in a wildlife sanctuary on the route into town, is the 1876 **Lyford House** (tel. 415/388–2524), a Victorian fantasy that is now the western headquarters for the National Audubon Society. House tours are conducted.

Dining

Tiburon's restaurants specialize in prime bay views and seafood prepared simply or with Mexican, Italian, or Chinese touches. The informal dining and drinking cafés along Main Street also serve a wide variety of lunch and brunch fare. Dress is casual.

Restaurants are listed according to price category.

Category	Cost*
$$$$	over $30
$$$	$20–$30

$$	$10–$20
$	under $10

per person, excluding drinks, service, and 7¹/₄% sales tax

$$ **Guaymas.** You won't find tacos on the menu here. In a large open kitchen the focus is on regional Mexican cuisine: fresh seafood, red meat, and poultry presented in a range of special sauces and served up with rice and beans. You are treated to hot tortillas and three different kinds of salsa the moment you are seated. The adobe walls are whitewashed and decorated with colorful Mexican toys; there is a bay view and a terrace bar. *5 Main St., at the ferry terminal, tel. 415/435–6300. Reservations advised. Sunday brunch. AE, DC, MC, V.*

Mr. Q's. Located on an upper level over the harbor, this casual and crowded restaurant is best known for the view from a deck that extends farther onto the bay than do its competitors. Jazz and rock groups play on weekends. Steaks, ribs, and fresh seafood are popular here; pasta, sandwiches, salads, and a variety of drinks are offered for lunch and dinner. Brunch is served every day. *25 Main St., tel. 415/435–5088. Reservations advised for dinner, not accepted for lunch. AE, DC, MC, V.*

Sam's Anchor Cafe. Mahogany wainscoting, old photos on the walls, and wonderful views of the bay from the outside deck make this place a perfect pick for lunch, dinner, or weekend brunch. Throw in a friendly, informal atmosphere, crayons and a color-in menu for the kids, and a tempting array of selections from fresh seafood to sandwiches, soups, and salads, and you're ready to settle in and stay awhile. *27 Main St., tel. 415/435–4527. Reservations for dinner only. AE, D, DC, MC, V.*

$ **Sweden House Bakery & Café.** Pastries, breakfast specialties, and sandwiches (asparagus tips and Danish ham; smoked Pacific salmon; avocado, bacon, and sprouts), along with espresso and cappuccino, are served here. There is a take-out bakery and a full-service café with seating inside or on a secluded deck where a sign warns, "Please Watch Your Food or the Birds Will Eat It." *35 Main St., tel. 415/435–9767. No reservations. Open for breakfast and lunch only. MC, V.*

The Marin Headlands

"The Golden Gate" originally referred not to a bridge painted "international orange" but to the grassy and poppy-strewn hills flanking the passageway into San Francisco Bay. This is the one break in the Coast Range Mountains that allows the rivers of California's 400-mile-long Central Valley to reach the ocean. The most dramatic scenery is on the north side of the gate—the Marin Headlands. Once the site of military installations, they are now open to the public as part of the Golden Gate National Recreation Area. The most spectacular photographs of San Francisco are taken from the headlands, with the Golden Gate Bridge in the foreground and the city skyline on the horizon.

There are remarkable views east across the bay, north along the coast, and out to sea, where the Farallon Islands are visible on a clear day.

Arriving and Departing

By Car   The headlands are a logical side trip on the way to Sausalito, but reaching them can be tricky. Take U.S. 101 across the Golden Gate Bridge to the first exit, Alexander Avenue, just past Vista Point. Then take the first left turn through a tunnel under the highway and look for signs to Fort Barry and Fort Cronkhite. Conzelman Road follows the cliffs that face the gate; Bunker Road is a less spectacular route through Rodeo to the headlands headquarters at Fort Cronkhite.

By Bus   **San Francisco Muni** (tel. 415/673–6864) No. 76 runs hourly from Fourth and Townsend streets on Sundays and holidays only. The trip takes 45 minutes one-way.

Exploring

Although they are only a short distance from San Francisco, the headlands are a world apart—a vast expanse of wild and open terrain. There are windswept ridges, stretches of shrubs and wildflowers, protected valleys, and obscure beaches. The views can be breathtaking, even when fog is rushing over the hills into the bay. The weather can change dramatically within a few hours, however. Dress warmly and wear appropriate shoes for walking. Stay on marked paths and park in designated areas.

The **Marin Headlands Visitors Center** at Fort Cronkhite is the center for exploring the region, which includes Rodeo Beach, Rodeo Lagoon, and the Point Bonita lighthouse. *Tel. 415/331–1540. Open daily 9:30–4:30.*

Also at Fort Cronkhite is the **California Marine Mammal Center** (tel. 415/289–7325), which rescues and rehabilitates sick and injured seals and sea lions. Campsites are available, and at nearby Fort Barry there is the Golden Gate Hostel (tel. 415/331–2777). For advance planning, detailed maps are available at the Golden Gate National Recreation Area headquarters in Fort Mason, Bay and Franklin streets, in San Francisco (tel. 415/556–0560).

Conzelman Road offers the most spectacular views of the gate, and craggy **Hawk Hill** is the best place on the West Coast from which to watch the migration of eagles, hawks, and falcons as they fly south for the winter from mid-August to mid-December. As many as 1,000 have been sighted in a single day. The viewing area is about 2 miles up Conzelman Road; look for a sign denoting former military Battery 129.

Muir Woods

One hundred and fifty million years ago, ancestors of redwood and sequoia trees grew throughout the United States. Today the *Sequoia sempervirens* can be found only in a narrow, cool coastal belt from Monterey to Oregon. (*Sequoiadendron gigantea* grows in the Sierra Nevada.) **Muir Woods National Monument,** 17 miles northwest of San Francisco, is a 550-acre park that contains one of the most majestic redwood groves in the world. Some redwoods in the park are nearly 250 feet tall and 1,000 years old. This grove was saved from destruction in 1908 and named for naturalist John Muir, whose campaigns helped to establish the National Park system. His response: "This is the best tree-lover's monument that could be found in all of the forests of the world. Saving these woods from the axe and saw is in many ways the most notable service to God and man I have heard of since my forest wandering began."

Arriving and Departing

By Car Take U.S. 101 north to the Mill Valley–Muir Woods exit. The trip takes 45 minutes one-way when the roads are clear, but traffic can be heavy on summer weekends, so allow more time. The park staff recommends visiting before 10 AM and after 4 PM to avoid congestion. Note that the narrow, winding entrance road cannot accommodate some larger recreation vehicles.

Guided Tours

Most tour companies include Muir Woods on excursions to the Wine Country, among them **Gray Line** (tel. 415/558–9400) and **Great Pacific** (tel. 415/626–4499).

Exploring

Muir Woods is a park for walking; no cars are allowed in the redwood grove itself. There are 6 miles of easy trails from the park headquarters. The main trail along Redwood Creek is 1 mile long, paved, and wheelchair accessible. The paths cross streams and pass through ferns and azaleas as well as magnificent stands of redwoods such as Bohemian Grove and the circular formation called Cathedral Grove. The trails connect with an extensive network of hiking tails in Mt. Tamalpais State Park. No picnicking or camping is allowed, but snacks are available at the visitor center, along with a wide selection of books and exhibits. The weather is usually cool and often wet, so dress warmly and wear shoes appropriate for damp trails. Pets are not allowed. *Tel. 415/388–2595. Open daily 8 AM–sunset.*

Mt. Tamalpais State Park

Although the summit of Mt. Tamalpais is less than 1/2-mile high, the mountain rises practically from sea level and dominates the topography of Marin County. Located about 18 miles northwest of San Francisco, adjacent to Muir Woods National Monument, Mt. Tamalpais offers views of the entire Bay Area and west to the Pacific Ocean from its summit. On foggy days lower elevations are sometimes blanketed by the fog, with other peaks just visible above. For years this 6,400-acre park has been a favorite destination for hikers. There are 50 miles of trails, some rugged but many developed for easy walking through meadows, grasslands, and forests, and along creeks.

Arriving and Departing

By Car Take U.S. 101 north over the Golden Gate Bridge to the Mill Valley–Muir Woods exit. From this road (Shoreline Hwy.), take Panoramic Highway into the park. The trip takes one hour one-way.

By Bus **Golden Gate Transit** (tel. 415/332–6600) departs from 1st and Mission streets and other points in the city.

Exploring

Panoramic Highway—the winding "Pan Toll Road" was once a toll road—eventually leads to the three peaks and the 2,571-foot summit of Mt. Tamalpais. Along the route are numerous parking areas, picnic spots, scenic overlooks, and trailheads. **The Mountain Theater** is a natural amphitheater with terraced stone seats that is used for plays and musicals in May and June. The relatively gentle **West Point Trail** begins here. A map of hiking trails is available from the ranger station, about 4 miles from the intersection of Panoramic Highway and the road down the hill to Muir Woods. *Tel. 415/388–2070. Open daily 8 AM–sunset.*

Point Reyes

By Dan Spitzer

Point Reyes frames the northern end of Drake's Bay. When Sir Francis sailed down the California coast in 1579 he missed the Golden Gate and San Francisco Bay, but he did land at what he described as a convenient harbor. It may have been Drake's Bay, Bolinas Bay, Bodega Bay, or somewhere else along Point Reyes. With its high rolling grassland above spectacular cliffs, Point Reyes probably reminded him of Scotland. Today Point Reyes National Seashore is a spectacularly beautiful park and a favorite spot for whale-watching.

Arriving and Departing

Take U.S. 101 north over the Golden Gate Bridge to the Mill Valley–Muir Woods exit and take Highway 1 north. You'll pass the turnoffs for Muir Woods and Mt. Tamalpais. If you have the energy for a long day of exploring, you can combine a trip to Point Reyes with a trip to Muir Woods or Mt. Tamalpais, but you'll need well over an hour to get to the visitor center and two hours to get all the way from San Francisco to the end of the point.

Exploring

Past the turnoff for Muir Woods, Highway 1 takes you past the town of **Stinson Beach,** which takes its name from one of the longest (4,500 ft) and most popular stretches of sand in Marin County. Along Bolinas Lagoon, just north of Stinson Beach, you'll find the **Audubon Canyon Ranch,** a 1,000-acre bird sanctuary. During the spring the public is invited to view great blue heron and great egret tree nests. There is also a small museum with a picnic area and displays on the geology and natural history of the region. *Tel. 415/868–9244. Admission free. Open mid-Mar.–mid-July, weekends and holidays only 10–4.*

At the northern edge of Bolinas Lagoon, a couple of miles beyond the Audubon Canyon Ranch, follow the unmarked road running west from Highway 1. This leads to the sleepy town of **Bolinas.** Some residents are so wary of tourism that whenever the state tries to post signs, they tear them down. Birders should take Mesa Road until they reach the **Point Reyes Bird Observatory,** a sanctuary that harbors nearly 350 species. *Tel. 415/868–0655. Admission free. Open daily.*

As you drive back to Bolinas, go right on Overlook Drive and right again on Elm Avenue until you come to Duxberry Reef, known for its fine tide pools.

Returning to Highway 1, you will pass a number of horse farms. About a third of a mile past Olema, look for a sign marking the turnoff for **Point Reyes National Seashore's Bear Valley Visitors Center.** The center has some fine exhibits of park wildlife, and helpful rangers can advise you on beaches, visits to the lighthouse for whale-watching (the season for gray-whale migration is mid-Dec.–Mar.), as well as on hiking trails and camping. Camping is free, but reservations should be made through the visitor center. A brilliantly reconstructed Miwok Indian Village is situated a short walk from the center. It provides insight into the daily lives of the first inhabitants of this region. The lighthouse is a very pretty, 30–40-minute drive from the visitor center, across rolling hills that resemble Scottish heaths. On busy weekends, parking at the lighthouse may be difficult. If you don't care to walk down—and back up—hundreds of steps, you may want to skip the descent to the lighthouse itself. You *can* see whales from the cliffs above the lighthouse, but it's worth the effort to get the lighthouse view. *Tel. 415/663–1092. Admission free. Open daily 9–5.*

Dining

Fresh seafood and local produce are best bets on a trip up to Point Reyes, and most of the following restaurants make good use of these ingredients in their meals. This area is also perfect for picnicking. So if you prefer the great outdoors, consider packing a lunch to take along on your wanderings. Restaurants hereabouts are generally casual and have no dress code.

Restaurants are listed according to price category.

Category	Cost*
$$$	$15–$20
$$	$10–$15
$	under $10

per person, excluding drinks, service and 7¹/₄% sales tax

$$$ **Manka's.** Regional cuisine featuring fresh-caught fish and wild game (venison, caribou, elk, quail) is served with style in this renovated 1917 hunting lodge. Candlelight, lush floral bouquets, food quotes on the wood-paneled walls, and a large fireplace provide an inimitable intimate atmosphere. Vegetarian specials are always available, and the small plate menu on Monday is a bargain. *Corner of Callendar Way and Argyll Way, Inverness, tel. 415/669–1034. Reservations advised. MC, V. Dinner Thurs.–Mon. Closed Thurs. in Jan. and Feb.*

$$ **Buckeye Roadhouse.** The atmosphere here is a blast from the past with a '90s twist: mahogany paneling, huge stone fireplace, hunting-lodge decor, and a view of the freeway. Hearty American fare includes burgers, malts, and barbecued-pork sandwiches. The Buckeye also uses prime native-Marin ingredients in dishes like roast Petaluma duck with wild rice and candied pumpkin. *15 Shoreline Hwy., Mill Valley, tel. 415/331–2600. Reservations advised. D, DC, MC, V. Sun. brunch.*

Sand Dollar. The owner is the local fire chief and this is the only bar in town, so you're sure to meet lots of locals lingering inside by the fire on foggy days or out on the deck when the sun breaks through. Burgers and fries, salads, and sandwiches are a good bet at lunch; fresh fish selections and pastas with scallops, mussels, and clams are an even better bet at dinner; the homemade soups and sinfully sweet mud pie are a hit anytime. *Hwy. 1, Stinson Beach, tel. 415/868–0434. Reservations advised on weekends. MC, V. Sun. brunch.*

$–$$ **Pelican Inn.** Delicious basic English fare—from fish-and-chips to prime rib and Yorkshire pudding—is served with a fine selection of imported beers and ales. The ambience is wonderful: a wood-paneled dining room warmed by a great stone fireplace and a glass-enclosed solarium ideal for sunny lunches. *10 Pacific Way, Muir Beach (off Hwy. 1), tel. 415/383–6000. Reservations advised for 6 or more. MC, V. Sun. brunch buffet. Closed Mon.*

Station House Cafe. Prints by local photographers decorate the light-filled, rust-and-green interior of this local favorite, and a garden offers alfresco dining in good weather. Breakfast, lunch, and dinner are served. The grilled chicken and salmon specialties and seafood pasta dishes like fettuccine and mussels are a predictable hit. *11180 Hwy. 1, Point Reyes Station, tel. 415/663–1515. Reservations advised. MC, V.*

$ **Grey Whale.** This is a good place for pizza, salad, vegetarian lasagna, pastries and coffee, for lunch or dinner. The patio overlooks the parking lot, but there's a view of paradise, complete with bay and mountains, just beyond. *Sir Francis Drake Blvd. in the center of Inverness, tel. 415/669–1244. No reservations. MC, V.*

Berkeley

By Robert Taylor

Berkeley and the University of California are not synonymous, although the founding campus of the state university system dominates the city's heritage and contemporary life. The city of 100,000 facing San Francisco across the bay has other interesting features for visitors. Berkeley is culturally diverse and politically adventurous, a breeding ground for social trends, a continuing bastion of the counterculture, and an important center for Bay Area writers, artists, and musicians. The city's liberal reputation and determined spirit have led detractors to describe it in recent years as the People's Republic of Berkeley. Wooded groves on the university campus, neighborhoods of shingled bungalows, and landscaped hillside homes temper the environment.

The city was named for George Berkeley, the Irish philosopher and clergyman who crossed the Atlantic to convert the Indians and wrote "Westward, the course of empire takes its way." The city grew with the university, which was created by the state legislature in 1868 and established five years later on a rising plain of oak trees split by Strawberry Canyon. The central campus occupies 178 acres of the scenic 1,282-acre property, with most buildings located from Bancroft Way north to Hearst Street and from Oxford Street east into the Berkeley Hills. The university has more than 30,000 students and a full-time faculty of 1,600. It is considered one of the nation's leading intellectual centers and a major site for scientific research.

Arriving and Departing

By Car Take I–80 east across the Bay Bridge, then the University Avenue exit through downtown Berkeley to the campus, or take the Ashby Avenue exit and turn left on Telegraph Avenue to the traditional campus entrance; there is a parking garage on Channing Way. The trip takes a half-hour one-way (except in rush hour).

By Public Transportation **BART** (tel. 415/788–2278) trains run under the bay to the downtown Berkeley exit; transfer to the Humphrey GoBart shuttle bus to campus. The trip takes from 45 minutes to one hour one-way.

Exploring

Numbers in the margin correspond to points of interest on the Berkeley map.

❶ The Visitors Center (tel. 510/642–5215) in **University Hall** at University Avenue and Oxford Street is open weekdays 8–5. There are maps and brochures for self-guided walks; 1½-hour student-guided tours leave Mondays, Wednesdays, and Fridays at 10 AM and 1 PM.

❷ The throbbing heart of the University of California is **Sproul Plaza,** just inside the campus at Telegraph Avenue and Bancroft Way. It's a lively panorama of political and social activists, musicians, food vendors along Bancroft Way, children, dogs, and students on their way to and from classes at this "university within a park."

Time Out Some people insist that without its cafés Berkeley would simply collapse. No fewer than 55 peacefully coexist within 1 square mile of the U.C. campus. There are cafés of all persuasions, serving every conceivable type of coffee concoction (with or without caffeine), along with teas, beverages of every stripe, desserts, and sometimes light meals. These are places for world-class hanging out, reading, discussing and debating the state of things, and eavesdropping on others doing the same. A few among the many: **Caffe Mediterraneum** (2475 Telegraph Ave., tel. 510/841–5634) is a relic of '60s-era Berkeley but far enough from campus to pull in a mostly nonstudent crowd. Allen Ginsberg wrote while imbibing here. **Caffe Strada** (2300 College Ave., tel. 510/843–5282) has a sprawling patio where frat boys, sorority sisters, and foreigners meet and greet. Try the iced white-chocolate mocha. **The Musical Offering** (2430 Bancroft Way, tel. 510/849–0211) serves light meals and coffee; in back there's a music store specializing in classical CDs and cassettes.

The university's suggested tour circles the upper portion of the central campus, past buildings that were sited to take advantage of vistas to the Golden Gate across the bay. The first campus plan was proposed by Frederick Law Olmsted, who designed New York's Central Park, and over the years the university's architects have included Bernard Maybeck and Julia Morgan (who designed Hearst Castle at San Simeon). Beyond Sproul
❸ Plaza is the bronze **Sather Gate,** built in 1909, and the former south entrance to the campus; the university expanded a block beyond its traditional boundary in the 1960s. Up a walkway to
❹ the right is vine-covered **South Hall,** one of two remaining buildings that greeted the first students in 1873.

❺ Just ahead is **Sather Tower,** popularly known as the Campanile, the campus landmark that can be seen for miles. The 307-foot tower was modeled on St. Mark's tower in Venice and was completed in 1914. The carillon, which was cast in England, is played three times a day. In the lobby of the tower is a photographic display of campus history. An elevator takes visitors 175 feet up

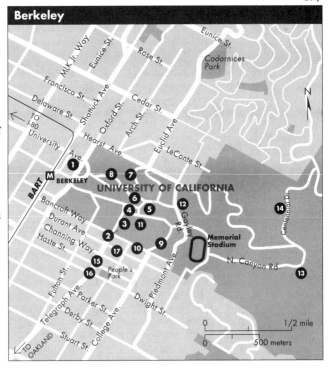

to the observation deck. *Admission: 50¢. Open daily except university holidays 10–3:15.*

6 Opposite the Campanile is **Bancroft Library,** with a rare-book collection and a changing series of exhibits that may include a Shakespeare first folio or a gold-rush diary. On permanent display is a gold nugget purported to be the one that started the rush to California when it was discovered on January 24, 1848.

7 Across University Drive to the north is the **Earth Sciences Building,** with a seismograph for measuring earthquakes. The build-
8 ing also contains the **Paleontology Museum,** which has displays of dinosaur bones and the huge skeleton of a plesiosaur. *Open when the university is in session, weekdays 8–5, weekends 1–5.*

The university's two major museums are on the south side of
9 campus near Bancroft Way. **The Phoebe Apperson Hearst Museum of Anthropology** (formerly the Lowie), in Kroeber Hall, has a collection of more than 4,000 artifacts. Items on display may cover the archaeology of ancient America or the crafts of Pacific Islanders. The museum also houses the collection of artifacts made by Ishi, the lone survivor of a California Indian tribe who was brought to the Bay Area in 1911. *Tel. 510/642–3681. Nominal admission charge. Open Tues.–Fri. 10–4:30, weekends noon–4:30.*

10 **The University Art Museum** is a fan-shaped building with a spiral of ramps and balcony galleries. It houses a collection of Asian and Western art, including a major group of Hans Hofmann's abstract paintings, and also displays touring exhibits. On the ground floor is the Pacific Film Archive, which offers daily programs of historic and contemporary films. *2626 Bancroft Way, tel. 510/642–0808 for film-program information. Museum admission $5, $4 senior citizens. Museum open Wed.–Sun. 11–5.*

Many of the university's notable attractions are outdoors. Just ⑪ south of the Campanile near the rustic Faculty Club is **Faculty Glade** on the south fork of Strawberry Creek, one of the best examples of the university's attempt to preserve a parklike atmosphere. East of the central campus, across Gayley Road, is ⑫ the **Hearst Greek Theatre,** built in 1903 and seating 7,000. Sarah Bernhardt once performed here; now it is used for major musical events.

Above the Greek Theatre in Strawberry Canyon is the 30-acre ⑬ **Botanical Garden,** with a collection of some 25,000 species. It's a relaxing gathering spot with benches and picnic tables. *Open daily 9–5, except Dec. 25.*

Perched on a hill above the campus on Centennial Drive is the ⑭ fortresslike **Lawrence Hall of Science,** which is a laboratory, a science education center, and—most important to visitors—a dazzling display of scientific knowledge and experiments. Displays are updated regularly. On weekends there are additional films, lectures, and demonstrations, especially for children. *Tel. 510/642–5132. Admission: $5 adults, $4 senior citizens and students. Open weekdays 10–4:30, weekends 10–5.*

Berkeley is a rewarding city to explore beyond the university. Just south of the campus on **Telegraph Avenue** is the busy student-oriented district, full of cafés, bookstores, poster shops, and street vendors with traditional and trendy crafts items. Shops come and go with the times, but among the neighborhood ⑮ landmarks are **Cody's Books** (2454 Telegraph Ave.), with its ad- ⑯ jacent café; **Moe's** (2476 Telegraph Ave.), with a huge selection ⑰ of used books; and **Leopold Records** (2518 Durant Ave.). This district was the center of student protests during the 1960s, and on the street it sometimes looks as if that era still lives (it can be unruly at night). People's Park, one of the centers of protest, is just east of Telegraph between Haste Street and Dwight Way.

Downtown Berkeley around University and Shattuck avenues is nondescript. However, there are shops for browsing along College Avenue near Ashby Avenue south of campus and in the Walnut Square development at Shattuck and Vine streets northwest of campus. Berkeley's shingled houses can be seen on tree-shaded streets near College and Ashby avenues. Hillside houses with spectacular views can be seen on the winding roads near the intersection of Ashby and Claremont avenues, around the Claremont Hotel (*see* Exploring in Oakland, *below*). At the opposite side of the city, on Fourth Street north of University Avenue, an industrial area has been converted into a pleasant shopping street with popular eateries such as **Bette's Oceanview Diner** and the **Fourth Street Grill.**

Dining

Berkeley is a food-lover's paradise full of specialty markets, cheese stores, charcuteries, coffee vendors, produce outlets, innovative restaurants, and ethnic eateries. The most popular gourmet ghetto is along Shattuck Avenue, a few blocks north of University Avenue. University Avenue itself has become a corridor of good Indian, Thai, and Cambodian restaurants. You'll find lots of students, interesting coffee houses, and cheap eats on Telegraph, Durant, and Berkeley avenues near the campus. Casual dress is considered politically correct wherever you dine.

Restaurants are listed according to price category.

Category	Cost
$$$$	over $30
$$$	$20–$30
$$	$10–$20
$	under $10

per person, excluding drinks, service, and 8¹/₄% sales tax

$$$–$$$$ **Chez Panisse Cafe & Restaurant.** President Clinton has joined the ranks of luminaries who have dined at this legendary eatery, but like anyone else without a reservation, he had to settle for a seat in the upstairs café. Alice Waters is still the mastermind behind the culinary wizardry, with Jean-Pierre Moullé supplying hands-on talent as head chef. In the downstairs restaurant, where redwood paneling, a fireplace, and lavish floral arrangements create the ambience of a private home, dinners are prix fixe and pricey, but the cost is lower on weekdays and almost halved on Mondays. The culinary entertainment includes creations like pasta with squid and leeks, grilled sea bream with black olives and anchovies, and roast truffled breast of guinea hen. Upstairs in the café the atmosphere is informal, the crowd livelier, the prices lower, and the flavors come through in dishes like calzone with goat cheese, mozzarella, prosciutto, and garlic. *1517 Shattuck Ave., north of University Avenue. Restaurant (downstairs): tel. 510/548–5525. Reservations required. Dinner only. Café (upstairs): tel. 510/548–5049. Same-day reservations. AE, D, DC, MC, V. Closed Sun.*

$$ **Spenger's Fish Grotto.** This is a rambling, boisterous seafood restaurant serving hearty portions of fairly ordinary food. It's a wildly popular place, though, so expect a wait in their combination oyster/sports bar, or opt for the take-out section next door and eat your fish alfresco on the Berkeley pier at the foot of University Avenue. *1919 Fourth St., near University Ave. and I-80, tel. 510/845–7771. Reservations for 5 or more. AE, D, DC, MC, V.*

Venezia Caffe & Ristorante. This family-friendly eatery was the first to serve fresh pasta in the Bay Area, and it continues to offer a wide range of tasty pasta selections (pick a dish that includes their house-made chicken sausage). The large dining room looks like a Venetian piazza, with a fountain in the middle, murals on the walls, and laundry hanging overhead. Children get their own menu, free antipasti, and crayons. *1799 University Ave., tel. 510/849–4681. Reservations advised. AE, MC, V. No lunch weekends.*

$–$$ **Pasand Madras Cuisine.** This informal restaurant serves south Indian fare from *masala dhosa* (spiced vegetables in a crispy thin pancake) and savory curries to exotically sticky sweets. There are several large dining rooms decorated with Indian art, and live sitar music is provided most nights. *2286 Shattuck Ave., tel. 510/549–2559. Reservations accepted. AE, MC, V.*

Saul's Delicatessen. Transplanted New Yorkers agree this is the best Jewish-style deli west of the Rockies. They've got it all from huge corned beef and pastrami sandwiches to chopped liver and chicken soup with table service, a take-out counter, and breakfast served all day. *1475 Shattuck Ave., tel. 510/848–3354. Reservations accepted. MC, V. Closed Yom Kippur.*

Oakland

Originally the site of ranches, farms, a grove of redwood trees, and, of course, clusters of oaks, Oakland has long been a warmer and more spacious alternative to San Francisco. By the end of the 19th century, Mediterranean-style homes and gardens had been developed as summer estates. With swifter transportation, Oakland became a bedroom community for San Francisco; then it progressed to California's fastest-growing industrial city. In recent decades, Oakland has struggled to redefine its identity. However, the major attractions remain: the parks and civic buildings around Lake Merritt, which was created from a tidal basin in 1898; the port area, now named Jack London Square, where the author spent much of his time at the turn of the century; and the scenic roads and parks along the crest of the Oakland-Berkeley hills. Also in the hills is the castlelike Claremont Resort Hotel, a landmark since 1915, as well as more sprawling parks with lakes and miles of hiking trails.

Arriving and Departing

By Car Take I–80 across the Bay Bridge, then I–580 to the Grand Avenue exit for Lake Merritt. To reach downtown and the waterfront, take the I–980 exit from I–580. The trip takes 45 minutes.

By Public Transportation Take the BART to Oakland City Center station or to Lake Merritt station for the lake and Oakland Museum. The trip takes 45 minutes one-way.

Exploring

Numbers in the margin correspond to points of interest on the Oakland map.

❶ If there is one reason to visit Oakland, it is to explore the **Oakland Museum,** an inviting series of landscaped buildings that display the state's art, history, and natural science. It is the best possible introduction to a tour of California, and its dramatic and detailed exhibits can help fill the gaps on a brief visit. The natural science department displays a typical stretch of California from the Pacific Ocean to the Nevada border, including plants and wildlife. A breathtaking film, *Fast Flight,* condenses the trip into five minutes. The museum's sprawling history section includes everything from Spanish-era artifacts and a gleaming fire engine that battled the flames in San Francisco in 1906 to 1960s souvenirs of the "summer of love." The California Dream exhibit recalls a century of inspirations. The museum's art department includes mystical landscapes painted by the state's pioneers, as well as contemporary visions. There is a pleasant museum café for lunch and outdoor areas for relaxing. *1000 Oak St. at 10th St., tel. 510/834–2413. Admission: $4 adults, $2 children. Open Wed.– Sat. 10–5, Sun. noon–7.*

❷ Near the museum, **Lake Merritt** is a 155-acre oasis surrounded by parks and paths, with several outdoor attractions on the
❸ north side. The **Natural Science Center and Waterfowl Refuge** attracts birds by the hundreds during winter months. *At the foot of Perkins St., tel. 510/238–3739. Open daily 10–5.*

❹ **Children's Fairyland** is a low-key amusement park with a puppet theater, small merry-go-round, and settings based on nursery rhymes. *Grand Ave. at Park View Terr., tel. 510/832–3609. Nominal admission charge. Open summer, daily 10–4:30; winter, weekends 10–4:30.*

❺ The **Lakeside Park Garden Center** includes a Japanese garden and many native flowers and plants. *666 Bellevue Ave., tel. 510/238–3208. Open daily 10–3 or later in summer. Closed Thanksgiving, Dec. 25, and Jan. 1.*

Jack London, although born in San Francisco, spent his early years in Oakland before shipping out for adventures that inspired *The Call of the Wild, The Sea Wolf, Martin Eden,* and *The Cruise of the Snark.* He is commemorated with a bronze bust on
❻ what is now called **Jack London's Waterfront,** at the foot of
❼ Broadway. A livelier landmark is **Heinhold's First and Last Chance Saloon,** one of his hangouts. Next door is the reassembled Klondike cabin in which he spent a winter. Restaurants cluster around the plaza, and a Barnes & Noble bookstore offers a wide selection of London's writings. Nearby, Jack London Village has specialty shops and restaurants. The best local collection of the author's letters, manuscripts, and photographs is in the Jack London Room at the Oakland Main Library (125 14th St., tel. 510/273–3134). Oakland's downtown has been undergoing redevelopment for many years. More stable and pleasant areas for shopping and browsing, with a selection of cafés, can be found on Lake Shore Avenue northeast of Lake Merritt, Piedmont Avenue near the Broadway exit from I–580, and College Avenue west of Broadway in North Oakland. College Avenue is lined with antiques stores, boutiques, and cafés. The

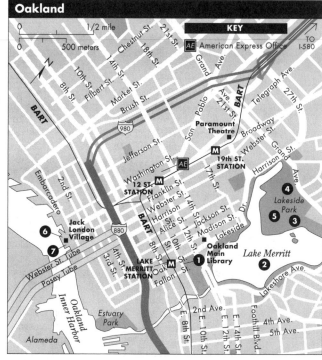

neighborhood surrounds BART's Rockridge station. Transferring there to the local No. 51 bus will take visitors to the University of California campus, about 1½ miles away in Berkeley.

The East Bay Regional Park District (tel. 510/562–7275) offers 46 parks in an area covering 60,000 acres to residents and visitors. In the Oakland hills is **Redwood Regional Park,** accessible from Joaquin Miller Road off Highway 13, to which Ashby Avenue will lead you. In the Berkeley hills is the 2,000-acre **Tilden Park,** which includes a lake and children's playground and is accessible from Grizzly Peak Boulevard off Claremont Avenue. There are scenic views of the Bay Area from roads that link the hilltop parks: Redwood Road, Skyline Boulevard, and Grizzly Peak Boulevard. Parks are open daily during daylight hours.

Off the Beaten Track

Given the city's reputation for Victorian and Craftsman housing, visitors to Oakland are generally surprised by the profusion of Art Deco architecture in the neighborhood around the 19th Street BART station downtown. Some of these buildings have fallen into disrepair, but the **Paramount Theater** (2025 Broadway, tel. 510/465–6400) is a masterpiece of the Art Deco style and remains open and operating as a venue for concerts and performances of all kinds. For $1 you can take a two-hour tour of the building, given the first and third Saturday of each month.

For information about performances, check the free weekly *East Bay Express,* or call the box office.

In the years just after the Second World War, Oakland gave birth to the gritty, hurts-so-bad-I-think-I'm-gonna-die soulful music known as West Coast blues, and the style still flourishes in clubs and bars all over town. One consistently good spot for blues is **Eli's Mile High Club** (3629 Martin Luther King Jr. Way, tel. 510/655–6661). Reputedly *the* birthplace of West Coast blues, it's a small, basic club with a pool table, soul food, and music Wednesday–Sunday. At **Your Place Too** (5319 Martin Luther King Jr. Way, tel. 510/652–5837) there are 50¢ beers and a warped pool table (complete with resident pool shark), along with nightly blues and the occasional hard-core band.

A drive through the Oakland Hills is spectacular, although a wide area north from Broadway is still recovering from the devastating 1991 firestorm. One landmark that was saved is the **Claremont Hotel** (Ashby and Domingo Aves., tel. 510/843–3000), which offers fine views, a spot in which to relax, and good food. Drive north on Claremont Avenue to Ashby Avenue and on up the hill to the hotel. From a distance, this sprawling white building with towers and gables looks like a castle. Surrounded by 22 acres of lush grounds tucked into the south Berkeley hills, the Claremont is on the Oakland-Berkeley border, and for years both cities have claimed it. When a new entrance was built on a different side of the building, the address changed from Berkeley to Oakland. The 1915 hotel has been restored and refurbished and turned into a resort spa facility. The dining room is large and elegant, with pressed linen, large contemporary paintings, and views across the bay to San Francisco and the peninsula and north to Mt. Tamalpais. Meals, which fall into the $$–$$$ category, feature California cuisine, with seasonal fresh seafood for Sunday brunch and creative sandwiches for lunch.

Dining

Oakland's ethnic diversity is reflected in its restaurants and cafés. There is a thriving Chinatown a few blocks northwest of the Oakland Museum, a number of seafood restaurants at Jack London Square, and fare to fit any palate, penchant, or pocketbook on Piedmont and College Avenues. Dress is, as usual, casual.

Restaurants are listed according to price category.

Category	Cost*
$$$$	over $30
$$$	$20–$30
$$	$10–$20
$	under $10

*per person, excluding drinks, service, and 8¹/₄% sales tax

$$–$$$ **The Bay Wolf.** A perpetual favorite, in a converted home with a redwood deck out front, elegantly understated dining rooms inside, and a kitchen garden out back. The menu changes frequently to feature fresh seasonal ingredients and innovative California-Mediterranean cuisine in selections like a pork loin salad with stuffed squash, grilled eggplant, peppers, and couscous; or pan-roasted salmon with artichokes, asparagus, spring carrots, and sorrel sauce. *3853 Piedmont Ave., tel. 510/655–6004. Reservations advised. MC, V. No lunch weekends.*

$$ **ZZA's Trattoria.** Pizzas, salads, house-smoked chicken, and homemade pasta, ravioli, and lasagna are served up in a wacko environment on the shore of Lake Merritt. There's a wild neon sign over the open kitchen, butcher-paper table covers and crayons, customers' artwork on the walls, and lines out the door. *552 Grand Ave., tel. 510/839–9124. Same-day reservations for 6 or more. MC, V. No lunch Mon., Tues., and weekends.*

$–$$ **Lantern Restaurant.** Fine Hong Kong cuisine can be had downstairs at the oldest restaurant in Oakland's Chinatown, but the dim sum (steamed dumplings, spring rolls, and assorted exotic delicacies) served in the enormous upstairs dining room is the big deal here. Point to what you want as the carts roll by and pay by the plate. *814 Webster St., tel. 510/451–0627. D, DC, MC, V.*

Oliveto Café & Restaurant. This is one of the East Bay's prime foodie hangouts, fashioned after a rustic stucco casa in Tuscany and situated on the corner of a bustling gourmet marketplace. Top-notch northern Italian cuisine is served in the formal dining room upstairs, where prices can edge into the $$$ category, but the café at street level is the place to see and be seen sipping wine or espresso and consuming pizzas, tapas, and pastry. *5655 College Ave., tel. 510/547–5356. Reservations advised for restaurant. AE, DC, MC, V. No lunch weekends in restaurant.*

Rockridge Cafe. A favorite standby for burgers, breakfasts, and mighty fine pie in a casual setting. *5492 College Ave., tel. 510/653–1567. Reservations for 6 or more. MC, V. Sun. brunch.*

The San Francisco Peninsula

During the morning and evening rush hours, the peninsula south of San Francisco resembles nothing so much as a vast commuter corridor. At other times and on the network of less-traveled roads, the area offers a remarkable variety of scenic attractions. Redwood forests still remain, though they were heavily logged during the 19th century. In San Mateo and Half Moon Bay there are small adobe houses from California's Spanish and Mexican eras.

The peninsula's most dramatic development came later with the grand country estates built by the "bonanza kings" who made their fortunes in mining and transportation. Many mansions survive: Ralston Hall, built by the owner of San Francisco's Palace Hotel, now the College of Notre Dame on Ralston Avenue in Belmont; La Dolphine on Manor Drive in Burlingame, inspired by Le Petite Trianon at Versailles; and the Uplands, built by banker C. Templeton Crocker, now the Crystal Springs School for Girls on Uplands Drive in Burlingame. The only estate open to the general public is Filoli in Woodside, which has 16 acres of gardens. Another major attraction is Stanford University at Palo Alto, with a campus that stretches from the flatlands of the Santa Clara Valley into the Santa Cruz Mountains.

Arriving and Departing

By Car   The most pleasant direct route down the peninsula is I–280, the Junipero Serra Freeway, which passes along Crystal Springs reservoir. Take the Edgewood Road exit for Filoli, and Alpine Road for Stanford. U.S. 101 along the bay shore can be congested, but from there take Highway 93 west to Filoli and University Avenue or Embarcadero Road to Stanford. Skyline Boulevard (Hwy. 35), which begins near the San Francisco Zoo, is the most scenic route through the peninsula, following the crest of the Santa Cruz Mountains and offering views of both the bay and the Pacific Ocean. Highway 1 follows a relatively unknown section of the coast from San Francisco to Santa Cruz, a route including rugged cliffs, public beaches, communities such as Pescadero that began as fishing villages, and several 19th-century lighthouses.

By Public Transportation   Take the **CalTrain** (tel. 415/557–8661) from 4th and Townsend streets to Palo Alto, then the shuttle bus to Stanford campus. Other attractions on the peninsula are difficult to reach except by car.

Exploring

One of the few great country houses in California that remains intact in its original setting is **Filoli** in Woodside. Built for wealthy San Franciscan William B. Bourn in 1916–1919, it was designed by Willis Polk in a Georgian style, with redbrick walls and a tile roof. The name is not Italian but Bourn's acronym for "fight, love, live." As interesting to visitors as the house (which you might remember from the television series "Dynasty") are the 16 acres of formal gardens. The gardens were planned and developed over a period of more than 50 years and preserved for the public when the last private owner, Mrs. William P. Roth, deeded Filoli to the National Trust for Historic Preservation.

The gardens rise south from the mansion to take advantage of the natural surroundings of the 700-acre estate and its vistas. Among the designs are a sunken garden, walled garden, woodland garden, yew alley, and a rose garden developed by Mrs. Roth with more than 50 shrubs of all types and colors. A focal point of the garden is a charming teahouse designed in the Italian Renaissance style. Spring is the most popular time to visit, but daffodils, narcissi, and rhododendrons are in bloom as early as February, and the gardens remain attractive in October and November. *Canada Rd., near Edgewood Rd., Woodside, tel.*

415/364–2880. Admission: $8. Children under 12 not admitted. Open for tours mid-Feb.–mid-Nov., Tues.–Sat. Reservations necessary; spring tours may fill several weeks in advance. Call for openings. Filoli is often open for unguided visits and nature hikes on the estate, but call for information.

Stanford University, 30 miles south of San Francisco, also has its roots among the peninsula's estates. Originally the property was former California governor Leland Stanford's farm for breeding horses. For all its stature as one of the nation's leading universities, Stanford is still known as "the farm." Founded and endowed by Leland and Jane Stanford in 1885 as a memorial to their son, Leland, Jr., who died of typhoid fever, the university was opened in 1891. Frederick Law Olmsted conceived the plan for the grounds and Romanesque sandstone buildings, joined by arcades and topped by red-tile roofs. Variations on this solid style persist in newer buildings, which, along with playing fields, now cover about 1,200 acres of the 8,200-acre campus. The center of the university is the inner quadrangle, a group of 12 original classroom buildings later joined by Memorial Church, with its facade and interior walls covered with mosaics of biblical scenes.

The university is organized into seven schools made up of 70 departments. In addition, there are several institutes on campus, including the Hoover Institution on War, Revolution, and Peace. Its 285-foot tower is a landmark; there is an elevator to an observation deck. Except for the central cluster of buildings, the campus is remarkably uncongested—enrollment is only about 15,000. Free walking tours leave daily at 11 AM and 3:15 PM from the **Visitor Information Booth** (tel. 415/723–2560 or 415/723–2053) at the front of the quadrangle. The main campus entrance, Palm Drive, is an extension of University Avenue from Palo Alto.

The **Stanford Art Gallery,** to the right of Hoover Tower near the campus entrance, features visiting shows, some student works, and a selection of the university's historical artifacts. At the Stanford Museum of Art on Lomita Drive, ¾ mile northwest of the Art Gallery, you can view a collection of Rodin bronzes in a garden outside. The museum, with its collection of 18th- and 19th-century art, has been closed for renovation since it was damaged in the 1989 Loma Prieta earthquake. It is expected to reopen in 1997. *Art Gallery tel. 415/723–3469. Donation requested. Open Tues.–Fri. 10–5, weekends 1–5.*

Two miles west of the main campus, on Sand Hill Road, is the **Stanford Linear Accelerator** (tel. 415/926–2204). There are tours of the 2-mile-long electron accelerator used for elementary-particle research.

Just north of the main campus, facing El Camino Real, is the **Stanford Shopping Center,** one of the Bay Area's first and still one of the most pleasant and inviting. The Nature Company has a fascinating collection of artifacts and gadgets reflecting an interest in the natural world, a large collection of natural-history books, and a good poster selection. The Palo Alto Coffee Roasting Company roasts a variety of coffees in three strengths. Crate and Barrel is a large kitchen and housewares store with a fine contemporary (and moderately priced) selection.

Dining

El Camino Real (Highway 82) is the peninsula's major commercial thoroughfare, with many cafés, restaurants, and fast-food franchises. There are several pleasant cafés, some with outdoor dining, in downtown Palo Alto along University Avenue and its cross streets, just east of El Camino Real. The Stanford Shopping Center has a variety of upscale cafés: Gaylord's serves moderately priced Indian food in a relaxed and elegant atmosphere, and the nearby Fresh Choice offers inexpensive gourmet salads and sandwiches.

Restaurants are listed according to price category.

Category	Cost*
$$$$	over $30
$$$	$20–$30
$$	$10–$20
$	under $10

per person, excluding drinks, service, and 8.25% sales tax

$$–$$$ **Flea Street Cafe.** The floral decor evokes a romantic, intimate country inn, and the fare is imaginative, featuring fresh organic produce and freshly baked breads. Specialties change seasonally and may include herb-roasted Cornish game hen with sage jalapeño gravy and red-onion cornbread stuffing, fettuccine with duck sausage and pippin apples, and—for Sunday brunch—house-baked buttermilk biscuits, homemade jams, and unbelievably seductive pancake, egg, and omelet creations. Young diners have access to a fully stocked toy chest. *Alameda de las Pulgas, Menlo Park (take Sand Hill Rd. west from the Stanford shopping center or east from I–280, turn right on Alameda), tel. 415/854–1226. MC, V. No lunch Sat. Closed Mon.*

Il Fornaio Cucina Italiana. Situated in a gorgeous Italianate setting on the ground floor of the Garden Court Hotel, this popular eatery has a rustic decor with food as the visual focus. Get gourmet fare to go or eat here and sample superb antipasti, pizza, and calzone baked to perfection in a wood-burning oven. Italian breads and irresistible bread sticks, biscotti, cakes, and tortes are prime attractions. *520 Cowper St., Palo Alto, tel. 415/853–3888. Reservations strongly advised. AE, DC, MC, V. Weekend brunch.*

MacArthur Park. A classic steak house favored by the Stanford crowd, specializing in mesquite-grilled steaks and oakwood-smoked ribs. Tasty renditions of chicken and fish entrées are also available, but those who like to send their cholesterol counts soaring will opt for ribs and finish off with mud pie (a chocolate cookie topped with ice cream, hot fudge, and chopped nuts). *27*

University Ave. (west side of the Caltrain station), Palo Alto, tel.
415/321–9990. AE, DC, MC, V. Sun. brunch. No lunch Sat.

Village Pub. This is a pleasant restaurant near Filoli where patrons elbow up to a carved oak bar to sample the ale, or relax in
a stylishly simple modern dining room to savor creative rustic-
California renditions of duck, fresh seafood, steak, and pasta.
*2967 Woodside Rd. (³/₄ mi from I–280W), Woodside, tel. 415/851–
1294. Reservations advised. AE, DC, MC, V. No lunch weekends.*

$ **Vicolo Pizzeria.** An upscale little hangout (hungry Stanford stu-
dents come here for breakfast, lunch, and dinner), Vicolo has
whimsical, faux-Italian decor, more than 30 varieties of gourmet
toppings on tasty cornmeal crust, and sidewalk seating in good
weather. *473 University Ave. (near Cowper St.), Palo Alto, tel.
415/324–4877. No reservations. No credit cards.*

Silicon Valley

*By Claudia
Gioseffi*

Like many famous rock bands, Silicon Valley began in a garage.
In the spring of 1938, Dave and Lucile Packard, joined by William Hewlett, made room in back of their house for what would
eventually become Hewlett-Packard, a pioneer company in the
high-tech and electronics revolutions. Another milestone was
marked 39 years later when Steve Jobs and Steve Wozniak
emerged from a small garage in Cupertino with something
called Apple. Ultimately these computer companies, and others
such as Intel, Tandem, and Microsystem, grew big enough to
replace sleepy Santa Clara County's fruit growers and cattle
ranchers with an industry that changed the world. Although
some companies have now relocated to less expensive regions of
the country, Silicon Valley remains the undisputed home of the
tiny chips which support the Information Superhighway.

The Valley is a sprawling community of spanking-new office
parks, business-lined highways, shopping malls, and Spanish-
style homes—their red-tiled roofs peeking through dense juni-
pers and magnolias. El Camino Real, Highway 101, and the
more picturesque I–280 link the area's key towns: Sunnyvale,
Cupertino, Santa Clara, and San Jose. Green hills that turn
khaki under the summer sun surround the valley. Many of the
sights here are suitable for a day-trip from San Francisco, but
the region's attractions warrant a closer look. Moderate year-
round temperatures make Silicon Valley ideal for viticulture—
and for enjoying the great outdoors. Take a weekend, rent a car,
open the windows or fold down the top, and head south.

The center of the Valley is San Jose—California's first town, and
now the state's third largest city. Despite its reputation as a
charmless, suburban Los Angeles of the north, San Jose is
buffered by city parks and gardens, and in addition to the industrial parks, computer companies, and corporate headquarters,
the city is home to museums, symphonies, theaters, and viner-
ies.

Tourist Information

For information about recreational events, contact the **Santa Clara Chamber of Commerce and Convention & Visitors Bureau** (2200 Laurelwood Rd., Santa Clara, 95054, tel. 408/970–9825) or the **Visitor Information Center** (1515 El Camino Real, Box 387, Santa Clara, 95050, tel. 408/296–7111). The **San Jose Visitor and Business Center** (tel. 408/283–8833) publishes a bimonthly calendar of ethnic festivals and outdoor events, and the **San Jose Convention and Visitors Bureau** (333 W. San Carlos St., Suite 1000, San Jose 95110, tel. 408/295–9600) produces an annual events calendar. For schedules for all activities around the clock, call the **San Jose Tourist Bureau's FYI Hotline** (tel. 408/295–2265).

Arriving and Departing

By Car   U.S. 101, I–280 (the Junipero Serra Freeway), and I–880 (Highway 17) connect the Valley with the San Francisco Bay Area. The drive south from San Francisco to San Jose on I–280 takes 60 minutes, depending on traffic, which tends to be heavy during rush hours. The drive north from Monterey, on U.S. 101 takes about 90 minutes. Highway 1, which runs along the California coast, takes longer, but is far more scenic.

By Public   Although Silicon Valley is as much a car culture as Los Angeles, **Transporta-** commuter services are available. **CalTrain** (tel. 800/660–4287) **tion** runs from 4th and Townsend streets in San Francisco to San Jose's light-rail system; **Amtrak** (tel. 800/872–7245), **BART** (Bay Area Rapid Transit, tel. 415/788–2278), and **Greyhound Lines** (tel. 800/231–2222) also provide public transportation.

By Plane   **San Jose International Airport** (tel. 408/277–4759) is just 3 miles from downtown San Jose and is served by the light rail system in addition to airport shuttle services such as **Express Airport Shuttle** (tel. 408/378–6270) and **South & East Bay Airport Shuttle** (tel. 408/559–9477).

Getting Around

In San Jose, **light-rail vehicles** serve most major attractions, shopping malls, historic sites, and downtown. Service is every 10 to 15 minutes between 4:30 AM and 1:30 AM on weekdays, every 15 to 30 minutes between 5:45 AM and 1:30 AM on weekends. **Historic trolleys** also operate in downtown San Jose from 11 to 7 daily. Buy tickets for both the light rail and the trolleys at vending machines in any transit station. Tickets for the light rail are valid for two hours; prices vary with destination. Trolley fare is 50¢ for ages 5 to 64, 25¢ for seniors and passengers with disabilities. For more information call or visit the **Transit Information Center** (4 N. 2nd St., San Jose, tel. 408/321–2300).

Guided Tours

Royal Coach Tours (644 Stockton Ave., San Jose, tel. 408/279–4801 or 800/443–7433) plans custom tours for individuals as well as groups.

Exploring

Santa Clara Santa Clara's offerings include two major attractions at opposite ends of the sightseeing spectrum: the mission, founded in 1777, and Paramount's Great America, Northern California's answer to Disneyland.

In **Paramount's Great America** 100-acre theme park, on the edge of San Francisco Bay, each section of the park recalls a familiar part of North America: Hometown Square, Yukon Territory, Yankee Harbor, County Fair, and Orleans Place. The double-decker carousel just inside the entrance, the "Columbia," is fairly tame, but the park's other rides would tempt Evel Knievel. There are six roller coasters, a triple-arm Ferris wheel, and several exciting water rides. The latest rides are the "Rip Roaring Rapids," which takes you on a white-water river in oversize inner tubes; the "Vortex" stand-up roller coaster; a movie-themed *Top Gun* roller coaster, whose cars travel along the outside of a 360-degree loop track; and a *Days of Thunder* racing-simulator theater, which combines film, a giant-screen image, special effects, and moving seats to simulate a stock-car race. Star Trek characters wander around the grounds, and movie and TV references are everywhere. The park is served by Santa Clara County Transit and BART (the Fremont station). *Great America Pkwy., between U.S. 101 and Hwy. 237 (6 mi north of San Jose), tel. 408/988–1776. Admission: $25.95 adults, $18.95 senior citizens, $12.95 children 3–6. Parking $5. Open weekends Mar. 19–May 29 and Sept. 3–Oct. 9; daily in summer. Opens at 10 AM; closing times vary with season. AE, MC, V.*

After a day at the park, you may be in the mood for some intellectual stimulation. Visitors to the **Intel Museum,** just a couple miles south of the Great America park, can learn how computer chips are made, and follow the development of Intel Corporation's microprocessor, memory, and systems product lines. Although the tour is designed to be self-guided, guided tours are available by reservation. *Robert Noyce Bldg., 2200 Mission College Blvd., tel. 408/765–0503. Admission free. Open Mon.–Fri. 8–5.*

Downtown Santa Clara's attractions are on or near the green campus of Santa Clara University. Founded in 1851 by Jesuits, this was California's first college.

Right in the center of the campus is the **Mission Santa Clara de Assis**, the eighth of 21 California missions founded under the direction of Father Junipero Serra. The mission has a dramatic history. Several early settlements were flooded by the Guadalupe River, the present site was the fifth chosen, and the permanent mission chapel was destroyed by fire in 1926. Roof tiles of the current building, a replica of the original, were salvaged

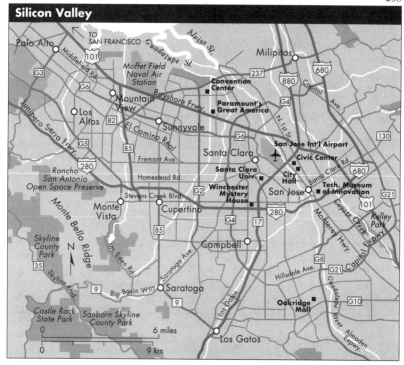

Silicon Valley

from earlier structures, which dated from the 1790s and 1820s. There is also a wooden **Memorial Cross** from 1777 set in front of the Santa Clara Mission church, and early adobe walls and gardens. In the mid-1770s, Franciscan friars raised grapes here for sacramental wines; the olive and fig trees that they planted at the same time remain. Also on the campus is a notable art museum, the **de Saisset,** with a permanent collection that includes California mission artifacts. The museum also has a full calendar of temporary exhibits. *Campus: 500 El Camino Real. Mission: tel. 408/554-4023. Admission free. Open weekdays 8–6. De Saisset Museum: tel. 408/554-4528. Admission free. Open Tues.–Sun. 11–4. Closed Mon.*

Several blocks east of campus is the **Carmelite Monastery.** Built in 1917, it's on the grounds of a historic ranch and is an example of Spanish Ecclesiastical architecture. The church and grounds are open from 7:15 to 4 daily; to see inside, ring the bell. Mass is open to the public, and is given at 7:15 AM Monday through Saturday, and 10:30 AM on Sunday. *1000 Lincoln St., tel. 408/296–8412. Admission free.*

From the monastery, a stroll up Lincoln Street will bring you to Civic Center Park to see a **statue of Saint Clare,** the patron saint of Santa Clara. The sculpture was cast in Italy in 1965 by Anne Van Kleeck, using an ancient wax process. It was then shipped around Cape Horn and dedicated on this site in 1985. *Civic Center Park, Lincoln St. at El Camino Real.*

Across from the Civic Center, skylights cast natural light for viewing the exhibitions in the **Triton Museum of Art.** A permanent collection of 19th- and 20th-century sculpture by artists from the Bay Area is displayed in a 7-acre garden, which you can see through a curved-glass wall at the rear of the building. Indoors there are rotating exhibits of contemporary works in a variety of media and a permanent collection of 19th- and 20-century American artists, many from California. *1505 Warburton Ave., tel. 408/247–3754. Admission free. Open Tues. 10–9, Wed.–Fri. 10–5, weekends noon–5.*

The **Santa Clara Historic Museum**, next door, exhibits artifacts and photos that trace the history of the region. *1509 Warburton Ave. (across from City Hall), tel. 408/248–2787. Admission free. Open daily 1–4.*

Walk over to the grounds of City Hall to see noted San Francisco sculptor Benny Bufano's primitive *Universal Child,* facing the museum. The statue, which depicts the children of the world standing as one, stands 85 feet tall.

The recently opened **Harris-Lass Historic Museum**, Santa Clara's last farmstead. A restored barn, summer kitchen, and house convey a sense of life on the farm from the early 1900s through the 1930s. *1889 Market St., tel. 408/249–7905. Admission: $3 adults, $2 senior citizens over 59, $1 children 6–12. Open weekends noon–4; guided tours every 1/2 hr; last tour at 3:30.*

San Jose As part of its plans to attract tourists and increase convention business, San Jose has embarked on a massive project to redefine its city center; it has completed a 20-mile light-rail transportation system, a convention center, a 17,000-seat arena for the San Jose Sharks hockey team, and a major addition to the San Jose Museum of Art and has begun to restore the few remaining 19th-century buildings downtown. The results of these attempts to marry the existing Old West and mission architecture with modern styles and materials are sights like a very traditional small-town clock tower constructed from marble and stainless steel.

A good method of exploring is to hop on the light rail that connects San Jose State University on one end with the Center for Performing Arts on the other; its route will give you a good overview of the city, and the convention center stop will drop you in the center of downtown so you can explore on foot.

The **Children's Discovery Museum**, near the convention center, exhibits interactive installations on space, technology, the humanities, and the arts. Children can dress up in period costumes, create jewelry from recycled materials, or play on a real fire truck. *180 Woz Way, at Auzerais St., tel. 408/298–5437. Admission: $6 adults, $5 senior citizens, $4 children 2–18. Open Tues.–Sat. 10–5, Sun. noon–5.*

The **Tech Museum of Innovation**, across from the convention center, presents high-tech information through hands-on lab exhibits that are fun and accessible, allowing visitors to discover and demystify disciplines such as microelectronics, biotechnology, robotics, and space exploration. *145 W. San Carlos St., tel. 408/279–7150. Admission: $6 adults, $4 students and senior citizens. Open Tues.–Sun. 10–5.*

In collaboration with New York's Whitney Museum, the **San Jose Museum of Art** is exploring the development of 20th-century American art with exhibits of pieces from the permanent collections of both. The series will run through the year 2000, and include works by such American artists as Andrew Wyeth, Edward Hopper, and Georgia O'Keeffe. Housed in a former post- office building, the museum also has a permanent collection that includes paintings, large-scale multimedia installations, photographs, and sculptures by local and nationally known artists. *110 S. Market St., tel. 408/294–2787. Admission: $5 adults, $3 senior citizens, students, and children 6–17. Open Tues.–Sun. 10–5, Thurs. 10–8.*

The following attractions are on the outskirts of town; the easiest way to reach them is by car.

On the north end of town lies the **Winchester Mystery House.** Convinced that spirits would harm her if construction ever stopped, firearms-heiress Sarah Winchester constantly added to her house. For 38 years beginning in 1884, she kept hundreds of carpenters working around the clock, creating a bizarre, 160-room Victorian labyrinth with stairs going nowhere and doors that open into walls. The brightly painted house and well-tended gardens are a favorite family attraction, and though the grounds are no longer dark and overgrown, the place retains an air of mystery. There is also an extensive firearms collection on exhibit. *525 S. Winchester Blvd. (between Stevens Creek Blvd. and I–280), tel. 408/247–2101. Admission: $12.50 adults, $9.50 senior citizens, $6.50 children 6–12. Open daily 9:30–4; later in summer.*

The **Egyptian Museum and Planetarium** offers some mysteries of its own in the West Coast's largest collection of Egyptian and Babylonian antiquities, including mummies and an underground replica of a pharaoh's tomb. The museum's entrance is a reproduction of the Avenue of Ram Sphinxes from the Temple at Karnak in Egypt, and the complex is surrounded by a garden filled with palms, papyrus, and other plants recalling ancient Egypt. The planetarium offers programs like the popular "Celestial Nile," which describes the significant role astrology played in ancient Egyptian myths and religions. *1600 Park Ave. at Naglee Ave., tel. 408/947–3636. Admission (museum only): $6 adults, $4 senior citizens and students, $3.50 children 7–15. Planetarium admission and show times vary. Open daily 9–5.*

On 176 acres of rolling lawns on the east side of San Jose, off I–280, is **Kelley Park,** which offers a variety of family attractions and shady picnic sites. On the grounds is the creative **Happy Hollow Park & Zoo,** with theme rides, puppet shows, a riverboat replica, and events specially planned for children from 2 to 10 years old. Also in the park is the **Japanese Friendship Garden** (free; open daily), with fish ponds and a teahouse inspired by

Japan's Korakuen Garden. Occupying 25 acres of the park is the **San Jose Historical Museum,** which recreates San Jose in the 1880s with a collection of original and replicate Victorian homes and shops, a firehouse, and a trolley line. The dusty Main Street recalls small-town America without the brightly painted gloss of amusement-park reproductions. *Kelley Park: 1300 Senter Rd. Admission to park free, parking $3 on holidays and in summer. Happy Hollow Park: tel. 408/295–8383, admission: $3.50, $3 seniors, free for visitors under 2 and over 75. Open Mon.–Sat. 10–5, Sun. 11–6 Apr.–Oct; 10–5 Nov.–Mar. Historical Museum: tel. 408/287–2290, admission: $4 adults, $3 senior citizens, $2 children 6–17. Open weekdays 10–4:30, weekends noon–4:30.*

On the sandy shores of Lake Cunningham, **Raging Waters Aquatic Park,** off the Capitol Expressway, offers all kinds of water features from children's wading pools to a water slide with a heart-stopping, 7-foot free fall. *Lake Cunningham Park, 2333 S. White Rd., tel. 408/270–8000. Admission: $16, $10 after 3 PM. Open weekends mid-May–mid-June 10–6; daily mid-June–Labor Day 10–7.*

Saratoga   Saratoga, 10 miles west of San Jose, is a quaint, former artists' colony chock-full of antiques shops, upscale jewelry stores, and art galleries. Just south of downtown, nestled on a steep hillside, are the **Hakone Gardens.** This Zen-style retreat was designed in 1918 by a man who had been an imperial gardener in Japan and has been carefully maintained. On the site are *koi* (carp) ponds, sculptured shrubs, and a traditional Japanese teahouse. *21000 Big Basin Way, tel. 408/741–4994. Admission: $3 per car weekends Mar.–Oct., free weekdays and all of Nov.–Feb. Open weekdays 10–5, weekends 11–5.*

Wineries

Although most people don't think of wine in connection with Silicon Valley, the area's vintages are gaining attention. Many of the wineries represent generations of vintners, whose families began making wine in Europe long before coming to California.

Cupertino   **Ridge Vineyards** is perched on Montebello Ridge in the Santa Cruz Mountains overlooking San Francisco Bay. Founded in 1959, the winery adheres to traditional wine-making techniques. *17100 Montebello Rd., Cupertino, tel. 408/867–3233. Tasting Sat. and Sun. 11–3. Tours by appointment.*
Fellom Ranch Vineyards, a bit farther down Montebello Road, is nestled on a terraced hillside at a 2,000-foot elevation with panoramic views of the valley. In the 1920s, when the Fellom family purchased the ranch, it consisted of a small vineyard of zinfandel grapes. Today, some of the finest cabernet sauvignon grapes in the world are grown here. High elevation, non-irrigated vines, and the unique microclimate of the Montebello mountain combine to create a very high-quality wine. *17075 Montebello Rd., Cupertino, tel. 408/741–0307. Tours and tasting weekends by appointment only.*

Los Gatos **Byington Winery and Vineyards** is one of the newest wineries in the region. Eight acres of pinot noir grapes are planted on an 80-acre estate with breathtaking views of the Pacific and Monterey Bay and a pastoral picnic area. The Italian-style chateau has a cozy fireplace in the tasting room and a veranda. *21850 Bear Creek Rd., tel. 408/354–1111. Tasting Wed.–Sun. 11–5. Tours by appointment.*

Mirassou Champagne Cellars, located in the hills of Los Gatos and run by members of the Mirassou family, is one of the pioneers in champagne-making in California. The winery offers samples of its award-winning sparkling wines, including a blanc de noir and a brut. Tours offer an in-depth look at production methods and let you explore the property's century-old cellars. *300 College Ave., tel. 408/395–3790. Open Wed.–Sun. noon–5, tours at 1:30 and 3:30.*

San Jose **J. Lohr Winery** is on the site of the old Falstaff and Fredericksburg breweries. Most of the winery's more than 1,000 acres of vineyards are located on California's central coast, in Monterey, the rest in the Napa Valley and the Sacramento Delta. J. Lohr produces many varietals but is best known for its Estate chardonnay, cabernet sauvignon, Johannisberg Riesling, and gamay. The brief tours of the facility include viewing the tanks and the bottling facilities; production methods are explained. *1000 Lenzen Ave., tel. 408/288–5057. Tasting daily 10–5, tours Sat. and Sun. at 11 and 2.*

Mirassou Vineyards, run by America's oldest wine-making family, has been in operation for 130 years and has produced several award-winning wines in the last few years. They include a reserve pinot noir, a chardonnay, a cru gamay, and a Petite Syrah. Mirassou also hosts three annual events, the Epicurean Fare in June, an American Pops Concert in July, and the Holiday Festival in November, in addition to a series of Bistro and Candlelight Dinners. (*See* Arts and Nightlife, *below.*) *3000 Aborn Rd., tel. 408/274–4000. Open noon–5, tours Mon.–Sat. 1:30 and 3:30, Sun. 1 and 3.*

Sport and the Outdoors

Participant Sports

Golf **Sunnyvale Golf Course** (605 Macara La., tel. 408/738–3666), **San Jose Municipal Golf Course** (1560 Oakland Rd., tel. 408/441–4653), and **Santa Clara Golf & Tennis Club** (5155 Stars & Stripes Dr., tel. 408/980–9515) are all 18-hole municipal courses. Serious golfers may be willing to travel farther afield; Pebble Beach courses are about 90 minutes from San Jose. Greens there include some that are world-class: **Poppy Hills** (tel. 408/625–2035), **Spyglass Hill** (tel. 408/625–8563), and **The Links at Spanish Bay** (tel. 408/624–3811). Tee times can be difficult to get despite high greens fees—$75 to $225—depending on the course.

Horseback Riding **Garrod Farms Stables** (22600 Mount Eden Rd., Saratoga, tel. 408/867–9527), has horse and pony rentals. Farther afield, **Molera Trail Rides** (Box 167, Big Sur, tel. 408/625–8664) caters to experienced riders.

Swimming The International Swim Center is a competitive swim facility open to adults 18 years and older. Olympian swimmers occasionally use it, but there are scheduled public lap-swimming times, and lessons are available. Take Homestead Avenue to the Santa Clara Public Library parking lot; the pool is just behind it. *2625 Patricia Dr., Santa Clara, tel. 408/246–5050. $3 drop-in fee. Open daily 5:30–8 AM, 6–7:30 PM.*

Spectator Sports Home to the San Jose Sharks hockey team, the 20,000-seat **San Jose Arena,** completed in 1993, looks like a giant hothouse with its glass entrance and skylight ceiling. The venue also hosts tennis matches, basketball games, concerts, and other events. *Santa Clara St. at Autumn St., San Jose, tel. 408/287–9200. Ticket office open weekdays 9:30–5:30, Sat. 9:30–1, or call BASS at 408/998–2277.*

Beaches About 45 minutes south of San Jose on Route 17 is the **Santa Cruz Beach and Boardwalk** (tel. 408/426–7433)—part Asbury Park and part Coney Island—with its huge weekend crowds of sun-scorched surfers and Bay Area residents. The mile-long boardwalk, lined with rides, amusements, and arcades, runs along Beach Street.

The San Mateo County coast state beaches run from Pacifica, just south of San Francisco, down to Big Basin Redwoods State Park. It's a 20–30 minute drive west over the mountains from just north of Santa Clara to the beaches at Half Moon Bay and others along the coast. The **Half Moon Bay State Parks District Office** (tel. 415/726–8800) has information on the state parks and beaches from Montara to Año Nuevo.

Shopping

The malls of Silicon Valley are a mind-blowing maze of shopping habitats: **Valley Fair Shopping Center** in Santa Clara (2855 Stevens Creek Blvd., tel. 408/248–4451), and **Pavilion Shops** (150 S. 1st St., tel. 408/286–2076) and **Eastridge Mall** (Capitol Expressway and Tully Rd., tel. 408/274–0360) in San Jose.

In downtown **Los Gatos,** boutiques, antiques shops, and restaurants are in restored buildings constructed when California was a young state. Call the **Los Gatos Chamber of Commerce** (tel. 408/354–9300) for details.

The **Factory Outlets at Gilroy** (8300 Arroyo Circle, tel. 408/842–3729) and **Pacific West Outlet Center** (8375 Arroyo Circle, No. 46, tel. 408/847–4155), both in Gilroy, 45 minutes south of San Jose, offer discounts of up to 75% on clothing and gear by Esprit, Brooks Brothers, Anne Klein, Nike, and Eddie Bauer.

The **San Jose Flea Market** looks, feels, and smells like Mexico's festive and colorful *mercados,* but it's on a larger scale. Some 2,700 booths spread over 125 acres sell handicrafts, leather, jewelry, furniture, produce, and just about anything else you could imagine. As in markets south of the border, it's smart to shop around and to examine merchandise before buying. *Berryessa Rd. between I–680 and Hwy. 101, tel. 408/453–1110. Open dawn to* *dusk, Wed.–Sun. Admission free. Parking $3 on weekends, free weekdays.*

Off the Beaten Track

The small town of **Gilroy,** which calls itself the Garlic Capital of the World, is 30 miles south of San Jose on U.S. 101, surrounded by rolling countryside crisscrossed by picturesque back roads. Multitudes follow their noses here every July when the world-renowned **Gilroy Garlic Festival** kicks off. The recipe for the three-day extravaganza calls for more than 4 tons of garlic. Contact the Gilroy Visitors Bureau (tel. 408/842–6436).

Dining

Though Silicon Valley's billboard-strewn highways lined with motels and fast-food franchises can look like a Nabokov landscape, the Bay Area's reputation as a world-class culinary center remains intact at its southernmost tip. Restaurants are listed according to price category.

Category	Cost*
$$$$	over $30
$$$	$20–$30
$$	$10–$20
$	under $10

*per person, excluding drinks, service, and 8.25% sales tax.

$$$$
San Jose
★ **Emile's.** Swiss chef and owner Emile Mooser is well-versed in the classic marriage of food and wine, and will make your wine selection from the restaurant's extensive list for you. House specialties include house-cured gravlax and fresh sturgeon; the menu emphasizes lighter cuisine. Lamps on every table and walls hand-painted with gold leaves create an intimate and elegant backdrop. *545 S. 2nd St., tel. 408/289–1960. Reservations advised. AE, DC, MC, V. Closed Sun. and Mon., lunch Fri. only.*

Saratoga **Le Mouton Noir.** Even President Clinton, who favors a Big Mac and fries, found his way to Saratoga's most famous restaurant during a visit to Silicon Valley. Anything but the black sheep that its name suggests, the place is filled with aspiring and established foodies and wine connoisseurs, and the kitchen turns out understated dishes that let the full flavor of the ingredients come through. Fine examples are the seafood dishes and the roast rack of lamb with a light, caramelized fennel and raspberry sauce. *14560 Big Basin Way, near Hwy. 9, tel. 408/867–7017. Reservations recommended. AE, DC, MC, V. No lunch Sun. and Mon.*

$$$
San Jose
Paolo's Restaurant. In this spot not far from local cultural centers, grazing is an art, and the the bar menu offers small plates that give you several different tastes in a hurry—great for a snack before or after the theater. Try the eggplant sandwich, antipasto plate, or the mixed salad topped with hearty serving

of shrimp. The Italian entrées and the parklike dining room—filled with plants and overlooking a patio, lush greenery, and the Guadalupe River—deserve more leisurely appreciation. *333 W. San Carlos St., tel 408/294–2558. Reservations advised. AE, DC, MC, V. No lunch weekends.*

Santa Clara **Birk's.** Silicon Valley's business people come to this sophisticated American grill to unwind after a hard day of paving the way to the future. It probably appeals to their high-tech sensibilities with its modern open kitchen and streamlined, multilevel dining area. Yet the menu is traditional, strong on grilled and smoked meat, fish, and fowl. Try the smoked prime rib, served with garlic-mashed potatoes and creamed spinach, or the rotisserie-grilled chicken or ribs. *3955 Freedom Circle at Hwy. 101 and Great America Pkwy., tel. 408/980–6400. Reservations advised. AE, DC, MC, V. No lunch weekends.*

$$
San Jose **Henry's World Famous Hi-Life.** This vintage rib-and-steak joint in a 120-year-old building, two blocks from San Jose Arena, has been owned and operated by the same family since 1960. The interior is funky and rustic, the atmosphere friendly and fun. Try the sweet barbecue sauce. *301 W. St. John St., tel. 408/295–5414. Reservations for 8 or more. AE, MC, V. No lunch Mon. and weekends.*

Scott's Seafood Grill & Bar. Young, upwardly mobile types fill the clean-lined, oak-and-brass dining room here. Seafood and shellfish is the specialty; the fresh calamari (dusted with flour and lightly fried in garlic, lemon butter, and wine) and the oyster bar are noted attractions. *185 Park Ave., 6th Floor, tel. 408/971–1700. Reservations accepted. AE, DC, MC, V. No lunch weekends.*

$
San Jose **Original Joe's.** Hearty Italian specialties, along with steaks, chops, and hamburgers, are served until 1:30 AM here in a warm cognac-and-green dining room with seating in cozy booths, and at a convivial counter overlooking the open kitchen. This downtown favorite has been in business since 1956. *301 S. 1st St., tel. 408/292–7030. No reservations. AE, D, MC, V.*

Santa Clara **Pizzeria Uno.** Some say that eating at one is eating at them all. Still, Pizzeria Uno is consistent, reliable, and tasty. You can get the same gourmet deep-dish pizzas here as in the Chicago flagship, classic pies that predate Wolfgang Puck's versions by 45 years. *2570 El Camino Real, tel. 408/241–5152. Reservations for 10 or more. AE, DC, MC, V.*

Lodging

All of the big hotel chains are represented in the valley: Best Western, Howard Johnson, Marriott, Days Inn, Hilton, Holiday Inn, Quality Inn, and Sheraton. Many dot the King's Highway—El Camino Real. If character is more important than luxury, seek out a smaller inn.

Category	Cost*
$$$$	over $175

$$$	$110—$175
$$	$75—$110
$	under $75

All prices are for a standard double room, excluding 9.5% room tax (10% in San Jose).

$$$$ **Fairmont Hotel.** If you're accustomed to the best, this is the place to stay. Affiliated with the famous San Francisco hotel of the same name, this downtown gem opened in 1987, and offers the utmost in luxury and sophistication. Get lost in the lavish lobby sofas under dazzling chandeliers while waiting for your Louis Vuitton collection to be delivered to your room, or dip your well-traveled feet in the rooftop pool, making rings in the exotic palms mirrored in the water. The rooms have every imaginable comfort, from down pillows and custom-designed comforters to oversize bath towels changed twice a day. The hotel offers complimentary HBO, and has accessible rooms for travelers with disabilities. *170 S. Market St. at Fairmont Pl., San Jose 95113, tel. 408/998–1900 or 800/527–4727, fax 408/280–0394. 500 rooms, 41 suites. Facilities: 5 restaurants, 24-hr room service, lounge, fitness center, business center, nonsmoking floors, currency exchange, valet parking. AE, D, DC, MC, V.*

$$$ **Hotel De Anza.** This lushly appointed French Mediterranean-style hotel, opened in 1931, has an Art Deco facade, hand-painted ceilings, and an enclosed terrace with towering palms and dramatic fountains. You'll also find many business amenities, including computers, cellular phones, and secretarial services. *233 W. Santa Clara St., San Jose 95113, tel. 408/286–1000 or 800/843–3700, fax 408/286–0500. 100 rooms. Facilities: restaurant, jazz club, exercise room, breakfast buffet, complimentary late-night snacks, valet parking. AE, DC, MC, V.*

★ **The Inn at Saratoga.** This five-story, European-style inn is actually only 10 minutes from the cultural action of Saratoga, yet it's far in spirit from bustling Silicon Valley, with its aura privacy and calm. All rooms have secluded sitting alcoves overlooking a peaceful creek, and the hotel's sun-dappled patio provides a quiet retreat. Modern business conveniences are available but discreetly hidden. *20645 Fourth St., Saratoga 95070, tel. 408/867–5020, 800/338–5020, or 800/543–5020 in CA, fax 408/741–0981. 46 rooms. Facilities: meeting room; executive services; complimentary breakfast, newspaper, and afternoon tea and wine. AE, DC, MC, V.*

$$ **Biltmore Hotel & Suites.** This hotel's central Silicon Valley location makes it a popular choice for business travelers. Completely renovated in 1993, it has an atrium lobby, ballroom, and a sports bar, in addition to 16 meeting rooms. *2151 Laurelwood Rd., Santa Clara 95054, tel. 408/988–8411 or 800/255–9925, fax 408/988–0225. 128 rooms, 134 suites. Facilities: restaurant, lounge, fitness center, heated outdoor pool, Jacuzzi, free parking, complimentary shuttle to airport, Paramount's Great America Park, and local businesses. AE, DC, MC, V.*

Madison Street Inn. Complimentary breakfast and afternoon tea are served on a brick garden patio with a bougainvillea-draped trellis at this refurbished Queen Anne Victorian. Light gray with blue and red trim, it's one of the few bed-and-breakfasts in Silicon Valley. *1390 Madison St., Santa Clara 95050, tel. 408/249–5541, fax 408/249–6676. 5 rooms, 3 with private baths. Facilities: outdoor pool, hot tub, meeting room. AE, D, DC, MC, V.*

Sundowner Inn. Exploiting the Valley's passion for high-tech machinery, this contemporary hotel offers voice mail, computer data ports, and remote-control televisions with ESPN, HBO, CNN, Nintendo, and VCRs, which you can use to play complimentary tapes from the library of 500. There's also a fleet of mountain bikes and a library full of best-sellers you can borrow. The complimentary breakfast buffet is served poolside. *504 Ross Dr., Sunnyvale 94089, tel. 408/734–9900 or 800/223–9901, fax 408/747–0580. 105 rooms, 12 suites. Facilities: exercise room, heated outdoor pool, sauna, laundry and valet service, nonsmoking rooms, meeting room. AE, DC, MC, V.*

$ **Motel 6.** Everything the name suggests, Motel 6 is the quintessential highway motel—basic and conveniently located. *3208 El Camino Real, Santa Clara, 95051, tel. 408/241–0200 or 800/437–7486. 99 rooms. Facilities: pool, parking, free local calls. AE, DC, MC, V.*

The Arts and Nightlife

Because of its size, it's not surprising that San Jose offers the richest mix of performing arts and other cultural attractions in Silicon Valley. The city's calendar is packed with everything from film festivals to jazz festivals, and there are many nightclubs and dance floors within the larger hotels. Throughout the rest of the valley there is plenty to do after the sun goes down.

Arts If you're traveling in summer, try not to miss the **Mountain Winery Concert Series** (14831 Pierce Rd., Box 1852, Saratoga 95070, tel. 408/741–5181). Music is performed under the moon and stars on a stage surrounded by grapevines. The series hosts internationally known country, jazz, blues, and opera acts. Be sure to buy tickets well in advance, as shows always sell out.

Mirassou Vineyards (tel. 408/274–4000) hosts a series of Pops Concerts each summer. The winery also offers four-course **Bistro Dinners** of informal, peasant fare ($45 per person) as well as more elegant, eight-course **Candlelight Dinners,** accenting food and wine pairings ($75 per person).

The **Flint Center at DeAnza College** (21250 Stevens Creek Blvd., Cupertino, tel. 408/864–8816) showcases nationally known dance, music, and theater acts. There is also a top-notch lecture series with celebrity speakers from the worlds of entertainment, education, and politics. Designed by the Frank Lloyd Wright Foundation, the **Center for Performing Arts** (255 Almaden Blvd., San Jose) is the venue for performances of the **San Jose Civic Light Opera** (1717 Technology Dr., tel. 408/453–7108), the **San Jose Symphony** (99 Almaden Blvd., Suite 400, tel. 408/288–2828), and the **San Jose Cleveland Ballet** (Almaden Blvd. and Woz Way, tel. 408/288–2800). **The San Jose Repertory Theatre** (1 N. 1st St., Suite 1, tel. 408/291–2255), the only professional resident theater in Silicon Valley, performs at the **Montgomery Theater** (corner of San Carlos and Market). To get schedules and reserve tickets for any of these performances, call the companies directly or phone BASS (tel. 408/998–2277). The season generally runs from September through June.

Nightlife **ComedySportz** (3428 El Camino Real, Santa Clara, tel. 408/725– 1356) is a comedy club and sports bar combined. The **Plumed Horse** (14555 Big Basin Way, Saratoga, tel. 408/867–4711; weekends only) is known for good jazz and blues. Try the **New West Melodrama and Comedy Vaudeville Show** (157 W. San Fernando St., San Jose, tel. 408/295–7469) for a fresh take on the Old West.

On and Around the Bay

A ferry ride to Sausalito or Tiburon or a drive across the Golden Gate or Bay bridges only suggests the many opportunities to enjoy and explore San Francisco Bay and its nearby waterways. The bay, 60 miles long and between 3 and 13 miles wide, was the area's transportation hub before there were passable roads and rails. Richard Henry Dana described sailing and shipping here during the 1830s in *Two Years Before the Mast.* The bay, the inland delta, and the Sacramento River were the gateways to the goldfields. Now they are an equally thriving area for weekend and vacation excursions. Around the bay are miles of shoreline parks and wildlife refuges, easily accessible but almost never seen by travelers on the busy Bayshore and East Shore freeways.

Yerba Island provides the center anchorage for the Bay Bridge and is connected by a causeway to man-made Treasure Island, with its military museum and relics of the island's 1939 World's Fair. There are excursions available to the Farallon Islands, which are rich with wildlife, 23 miles outside the Golden Gate. Other boating excursions explore the bay and the delta's maze of waterways as far as Stockton and Sacramento. Back on land is the town of Benicia, about an hour's drive northeast of San Francisco, where an early state capitol has been meticulously restored. Across Carquinez Strait is the former home of naturalist John Muir. Scenic river roads, particularly Highway 160, offer slower-paced alternatives to freeway travel between the Bay Area and Sacramento.

Exploring

Every day 250,000 people pass through **Yerba Buena Island** on their way across the San Francisco–Oakland Bay Bridge, yet it remains a mystery to most of them. Yerba Buena and the adjacent Treasure Island are primarily military bases, but they are accessible to the public. **Treasure Island** provides a superb bay-level view of the San Francisco skyline. The **Navy–Marine Corps–Coast Guard Museum** focuses on the military role in the Pacific;

it is housed in one of the remaining buildings from the 1939 Golden Gate International Exposition. *Bldg. 1, Treasure Island, tel. 415/395–5067. Admission free. Open daily 10–3:30.*

Recently developed wildlife refuges offer welcome access to the bay's shore, which can appear to be a congested commercial strip from surrounding freeways. Among the best of the free public parks are **Coyote Point Nature Museum** just off U.S. 101 south of San Francisco Airport (tel. 415/342–7755; open Tues.–Sat. 10–5, Sun. noon–5); the **Baylands Nature Interpretive Center** (tel. 415/329–2506; open Tues. and Wed. 10–5, Thurs. and Fri. 2–5, Sat. and Sun. 1–5) in the marshes at the east end of Embarcadero Road in Palo Alto; the **San Francisco Bay National Wildlife Refuge** on Thornton Avenue in Fremont, at the east end of the Dumbarton Bridge/Highway 84 (tel. 510/792–0222; open Tues.–Sun. 10–5); and the **Hayward Regional Shoreline** (open daily 6 AM–sunset; for guided walks, call the Interpretive Center, tel. 510/881–6751), the largest marsh restoration project on the West Coast, on West Winton Avenue at the east end of the San Mateo Bridge/Highway 92.

Another major wildlife center is outside the bay, the islands of the **Gulf of the Farallones National Maritime Sanctuary.** Rare nesting birds and passing seals and whales are visible from cruise boats, but the islands are off limits to visitors. Cruises are operated June–November by Oceanic Society Expeditions (tel. 415/474–3385). Fares are $49–$58.

A cruise line offers riverboat excursions through San Francisco, San Pablo, and Suisun bays, and along the Sacramento–San Joaquin River Delta as far as Sacramento. **Delta Riverboats** uses Harbor Tours ferries for the day-long voyage, two weekends a month May through October, with sightseeing on land in Old Sacramento before returning to San Francisco by bus. Passengers can also stay overnight and return on the ferry. *1540 W. Capitol Ave., Box 813, West Sacramento 95691, tel. 916/372–3690. Cost: $68, overnight $153.*

Houseboats can be rented to explore the 1,000 miles of delta waterways. Prices are about $600–$2,000 a week. Boats accommodate up to 14 persons, and a "test drive" with an operator is included in the rental. "The California Adventure Guide," covering houseboating, white-water rafting, and hot-air ballooning, is available from the California Office of Tourism (801 K St., Suite 1600, Sacramento 95814, tel. 800/862–2543).

The historic port city of **Benicia** is worth a detour for travelers on I–80 between San Francisco and Sacramento. (Take the I–780 exit in Vallejo, then Benicia's E. 2nd St. exit.) The old town center is on 1st Street, and at the foot of the street there is a fishing pier with a view through Carquinez Strait to San Pablo Bay. Benicia was named for the wife of General Mariano Vallejo, who owned the surrounding 99,000 acres. Benicia was the state capital in 1852 and 1853, and the handsome brick Greek Revival **capitol** has been splendidly restored. *1st and W. G Sts., tel. 707/745–3385. Nominal admission fee. Open daily 10–5.*

There is a pleasant garden and Federal-style home next door to the capitol that is open to the public. Nearby are scattered historic buildings, art galleries, crafts workshops, and antiques stores. The **Chamber of Commerce** (601 1st St.) distributes a helpful map and guide to the old waterfront district—including a list of former brothels. The restored Union Hotel (401 1st St., tel. 707/746–0100) is a prime example of restoration, and its restaurant is the area's finest.

Just across Carquinez Strait from Benicia is Martinez, another historic port city (now increasingly industrial) with at least one inviting landmark: **John Muir National Historic Site,** the Victorian-era residence of conservationist John Muir. Carefully restored and maintained, it sits atop a hill and is still surrounded by orchards and gardens. *Alhambra Valley Rd., near Hwy. 4, tel. 510/228–8860. Nominal admission fee. Open Wed.–Sun. 10–4:30. Closed Thanksgiving, Dec. 25, and Jan. 1.*

Another historic note: Martinez claims to be the birthplace of the martini, which according to legend was invented as the "Martinez cocktail" and was later slurred into its present designation.

North of the delta, about halfway between San Francisco and Sacramento, is the **Western Railway Museum,** which has collected and restored more than 100 pieces of railway equipment, including steam engines, suburban railroad commuter cars, and a variety of streetcars that make excursions around the 25-acre site. *Hwy. 12 at Rio Vista Junction, 10 mi east of Fairfield, tel. 707/374–2978. Admission: $2–$5. Open 11–5 weekends and most holidays.*

Marine World Africa USA

This wildlife theme park is one of Northern California's most popular attractions. It has been a phenomenal success since moving in 1986 from a crowded site south of San Francisco to Vallejo, about an hour's drive northeast. The 160-acre park features animals of the land, sea, and air performing in shows, roaming in natural habitats, strolling among park visitors with their trainers. Among the "stars" are killer whales, dolphins, camels, elephants, sea lions, chimpanzees, and a troupe of human water-skiers (April–October) The newest attraction, "Shark Experience," takes visitors on a walk in an acrylic tunnel through a 300,000-gallon coral reef habitat with 15 species of sharks and rays and 100 species of tropical fish.

The park is owned by the Marine World Foundation, a nonprofit organization devoted to educating the public about the world's wildlife. The shows and close-up looks at exotic animals serve that purpose without neglecting entertainment. The park is a family attraction, so it's not just for youngsters. For additional sightseeing, visitors can reach the park on a high-speed ferry from San Francisco, a trip that offers unusual vistas through San Francisco Bay and San Pablo Bay. *Marine World Pkwy., Vallejo, tel. 707/643–6722. Admission: $23.95 adults, $19.95 senior citizens*

60 and over, $16.95 children 4–12. Open summer, daily 9:30–6:45; rest of year and some school holidays, Wed.–Sun. 9:30–5.

Arriving and Departing

By Car Take I–80 east to Marine World Parkway in Vallejo. The trip takes one hour one-way. Parking is $3 at the park.

By Bus **Greyhound Lines** (tel. 800/231–2222) runs buses from downtown San Francisco to Vallejo. You can take the **BART** train (415/992–2278) to El Cerrito Del Norte Station and transfer to **Vallejo Transit** line (tel. 707/648–4666) to get to the park.

By Ferry **Red and White Fleet**'s (tel. 415/546–2896) high-speed ferry departs mornings each day that the park is open, from Pier 41 at Fisherman's Wharf. It arrives in Vallejo an hour later. Round-trip service allows five hours to visit the park. Excursion tickets are $21–$38 and include park admission.

10 The Wine Country

*Updated by
Claudia
Gioseffi*

In 1862, after an extensive tour of the wine-producing areas of Europe, Count Agoston Haraszthy de Mokcsa reported to his adopted California with a promising prognosis: "Of all the countries through which I passed," wrote the father of California's viticulture, "not one possessed the same advantages that are to be found in California. . . . California can produce as noble and generous a wine as any in Europe; more in quantity to the acre, and without repeated failures through frosts, summer rains, hailstorms, or other causes."

The "dormant resources" that Haraszthy saw in the temperate valleys of Sonoma and Napa, with their balmy days and cool nights, are in full fruition today. While the wines produced here are praised and savored by connoisseurs throughout the world, the area continues to be a fermenting vat of experimentation, a proving ground for the latest techniques of grape-growing and wine-making.

In Napa Valley, it seems that every available inch of soil is combed with neat rows of vines; would-be wine-makers with very little acreage can rent the cumbersome, costly machinery needed to stem and press the grapes. Many say making wine is a good way to turn a large fortune into a small one, but that hasn't deterred the doctors, former college professors, publishing tycoons, and airline pilots who come to try their hand at it.

Twenty years ago, Napa Valley had no more than 20 wineries; today there are almost 10 times that number. In Sonoma County, where the web of vineyards is looser, there are more than 100 wineries, and development is now claiming the cool Carneros region at the head of the San Francisco Bay, deemed ideal for growing the currently favored chardonnay grape.

All this has meant some pretty stiff competition, and the wine-makers are constantly honing their skills, aided by the scientific know-how of graduates of the nearby University of California at Davis, as well as by the practical knowledge of the grape-growers. They experiment with planting the vine stock closer together and with "canopy management" of the grape cluster, as well as with "cold" fermentation in stainless steel vats and new methods of fining, or filtering, the wine.

Recently phylloxera (a root louse) has caused quite a bit of re-planting in the valley. This is not necessarily bad, because only the finest and most disease-resistant grapes are now being re-planted. This selection process ensures the survival of the finer wines and eases the glut on the market. Another development is that grape growers are now producing outstanding wines themselves instead of selling their grapes to larger wineries. As a result, smaller producers can make excellent, reasonably-priced wines, while the larger wineries consolidate own land and expand their varietals.

In the past, the emphasis was on creating wines to be cellared, but today "drinkable" wines that can be enjoyed relatively rapidly are in demand. This has led to the celebration of dining as an art in the Wine Country. Many wineries boast first-class restaurants, which showcase excellent California cuisine and their own fine wines.

The stretch of highway from Napa to Calistoga rivals Disneyland as the biggest tourist draw in the state. Two-lane Highway 129 slows to a sluggish crawl on weekends throughout the year, and there are acres of vehicles parked at the picnic places, upscale gift shops, and restaurants in the area.

The pace in Sonoma County is less frenetic. While Napa is upscale and elegant, Sonoma is overalls-and-corduroy, with an air of rustic innocence. But the county's Alexander, Dry Creek, and Russian River valleys are no less productive of award-winning vintages. The Sonoma countryside also offers excellent opportunities for hiking, biking, camping, and fishing.

In addition to state-of-the-art viticulture, the Wine Country also provides a look at California's history. In the town of Sonoma, you'll find remnants of Mexican California and the solid, ivy-covered, brick wineries built by Haraszthy and his disciples. The original attraction here was the water, and the rush to the spas of Calistoga, promoted by the indefatigable gold-rush entrepreneur Samuel Brannan in the late 19th century, left a legacy of fretwork, clapboard, and Gothic architecture. More recent architectural details can be found at the Art Nouveau mansion of the Beringer brothers in St. Helena and the latter-day postmodern extravaganza of Clos Pegase in Calistoga.

The courting of the tourist trade has produced tensions, and some residents wonder whether projects like the Wine Train, running between Napa and St. Helena, brings the theme-park atmosphere a little too close to home. These fears may or may not be realized, but the natural beauty of the landscape will always draw tourists. Whether in the spring, when the vineyards bloom yellow with mustard flowers, or in the fall, when fruit is ripening, this slice of California has a feel reminiscent of the hills of Tuscany or Provence. Haraszthy was right: This is a chosen place.

Essential Information

Getting Around

By Plane The San Francisco and Oakland airports are closest to the Wine Country.

By Bus **Greyhound-Trailways** (tel. 800/231–2222) runs buses from the Transbay Terminal at 1st and Mission streets to and from Sonoma (two each day) and Santa Rosa (two each day). **Sonoma County Area Transit** (tel. 707/585–7516) and **Napa Valley Transit** (tel. 707/255–7631) provide local transportation within towns in the Wine Country.

By Car Although traffic on the two-lane country roads can be heavy, the best way to get around the Wine Country is by private car. Rental cars are available at the airports and in San Francisco, Oakland, Santa Rosa, and Napa.

The Rider's Guide (484 Lake Park Ave., Suite 255, Oakland 94610, tel. 510/653–2553) produces tapes about the history, landmarks, and wineries of the Sonoma and Napa valleys that you can play in your car (maps also provided). The tapes are available at some local bookstores or can be ordered directly from the Rider's Guide for $12.95, plus $2 postage.

Guided Tours

Full-day guided tours of the Wine Country usually include lunch and cost about $50. The guides, some of whom are winery owners themselves, know the area well and may show you some lesser-known cellars.

Wine Country Wagons (Box 1069, Kenwood 95452, tel. 707/833–2724, fax 707/833–1041) offers four-hour horse-drawn wagon tours that take in three wineries and end at a private ranch for a lavish buffet lunch. Tours depart daily at 10 AM, May–October; advance reservations are required.

Gray Line Inc. (350 8th St., San Francisco 94103, tel. 415/558–9400) has bright-red double-deckers that tour the Wine Country. Reservations are required.

Great Pacific Tour Co. (518 Octavia St., San Francisco 94102, tel. 415/626–4499) offers full-day tours, including a picnic lunch, to Napa and Sonoma, in passenger vans that seat 13.

HMS Tours (707 Fourth St., Santa Rosa 95404, tel. 707/526–2922 or 800/367–5348) offers customized tours of the Wine Country by appointment.

California Wine Adventures (1258 Arroyo Sarco, Napa 94558, tel. 707/257–0353) is a twenty-year-old family-owned operation which designs private tours for groups of at least two people. Cost includes a gourmet picnic lunch. Tours are available daily all year long. By appointment only.

Napa Valley Wine Train (1275 McKinstry St., Napa 94559, tel. 707/253–2111, 800/522–4142, or 800/427–4124 in CA) allows you to enjoy lunch, dinner, or a weekend brunch on one of several restored 1915 Pullman railroad cars that now run between Napa and St. Helena on tracks that were formerly owned by the Southern Pacific Railroad. Round-trip fare is $29; a three-course brunch costs $22, a three-course lunch is $25 and a five-course dinner is $45 (train fare is reduced to $14.50 for dinner parties of two or more). During the winter, service is limited to Thursday–Sunday. There is a special car for families with children on the weekend brunch trips.

Superior Sightseeing (642 Alvarado St., Suite 100, San Francisco 94114, tel. 415/550–1352) limits its full-day excursions to 20 passengers. The company offers personalized itineraries on request and provides free hotel pickup as well as group and senior-citizen rates. Reservations are required.

Important Addresses and Numbers

Tourist Information | **Calistoga Chamber of Commerce** (1458 Lincoln Ave., Calistoga 94515, tel. 707/942–6333). **Healdsburg Chamber of Commerce** (217 Healdsburg Ave., Healdsburg 95448, tel. 707/433–6935 or 800/648–9922 in CA).

Napa Valley Conference and Visitors Bureau (1310 Napa Town Center, Napa 94559, tel. 707/226–7459).

Redwood Empire Association (785 Market St., 15th Floor, San Francisco 94103, tel. 415/543–8334, fax 415/543–8337). The Redwood Empire Visitors' Guide is available free at the office or for $3 by mail.

St. Helena Chamber of Commerce (1080 Main St., Box 124, St. Helena 94574, tel. 707/963–4456 or 800/767–8528, fax 707/963–5396).

Sonoma County Convention and Visitors Bureau (5000 Roberts Lake Rd., Rohnert Park 94928, tel. 707/586–8100 or 800/326–7666, fax 707/586–8111).

Sonoma Valley Visitors Bureau (453 1st St. E, Sonoma 95476, tel. 707/996–1090).

Emergencies | The emergency number for fire, police, ambulance, and paramedics is 911; or dial 0 for operator and ask to be connected with the appropriate agency.

Exploring

There are three major paths through the Wine Country: U.S. 101 north from Santa Rosa, Highways 12 and 121 through Sonoma County, and Highway 29 north from Napa.

From San Francisco, cross the Golden Gate Bridge and follow U.S. 101 to Santa Rosa and points north. Or cross the Golden Gate, go north on U.S. 101, east on Highway 37, and north on Highway 121 into Sonoma. Yet another route runs over the San Francisco Bay Bridge and along I–80 to Vallejo, where Highway 29 leads north to Napa.

If you approach the Wine Country from the east, you'll travel along I–80 and then turn northwest on Highway 12 for a 10-minute drive through a hilly pass to Highway 29. From the north, take U.S. 101 south to Geyserville, turn southeast on Highway 128, and drive down into the Napa Valley.

Wineries

Choosing which of the 400 or so wineries to visit will be difficult, and the range of opportunities makes it tempting to make multiple stops. Being adventurous will pay off. The wineries along Napa Valley's more frequented arteries tend to charge nominal fees for tasting, but in Sonoma County, where there is less tourist traffic, fees are the exception rather than the rule. In Sonoma, you are more likely to run into a winegrower who is willing to spend part of an afternoon in convivial conversation than you are along the main drag of Napa Valley, where the waiter serving the bar has time to do little more than keep track of the rows of glasses.

Unless otherwise noted, visits to the wineries listed are free.

Highway 29 The town of **Napa** is the gateway into the famous valley, with its unrivaled climate and neat rows of vineyards. The towns in the area are small, and their Victorian Gothic architecture adds to the self-contained and separate feeling that permeates the valley.

A few miles north of Napa is the small town of **Yountville.** Turn west off Highway 29 at the Veterans Home exit and then up California Drive to **Domaine Chandon,** owned by the French champagne producer Moet-Hennessy and Louis Vuitton. You can tour the sleek modern facilities of this beautifully maintained property and sample flutes of the méthode champenoise sparkling wine. Champagne is $3–$4 per glass, the hors d'oeuvres are complimentary, and there is an elegant restaurant. *California Dr., Yountville, tel. 707/944–2280. Restaurant closed Mon. and Tues. Nov.–Apr. and closed entirely Jan. 1-19. No dinner Mon. and Tues. May–Oct. Tours daily 11–5 except Mon. and Tues. Nov.–Apr. Closed major holidays.*

Vintage 1870, a 26-acre complex of boutiques, restaurants, and gourmet stores, is on the east side of Highway 29. The vine-covered brick buildings were built in 1870 and originally housed a winery, livery stable, and distillery. The original mansion of the property is now **Compadres Bar and Grill,** and the adjacent **Red Rock Cafe** is housed in the train depot Samuel Brannan built in 1868 for his privately owned Napa Valley Railroad. The remodeled railroad cars now accommodate guests at the Napa Valley Lodge (*see* Lodging, *below*).

Washington Square, at the north end of Yountville, is a complex of shops and restaurants; **Pioneer Cemetery,** where the town's founder, George Yount, is buried, is across the street.

Many premier wineries lie along the route from Yountville to St. Helena.

At **Robert Mondavi,** tasters are encouraged to take the 60-minute production tour with complimentary tasting before trying the reserved wines ($1–$5 per glass). In-depth, 3- to 4-hour tours and gourmet lunch tours are also popular. There is an art gallery, and in summer there are concerts on the grounds. *7801 St. Helena Hwy., Oakville, tel. 707/963–9611. Open May–Oct., daily 9–5:30; Nov.–Apr., daily 9:30–4:30. Reservations advised in summer. Closed major holidays.*

The **Charles Krug Winery** opened in 1861 when Count Haraszthy loaned Krug a small cider press. It is the oldest winery in the Napa Valley, and is run by the Peter Mondavi family. There is also a gift shop. *2800 N. Main St., St. Helena, tel. 707/963–5057. May–Oct. open Mon.–Thurs. 10–5, Fri.–Sun. 10–6; Nov.–Apr. Mon.–Thurs. 10:30–4:30, Fri.–Sun. 10–5. Closed major holidays.*

Benziger Family
Winery, **23**
Beringer
Vineyards, **15**
Buena Vista
Carneros Winery, **27**
Charles Krug, **14**
Chateau Montelena, **9**
Clos du Bois, **4**
Clos du Val, **21**
Clos Pegase, **10**
Cuvaison, **11**
Davis Bynum
Winery, **7**
Domaine Chandon, **19**
Dry Creek
Vineyard, **1**
Freemark Abbey
Winery, **13**
Gloria Ferrer
Champagne Caves, **24**
Hop Kiln Winery, **5**
Kenwood
Vineyards, **22**
Korbel
Champagne Cellars, **8**
Lytton Springs, **2**
Piper Sonoma, **6**
Robert Mondavi, **18**
Robert Stemmler
Winery, **3**
Rutherford Hill
Winery, **17**
Sebastiani
Vineyards, **26**
Stag's Leap Wine
Cellars, **20**
Sterling Vineyards, **12**
V. Sattui, **16**
Viansa, **25**

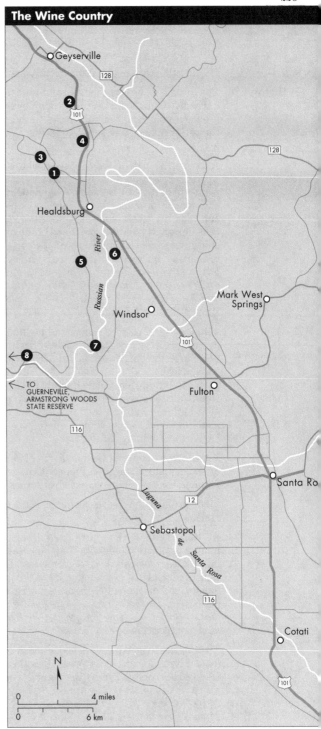

The Wine Country

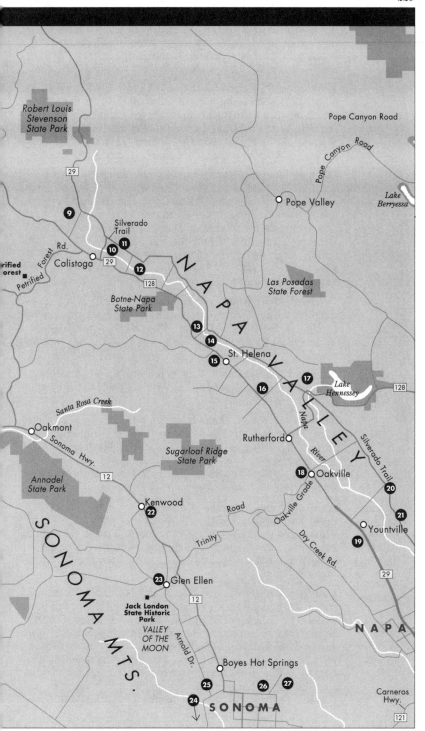

The wine made at **V. Sattui** is sold only on the premises; the tactic draws crowds, as does the huge gourmet delicatessen with its exotic cheeses and pâtés. Award-winning wines include dry Johannisberg Rieslings, zinfandels, and Madeiras. *1111 White La., St. Helena, tel. 707/963-7774. Open daily 9-5. Closed Christmas.*

The town of St. Helena boasts many Victorian buildings. Don't overlook the **Silverado Museum,** two blocks east from Main Street on Adams. Its Robert Louis Stevenson memorabilia consist of more than 8,000 artifacts, including first editions, manuscripts, and photographs. *1490 Library La., tel. 707/963-3757. Admission free. Open Tues.-Sun. noon-4. Closed major holidays.*

Beringer Vineyards has been operating continually since 1876. Tastings are held in the Rhine House mansion, where hand-carved oak and walnut and stained glass show Belgian Art Nouveau at its most opulent. The Beringer brothers, Frederick and Jacob, built the mansion in 1883 for the princely sum of $30,000. Tours are given every 30 minutes, and include a visit to the deep limestone tunnels in which the wines mature. *2000 Main St., St. Helena, tel. 707/963-4812. Open daily 9:30-4; summer hours are sometimes extended to 5. Closed major holidays.*

Freemark Abbey Winery was founded in the 1880s by Josephine Tychson, the first woman to establish a winery in California. *3022 St. Helena Hwy. N, St. Helena, tel. 707/963-9694. Open Mar.-Dec., daily 10-4:30; Jan. and Feb., Thurs.-Sun. 10-4:30. One tour daily at 2 PM.*

The **Hurd Beeswax Candle Factory** is next door, with two restaurants and a gift shop that specializes in handcrafted candles made on the premises.

The **Sterling Vineyards** sits on a hilltop to the east near Calistoga. The pristine white Mediterranean-style buildings are reached by an enclosed gondola from the valley floor; the view from the tasting room is superb. *1111 Dunaweal La., Calistoga, tel. 707/942-5151. Tram fee: $6 adults, children under 16 free. Open daily 10:30-4:30. Closed major holidays.*

At **Clos Pegase,** neoclassicism sets the tone. The winery, designed by architect Michael Graves, the exemplar of postmodernism, and commissioned by Jan Schrem, a publisher and art collector, pays homage to art, wine, and mythology. *1060 Dunaweal La., Calistoga, tel. 707/942-4981. Open 10:30-5. Closed major holidays.*

Calistoga, at the head of the Napa Valley, is noted for its mineral water, hot mineral springs, mud baths, steam baths, and massages. The Calistoga Hot Springs Resort was founded in 1859 by maverick entrepreneur Sam Brannan, whose ambition was to found "the Saratoga of California." He tripped up the pronunciation of the phrase at a formal banquet—it came out "Calistoga"—and the name stuck. One of his cottages, preserved as the Sharpsteen Museum, has a magnificent diorama of the resort in its heyday. *1311 Washington St., tel. 707/942-5911. Dona-*

tions accepted. Open May–Oct., daily 10–4; Nov.–Apr., daily noon–4.

Chateau Montelena is a vine-covered 1882 building set amid Chinese-inspired gardens, complete with a lake, red pavilions, and arched bridges. It's a romantic spot for a picnic, but you must reserve in advance. *1429 Tubbs La., Calistoga, tel. 707/942–5105 or 800/222–7288. Open daily 10–4. Tours at 11 and 2 by appointment only.*

The **Silverado Trail,** which runs parallel to Highway 29, takes you away from the madding crowd to some distinguished wineries as you travel north from Napa.

Clos du Val. Bernard Portet, the French owner, produces a celebrated cabernet sauvignon at this winery on the Silverado Trail. *5330 Silverado Trail, tel. 707/259–2200. Open daily 10–5.*

Stag's Leap Wine Cellars. In 1993, the winery's 1990 Reserve Chardonnay garnered a platinum award designating it the highest ranked premium Chardonnay in the world by the World Wine Championships. Also in 1993, *Bon Appetit*'s "Best Wines of the Year" featured both the 1990 Chardonnay and the Stag's Leap 1989 Cabernet. *5766 Silverado Trail, tel. 707/944–2020. Tasting fee: $3. Open daily 10–4. Tours by appointment. Closed major holidays.*

Rutherford Hill Winery. The wine here is aged in French oak barrels stacked in more than 30,000 square feet of caves. You can tour the nation's largest such facility and picnic on the grounds. *200 Rutherford Hill Rd., Rutherford, tel. 707/963–7194. Open weekdays 10–4:30, weekends 10–5, summer weekends (Fri.–Sun.) 11–6. Tour times vary seasonally; call ahead for detailed information.*

Cuvaison. This Swiss-owned winery specializes in chardonnay, merlot, and cabernet sauvignon for the export market. There are several picnic areas on the grounds, all with views of Napa Valley. *4550 Silverado Trail, tel. 707/942–6266. Open daily 10–5. Tours by appointment.*

Calistoga Gliders will give you a bird's-eye view of the entire valley, and on a clear day you can also see the San Francisco skyline, snowcapped Sierra peaks, and the Pacific Ocean. *1546 Lincoln Ave., tel. 707/942–5000. Fees: $110–$150 for 2 passengers, depending on length of ride. Open daily 9 AM–sunset, weather permitting. Closed Thanksgiving and Christmas.*

You don't have to be a registered guest at a spa to experience a mud bath. At **Dr. Wilkinson's Hot Springs** a $45 fee gets you "The Works": mud baths, individual mineral-water showers and a mineral-water whirlpool, followed by time in the steam room and a blanket wrap. For $65, you also get a half-hour massage. *1507 Lincoln Ave., Calistoga, tel. 707/942–4102. Open daily 8–3:30. Reservations are recommended.*

Highway 12   Rustic Sonoma is anchored by its past. It is the site of the last and the northernmost of the 21 missions established by the

Franciscan order of Fra Junipero Serra, and its central plaza includes the largest group of old adobes north of Monterey. The **Mission San Francisco Solano,** whose chapel and school labored to bring Christianity to the Indians, is now a museum that displays a collection of 19th-century watercolors. *114 Spain St. E, tel. 707/938–1519. Admission: $2 adults, $1 children 6–12; includes the Sonoma Barracks on the central plaza and General Vallejo's home, Lachryma Montis (*see below*). Open daily 10–5. Closed major holidays.*

Time Out | The four-block **Sonoma Plaza** is an inviting array of shops and food stores that overlook the shady park and attract gourmets from miles around. You can pick up the makings for a first-rate picnic here. The **Sonoma French Bakery** (466 1st St. E) is famous for its sourdough bread and cream puffs. The **Sonoma Sausage Co.** (453 1st St. W) produces a mind-boggling selection of bratwurst, bologna, boudin, bangers, and other Old World sausages. There are good cold cuts, too. The **Sonoma Cheese Factory** (2 Spain St.), run by the same family for four generations, makes Sonoma jack cheese and a tangy new creation, Sonoma Teleme. You can peer through the windows at the cheese-making process: great swirling baths of milk and curds and the wheels of cheese being pressed flat to dry.

A few blocks west (and quite a hike) is the tree-lined approach to **Lachryma Montis,** which General Mariano Vallejo, the last Mexican governor of California, built for his large family in 1851. The Victorian Gothic house is secluded in the midst of beautiful gardens; opulent Victorian furnishings, including a white marble fireplace in every room, are particularly noteworthy. The state purchased the home in 1933. *Spain St. W, tel. 707/938–1519. Admission: $2 adults, $1 children 6–12. Open daily 10–5. Closed major holidays.*

The **Sebastiani Vineyards,** originally planted by Franciscans of the Sonoma Mission in 1825, were bought by Samuele Sebastiani in 1904. The Sebastianis are renowned producers of red wines, and Sylvia Sebastiani has recorded her good Italian home cooking in a family recipe book, *Mangiamo,* to complement them. Tours include a look at an unusual collection of impressive carved oak casks. *389 4th St. E, tel. 707/938–5532. Open daily 10–5; last tour at 4:30. Closed major holidays.*

The landmark **Buena Vista Carneros Winery** (follow signs from the plaza), set among towering trees and fountains, is a must-see in Sonoma. It was here, in 1857, that Count Agoston Haraszthy de Mokcsa laid the basis for modern California wine-making, bucking the conventional wisdom that vines should be planted on well-watered ground by instead planting on well-drained hillsides. Chinese laborers dug the cool aging tunnels 100 feet into the hillside, and the limestone they extracted was used to build the main house. Although the wines are produced elsewhere in the Carneros region today, there are tours, a gourmet shop, an art gallery, and great picnic spots. *18000 Old Winery Rd., tel. 707/938–1266. Open daily 10–4:30.*

In the Carneros region of the Sonoma Valley, south of Sonoma, the wines at **Gloria Ferrer Champagne Caves** are aged in a "cava," or cellar, where several feet of earth maintain a constant temperature. *23555 Carneros Hwy. 121, tel. 707/996–7256. Tasting fees by the glass and the type of champagne. Open daily 10:30–5:30, tours every hour from 11 to 4.*

One of the newer wineries in Sonoma Valley is **Viansa,** opened by a son of the famous Sebastiani family, who decided to strike out on his own. Looking like a transplanted Tuscan villa, the winery's ocher-colored building is surrounded by olive trees and overlooks the valley. Inside is an Italian food and gift market. *25200 Arnold Dr., Sonoma, tel. 707/935–4700. Open daily 10–5.*

Continue north on Highway 12 through lush Sonoma Valley, where writer Jack London lived for many years; much around here has been named for him. The drive along Highway 12 takes you through orchards and rows of vineyards, with oak-covered mountain ranges flanking the valley. Some 2 million cases of wine are bottled in this area annually, and the towns of Glen Ellen and Kenwood are rich in history and lore. **Glen Ellen,** with its century-old Jack London Bar, is nestled at the base of the hill leading to Jack London State Park and the Benziger Family Winery. Nearby is Grist Mill Inn, a historic landmark with shops, and Jack London Village, with a charming bookstore filled with London's books and memorabilia. **Kenwood** is home to several important wineries, a historic train depot, and several eateries and shops specializing in locally produced gourmet products.

In the hills above Glen Ellen, known as the Valley of the Moon, is **Jack London State Historic Park.** The House of Happy Walls is a museum of London's effects, including his collection of South Sea artifacts. The ruins of Wolf House, which London designed and which mysteriously burned down just before he was to move in, are nearby, and London is buried on the property. *2400 London Ranch Rd., tel. 707/938–5216. Parking: $5 per car, $4 per car driven by senior citizen. Park open daily 9:30–sunset, museum daily 10–5. Museum closed major holidays.*

The Glen Ellen Winery is now the **Benziger Family Winery,** specializing in premium estate and Sonoma County wines. Their Imagery Series is a low-volume release of unusual red and white wines distributed in bottles with art labels by well-known artists from all over the world. *1883 London Ranch Rd., Glen Ellen, tel. 707/935–3000. Complimentary tasting of Sonoma County wines; fees vary for tasting estate and Imagery wines. Open daily 10–4:30.*

The beautifully rustic grounds of **Kenwood Vineyards** perfectly match the winery's approach to presenting wine, from the tasting room to bottle labels. While they produce all premium varietals, they are best known for their signature Jack London Vineyard reds—pinot noir, zinfandel, cabernet and merlot, and their Artist Series Cabernet. *9592 Sonoma Hwy., Kenwood, tel. 707/833–5891. Tasting available, no tours. Open daily 10–4:30.*

U. S. 101 Santa Rosa is the Wine Country's largest city and your best bet for a moderately priced hotel room, especially if you haven't reserved in advance.

The **Luther Burbank Home and Gardens** commemorate the great botanist, who lived and worked on these grounds for 50 years, single-handedly developing modern techniques of hybridization. Arriving as a young man from New England, he wrote: "I firmly believe . . . that this is the chosen spot of all the earth, as far as nature is concerned." The Santa Rosa plum, the Shasta daisy, and the lily of the Nile agapanthus are among the 800 or so plants he developed or improved. In the music room of his house, a Webster's Dictionary of 1946 lies open to a page on which the verb "burbank" is defined as "to modify and improve plant life." *Santa Rosa and Sonoma Aves., tel. 707/524–5445. Gardens free and open Nov.–Mar., daily 8–5; Apr.-Oct., daily 8–7. Guided tours: $2, children under 12 free; tours Apr.–Oct., Wed.–Sun. 10–4.*

The wineries of Sonoma County are located along winding roads and are not immediately obvious to the casual visitor; a tour of the vineyards that lie along the Russian River is a leisurely and especially bucolic experience. For a free map of the area, contact **Russian River Wine Road** (Box 46, Healdsburg 95448, tel. 707/433–6782).

For a historical overview, start at the imposing **Korbel Champagne Cellars,** which displays photographic documents of the North West Railway in a former train stop on its property. *13250 River Rd., Guerneville, tel. 707/887–2294. Open Oct.–Apr., daily 9–4:30; May–Sept., daily 9–5. Tours on the hour 10–3.*

Armstrong Woods State Reserve, just outside of Guerneville, contains 752 acres of virgin redwoods and is the best place in the Wine Country to see California's most famous trees. West of Guerneville along the Russian River Road (Highway 116) that leads to the Pacific Ocean and the rugged Sonoma coast is more redwood country, and a string of small towns. **Duncans Mills** is an old logging and railroad town with a complex of shops and a small museum in an old train depot. At the coast is **Jenner,** where the Russian River meets the Pacific. A colony of harbor seals makes its home here March through June. There are several bed-and-breakfasts here, and restaurants specializing in seafood.

Traveling down the River Road east of Guerneville, turn left down Westside Road and follow it as it winds past a number of award-winning wineries.

Davis Bynum Winery is an up-and-coming label that offers a full line of varietal wines that have done well in recent competitions. *8075 Westside Rd., Healdsburg, tel. 707/433–5852. Open daily 10–5.*

The **Hop Kiln Winery** is in an imposing hops-drying barn, which was built during the early 1900s and used as the backdrop for such films as the 1960 *Lassie* with James Stewart. *6050 Westside Rd., Healdsburg, tel. 707/433–6491. Open daily 10–5.*

Dry Creek Vineyard is one of California's leading producers of white wines and well known for its fumé blanc. Their reds, especially zinfandels and cabernets, have also begun to earn notice. There is a lovely picnic area. *3770 Lambert Bridge Rd., Healdsburg, tel. 707/433–1000. Open daily 10:30–4:30.*

The **Robert Stemmler Winery** draws on German traditions of wine-making and specializes in pinot noir. There are picnic facilities on the grounds. *3805 Lambert Bridge Rd., Healdsburg (Dry Creek Rd. exit from Hwy. 101, northwest 3 mi to Lambert Bridge Rd.), tel. 707/433–6334. Open 10:30–4:30 by appointment only.*

Lytton Springs Winery produces the archetype of the Sonoma Zinfandel, a dark, fruity wine with a high alcohol content. There is still dispute over the origin of this varietal and whether it was transplanted from stock in New England, but the vines themselves are distinctive, gnarled, and stocky, many of them over a century old. *650 Lytton Springs Rd., Healdsburg, tel. 707/433–7721. Open daily 10–4.*

In its new location five miles north of Healdsburg, **Clos du Bois** continues to produce the fine estate chardonnays of the Alexander and Dry Creek Valleys that have been mistaken for great French wines. *19410 Geyserville Ave., Box 940, Geyserville, tel. 707/857–1651 or 800/222–3189. Open daily 10–4:30. Call for tasting appointments.*

South of Healdsburg, off U.S. 101, is **Piper Sonoma,** a state-of-the-art winery that specializes in méthode champenoise sparkling wines. *11447 Old Redwood Hwy., Healdsburg, tel. 707/433–8843. Open daily 10–5.*

Time Out   Once you've seen, heard about, and tasted enough wine for one day, head over to **Kozlowski's Raspberry Farm** (5566 Gravenstein, Hwy. 116N), in Forestville, where jams are made from every berry imaginable.

Also in Forestville, **Brother Juniper's** makes a heavenly Struan bread of polenta, malted barley, brown rice, buttermilk, wheat bran, and oats. *6544 Front St., Hwy. 116, tel. 707/887–7908; 463 Sebastopol Ave., Santa Rosa, tel. 707/542–9012. Open Mon.–Sat. 9–3.*

What to See and Do with Children

In the **Bale Grist Mill State Historic Park** there is a partially restored 1846 flour mill powered by a 36-foot overshot water wheel. Short paths lead from the access road to the mill and the old pond site. *3 mi north of St. Helena on Hwy. 29, tel. 707/942–4575. Day use: $2 adults, $1 children 6–17. Open daily 10–5. Waterwheel demonstrations on weekends. Call ahead for special tour arrangements.*

Old Faithful Geyser of California blasts a 60-foot tower of steam and vapor about every 40 minutes; the pattern is disrupted if there's an earthquake in the offing. One of just three regularly erupting geysers in the world, it is fed by an underground river that heats to 350°F. The spout lasts three minutes. Picnic facilities are available. *1299 Tubbs La., 1 mi north of Calistoga, tel. 707/942–6463. Admission: $4.50 adults, $3.50 senior citizens, $2 children 6–11. Open daily 9–6 during daylight saving time, 9–5 in winter.*

In the **Petrified Forest** you can see the result of volcanic eruptions of Mount St. Helena 3.4 million years ago. The force of the explosion uprooted the gigantic redwoods, covered them with volcanic ash, and infiltrated the trees with silicas and minerals, causing petrification. There is a museum, and picnic facilities are available. *4100 Petrified Forest Rd., 5 mi west of Calistoga, tel. 707/942–6667. Admission: $3 adults, $2 senior citizens, $1 children 4–11. Open summer, daily 10–6; winter, daily 10–5.*

The Redwood Empire Ice Arena in Santa Rosa is not just another skating rink. It was built by local resident Charles Schulz, creator of *Peanuts.* The Snoopy Gallery and gift shop, with Snoopy books, clothing, and life-size comic strip characters, is delightful. *1667 W. Steele La., tel. 707/546–7147. Public skating in the afternoons.*

A scale steam train at **Train Town** runs for 20 minutes through a forested park with trestles, bridges, and small animals. *20264 Broadway (Hwy. 12), 1 mi south of Sonoma Plaza, tel. 707/938–3912. Admission: $3.50 adults, $2.50 children under 16 and senior citizens. Open mid-June–Labor Day, daily 10:30–5; Sept.–mid-June, Fri.–Sun. and holidays 10:30–5. Closed Christmas.*

Howarth Memorial Park, in Santa Rosa, has a lake where canoes, rowboats, paddleboats, and small sailboats can be rented for $6 an hour. The children's area has a playground, pony rides, a petting zoo, a merry-go-round, and a miniature train. Fishing, tennis, and hiking trails are also available. *Summerfield Rd. off Montgomery Rd., tel. 707/543–3282. Amusements: 75¢–$1. Park open daily; children's area open summer, Wed.–Sun.; spring and fall, weekends.*

Off the Beaten Track

You'll see breathtaking views of both the Sonoma and Napa valleys along the hairpin turns of the **Oakville Grade,** which twists along the range dividing the two valleys. The surface of the road is good, and if you're comfortable with mountain driving, you'll enjoy this half-hour excursion. Driving the road at night however, can be difficult. Trucks are advised not to take this route at any time.

Robert Louis Stevenson State Park, on Highway 29, 3 miles northeast of Calistoga, encompasses the summit of Mount St. Helena. It was here, in an abandoned bunkhouse of the Silverado Mine, that Stevenson and his bride, Fanny Osbourne, spent their honeymoon in the summer of 1880. The stay inspired Stevenson's "The Silverado Squatters," and Spyglass Hill in *Treasure Island* is thought to be a portrait of Mount St. Helena. The park's 3,000 acres are undeveloped except for a fire trail leading to the site of the cabin, which is marked with a marble tablet, and then on to the summit. Picnicking is permitted, but fires are not.

Shopping

Most wineries will ship purchases. Don't expect bargains at the wineries themselves, where prices are generally as high as at retail outlets. Residents report that the area's supermarkets stock a wide selection of local wines at lower prices. For connoisseurs seeking extraordinary values, the **All Seasons Cafe Wine Shop** (tel. 707/942–6828) in Calistoga is a true find. Gift shops in the larger wineries offer the ultimate in gourmet items—you could easily stock up early on Christmas presents.

Sports and the Outdoors

Ballooning This sport has fast become part of the scenery in the Wine Country, and many hotels arrange excursions. Most flights take place soon after sunrise, when the calmest, coolest time of day offers maximum lift and soft landings. Prices depend on the duration of the flight, number of passengers, and services (some companies provide pickup at your lodging, champagne brunch after the flight, and so forth). Expect to spend about $165 per person. Companies that provide flights include **Balloons Above the Valley** (Box 3838, Napa 94558, tel. 707/253–2222 or 800/464–6824 in CA), **Napa Valley Balloons** (Box 2860, Yountville 94599, tel. 707/944–0228 or 800/253–2224), **Once in a Lifetime** (Box 795, Calistoga 94515, tel. 707/942–6541 or 800/659–9915), and **Napa's Great Balloon Escape** (Box 795, Calistoga 94515, tel. 707/253–0860 or 800/564–9399), featuring a catered brunch finale at the Silverado Country Club overlooking the golf course.

Bicycling One of the best ways to experience the countryside is on two wheels, and the Eldorado Bike Trail through the area is considered one of the best. Reasonably priced rentals are available in most towns.

Golf Although the weather is mild year-round, rain may occasionally prevent your teeing off in the winter months. Call to check on greens fees at **Fountaingrove Country Club** (1525 Fountaingrove Pkwy., Santa Rosa, tel. 707/579–4653), **Oakmont Golf Club** (west course: 7025 Oakmont Dr., Santa Rosa, tel. 707/539–0415; east course: 565 Oak Vista Ct., Santa Rosa, tel. 707/538–2454), **Silverado Country Club** (1600 Atlas Peak Rd., Napa, tel. 707/257–0200), or **The Chardonnay Club** (2555 Jameson Canyon Rd., Napa, tel. 707/257–8950), a favorite among Bay Area golfers.

Dining

Revised by Catherine McEver

A Bay Area resident for over 20 years and a freelance writer, Catherine McEver has covered every aspect of the local food scene—from appetizers to ambience— for SF Magazine *and the* East Bay Express.

The restaurants in the Wine Country have traditionally reflected the culinary heritage of early settlers from Italy, France, and Mexico. Star chefs from urban areas are the most recent influx of immigrants, bringing creative California cuisine, seafood, and an eclectic range of American-regional and international fare. Food now rivals wine as the prime attraction in the region. A common element in today's Wine Country restaurants is reliance on fresh produce, meats, and prime ingredients from local farms. Those on a budget will find an appealing range of reasonably priced eateries. Gourmet delis offer superb picnic fare, and brunch is a cost-effective strategy at high-end restaurants.

With few exceptions (which are noted), dress is informal. Where reservations are indicated to be essential, you may need to reserve a week or more ahead; during the summer and early fall harvest seasons you may need to book several months ahead.

Category	Cost*
$$$$	over $40
$$$	$25–$40
$$	$16–$25
$	under $16

per person, excluding drinks, service, and 7.25% sales tax

The following credit card abbreviations are used: AE, American Express; D, Discover; DC, Diners Club; MC, MasterCard; V, Visa.

Calistoga
$$$$

All Seasons Cafe. Bistro cuisine has a California spin in this sun-filled setting with marble tables and a black-and-white checkerboard floor. A seasonal menu featuring organic greens, wild mushrooms, local game birds, house-smoked beef and salmon, and homemade breads, desserts, and ice cream from their on-site ice-cream plant, is coupled with a superb listing of local wines at bargain prices. For lunch there's a tempting selection of pizza, pasta, and sandwiches. *1400 Lincoln Ave., tel. 707/942–9111. Reservations advised on weekends. MC, V. Brunch Fri.–Sun. Closed Tues. dinner and Wed.*

$–$$

Silverado Restaurant & Tavern. In a setting straight out of a spaghetti western, savvy locals and seasoned wine connoisseurs linger over an award-winning wine list with over 700 selections priced just above retail. The eclectic menu includes egg rolls, chicken-salad sandwiches, Caesar salad, and great burgers. *1373 Lincoln Ave., tel. 707/942–6725. Reservations advised. MC, V. Closed Wed.*

$

Boskos Ristorante. Settling nicely into its second decade and its second home—a restored sandstone building that dates back to the 1800s—this popular eatery continues to dish up homemade pasta, pizza, and garden-frsh salads. *Glorioso* (pasta shells with garlic, mushrooms, and red chilies), is a favorite entrée. Leave room for the homemade chocolate cheesecake. *1364 Lincoln Ave., tel. 707/942-9088. No reservations. No credit cards.*

Geyserville **Château Souverain Café.** Those who mourned the closing of the
$–$$ Château's restaurant now have reason to celebrate. The new café has the same spectacular view of Alexander Valley vineyards and the same outdoor terrace for tranquil summer lunches, but now features radically reduced prices. The low tab makes chef Martin Courtman's seductive menu of French country fare such as braised lamb shanks, Sonoma roast chicken, or grilled buckwheat polenta with gorgonzola cheese irresistible. Check for expanded hours as café matures. *400 Souverain Rd. (Independence La. exit west from Hwy. 101), tel. 707/433-3141. Reservations advised. AE, MC, V. Closed Mon.–Thurs.*

Healdsburg **The Restaurant at Madrona Manor.** A brick oven, smoke-
$$$$ house, orchard, and kitchen garden on-site, paired with fresh Sonoma produce, Campbell lamb, and choice seafood, enable chef Todd Muir to turn out dishes fit for a wine baron: smoked lamb salad, Dungeness crab mousse, acorn squash soup, oven-roasted pork tenderloin, and Grand Marnier crème caramel. The 1881 Victorian mansion surrounded by 8 acres of wooded and landscaped grounds provides a storybook setting for a candlelight dinner in one of the formal dining rooms, or brunch on the outdoor deck. A la carte and prix fixe selections are available. *1001 Westside Rd. (take central Healdsburg exit from Hwy. 101, turn left on Mill St.), tel. 707/433-4231. Reservations advised. AE, D, DC, MC, V. Dinner only. Sun. brunch.*

$$ **Tre Scalini Ristorante.** Neo-Tuscan decor with mellow golden hues and live classical music Friday and Saturday nights provide the perfect backdrop for chef-owner Fernando Urroz's contemporary take on northern Italian cuisine. The menu changes quarterly to feature dishes such as fresh sea scallops baked in paper with saffron-infused polenta and sweet roasted peppers; wild mushroom fettuccine with crushed chilies, garlic, essence of white peppers and truffle oil; and braised Sonoma rabbit with a sauce of red wine, balsamic vinegar, and sweet onions. *241 Healdsburg Ave. (¼ block south of town plaza), tel. 707/433-1772. Reservations advised. AE, MC, V. Dinner only. Closed Tues.*

$–$$ **Bistro Ralph.** Ralph Tingle, once executive chef of the defunct Fetzer Vineyards Sun Dial Grill in Mendocino, has created a culinary hit with his California homestyle cuisine. The small, frequently changing menu includes Szechuan pepper calamari, braised lamb shanks with mint essence (using locally ranched Bruce Campbell lamb), and sea bass braised with ginger and carrot juice. Wine is used liberally in the cooking and the wine list features picks from small local wineries. The stark industrial setting is tempered by a couple of trees perched incongruously on the bar and an exceedingly friendly wait staff. *109 Plaza St., tel. 707/433-1380. Reservations advised. MC, V. No lunch weekends.*

Samba Java. This lively café manages to cram a lot of tables, colorful decor, and culinary action into a very small space. The menu covers an eclectic range of California-American cuisine, is based exclusively on Sonoma ingredients, and changes daily. Everything on it is made from scratch: from breads and preserves to a succulent roasted pork loin with a sweet-potato *galette* (razor-thin slices layered with olive oil and herbs) and wilted bitter greens to a coconut *tuille* (delicate cookie cup) filled with chocolate mousse and raspberry sauce. *109A Plaza St., tel. 707/433–5282. Reservations accepted for dinner; lunch reservations for 6 or more only. AE, MC, V. No lunch Mon. No dinner Sun.–Wed. Breakfast served Tues.–Sun.*

Napa **Silverado Country Club.** There are two restaurants and a bar and
$$$ grill at this large, famous resort. Vintner's Court, with California-Continental cuisine, serves dinner only; there is a seafood buffet on Friday night and a champagne brunch on Sunday. Royal Oak serves steak and seafood for dinner nightly. The bar and grill is open for breakfast and lunch year-round; in the summer, lunch offerings include an outdoor barbecue with chicken and hamburgers. *1600 Atlas Peak Rd. (follow signs to Lake Berryessa), tel. 707/257–0200. Reservations required for 2 restaurants only. Jackets suggested in Vintner's Court. AE, D, DC, MC, V. Vintner's Court closed Mon. and Tues. No dinner Sun.*

$$–$$$ **La Boucane.** Chef-owner Jacques Mokrani has created a gorgeous little gem of a restaurant in a restored 1885 Victorian decorated with period antiques. Classic French cuisine (rack of lamb, champagne-crisp duck) is delivered with style in a candlelit dining room enhanced by silver, linen, and a red rose on each table. *1778 2nd St. (at Jefferson St. in downtown Napa), tel. 707/253–1177. Reservations advised. MC, V. Dinner only. Closed Sun. and month of January.*

$–$$ **Bistro Don Giovanni.** Rumor has it that Alice Waters' first venture in the Wine Country, Table 29, failed because there weren't enough Napa Valley selections on the wine list. Giovanni and Donna Scala, the culinary couple behind the success of Ristorante Piatti, have created a new hit on this site, dishing up Italian and French fare with a California twist. The atmosphere is casual Mediterranean, with terra-cotta tile floors, high ceilings, and a full bar (with plenty of Napa wines). Ingredients such as pesto, goat cheese, and shrimp top individual pies from the wood-burning pizza oven. The carpaccio is a standout. Winning items include pastas and grilled entrées such as pork chops with garlic-infused mashed potatoes. Don't miss the delectable fruit-crisp dessert, which changes daily. *4110 St. Helena Hwy., tel. 707/224–3300. Reservations advised. AE, DC, MC, V.*

$ **Jonesy's Famous Steak House.** This spacious and informal local favorite has been providing lots of entertainment for aviation buffs, steak lovers, and kids of all ages since 1946. One entire wall has an expanse of windows with a prime view of the landing strip. Inside, prime steaks weighted down with Sacramento River rocks are seared over a dry grill. Broasted chicken, homemade soups, and fresh fish round out the fare. Kids get their own menu. *2044 Airport Rd. (halfway between Napa and Vallejo, off Hwy. 29), tel. 707/255–2003. Reservations advised. AE, D, DC, MC, V. Closed Mon. and a week at Christmas.*

Oakville **Stars Oakville Cafe.** Jeremiah Tower, father of California Cui-
$$ sine, and Marc Franz (executive chef of Tower's legendary Stars
Restaurant in San Francisco) have transformed an old building
next to the Oakville Grocery store into a Mediterranean café
with glazed tile floors, white walls, lots of flowers, and picture
windows that look into the kitchen. Franz designed the wood-
burning ovens to turn out rustic fare such as roasted leg of lamb,
roast salmon, and roast pumpkin-filled pasta with white truffle
oil, for a menu that changes daily. A stellar wine list comple-
ments the cuisine; the desserts (brownie-steamed pudding,
pumpkin cheesecake) are sublime. Space heaters on the tented
outdoor patio add comfort to al fresco dining, and the adjacent
garden with lemon trees, lavender, and an antique aviary is the
perfect setting for an after-dinner stroll. *7848 St. Helena Hwy.
29 (corner of Hwy. 29 and Oakville Crossroad), tel. 707/944–8905.
Reservations required weekends, advised weekdays. AE, D, DC,
MC, V. No lunch Mon. and Tues.*

Rutherford **Auberge du Soleil.** The dining room is a setting of rustic ele-
$$–$$$$ gance: earth tones, wood beams, and outdoor deck with panoramic views of the valley. The menu changes monthly and
features local produce and American Wine Country cuisine with
some innovative twists. House specialties include roasted lobster sausage and braised California pheasant. There is a moderately priced bar menu (Dungeness crab quesadillas, black-
bean chili) and a fine list of wines from California, France, and
Italy. This place is also a 48-room inn (*see* Lodging, *below*). *180
Rutherford Hill Rd. (off Silverado Trail just north of Rte. 128), tel.
707/963–1211. Reservations advised. AE, D, MC, V. Breakfast
daily.*

St. Helena **The Restaurant at Meadowood.** This sprawling resort looks like
$$$$ a scene from an F. Scott Fitzgerald novel, complete with croquet
lawns, and provides the perfect setting for weekend brunch.
Classic French cuisine is offered at dinner in either a dining
room that sports a fireplace, lush greenery, and skylights in a
cathedral ceiling or outdoors on a terrace overlooking the golf
course. A lighter menu of American and French bistro fare can
be had at breakfast and lunch (and early dinners Friday and
Saturday) at a second, less formal and less expensive Meadowood restaurant, the Grill. *900 Meadowood La., tel. 707/963–
3646. Reservations required. Jacket recommended for The
Restaurant. AE, D, DC, MC, V.*

Terra. The delightful couple who owns this lovely, unpretentious
restaurant housed in a century-old stone foundry learned their
culinary skills at the side of chef Wolfgang Puck. Hiro Sone was
head chef at L.A.'s Spago, and Lissa Doumanie was the pastry
chef. The menu has an enticing array of southern French and
northern Italian favorites, prepared with Hiro's Japanese-
French-Italian finesse. Favorites include pear and goat cheese
salad with warm pancetta and sherry vinaigrette, and filet of

salmon with Thai red-curry sauce and basmati rice. Save room for Lissa's desserts. *1345 Railroad Ave., tel. 707/963–8931. Reservations advised. MC, V. Dinner only. Closed Tues.*

Trilogy. Chef-owner Diane Pariseau pairs one of the best and most extensive contemporary wine lists in the valley with superb renditions of California-French cuisine on a prix-fixe menu that changes daily. Pariseau has a deft touch at juxtaposing flavors, textures, and artful presentation in her soups, appetizers, salads, and all-star entrées, such as grilled chicken breast on a nest of sautéed apples and green peppercorns or grilled tuna steak with olive oil and sweet red pepper puree. The atmosphere is that of a gracious home: There are just 10 tables tucked away in semiprivate dining areas on two different levels. *1234 Main St., tel. 707/963–5507. Reservations required. MC, V. No lunch weekends. Closed Mon. and 3 wks in Dec.*

$$ **Brava Terrace.** Owner Fred Halpert is part of the recent influx of all-star chefs who are creating a culinary renaissance in the Wine Country. American-born, French-trained Halpert has worked with head chef Peter McCaffrey to create a menu featuring pasta, risotto, and a trademark lentil cassoulet. The chocolate-chip crème brûlée provides a grand finale. The restaurant has a comfortably casual ambience, a full bar, a large stone fireplace, an outdoor terrace, and an enclosed, heated deck with views of the valley floor and Howell Mountain. *3010 St. Helena Hwy. (Hwy. 29, 1/2 mi north of St. Helena), tel. 707/963–9300. Reservations advised. AE, D, DC, MC, V. Closed Wed. Nov.–Apr. and Jan. 17–26.*

Tra Vigne. A Napa Valley fieldstone building has been transformed into a striking trattoria with beaded lamps and plush banquettes. Homemade breads, pastries, mozzarella, pastas, sauces, olive oils, and vinegar, and house-cured pancetta and prosciutto contribute to a one-of-a-kind tour of Tuscan cuisine. Seating is hopeless without a reservation, but drop-ins are welcome at the bar. The courtyard offers alfresco dining and Mediterranean ambience, and the Cantinetta delicatessen in the corner of the courtyard offers wine by the glass and gourmet picnic fare. *1050 Charter Oak Ave. (off Hwy. 29), tel. 707/963–4444. Reservations required in dining room. D, DC, MC, V.*

Santa Rosa **John Ash & Co.** The thoroughly regional cuisine here emphasizes
$$–$$$ beauty, innovation, and the seasonal availability of food products grown in Sonoma County and in the restaurant's organic garden. In spring, local lamb is roasted with hazelnuts and honey; in fall, farm pork is roasted with fresh figs and Gravenstein apples. There are fine desserts and an extensive wine list. The place looks like a Spanish villa amid the vineyards, with patio seating outside and a cozy fireplace indoors. This is a favorite spot for Sunday brunch. *4330 Barnes Rd. (River Rd. exit west from Hwy. 101), tel. 707/527–7687. Reservations advised. Jacket preferred. D, MC, V. Closed Mon.*

$–$$ **Lisa Hemenway's.** A shopping center on the outskirts of town seems an unlikely location for a restaurant find, but Hemenway, who trained under John Ash (*see* John Ash & Co., *above*) has created a light and airy eatery with soft wine-country colors, works by local artists on the walls, and a garden view from the patio. The fare (updated every four months) provides a deliciously eclectic tour through American and international cuisine, from grilled Indonesian chicken served over angel hair pasta to vegetable tamales with ancho-chili sauce, black beans, salsa, and sour cream. The adjacent deli, Tote Cuisine, has a vast selection of tempting takeouts for picnickers. *714 Village Ct. Mall (east on Hwy. 12, north on Farmer's La., right on Sonoma), tel. 707/526–5111. Reservations advised. D, MC, V. Sun. brunch.*

$ **Omelette Express.** As the name implies, some 300 omelet possibilities are offered in this friendly no-frills eatery in historic Railroad Square. *112 4th St., tel. 707/525–1690. No reservations weekends. MC, V. Breakfast and lunch only.*

Sonoma **The Grille at Sonoma Mission Inn & Spa.** There are two restau-
$$$ rants at this famed resort (*see* The Cafe, *below*). The Grille offers formal dining in a light, airy setting with original art on the walls, French windows overlooking the pool and gardens, and a patio for alfresco dining. Wine Country cuisine changes seasonally to feature favorites like Sonoma leg of lamb and basil-roasted chicken with garlic mashed potatoes. On weekends there's a prix-fixe menu, pairing each course with the appropriate wine from the restaurant's extensive selection. The special spa menu provides a tempting way to stay in shape. *18140 Hwy. 12 (2 mi north of Sonoma at Boyes Blvd.), tel. 707/938–9000. Reservations strongly advised. AE, DC, MC, V. Sun. brunch.*

$$–$$$ **L'Esperance.** The dining room is small and pretty, with flowered tablecloths, burgundy overcloths, and burgundy chairs. There is a choice of classic French entrées, such as rack of lamb, plus a prix-fixe "menu gastronomique" that includes hot and cold appetizers, salad, entrée, dessert, and coffee. *464 1st St. E (down a walkway off the plaza, behind the French bakery), tel. 707/996–2757. Reservations required weekends. AE, MC, V. Sun. brunch. Closed Mon. and Tues.*

$$ **Eastside Oyster Bar & Grill.** Chef-owner Charles Saunders, renowned for his stint at the Sonoma Mission Inn (*see above*), received rave reviews for his creative culinary flair (and health-conscious approach) when this place opened in the fall of 1992. The California fare incorporates fresh fish, local meat and poultry, and produce from an organic kitchen garden. Hits here include a surprisingly delicate hangtown fry (plump oysters on a bed of greens and beets with a Sonoma mustard vinaigrette); creative renditions of roast chicken or Sonoma lamb; and stellar salads and vegetarian dishes. Inside, the restaurant has a fireplace and an intimate bistro atmosphere; outside there's a wisteria-draped terrace where diners enjoy a picture-window view into the pastry kitchen. *133 E. Napa St. (just off downtown plaza square), tel. 707/939–1266. Reservations advised. AE, DC, MC, V. Sun. brunch.*

Kenwood Restaurant & Bar. This place's highest recommendation is the fact that when Napa and Sonoma chefs take their night off, they come here. Both in tastes and looks it will remind you of a sunny hotel dining room in the south of France. Patrons indulge in country French cuisine such as braised rabbit and warm sweetbread salad in the airy dining room, or head through the French doors to the patio where there's a memorable view of the vineyards. *9900 Hwy. 12, Kenwood, tel. 707/833–6326. Reservations advised. MC, V. Sun. brunch. Closed Mon.*

Ristorante Piatti. On the ground floor of the remodeled El Dorado Hotel, a 19th-century landmark building, this is the Sonoma cousin of the Yountville Piatti (*see below*). Pizza from the wood-burning oven and northern Italian specials (spit-roasted chicken, ravioli with lemon cream) are served in a rustic Italian setting with an open kitchen and bright wall murals, or on the outdoor terrace. *405 First St. W (facing the plaza), tel. 707/996–2351. Reservations advised. AE, MC, V.*

$ **The Cafe.** This is Sonoma Mission Inn's (*see above*) second restaurant, with an informal bistro atmosphere, overstuffed booths, ceiling fans, and an open kitchen renowned for its country breakfasts, pizza from the wood-burning oven, and tasty California renditions of northern Italian cuisine. *18140 Sonoma Hwy. (2 mi north of Sonoma on Hwy. 12 at Boyes Blvd.), tel. 707/938–9000. Reservations recommended at dinner; accepted for 6 or more for breakfast and lunch. AE, DC, MC, V. Weekend brunch.*

La Casa. "Whitewashed stucco, red tile, serapes, and Mexican glass" describes this restaurant just around the corner from Sonoma's plaza. There's bar seating, a patio out back, and an extensive menu of traditional Mexican food: chimichangas and snapper Veracruz for entrées, sangria to drink, and flan for dessert. *121 E. Spain St., tel. 707/996–3406. Reservations advised. AE, DC, MC, V.*

Yountville **Domaine Chandon.** The menu of expertly prepared, artfully pre-
$$$$ sented light French cuisine (featuring seafood, poultry, venison, and lamb) has a California accent and changes daily. The architecturally dramatic dining room has views of vineyards and carefully preserved native oaks. There is also outdoor service on a tree-shaded patio. *California Dr. (Yountville exit off Hwy. 29, toward Veterans' Home), tel. 707/944–2892. Reservations essential. Jacket required at dinner. AE, D, DC, MC, V. No dinner Mon. and Tues. year-round; no lunch Mon. and Tues. Oct.–May.*

$$ **Anesti's Grill and Rotisserie.** Specialties at this spacious, cheerful restaurant include leg of lamb and duckling roasted to perfection on the only French rotisserie in Napa and rack of lamb from the mesquite grill. The open kitchen provides entertainment indoors; a patio offers alfresco dining and vistas of vineyards and hills. *6518 Washington St., tel. 707/944–1500. Reservations advised. AE, DC, MC, V.*

Mustard's Grill. Grilled fish, hot smoked meats, fresh local produce, and a good wine list are offered in a boisterous, noisy bistro with a black-and-white marble floor and upbeat artwork. Expect to encounter a crowd. *7399 St. Helena Hwy., Napa Valley (Hwy. 29, 1 mi north of Yountville), tel. 707/944–2424. Reservations advised (2 months in advance). D, DC, MC, V.*

Ristorante Piatti. A small, stylish trattoria with a pizza oven and open kitchen, this cheery place is full of good smells and happy people. Its authentic regional Italian cooking—from the antipasti to the grilled chicken to the tiramisu—is the perfect cure for a jaded appetite. The homemade pastas are the best bet. *6480 Washington St., tel. 707/944–2070. Reservations advised. AE, MC, V.*

$ **The Diner.** This is probably the best-known and most-appreciated stop-off in the Napa Valley, especially for breakfast. Be sure to have the local sausages and the house potatoes. At night, you'll find healthful, California-cuisine versions of Mexican and American classics. *6476 Washington St., tel. 707/944–2626. Reservations accepted for 6 or more; expect a wait for seating. No credit cards. Closed Mon.*

Lodging

Make no mistake, staying in the Wine Country is expensive. The inns, hotels, and motels are usually exquisitely appointed, and many are fully booked long in advance of the summer season. Since Santa Rosa is the largest population center in the area, it has the largest selection of rooms, many at moderate rates. Try there if you've failed to reserve in advance or have a limited budget. For those seeking romantic and homey atmospheres, check out the dozens of bed-and-breakfast inns that have been established in the Victorian homes and old hotels of the wine country (the tourist bureaus of Sonoma and Napa counties both provide information and brochures on B&Bs). Families should note, however, that small children are often discouraged as guests. Aside from the charm and romance, an advantage of B&Bs (which cost more than the average motel) is the often sumptuous breakfast that is included in the price. In the Wine Country, the morning meal often features local produce and specialties. For all accommodations in the area, rates are lower on weeknights and about 20% less in the winter.

Highly recommended hotels are indicated by a star ★.

Category	Cost*
$$$$	over $100
$$$	$80–$100
$$	$50–$80
$	under $50

All prices are for a standard double room, excluding 12% tax.

The following credit card abbreviations are used: AE, American Express; D, Discover; DC, Diners Club; MC, MasterCard; V, Visa.

Calistoga **Brannan Cottage Inn.** This exquisite Victorian cottage with
$$$–$$$$ lacy white fretwork, large windows, and a shady porch is the
★ only one of Sam Brannan's 1860 resort cottages still standing on
its original site. The restoration is excellent and includes elegant
stenciled friezes of stylized wildflowers. All rooms have private
entrances. Full breakfast is included. *109 Wapoo Ave., 94515, tel.*
707/942–4200. 6 rooms. MC, V (for room payment; reservations
held by mailed check only).

Mount View Hotel. Once simply a refurbished 1930s hotel with
character, the Mount View is now one of the more elegant places
to stay in the valley. A full-service European spa offers state-of-
the-art pampering, and if you prefer a cottage to a room, there
are three—each equipped with private redwood deck, Jacuzzi,
and wet bar. A brand new restaurant/saloon, Catahoula's, offers
southern-inspired American cuisine. The poolside grill and ca-
bana bar showcase a live "blues brunch" on weekends. *1457 Lin-*
coln Ave., 94515, tel. 707/942–6877, fax 707/942–6904. 33 rooms with
bath. Facilities: spa, pool, restaurant. AE, MC, V.

$$–$$$ **Dr. Wilkinson's Hot Springs.** This hot springs spa resort has been
in operation for more than 40 years. Reserve ahead for week-
ends, when there are separate fees for mud baths, massages,
facials, and steam rooms. Midweek packages include room and
full spa services. *1507 Lincoln Ave., 94515, tel. 707/942–4102, fax*
707/942–6110. 42 rooms. Facilities: 3 mineral pools. AE, MC, V.

$$ **Comfort Inn Napa Valley North.** All the rooms in this motel have
one king- or two queen-size beds, and many have vineyard views.
Continental breakfast is included. There are rooms for nonsmokers and travelers with disabilities and discounts for senior
citizens. *1865 Lincoln Ave., 94515, tel. 707/942–9400 or 800/228–*
5150, fax 707/942–5262. 54 rooms with bath. Facilities: natural
mineral-water pool, spa sauna, steam room. AE, D, DC, MC, V.

Mountain Home Ranch. This rustic ranch, built in 1913, is set
on 300 wooded acres, with hiking trails, a creek, and a fishing
lake. There is just one TV, in the dining room, and no phones. In
summer, the modified American plan (full breakfast and dinner)
is used; otherwise, Continental breakfast is included. The seven
cabins spread over the grounds are ideal for families; each has
a full kitchen and bath, and the majority have wood-burning fireplaces. Special children's rates are available. *3400 Mountain*
Home Ranch Rd., 94515 (north of town on Hwy. 128, left on Petri-
fied Forest Rd., right on Mountain Home Ranch Rd., to end; 3 mi
from Hwy. 128), tel. 707/942–6616. 6 rooms in main lodge; 7 cabins,
all with private bath. Facilities: 2 pools, tennis. MC, V. Closed Dec.
and Jan.

Glen Ellen **Beltane Ranch.** On a slope of the Mayacamas range on the east-
$$$–$$$$ ern side of the Sonoma Valley is this 100-year-old house built by
a retired San Francisco madam. The inn is part of a working
cattle and grape-growing ranch (the nearby Kenwood Winery
has a chardonnay made from the ranch's grapes), and the family
of innkeeper Rosemary Woods has lived here for 50 years. The
inn's location is the big draw; miles of trails wander through the
oak-studded hills around the property. The comfortable living

room has dozens of books on the area. The rooms all have private baths and antique furniture and open onto the building's wraparound porch. *11775 Sonoma Hwy. (Hwy. 12), 95442, tel. 707/996–6501. 4 rooms. Facilities: tennis. No credit cards, but personal checks accepted.*

Glenelly Inn. Just outside the hamlet of Glen Ellen is this sunny little establishment, built as an inn in 1916. Rooms are cozy and furnished with country antiques. Most bathrooms have clawfoot tubs. Mother and daughter innkeepers Ingrid and Kristi Hallamore serve breakfast in front of the common room's cobblestone fireplace and local delicacies in the afternoons. If the weather is warm, ask to have breakfast outside under one of the shady oak trees; it's a tranquil way to begin your day. The inn's hot tub is enclosed in a small garden. *5131 Warm Springs Rd., 95442, tel. 707/996–6720. 8 rooms. MC, V.*

Healdsburg
$$$$

Madrona Manor. A splendid, three-story, 1881 Gothic mansion, carriage house, and outbuildings sit on 8 wooded and landscaped acres. Mansion rooms are recommended: All nine have fireplaces, and five contain the antique furniture of the original owner. The approach to the mansion leads under a stone archway and up a flowered hill; the house overlooks the valley and vineyards. Full breakfast is included, and there's a fine restaurant on the premises that serves dinner. Pets are allowed. *1001 Westside Rd., Box 818, 95448, tel. 707/433–4231 or 800/258–4003, fax 707/433–0703. 21 rooms with bath. Facilities: pool, restaurant. AE, DC, MC, V.*

$$–$$$$

Healdsburg Inn on the Plaza. This renovated 1900 brick building on the attractive town plaza has a bright solarium and a roof garden. The rooms are spacious, with quilts and pillows piled high on antique beds, and in the bathrooms, claw-foot tubs are outfitted with rubber ducks. Full breakfast, afternoon coffee and cookies, and early evening wine and popcorn are included. *110 Matheson St., Box 1196, 95448, tel. 707/433–6991. 9 rooms. Facilities: fireplaces in most rooms. MC, V.*

$$

Best Western Dry Creek Inn. Continental breakfast and a bottle of wine are complimentary at this three-story Spanish Mission-style motel. There is a coffee shop next door. Small pets are allowed. Midweek discounts are available, and direct bus service from San Francisco Airport can be arranged. *198 Dry Creek Rd., 95448, tel. 707/433–0300, 800/528–1234, or 800/222–5784 in CA, fax 707/433–1129. 102 rooms with bath. Facilities: pool, spa, laundry. AE, D, DC, MC, V.*

Napa
$$$$

Sheraton Inn Napa Valley. This modern, comfortable motel was completely renovated in late 1993. A convenient restaurant and lounge are on the premises, with live music in the lounge. Movies and rooms for travelers with disabilities are also available. *3425 Solano Ave., 94558 (1 block west off Hwy. 29; take Redwood-Trancas exit), tel. 707/253–7433 or 800/325–3535, fax 707/258–1320. 191 rooms. Facilities: heated pool, spa, lighted tennis courts. AE, D, DC, MC, V.*

Silverado Country Club. This luxurious 1,200-acre resort in the hills east of the town of Napa offers cottages, kitchen apartments, and one- to three-bedroom efficiencies, many with fireplaces. There are also two dining rooms, a lounge, a sundries store, seven pools, 20 tennis courts, and two championship golf courses designed by Robert Trent Jones. Fees are charged for golf, tennis, and bike rentals. *1600 Atlas Peak Rd., 94558 (6 mi east of Napa via Hwy. 121), tel. 707/257–0200 or 800/532–0500, fax 707/257–5425. 277 condo units. Facilities: 3 restaurants. AE, D, DC, MC, V.*

$$–$$$$ **Best Western Inn Napa.** This immaculate modern redwood motel with spacious rooms has a restaurant on the premises and same-day laundry and valet service. There are suites, as well as rooms for nonsmokers and travelers with disabilities. Small pets are allowed. *100 Soscol Ave., 94558 (from the direction of the Golden Gate Bridge, take Imola Ave./Hwy. 121 exit east from Hwy. 29 to junction of Hwy. 121 and Soscol), tel. 707/257–1930 or 800/528–1234, fax 707/255–0709. 68 rooms. Facilities: pool, spa. AE, D, DC, MC, V.*

John Muir Inn. Continental breakfast and in-room coffee are included at this new, well-equipped, three-story motel that has kitchenettes, refrigerators, movies, valet service, and some whirlpool tubs. Discounts for senior citizens and rooms for nonsmokers and guests with disabilities are available. *1998 Trower Ave., 94558 (corner of Hwy. 29), tel. 707/257–7220 or 800/522–8999, fax 707/258–0943. 59 rooms. Facilities: pool, spa. AE, D, DC, MC, V.*

$$$ **Chateau.** There's a French country-inn atmosphere at this modern motel. Continental breakfast, in-room refrigerators, facilities for travelers with disabilities, and discounts for senior citizens are offered. *4195 Solano Ave., 94558 (west of Hwy. 29; exit at Trower Ave.), tel. 707/253–9300 or 800/253–6272 in CA. 115 rooms. Facilities: outdoor pool and spa. AE, D, DC, MC, V.*

Rutherford **Auberge du Soleil.** As you sit on a wisteria-draped deck sipping
$$$$ a late-afternoon glass of wine, with acres of terraced olive groves
★ and rolling vineyards at your feet, you'll swear you're in Tuscany. The Mediterranean spell continues inside, with Sante Fe accents, and even extends to the hotel's superb restaurant. *180 Rutherford Hill Rd., 94573, tel. 707/963–1211 or 800/348–5406, fax 707/963–8764. 50 rooms. Facilities: outdoor pool, spa, tennis, masseuse, nature trail, exercise room. AE, MC, V.*

$$$–$$$$ **Rancho Caymus Inn.** California-Spanish in style, this inn has well-maintained gardens and large suites with kitchens and whirlpool baths. Also of note are the home-baked breads, an emphasis on decorative handicrafts, unusual beehive fireplaces, tile murals, stoneware basins, and llama-hair blankets. *1140 Rutherford Rd., 94573 (junction of Hwys. 29 and 128), tel. 707/963–1777 or 800/845–1777, fax 707/963–5387. 26 rooms. Facilities: restaurant. 2-night minimum Apr. 1–Nov. 30. AE, MC, V.*

St. Helena **Harvest Inn.** This English Tudor inn with many fireplaces
$$$$ overlooks a 14-acre vineyard and hills beyond. Although the property is flat and set close to a main highway, the award-winning landscaping creates an illusion of remoteness. The

furnishings are antiques, and most rooms have wet bars, refrigerators, and fireplaces. Pets are allowed in certain rooms for a $20 fee. Complimentary breakfast is served in the breakfast room and on the patio overlooking the vineyards. *1 Main St., 94574, tel. 707/963–9463 or 800/950–8466, fax 707/963–4402. 55 rooms. Facilities: 2 pools, 2 whirlpools. AE, D, MC, V.*

Meadowood Resort. The resort is set on 256 wooded acres, with a golf course, croquet lawns, and hiking trails. The hotel is a rambling country lodge reminiscent of a turn-of-the-century New England seaside cottage, and separate bungalow suites are clustered on the hillside. Half the suites and some rooms have fireplaces. *900 Meadowood La., 94574, tel. 707/963–3646 or 800/458–8080, fax 707/963–3532. 82 rooms. Facilities: 2 restaurants, lounge, room service, 2 pools, saunas, 9-hole and par golf courses, tennis, masseuse, wine school. AE, DC, MC, V.*

The Wine Country Inn. Surrounded by a pastoral landscape of vineyards and hills dotted with old barns and stone bridges, this New England–style inn feels peaceful. Rural antiques fill all of the rooms, and most face the splendid view with either a balcony, patio, or deck. There are fireplaces in almost every room, and private hot tubs in a few of the higher-priced rooms. A hearty country breakfast is presented buffet-style in the sun-splashed common room. There is no TV; this is a place for readers and dreamers. *1152 Lodi La., 94574, tel. 707/963–7077 or 800/473–3463, fax 707/963–9018. 24 rooms with bath. Facilities: outdoor pool and Jacuzzi with shower, gift shop, complimentary breakfast, kitchen will pack a picnic lunch. MC, V.*

$$$–$$$$ **Hotel St. Helena.** The oldest standing wooden structure in St. Helena, this restored 1881 hostelry aims at Old World comfort. It is completely furnished with antiques and decorated in rich, appealing tones of burgundy. Complimentary Continental breakfast is included. Smoking is discouraged—the only evidence of the New World. *1309 Main St., 94574, tel. 707/963–4388, fax 707/963–5402. 14 rooms with bath, 4 rooms with shared bath. AE, DC, MC, V.*

$$–$$$$ **Cinnamon Bear Bed and Breakfast.** Built in 1904 as a wedding gift, this house is decorated with a period flavor, from the antique quilts and toys to the claw-foot tubs, and there's a cozy fireplace in the parlor. Full breakfast is included. Rooms for nonsmokers are available. *1407 Kearney St., 94574 (from Main St., Hwy. 29, turn west on Adams St., then 2 blocks to Kearney), tel. 707/963–4653. 4 rooms with bath. MC, V.*

$$ **El Bonita Motel.** Remodeled throughout 1992 and 1993, this roadside motel now boasts 20 additional rooms, most with whirlpool spas, and a new look. Hand-painted grapevines surround the windows, and flower boxes overflow with new colors every season. Although sauna and Jacuzzi facilities are offered all year, the outdoor pool is only available in summer. There are 16 rooms in the main motel and six smartly furnished garden rooms with kitchenettes. *195 Main St., 94574, tel. 707/963–3216 or 800/541–3284, fax 707/963–8838. 42 rooms. AE, MC, V.*

Santa Rosa
$$$$

Vintner's Inn. Set on 50 acres of vineyards, this attractive inn has large rooms, French-provincial furnishings, and wood-burning fireplaces. The trellised sundeck is delightful. Breakfast is complimentary, and there is an excellent restaurant on the premises. There are rooms for travelers with disabilities. VCRs are available for a small fee. *4350 Barnes Rd., 95403 (River Rd. exit west from U.S. 101), tel. 707/575–7350 or 800/421–2584, fax 707/575–1426. 44 rooms. Facilities: restaurant, spa and outdoor showers, affiliated full-service health club nearby. AE, DC, MC, V.*

$$–$$$$

Doubletree Hotel. Many rooms in this large, modern, multistory hotel on a hilltop have views of the valley and vineyards; the Burgundy, Cabernet, Chardonnay, Chablis, and Riesling buildings have especially fine views. The spacious rooms have work-size desks and functional, comfortable furnishings. There are rooms for nonsmokers and travelers with disabilities. Golf and tennis are available at the adjacent Fountaingrove Country Club for additional fees, and there's a jogging path. *3555 Round Barn Blvd., 95401 (exit Mendocino Ave. from U.S. 101), tel. 707/523–7555 or 800/528–0444, fax 707/545–2807. 247 rooms with bath, 14 suites. Facilities: restaurant, bar, lounge, pool, spa, valet service. AE, D, DC, MC, V.*

$$$
★

Fountaingrove Inn. This elegant, comfortable inn located in the heart of the Sonoma valley boasts a redwood sculpture, *Equus III,* and a wall of cascading water in the lobby. Rooms have work spaces with modem jacks. Buffet breakfast is included, and there's an exceptional restaurant. Discounts for senior citizens and rooms for nonsmokers and travelers with disabilities are available. *101 Fountaingrove Pkwy. (near U.S. 101), 95403, tel. 707/578–6101 or 800/222–6101, fax 707/544–3126. 85 rooms. Facilities: complimentary health club nearby, golf and tennis, lap pool, spa, lounge, room service, movies. AE, DC, MC, V.*

$$–$$$
★

Los Robles Lodge. This pleasant, relaxed motel has comfortable rooms overlooking a pool set into a grassy landscape. Rooms for the handicapped and nonsmokers are available. Pets are allowed, except in executive rooms, which have whirlpools. *925 Edwards Ave., 95401 (Steele La. exit west from Hwy. 101), tel. 707/545–6330 or 800/255–6330, fax 707/575–5826. 105 rooms. Facilities: restaurant, coffee shop, lounge with nightly entertainment, pool, outdoor whirlpool, fitness center nearby, laundry. AE, D, DC, MC, V.*

$

Best Western Hillside Inn. Some rooms at this cozy, nicely landscaped, small motel have balconies or patios. Kitchenettes and suites are available. *2901 4th St., 95409 (at Farmers La., 2 mi east off U.S. 101 on Hwy. 12), tel. 707/546–9353 or 800/528–1234. 35 rooms. Facilities: pool, restaurant, sauna, shuffleboard. AE, DC, MC, V.*

Sonoma
$$$$

Sonoma Mission Inn. This elegantly restored, nicely landscaped 1920s resort blends Mediterranean and old-California architecture for a result that's early Hollywood—you half expect Gloria Swanson to sweep through the lobby. The location is a surprise, off the main street of tiny, anything-but-posh Boyes Hot

Springs. The rooms in the newer buildings are much larger and more attractive than the smallish standard rooms in the main building. The hotel is known for its extensive spa facilities and treatments. In 1993, the hotel again began pumping warm mineral water from underground wells into one of its swimming pools and added a new fitness pavilion. *18140 Hwy. 12 (just north of Sonoma), Box 1447, 95476, tel. 707/938–9000, 800/358–9022, or 800/862–4945 in CA, fax 707/996–5358. 170 rooms. Facilities: restaurant, coffee shop, 2 bars, lounge, 2 pools, weight room, steam room, whirlpools, sauna, tennis. AE, DC, MC, V.*

Thistle Dew Inn. A half-block from Sonoma Plaza is this turn-of-the-century Victorian home filled with collector-quality arts-and-crafts furnishings. Owners Larry and Norma Barnett live on the premises, and Larry cooks up creative, sumptuous breakfasts and serves hors d'oeuvres in the evenings. Upgraded in 1993, four of the six rooms now have private entrances and decks. Every room has queen-size beds with antique quilts, private baths, and air-conditioning. There is a hot tub, and bicycles are provided free to guests. Smoking is not permitted indoors. *171 W. Spain St., 95476, tel. 707/938–2909 or 800/382–7895 in CA. 6 rooms. AE, MC, V.*

$$$–$$$$ **Best Western Sonoma Valley Inn.** Just one block from the historical town plaza, this motel features balconies, hand-crafted furniture, wood-burning fireplaces, and whirlpool baths. Continental breakfast and a complimentary split of wine are included. Kitchenettes and rooms for nonsmokers and travelers with disabilities are available. *550 2nd St. W, 95476, tel. 707/938–9200 or 800/334–5784, fax 707/938–0935. 72 rooms. Facilities: pool, whirlpool, laundry. AE, D, DC, MC, V.*

★ **El Dorado Hotel.** In 1990, Claude Rouas, the owner of Napa's acclaimed Auberge du Soleil, entered the Sonoma scene with this fine small hotel and its popular restaurant, Piatti (*see* Dining, *above*). Rooms reflect Sonoma's mission era, with Mexican-tile floors and white walls. The best rooms are numbers 3 and 4, which have big balconies overlooking Sonoma Plaza. Only four of the rooms—the ones in the courtyard by the pool—have bathtubs; the rest have showers only. *405 1st St. W (on Sonoma Plaza), tel. 707/996–3030 or 800/289–3031, fax 707/996–3148. 27 rooms. Facilities: restaurant, heated pool. AE, MC, V.*

$$–$$$ **Vineyard Inn.** Built as a roadside motor court in 1941, this red-tiled-roof inn has been refurbished to add Mexican village charm to an otherwise lackluster location at the junction of two main highways. The inn is in the heart of Sonoma's Carneros region, across from two vineyards. It is also the closest lodging to Sears Point Raceway. Rooms have queen-size beds. Continental breakfast is provided. *23000 Arnold Dr. (at the junction of Hwys. 116 and 121), 95476, tel. 707/938–2350 or 800/359–4667. 9 rooms, 3 suites with wet bar, 1 resident suite with kitchenette. AE, MC, V.*

Yountville **Vintage Inn.** All the rooms at this luxurious inn have fireplaces,
$$$$ whirlpool baths, refrigerators, private verandas or patios, hand-painted fabrics, window seats, and shuttered windows. A welcome bottle of wine, Continental breakfast with champagne, and

afternoon tea are all complimentary. In season, bike rentals and hot-air ballooning are available. *6541 Washington St., 94599, tel. 707/944–1112 or 800/351–1133, fax 707/944–1617. 80 rooms with bath. Facilities: lap pool, spa, tennis. AE, D, DC, MC, V.*

$$$–$$$$ **Napa Valley Lodge.** Spacious rooms overlook vineyards and the valley in this hacienda-style lodge with a tile roof, covered walkways, balconies, patios, and colorful gardens. Freshly brewed coffee is provided in rooms, as is Continental breakfast and the morning paper. Some rooms have fireplaces. Rooms with wet bars and rooms for nonsmokers and travelers with disabilities are available. *2230 Madison St. at Hwy. 29, 94599, tel. 707/944–2468 or 800/368–2468, fax 707/944–9362. 55 rooms. Facilities: exercise room, pool, spa, sauna, refrigerators, refreshment bars. AE, D, DC, MC, V.*

The Arts and Nightlife

Galleries throughout the Wine Country display the work of local artists: painters, sculptors, potters, and jewelry makers. The **Luther Burbank Performing Arts Center** in Santa Rosa (50 Mark West Springs Rd., 95403, tel. 707/546–3600; box office open Mon.–Sat. noon–6) offers a full events calendar featuring concerts, plays, and other performances by locally and internationally known artists. Write for the calendar in advance if you're planning a trip. For the symphony, ballet, and other live theater performances throughout the year, call the **Spreckels Performing Arts Center** in Rohnert Park (tel. 707/584–1700 or 707/586–0936; box office open Tues.–Sat. noon–5). The most highly recommended theater groups among the valley's 30 ensembles include: Cinnebar in Petaluma (tel. 707/763–8920), Main Street Theatre in Sebastopol (tel. 707/823–0177), SRT (Summer Repertory Theatre) in Santa Rosa (tel. 707/527–4307), and the Actors Theatre also in Santa Rosa (tel. 707/523–4185). In addition to the sounds at local music clubs and the larger hotels, wineries often schedule concerts and music festivals during the summer. Popular music aficionados might also try the Mystic Theatre in Petaluma where Chris Isaak plays now and then (tel. 707/765–6665), and movie lovers can take in a foreign or first-run film at the Raven Theatre in Healdsburg (tel. 707/433–5448). The Sebastiani Theatre on historic Sonoma square (tel. 707/996–2020) features first-run movies and hosts special events during the year.

Many believe that the best way to savor evenings in the Wine Country is to linger over an elegant dinner, preferably on a patio under the stars, at one of the restaurants for which the area is justly famous.

Index

The only guide to explore a *Disney World®* you've never seen before:
The one for grown-ups.

THE ONLY GUIDE WITH A GROWN-UP POINT OF VIEW

RESORTS • DINING • ITINERARIES

WALT
DISNEY
WORLD
for
ADULTS

THE FIRST COMPLETE HANDBOOK
FOR COUPLES, SINGLES, HONEYMOONERS,
BUSINESS TRAVELERS, SPORTS AND
NATURE LOVERS, AND THE
YOUNG AT HEART

• ATTRACTIONS • SPORTS • SHOPS •

Rita Aero

0-679-02490-5 $14.00 ($18.50 Can)

This is the only guide written specifically for the millions of adults who visit Walt Disney World® each year <u>without</u> kids. Upscale, sophisticated, packed full of facts and maps, *Walt Disney World® for Adults* provides up-to-date information on hotels, restaurants, sports facilities, and health clubs, as well as unique itineraries for adults. With *Walt Disney World® for Adults* in hand, you'll get the most out of one of the world's most fascinating, most complex playgrounds.

At bookstores everywhere, or call **1-800-533-6478.**

Fodor's Travel Guides

Available at bookstores everywhere, or call 1–800–533–6478, 24 hours a day.

U.S. Guides

Alaska

Arizona

Boston

California

Cape Cod, Martha's Vineyard, Nantucket

The Carolinas & the Georgia Coast

Chicago

Colorado

Florida

Hawaii

Las Vegas, Reno, Tahoe

Los Angeles

Maine, Vermont, New Hampshire

Maui

Miami & the Keys

New England

New Orleans

New York City

Pacific North Coast

Philadelphia & the Pennsylvania Dutch Country

The Rockies

San Diego

San Francisco

Santa Fe, Taos, Albuquerque

Seattle & Vancouver

The South

The U.S. & British Virgin Islands

USA

The Upper Great Lakes Region

Virginia & Maryland

Waikiki

Walt Disney World and the Orlando Area

Washington, D.C.

Foreign Guides

Acapulco, Ixtapa, Zihuatanejo

Australia & New Zealand

Austria

The Bahamas

Baja & Mexico's Pacific Coast Resorts

Barbados

Berlin

Bermuda

Brittany & Normandy

Budapest

Canada

Cancún, Cozumel, Yucatán Peninsula

Caribbean

China

Costa Rica, Belize, Guatemala

The Czech Republic & Slovakia

Eastern Europe

Egypt

Euro Disney

Europe

Florence, Tuscany & Umbria

France

Germany

Great Britain

Greece

Hong Kong

India

Ireland

Israel

Italy

Japan

Kenya & Tanzania

Korea

London

Madrid & Barcelona

Mexico

Montréal & Québec City

Morocco

Moscow & St. Petersburg

The Netherlands, Belgium & Luxembourg

New Zealand

Norway

Nova Scotia, Prince Edward Island & New Brunswick

Paris

Portugal

Provence & the Riviera

Rome

Russia & the Baltic Countries

Scandinavia

Scotland

Singapore

South America

Southeast Asia

Spain

Sweden

Switzerland

Thailand

Tokyo

Toronto

Turkey

Vienna & the Danube Valley

At last — a guide for Americans with disabilities that makes traveling a delight

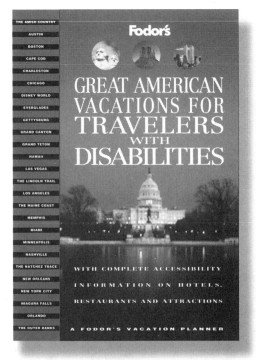

0-679-02591-X $18.00 ($24.00 Can)

This is the first and only complete guide to great American vacations for the 35 million North Americans with disabilities, as well as for those who care for them or for aging parents and relatives. Provides:

- Essential trip-planning information for travelers with mobility, vision, and hearing impairments
- Specific details on a huge array of facilities, along with solid descriptions of attractions, hotels, restaurants, and other destinations
- Up-to-date information on ISA-designated parking, level entranceways, and accessibility to pools, lounges, and bathrooms

 At bookstores everywhere, or call **1-800-533-6478**

AT LAST

YOUR OWN PERSONALIZED LIST
OF WHAT'S GOING ON IN THE
CITIES YOU'RE VISITING.

KEYED TO THE DAYS WHEN
YOU'LL BE THERE, CUSTOMIZED
FOR YOUR INTERESTS,
AND SENT TO YOU BEFORE YOU
LEAVE HOME.

GET THE INSIDER'S
PERSPECTIVE. . .

UP-TO-THE-MINUTE
ACCURATE
EASY TO ORDER
DELIVERED WHEN YOU NEED IT

Now there is a revolutionary way to get customized, time-sensitive travel information just before your trip.

Now you can obtain detailed information about what's going on in each city you'll be visiting <u>before</u> you leave home—up-to-the-minute, objective information about the events and activities that interest you most.

Travel Updates contain the kind of time-sensitive insider information you can get only from local contacts – or from city magazines and newspapers once you arrive. But now you can have the same information before you leave for your trip.

The choice is yours: current art exhibits, theater, music festivals and special concerts, sporting events, antiques and flower shows, shopping, fitness, and more.

The information comes from hundreds of correspondents and thousands of sources worldwide. Updated continuously, it's like having your own personal concierge or friend in the city.

You specify the cities and when you'll be there. We'll do the rest — personalizing the information for you the way no guidebook can.

It's the perfect extension to your Fodor's guide and the best way to make the most of your valuable travel time.

**Use Order Form on back
or call 1-800-799-9609**

Your Itinerary:
Customized reports
available for 160
destinations

a.
tou
9902
Regent
The ann
in this ar
domain of
tion as Joe F
worthwhile. I
the perfomance
Tickets are usual,
venue. Alternate
mances are cancelle
given. For more infor
Open-Air Theatre, Inner
NW1 4NP Open Air Th
Tel: 935-5756. Ends: 9-11-9
International Air Tattoo
Held biennially, the wor
military air display
demostra
tions, m
ba

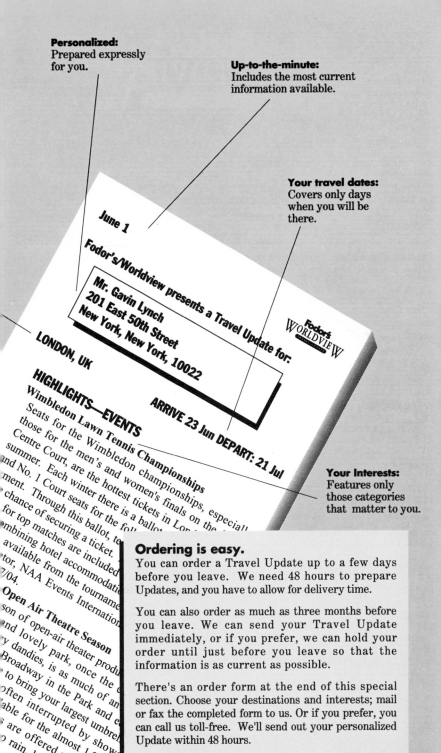

Personalized:
Prepared expressly for you.

Up-to-the-minute:
Includes the most current information available.

Your travel dates:
Covers only days when you will be there.

June 1

Fodor's/Worldview presents a Travel Update for:

Mr. Gavin Lynch
201 East 50th Street
New York, New York, 10022

Fodor's
WORLDVIEW

LONDON, UK

ARRIVE 23 Jun DEPART: 21 Jul

HIGHLIGHTS—EVENTS

Wimbledon Lawn Tennis Championships

Seats for the Wimbledon championships, especiall
those for the men's and women's finals on the
Centre Court, are the hottest tickets in Lon
summer. Each winter there is a ballot
and No. 1 Court seats for the foll
ment. Through this ballot, te
chance of securing a ticket.
for top matches are included
combining hotel accommodati
available from the tourname
tor, NAA Events Internation
7/04.

Open Air Theatre Season

son of open-air theater produ
and lovely park, once the
y dandies, is as much of an
Broadway in the Park and e
to bring your largest umbre
often interrupted by showe
able for the almost 1,200-seat
are offered when perfor-
rain, but refunds are not
contact Sheila Benjan
Regent's Park
Regent'

Your Interests:
Features only those categories that matter to you.

Ordering is easy.

You can order a Travel Update up to a few days before you leave. We need 48 hours to prepare Updates, and you have to allow for delivery time.

You can also order as much as three months before you leave. We can send your Travel Update immediately, or if you prefer, we can hold your order until just before you leave so that the information is as current as possible.

There's an order form at the end of this special section. Choose your destinations and interests; mail or fax the completed form to us. Or if you prefer, you can call us toll-free. We'll send out your personalized Update within 48 hours.

**Special concerts—
who's performing
what and where**

**One-of-a-kind,
one-time-only events**

**Special interest,
in-depth listings**

Children — Events

Angel Canal Festival
The festivities include a children's funfair entertainers, a boat rally and displays on the water. Regent's Canal. Islington. N1. Tube Angel. Tel: 267 9100. 11:30am-5:30pm. 7/04.

Blackheath Summer Kite Festival
Stunt kite displays with parachuting teddy bears and trade stands. Free admission. SE3. BR: Blackheath. 10am. 6/27.

Megabugs
Children will delight in this infestation of giant robotic insects, including a praying mantis 60 times life size. Mon-Sat 10am-6pm; Sun 11am-6pm. Admission 4.50 pounds. Natural History Museum, Cromwell Road. SW7. Tube: South Kensington. Tel: 938 9123. Ends 10/01.

Childminders
This establishment employs only women, providing nurses and qualified nannies to

Music — Jazz & Blues

Tito Puente's Golden Men of Latin Jazz
The father of mambo and Cuban rumba king comes to town. Royal Festival Hall. South Bank. SE1. Tube: Waterloo. Tel: 928 8800. 8pm. 7/15.

Georgie Fame and The New York Band
Riding a popular tide with his latest album, the smoky-voiced Fame and his keyboard are on a tour yet again. The Grand. Clapham Junction. SW11. BR: Clapham Junction. Tel: 738 9000. 7:30pm. 7/07.

Jacques Loussier Play Bach Trio
The French jazz classicist and colleagues. Kenwood Lakeside. Hampstead Lane. Kenwood. NW3. Tube: Golders Green, then bus 210. Tel: 413 1443. 7pm. 7/10.

Tony Bennett and Ronnie Scott
Royal Festival Hall. South Bank. SE1. Tube: Waterloo. Tel: 928 8800. 8pm. 7/11.

Santana
Royal Festival Hall. South Bank. SE1. Tube: Waterloo. Tel: 928 8800. 8pm. 7/12.

Count Basie Orchestra and Nancy Wilson Trio
Royal Festival Hall. South Bank. SE1. Tube: Waterloo. Tel: 928 8800. 8pm. 7/14.

King Pleasure and the Biscuit Boys
Royal Festival Hall. South Bank. SE1. Tube: Waterloo. Tel: 928 8800. 6:30 and 9pm. 7/16.

Al Green and the London Community Gospel Choir
Royal Festival Hall. South Bank. SE1. Tube: Waterloo. Tel: 928 8800. 8pm. 7/13.

BB King and Linda Hopkins
Mother of the blues and successor to Bessie Smith, Hopkins meets up with "Blues Boy" King. Royal Festival Hall. South Bank. SE1. 6:30 and 9pm.

Music — Classical

Marylebone Sinfonia
Kenneth Gowen conducts music by Puccini and Rossini. Queen Elizabeth Hall. South Bank. SE1. Tube: Waterloo. Tel: 928 8800. 7:45pm. 7/16.

London Philharmonic
Franz Welser-Moest and George Benjamin conduct selections by Alexander Goehr, Messiaen, and some of Benjamin's own compositions. Queen Elizabeth Hall. South Bank. SE1. Tube: Waterloo. Tel: 928 8800. 8pm.

London Pro Arte Orchestra and Forest Choir
Murray Stewart conducts selections by Rossini, Haydn and Jonathan Willcocks. Queen Elizabeth Hall. South Bank. SE1. Tube: Waterloo. Tel: 928 8800. 7:45pm.

Kensington Symphony Orchestra
Russell Keable conducts Dvorak's music. South Bank.

Here's what you get . . .

Detailed information about what's going on — precisely when you'll be there.

Show openings during your visit

Handy pocket-size booklet

Reviews by local critics

Exhibitions & Shows—Antique & Flower

Westminster Antiques Fair

Over 50 stands with pre-1830 furniture and other Victorian and earlier items. Thu-Fri 11am-8pm; Sat-Sun 11am-6pm. Admission 4 pounds, children free. Old Royal Horticultural Hall. Vincent Square. SW1. Tel: 0444/48 25 14. 6-24 thru 6/27.

Royal Horticultural Society Flower Show

The show includes displays of carnations, summer fruit and vegetables. Tue 11am-7pm; Wed 10am-5pm. Admission Tue 4 pounds, Wed 2 pounds. Royal Horticultural Halls. Greycoat Street and Vincent Square. SW1. Tube: Victoria. 7/20 thru 7/21.

Hampton Court Palace International Flower Show

Major international garden and flower show taking place in conjunction with

Theater — Musical

Sunset Boulevard

In June, the four Andrew Lloyd Webber musicals which dominated London's stages in the 1980s (Cats, Starlight Express, Phantom of the Opera and Aspects of Love) are joined by the composer's latest work, a show rumored to have his best music to date. The 1950 Billy Wilder film about a helpless young writer who is drawn into the world of a possessive, aging silent screen star offers rich opportunities for Webber's evolving style. Soaring, aching melodies, lush technical effects and psychological thrills are all expected. Patti Lupone stars. Mon-Sat at 8pm; matinee Thu-Sat at 3pm. In-person sales only at the box office; credit card bookings, Tel: 344 0055. Admission 15-32.50 pounds. Adelphi Theatre. The Strand. WC2. Tube: Charing Cross. Tel: 836 7611. Starts: 6/21.

Leonardo A Portrait of Love

A new musical about the great Renaissance artist and inventor comes in for a London pre-... tested by a brief run at Oxford's Old ... The work explores ...

Spectator Sports — Other Sports

Greyhound Racing: Wembley Stadium

This dog track offers good views of greyhound racing held on Mon, Wed and Fri. No credit cards. Stadium Way. Wembley. HA9. Tube: Wembley Park. Tel: 902 8833.

Benson & Hedges Cricket Cup Final

Lord's Cricket Ground. St. John's Wood Road. NW8. Tube: St. John's Wood. Tel: 289 1611. 11am. 7/10.

Business-Fax & Overnight Mail

Post Office, Trafalgar Square Branch

Offers a network of fax services, the Intelpost system, throughout the country and abroad. Mon-Sat 8am-8pm, Sun 9am-5pm. William IV Street. WC2. Tube: Charing Cross. Tel: 930 ...

Fodor's WORLDVIEW
TRAVEL UPDATE

London, England
Arriving: June 23
Departing: July 21

Interest Categories

For <u>your</u> personalized Travel Update, choose the categories you're most interested in from this list. Every Travel Update automatically provides you with *Event Highlights* - the best of what's happening during the dates of your trip.

1.	**Business Services**	Fax & Overnight Mail, Computer Rentals, Photocopying, Protocol, Secretarial, Messenger, Translation Services

Dining

2.	**All Day Dining**	Breakfast & Brunch, Cafes & Tea Rooms, Late-Night Dining
3.	**Local Cuisine**	In Every Price Range—from Budget Restaurants to the Special Splurge
4.	**European Cuisine**	Continental, French, Italian
5.	**Asian Cuisine**	Chinese, Far Eastern, Japanese, Other
6.	**Americas Cuisine**	American, Mexican & Latin
7.	**Nightlife**	Bars, Dance Clubs, Casinos, Comedy Clubs, Ethnic, Pubs & Beer Halls
8.	**Entertainment**	Theater—Comedy, Drama, English Language, Musicals, Dance, Ticket Agencies
9.	**Music**	Country/Western/Folk, Classical, Traditional & Ethnic, Opera, Jazz & Blues, Pop, Rock
10.	**Children's Activities**	Events, Attractions
11.	**Tours**	Local Tours, Day Trips, Overnight Excursions, Cruises
12.	**Exhibitions, Festivals & Shows**	Antiques & Flower, History & Cultural, Art Exhibitions, Fairs & Craft Shows, Music & Art Festivals
13.	**Shopping**	Districts & Malls, Markets, Regional Specialities
14.	**Fitness**	Bicycling, Health Clubs, Hiking, Jogging
15.	**Recreational Sports**	Boating/Sailing, Fishing, Golf, Ice Skating, Skiing, Snorkeling/Scuba, Swimming, Tennis & Racquet
16.	**Spectator Sports**	Auto Racing, Baseball, Basketball, Boating & Sailing, Football, Golf, Horse Racing, Ice Hockey, Rugby, Soccer, Tennis, Track & Field, Other Sports

Please note that interest category content will vary by season, destination, and length of stay.

Destinations

The Fodor's/Worldview Travel Update covers more than 160 destinations worldwide. Choose the destinations that match your itinerary from this list. (Choose bulleted destinations only.)

Europe
- Amsterdam
- Athens
- Barcelona
- Berlin
- Brussels
- Budapest
- Copenhagen
- Dublin
- Edinburgh
- Florence
- Frankfurt
- French Riviera
- Geneva
- Glasgow
- Istanbul
- Lausanne
- Lisbon
- London
- Madrid
- Milan
- Moscow
- Munich
- Oslo
- Paris
- Prague
- Provence
- Rome
- Salzburg
- * Seville
- St. Petersburg
- Stockholm
- Venice
- Vienna
- Zurich

United States (Mainland)
- Albuquerque
- Atlanta
- Atlantic City
- Baltimore
- Boston
- * Branson, MO
- * Charleston, SC
- Chicago
- Cincinnati
- Cleveland
- Dallas/Ft. Worth
- Denver
- Detroit
- Houston
- * Indianapolis
- Kansas City
- Las Vegas
- Los Angeles
- Memphis
- Miami
- Milwaukee
- Minneapolis/ St. Paul
- * Nashville
- New Orleans
- New York City
- Orlando
- Palm Springs
- Philadelphia
- Phoenix
- Pittsburgh
- Portland
- * Reno/ Lake Tahoe
- St. Louis
- Salt Lake City
- San Antonio
- San Diego
- San Francisco
- * Santa Fe
- Seattle
- Tampa
- Washington, DC

Alaska
- Alaskan Destinations

Hawaii
- Honolulu
- Island of Hawaii
- Kauai
- Maui

Canada
- Quebec City
- Montreal
- Ottawa
- Toronto
- Vancouver

Bahamas
- Abaco
- Eleuthera/ Harbour Island
- Exuma
- Freeport
- Nassau & Paradise Island

Bermuda
- Bermuda Countryside
- Hamilton

British Leeward Islands
- Anguilla
- Antigua & Barbuda
- St. Kitts & Nevis

British Virgin Islands
- Tortola & Virgin Gorda

British Windward Islands
- Barbados
- Dominica
- Grenada
- St. Lucia
- St. Vincent
- Trinidad & Tobago

Cayman Islands
- The Caymans

Dominican Republic
- Santo Domingo

Dutch Leeward Islands
- Aruba
- Bonaire
- Curacao

Dutch Windward Island
- St. Maarten/ St. Martin

French West Indies
- Guadeloupe
- Martinique
- St. Barthelemy

Jamaica
- Kingston
- Montego Bay
- Negril
- Ocho Rios

Puerto Rico
- Ponce
- San Juan

Turks & Caicos
- Grand Turk/ Providenciales

U.S. Virgin Islands
- St. Croix
- St. John
- St. Thomas

Mexico
- Acapulco
- Cancun & Isla Mujeres
- Cozumel
- Guadalajara
- Ixtapa & Zihuatanejo
- Los Cabos
- Mazatlan
- Mexico City
- Monterrey
- Oaxaca
- Puerto Vallarta

South/Central America
- * Buenos Aires
- * Caracas
- * Rio de Janeiro
- * San Jose, Costa Rica
- * Sao Paulo

Middle East
- * Jerusalem

Australia & New Zealand
- Auckland
- Melbourne
- * South Island
- Sydney

China
- Beijing
- Guangzhou
- Shanghai

Japan
- Kyoto
- Nagoya
- Osaka
- Tokyo
- Yokohama

Pacific Rim/Other
- * Bali
- Bangkok
- Hong Kong & Macau
- Manila
- Seoul
- Singapore
- Taipei

* Destinations available by 1/1/95

Fodor's WORLDVIEW TRAVEL UPDATE **Order Form**

THIS TRAVEL UPDATE IS FOR (Please print):

Name

Address

City	State	Country	ZIP

Tel # ( ) -   Fax # ( ) -

Title of this Fodor's guide:

Store and location where guide was purchased:

INDICATE YOUR DESTINATIONS/DATES: You can order up to three (3) destinations from the previous page. Fill in your arrival and departure dates for each destination. <u>**Your Travel Update itinerary (all destinations selected) cannot exceed 30 days from beginning to end.**</u>

		Month	Day		Month	Day
(Sample) LONDON	From:	6 /	21	To:	6 /	30
1	From:	/		To:	/	
2	From:	/		To:	/	
3	From:	/		To:	/	

CHOOSE YOUR INTERESTS: Select up to eight (8) categories from the list of interest categories shown on the previous page and circle the numbers below:

1   2   3   4   5   6   7   8   9   10   11   12   13   14   15   16

CHOOSE WHEN YOU WANT YOUR TRAVEL UPDATE DELIVERED (Check one):
❑ Please send my Travel Update immediately.
❑ Please hold my order until a few weeks before my trip to include the most up-to-date information.
   Completed orders will be sent within 48 hours. Allow 7-10 days for U.S. mail delivery.

ADD UP YOUR ORDER HERE. *SPECIAL OFFER FOR FODOR'S PURCHASERS ONLY!*

	Suggested Retail Price	Your Price	This Order
First destination ordered	$ 9.95	$ 7.95	$ 7.95
Second destination (if applicable)	$ 6.95	$ 4.95	+
Third destination (if applicable)	$ 6.95	$ 4.95	+

DELIVERY CHARGE (Check one and enter amount below)

	Within U.S. & Canada	Outside U.S. & Canada
First Class Mail	❑ $2.50	❑ $5.00
FAX	❑ $5.00	❑ $10.00
Priority Delivery	❑ $15.00	❑ $27.00

ENTER DELIVERY CHARGE FROM ABOVE: +

TOTAL: $

METHOD OF PAYMENT IN U.S. FUNDS ONLY (Check one):
❑ AmEx   ❑ MC   ❑ Visa   ❑ Discover   ❑ Personal Check (U. S. & Canada only)
❑ Money Order/ International Money Order
   Make check or money order payable to: Fodor's Worldview Travel Update

Credit Card —/—/—/—/—/—/—/—/—/—/—/—/—/—/—/—/ Expiration Date:___/___

Authorized Signature

SEND THIS COMPLETED FORM WITH PAYMENT TO:
Fodor's Worldview Travel Update, 114 Sansome Street, Suite 700, San Francisco, CA 94104

OR CALL OR FAX US 24-HOURS A DAY
Telephone **1-800-799-9609** • Fax **1-800-799-9619** (From within the U.S. & Canada)
(Outside the U.S. & Canada: Telephone 415-616-9988 • Fax 415-616-9989)

(Please have this guide in front of you when you call so we can verify purchase.)
Code: FTG   Offer valid until 12/31/95.